This is the first book to provide a synthesizing study of Russian writing about the Caucasus during the nineteenth-century age of empire-building. From Pushkin's ambivalent portrayal of an alpine Circassia to Tolstoy's condemnation of tsarist aggression against Muslim tribes in *Hadji Murat*, the literary analysis is firmly set in its historical context, and the responses of the Russian readership too receive extensive attention. As well as exploring literature as such, Susan Layton introduces material from travelogues, oriental studies, ethnography, memoirs, and the utterances of tsarist officials and military commanders. While showing how literature often underwrote imperialism, the book carefully explores the tensions between the Russian state's ideology of a European mission to civilize the Muslim mountain peoples, and romantic perceptions of those tribes as noble primitives whose extermination was no cause for celebration. By dealing with imperialism in Georgia as well, the study shows how the varied treatment of the Caucasus in literature helped Russians construct a satisfying identity for themselves as a semi-European, semi-Asian people.

CAMBRIDGE STUDIES IN RUSSIAN LITERATURE

RUSSIAN LITERATURE AND EMPIRE

CAMBRIDGE STUDIES IN RUSSIAN LITERATURE

General editor MALCOLM JONES

Editorial board: ANTHONY CROSS, CARYL EMERSON, HENRY GIFFORD, BARBARA HELDT, G. S. SMITH, VICTOR TERRAS

Recent titles in this series include

The Brothers Karamazov and the poetics of memory
DIANE OENNING THOMPSON

Andrei Platonov
THOMAS SEIFRID

Nabokov's early fiction
JULIAN W. CONNOLLY

Iurii Trifonov
DAVID GILLESPIE

Mikhail Zoshchenko
LINDA HART SCATTON

Andrei Bitov
ELLEN CHANCES

Nikolai Zabolotsky
DARRA GOLDSTEIN

Nietzsche and Soviet Culture
edited by BERNICE GLATZER ROSENTHAL

For a complete list of books in the series, see the end of this volume

RUSSIAN LITERATURE AND EMPIRE

Conquest of the Caucasus from Pushkin to Tolstoy

SUSAN LAYTON

CAMBRIDGE
UNIVERSITY PRESS

Published by the Press Syndicate of the University of Cambridge
The Pitt Building, Trumpington Street, Cambridge CB2 1RP
40 West 20th Street, New York, NY 10011–4211, USA
10 Stamford Road, Oakleigh, Melbourne 3166, Australia

First published 1994

Printed in Great Britain at the University Press, Cambridge

A catalogue record for this book is available from the British Library

Library of Congress cataloguing in publication data

Layton, Susan. Russian literature and empire: conquest of the Caucasus from
Pushkin to Tolstoy / Susan Layton.
p. cm. – (Cambridge studies in Russian literature)
Includes bibliographical references and index.
ISBN 0 521 44443 8
1. Russian literature – 19th century – History and criticism.
2. Caucasus – In literature. 3. Orient – In literature.
4. Romanticism – Russia. 5. Russia – Relations – Caucasus.
6. Caucasus – Relations – Russia. I. Title. II. Series.
PG3015.5.C3L39 1995
891.709'32479'09034–dc20 93–47121 CIP

ISBN 0521 44443 8 hardback

WV

To my mother and the memory of my father

Contents

Acknowledgments

My greatest intellectual debt for *Russian Literature and Empire* is to Marc Raeff who encouraged this project from the outset and provided invaluable observations on an initial draft of the manuscript. I also wish to thank Ilya Serman for suggesting helpful guidelines for this study in its earliest stages and for making useful comments on the first version of chapter 2. Special gratitude goes to Lauren Leighton and Neil Cornwell, my two readers at Cambridge who stimulated better formulations of some fundamental issues, steered me back onto fruitful paths when I began to wander and supplied references I had missed. The book's final form also owes a good deal to Jacques Melitz who read successive drafts of most chapters and prodded me to make many improvements. Of course, none of these insightful critics bears responsibility for any errors or shortcomings in my work. In addition to my various readers, I would like to thank Helen Sullivan and other reference librarians at the University of Illinois, who regularly supplied me with bibliographical information and copies of obscure Russian texts. Librarians at Indiana University, the Library of Congress and the Library of the Academy of Sciences in St. Petersburg also courteously performed these vital services.

Russian Literature and Empire began taking shape in my mind while I was doing research on *Hadji Murat* with a grant from the International Research and Exchanges Board (IREX) in Russia between 1979 and 1980. On the basis of my proposal for study of the literary Caucasus, I became a Mellon Fellow at Columbia University between 1981 and 1983, a time I conducted further investigation and began preliminary writing, while also teaching in the Humanities program. A second subsidy from IREX then allowed me to pursue my Caucasian project on a full-time basis the following year. Short-term grants from the Kennan Institute for Advanced Russian Studies permitted me to do additional work in Washington in 1985 and 1986. A grant from the American Philosophical Society also provided support in 1986. I am extremely grateful to all these institutions for having made this book possible.

Chapter 11 and a portion of chapter 3 appeared in earlier drafts in the following articles: "Eros and Empire in Russian Literature about Georgia," *Slavic Review* 51 (Summer 1992), 195–213; and "The Creation of an Imaginative Caucasian Geography," *Slavic Review* 45 (Fall 1986), 470–85. My thanks to the American Association for the Advancement of Slavic Studies for permission to reprint this material. Chapter 7 appears with permission of Macmillan Press and its United States copublisher St. Martin's Press who printed an earlier draft in the following book: *The Golden Age of Russian Literature and Thought. Selected Papers from the Fourth World Congress for Soviet and East European Studies, Harrogate, 1990*, ed. Derek Offord (1992).

Throughout *Russian Literature and Empire* translations are my own unless otherwise indicated. Transliteration follows the Library of Congress system, with some modifications in Russian names in the text and explanatory notes.

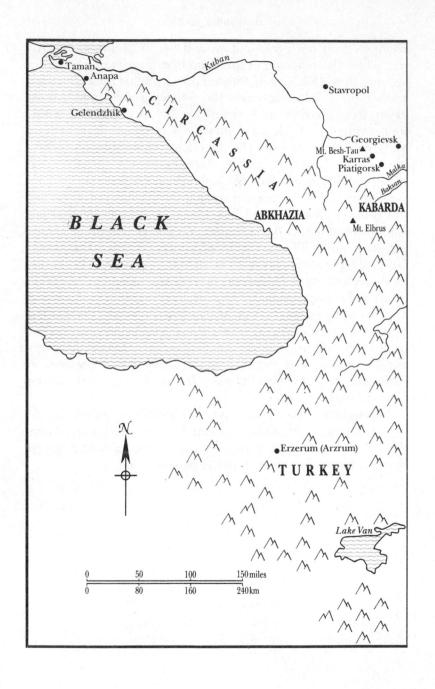

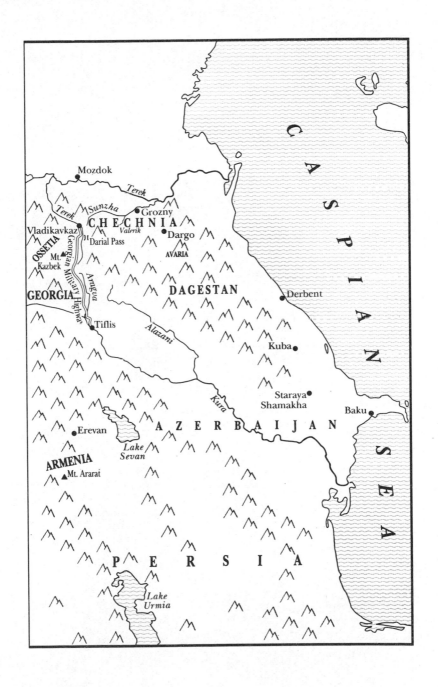

CHAPTER I

Introduction

The Russian empire included realms so diverse as Poland and Central Asia in the nineteenth century. But among all the assertions of imperial tsarist authority, the conquest of the Caucasus stimulated an incomparably rich body of literature and an exceptionally lively engagement with questions of Russian cultural identity. This book explores those literary and cultural ramifications of empire-building by focusing on Russian perceptions of the Caucasus as the orient. Russia's periphery offered other candidates for orientalization, as the Crimea illustrates. On her first visit to this land of Muslim Tatars which she annexed in 1783, Catherine II proclaimed it a "fairy tale from *The Thousand and One Nights*."[1] The Crimea would indeed acquire an aura of eastern exoticism in Russian literature and *récits de voyage*. The Caucasus, however, upstaged its rivals in the oriental domain. The explanation lies largely in historical timing: aggressive tsarist penetration into the Caucasus in the early decades of the nineteenth century coincided with the rise of Russian romanticism, a cultural phenomenon which entailed an extensive interplay with Europe's *renaissance orientale*. The processes of empire-building brought an unprecedented number of Russians to the Caucasus as civil servants, travelers, soldiers and exiles (so many of the latter, in fact, that the territory was nicknamed the "southern Siberia" already in the time of Alexander I).[2] Given these new contacts, Russians conversant with western orientalia and the European imperial manner in Asia readily latched onto the Caucasus as their "own" orient.[3]

I

But if frequently enough remarked in Russian literary criticism since the 1920s, the Caucasus' oriental status has not been thoroughly probed as a cultural offshoot of imperialism. What varied cultural and psychological satisfactions did semi-Europeanized Russians derive by consigning the Caucasus to the orient? What tensions existed between Asia and the Alps in Russian writing about the mountainous borderland? How did orientalization of the Caucasus evolve with the escalating war against the Muslim tribes? And did Russian writers not impose varying types and degrees of oriental identity on the Caucasus' highly diversified peoples?

Before outlining my approach to these questions, the book's regional and historical fields should be mapped in some detail. I deal mainly with literary responses to Russian conflict with the tribes of Circassia, Kabarda, Chechnia and Dagestan. The main targets of the "pacification" program undertaken by General Alexei Ermolov in 1818, Chechnia and Dagestan became the bastions of power of Shamil, the Caucasian imam who led the jihad from 1834 until his surrender in 1859.[4] The war proceeded on two flanks, however, since tribal resistance to Russia occurred in the northwestern Caucasus as well, right into the 1860s. While concentrating on literature about the Muslim tribes, I also give extensive treatment to Russian writing about Georgia. Voluntarily taken under the protection of Catherine II in 1783, the kingdom of eastern Georgia was annexed by Alexander I in 1801. The rest of Georgia soon went the same route, and the whole country was subjected to heavy-handed imperial rule for about twenty years. At one time or another, every segment of Georgian society resisted tsarist domination, and as late as 1832, a group of Georgian noblemen abortively conspired to reclaim their national independence. My book's two focuses thus illustrate the diversified nature of tsarist expansion: relentless war against the "savage" Muslim tribes and embattled protectoral relations with Christian Georgia.

In addition to the diversity of regional history, the annexation of the Caucasus spanned nearly three centuries. Russia began asserting power over the borderland in the mid-1550s when Ivan IV took the northwestern region of Kabarda under a protectorate and vassalized the tribes of the Kuban river basin. The nineteenth-century military conquest virtually ended with Shamil's defeat, but a small piece of territory remained to be won in the Russo-Turkish War of 1877–78, the last of many tsarist campaigns mounted against the two traditional forces of Islam in the Caucasus – the Ottoman empire and Persia. The whole process of annexation thus occurred under a long succession of Russian rulers with differing objectives and motivations.

The complex history requires clarifying the sense in which the term "imperialism" is used throughout the study. In the late nineteenth century the Russian historian Adolf Berzhe objected to the very word "conquest" (not to mention the qualifier "imperialist") by arguing that the annexation of the Caucasus had unfolded over the centuries in a haphazard, virtually unwilled manner: there was no grand design of subjugation, masterminded and executed by a Napoleon or an Alexander the Great.[5] According to this exercise in semantics, no conquest took place because there was no single conqueror. It is true, of course, that Russia's southern frontier began advancing in an unplanned, gradual way in the sixteenth century, with Cossacks playing the primary role.[6] Mainly Russian and Ukrainian peasants who fled the Muscovite state and Poland in order to evade high taxes, enserfment or military conscription, the Cossacks lived initially as nomadic bands and then formed settlements along the Don, Dnieper, Yaik (now Ural), Volga and Terek rivers. These communities were originally independent, self-governing groups. Their members lived as mercenaries and freebooters and frequently skirmished with the Caucasian or Tatar peoples of contiguous regions. Especially prominent in the literary Caucasus, the Grebensk Cossacks along the Terek were granted autonomy by Ivan IV in return for repelling marauders from across the river. In the course of the seventeenth and eighteenth centuries, however, the central tsarist state increasingly interfered in the affairs of all the Cossack groups. The most drastic curtailment of freedom followed the massive peasant rebellion led by Emelian Pugachev in 1773–74. After this event, large numbers of Cossacks were compelled to leave their chosen habitats and resettle along the Caucasian frontier, deprived of autonomy and pressed into service as border guards. But if the annexation of the Caucasus had its haphazard aspect, as some historians insist, the empress Catherine's concerted policy of southern expansion laid the base of the nineteenth-century imperialist agenda. The policy had economic, military, political, religious and moral dimensions which are virtually impossible to disentangle from one another. Marc Raeff's essay "In the Imperial Manner" argues that a concern with developing the economic resources and potential of the empire was ever present in Catherine's mind, whether in the formulation of domestic or foreign policy.[7] The objective was furthered by the settlement and development of underpopulated lands to the south and southwest, including the fertile plains of Ukraine. This push to the south was an exploitation of territory already under Russian sovereignty, but none the less it had an expansionist ramification: in order to derive economic benefit from the lands in question, the state had to protect them from foreign incursions and assure access to waterways. The resultant pursuit of border security in the south led to two wars with Turkey (1768–74, 1787–92) through which Russia gained control over the northern shores of the Black Sea. The annexation of the Crimea was another consequence of the same expansionist policy.

The quest for a secure southern border also largely explained Catherine's penetration of the Caucasus. Eastern Georgia became the empress' ally in war against Turkey in 1769, fourteen years before formally accepting Russian protection. Immediately after the protectorate was established, Russia founded Vladikavkaz, the northern terminus of the road to Tiflis (now Tbilisi) known as the Georgian Military Highway. Traditionally antagonistic to the Ottoman empire, Catherine's government gave Russian incursion into the Caucasus a moral and religious rationale – the defense of Christian civilization against Islam. In addition to establishing military outposts in the Caucasus, gaining a foothold in Georgia and articulating the goal of safeguarding Christianity, Catherine mapped out a stunning plan for reaping economic benefits from the southern territory. Her "oriental project" of 1796 called for full-scale invasion of the Caucasus and Persia, the seizure of trade stations between Turkey and Tibet, the consequent opening of a direct route to India and the isolation of Constantinople from the East. While utterly unrealistic ("truly fantastic," in Michael Florinsky's words), the "oriental project" was, of course, an unforgettable expression of apparently boundless imperial ambition.[8]

Catherine's objectives in the Caucasus defined the shape of nineteenth-century Russian imperialism, as expressed in tense protectoral relations with Georgia and prolonged war against the Muslim tribes. The major components of this imperialist outlook and course of action were a commitment to the multinational tsarist empire already in existence; territorial aggrandizement and the assertion of political sovereignty over subject peoples; a reliance on force to subjugate the tribes (and frequently to quell unrest in Georgia); an interest in economic enrichment; and an avowed dedication to a civilizing mission in Asia. One might define differences in the attitudes of key political actors. Alexander I, for example, reluctantly yielded to General Ermolov's demand for a bigger Caucasian army, whereas Nicholas I, with no prompting, offered the high command an unlimited supply of Russian troops to fight the Muslim mountaineers. But despite such distinctions, imperialist attitudes, ideas and beliefs generally pervaded nineteenth-century tsarist policy toward the Caucasus: the political, military, economic, moral and religious factors all operated synchronically, even though they did not assume exactly the same configuration or have equal intensity in the mind of every official.

The conquest produced a vast literary Caucasus whose chronology is readily delineated. Alexander Pushkin's poem "The Prisoner of the Caucasus" securely fixed the territory on the readership's cultural horizon in 1822. At the other end of the temporal framework stands Lev Tolstoy's *Hadji Murat*, written during 1896 and 1904 and first published in Russia in 1912 in a heavily censored form. In between young Pushkin and old Tolstoy, Alexander Bestuzhev-Marlinsky and Mikhail Lermontov dominated the literary Caucasus in the 1830s and 1840s. These four writers provide logical points of departure around which a massive amount of Russian writing can be organized. Further adding to the tractability of the sizeable literary corpus is the fact that the relevant output of the four primary producers was so concentrated in the period from 1822 to 1863, when Tolstoy's short novel *The Cossacks* was published. After that time, no nineteenth-century Russian literature of enduring aesthetic interest treated the Caucasian conquest, with the enormous exception of *Hadji Murat*.

Although concern with the subject is growing in the West, the literary Caucasus' relations to imperialism have so far been investigated mainly by Russian critics. The collapse of the Soviet Union promises to infuse fresh life into this field, not least by maximizing the freedom of scholars from the decolonized Caucasus. However, as for the commentary accumulated in the USSR between the late 1930s and early 1980s, much of it is marred by an ideological legacy from Stalin's time. By rapidly surveying this critical corpus in political context, I will start articulating my own assumptions about literature's relation to the state's imperialist agenda.

Lenin once called tsarist Russia a "prisonhouse of peoples" where a multitude of nationalities suffered oppression. In the late 1930s, though, Soviet ideologues formulated a new notion of tsarist imperialism as a lesser evil.[9] According to this view, conquering the Caucasus entailed reprehensible aggression but nevertheless had a fortunate outcome: by wrenching backward peoples from underdevelopment (and the "reactionary" religious rule of Shamil), Russia protected them from the nefarious expansionist designs of Turkey and Great Britain and thereby set them on the path to membership in the USSR.[10] The theory of lesser evil was progressively modified to underplay aggression and accentuate the strictly positive. Under Stalin, the new drift led to the doctrine of the happy family of nations, united under the leadership of the Russian "big brother." This metaphor eventually fell into disuse, and yet as of 1984, certain Russian historians still proclaimed the "friendship of peoples" in the USSR and protested that what "bourgeois" detractors call the Caucasian "conquest" was in truth an "annexation" immeasurably beneficial to the territory in the long run.[11]

Russian criticism about the literary Caucasus recapitulated this ideological passage from the "prisonhouse" to the "friendship of peoples." The reputations of problematic authors consequently underwent dramatic reversals, as best illustrated by the case of Pushkin. In 1934, prior to the formulation of the lesser evil theory, Nikolai Svirin viewed Pushkin's Caucasian and Crimean poems as major instances of "Russian colonial literature."[12] While betraying certain convictions about Asian alterity, S. Veltman's *Literature and the Orient* also chastised Pushkin and Lermontov for participating in "reactionary" tendencies of "colonial literature," as witnessed by their "false representation of our Orient."[13] Similarly, in a collection of memoirs about Pushkin compiled in the USSR in 1936, an editorial annotation associated the poet and the Decembrist revolutionaries with the brutal forces of empire-building.[14] To quote the none-too-elegant formulation: "With respect to Russia's war of aggression in the Caucasus, Pushkin displayed a solidarity with the overwhelming majority of the Decembrists, whose bourgeois-national program placed them among the ranks of proponents of the tsarist colonial policy in the Near East and made them try to justify Russia's atrocities through references to the tribesmen's 'savagery.'"[15]

Once the theory of lesser evil was in the air in the late 1930s, a loud chorus of international friendship drowned out such tunes. In this climate Pushkin emerged as a writer who wanted amical relations among all peoples of the Russian empire, regretted the oppression of Muslim tribeswomen and foretold the multinational state's "joyful life" inaugurated by the Stalin constitution.[16] International fraternity reigned in the 1950s' non-scholarly publications about the travels of famous Russian writers in the Caucasus.[17] More importantly, the friendship of peoples was a guiding assumption in two massive, heavily researched books of the period – the studies of Decembrist writers by Vasily Bazanov and Vano Shaduri.[18]

The critical edifice built on the doctrine of the friendship of peoples erected a rigid protective wall between the tsarist state and writers of the canon. In the concluding section of his book on Decembrists, Bazanov formulated the influential notion of "two Russias" – the "official Russia" of Nicholas I and a "second Russia," the "Decembrist, Pushkinian Russia." According to this view, the tsar's Russia was viciously hostile to the Caucasus, whereas the other Russia "wanted every possible good" for the territory and "was ready to struggle along with it against autocracy." But conquest itself turned out to be one of the purported goods: Bazanov attributed to the "Decembrist, Pushkinian" camp a recognition of tsarist expansion as a historically progressive phenomenon, boding well for the subjugated nationalities in the future. The conceptual framework of "two Russias" remained in force in the last pertinent study written prior to the collapse of the Soviet Union, Agil Gadzhiev's *The Caucasus in Russian Literature of the First Half of the Nineteenth Century* (1982).[19] Without repeating Bazanov's phrase, Gadzhiev built a similar dichotomy derived from a prevalent Soviet view of romanticism as a broad tendency split between "conservatives" and "progressives." In this scheme, Pushkin, Bestuzhev-Marlinsky and Lermontov were humanitarian "revolutionaries" antipathetic to the "reactionary" state's imperialism. The canonical triumvirate was equally protected from contamination by "low" literature: Gadzhiev dealt with some purveyors of pulp but dismissed them as conniving servants of Nicholas I, fundamentally disconnected from the "great" writers.

To re-examine the literary Caucasus in relation to imperialism, I have taken initial methodological inspiration from Edward Said's explication of discourse in *Orientalism*. Essentially a cultural monologue, Russian writing about the Caucasus engaged in ideologically significant discursive practices which transmitted and reproduced themselves from one epoch to another in various genres – in fiction and non-fiction, in the canonical and the "low." These practices included rhetorical postures, symbolic diction and tropes, specific concepts and a whole mental tendency to compare "us" to "them." While viewing literature in such a broad framework, I follow *Orientalism* and some other pertinent studies in distancing myself from Michel Foucault's conception of discourse as power. Foucaldian analysis tends to see culture hopelessly enmeshed in the structures of political and socioeconomic dominance. Literature retains no independence in this scheme, individual authors count for very little, and just about any protest against the power structure is all too liable to be maligned as some form of complicity with official discourse. As an alternative to Foucault's notion of discourse as power, Said's *Orientalism* proposed a theory of "dynamic exchange" between individual writers or texts and the complex processes of empire-building with which they interact.[20] By granting culture a vital measure of autonomy, this perspective allows for resistance to the state's political agenda. Jonathan Arac has forcefully insisted on the latter possibility in a recent polemic with Foucault: like other forms of writing, literature is a social practice which cannot be assured a pure, "radical autonomy" from politics; but writers may none the less utter real, meaningful protests against the given system of power and even effect changes in it.[21]

Russian literature does indeed run a gamut between underwriting and resisting the Caucasian conquest: writers were sovereign in their textual domains but wielded their representational authority to different ends. Total complicity in imperialism was the mode of ephemeral orientalia, especially prominent in the 1830s. At the polar opposite, *Hadji Murat* denounced the subjugation of the Muslim tribes as vile aggression. The particularly intriguing middle ground between the little orientalizers and old Tolstoy was occupied by young Pushkin, Bestuzhev-Marlinsky and Lermontov who all encountered the Caucasus as exiles. These three romantic outcasts endorsed imperialism in certain ways, while taking issue with it in others. The first part of this two-sided proposition was best illustrated in their treatment of Georgia. Although Pushkin, Bestuzhev-Marlinsky and Lermontov dealt with Georgia to greatly differing extents, they all helped to marginalize it as a "little corner of Asia forgotten by Europe" and awaiting Russian overlords.[22] But while underwriting tsarist domination of Georgia, Pushkin, Bestuzhev-Marlinsky and Lermontov produced the Muslim tribes as unusually problematic noble primitives who raised restive issues of Russia's own semi-Asian identity. The noble savage has in recent times been deconstructed as a "fetish" invented and worshiped by people blind to the ways their creation enables imperialism.[23] Chapter 14 of my book provides the most grist for this mill by documenting how popular history and literature used Pushkin, Bestuzhev-Marlinsky and Lermontov to constitute the Caucasian conquest as a civilizing mission in the post-war decades. For the most part, however, my study seeks to demonstrate that in their own times the tribesmen of Pushkin, Bestuzhev-Marlinsky and Lermontov disrupted ideology about Russia's European stature and the derivative right to subjugate the orient. If cultural and psychological divisions between "us" and the "orientals" do not hold fast, imperialism loses its moral justification as a civilizing mission.[24] In various ways, Pushkin, Bestuzhev-Marlinsky and Lermontov exposed this abyss by dissolving boundaries between Russia and Asia, for better or worse. The convergence flattered Russian national pride in certain respects. On the other hand, however, troubled recognition of war's manifestation of culturally non-specific "savagery" degraded the tsarist conquest itself. Most dramatic in writings of the military exiles Bestuzhev-Marlinsky and Lermontov, a revulsion from the extermination of the admirable Caucasian mountaineers deflated a central myth of imperialism – the conviction that violence is regenerative, if committed to further "civilization."[25]

As these remarks would indicate, in dealing with the literary Caucasus' relations to imperialism, I strive to confront the evolving nineteenth-century epoch in its own terms. While bound to remain an imperfectly realized project, any attempt to make a historical judgment of this literature must begin with the basic assumption that the milieux of empire-building created their own meanings for the texts.[26] The milieux shifted, of course. In moving from young Pushkin to old Tolstoy, my study ranges over a vast amount of literary and political history, not all of which can be recapitulated. The changing social composition of the readership provides just one example. At the literary Caucasus' birth in the 1820s, the readership was tiny.[27] But in the second half of the nineteenth century, the rise of literacy in Russia brought the wide dissemination of certain features of the old romantic discourse. Such important aspects of the sociology of reader reception are evoked in my study but cannot be tracked continuously from one period to the next. What I have tried to do instead is provide a sequence of historical moments which created meanings for the texts in question. The issue of historical conditioning pertains primarily to values perceived in the writings (most pervasively, as concerns the relative merits of mutually conditioned "civilization" and "savagery"). But in addition, the cultural context may even delineate formal, generic properties of a piece of writing (and indeed determine just what passes for literature). Russian readers of the 1820s, for instance, perceived reliable ethnography in Pushkin's "The Prisoner of the Caucasus" and thereby imparted to the poem an extra-literary quality entirely lost for us today.[28]

For all its self-evident importance, entering into the nineteenth century is only the first step towards fresh understanding of the literary Caucasus. Every good historian creatively interrogates the past from vantage points in the present. As Mikhail Bakhtin stressed in his "Response to a Question from the *Novy Mir* Editorial Staff," full immersion in a foreign culture or remote epoch would produce merely a replication of the object under study. Indeed, we can detect "new semantic depths" in a literary artifact only by standing outside it in time and place.[29] Bakhtin thus defined literary history as a process of dialogue between two eras, two cultures. In trying to realize this ideal, *Russian Literature and Empire* grounds textual analysis in particularized cultural contexts but seeks to ask the literary Caucasus enriching new questions – ones that nineteenth-century Russians were not able to pose about it themselves.

This historical study raises a variety of issues, without treating the whole configuration in any chapter. Bakhtinian dialogism plays a pervasive role in the assemblage of many different texts, the tracking of romantic discourse and the investigation of exchanges between authors and readers (both historical and implied). A special concern with the psychology of reader-response has led me to stress frequently the literary Caucasus' irrational, affective power.[30] Fact-oriented writings about the territory grew massively in the course of the nineteenth century, but readers consistently gravitated to the most artful, entertaining texts, exactly as common sense would predict. Where, after all, is the nation of readers who prefer scholarly monographs to pleasurable literature? But if hardly startling, the primary allegiance to literary pleasures was particularly pronounced in the evolution and consolidation of the cultural mythology of the Caucasian conquest. Certain Russian critics with a normative commitment to "realism" have thrust this crucial factor into the background by insisting that all the pertinent major contributors, from young Pushkin onward, performed an educative function for readers by dispensing empirical knowledge about the Caucasus. Such views of triumphant factuality grossly exaggerate the amount of reliable information available in these writings. But more importantly, no matter how accurate the literature may have been, it exerted its biggest impact not by satisfying readers' intellectual curiosity but rather by supplying them with unverifiable affective meanings about their relation to untamed Asia. Indeed, the history of the production and consumption of the Caucasus as the orient adds much concrete substance to Dmitri Likhachev's recent generalization that in Russian culture, in contrast to the West, "emotional principles" have always meant more than logical ones.[31]

Issues of gender accounted for many of the mythology's affective pleasures. The literary Caucasus had a good number of oriental love slaves whom some nineteenth-century Russian men were especially ready to promote as ideals of universally valid, "natural" femininity. Of even greater note, however, the producers and consumers of the literary Caucasus exhibited an enormous fondness for oriental machismo, if sometimes only covertly. By far the most dominant personages of the romantic Caucasus, dashing mountain warriors have particularly interesting stories to tell us about gender gaps in nineteeth-century Russian audiences, as readings of "Ammalat-Bek" and "Izmail-Bey" will stress. Last but not least, besides suggesting how the literary Caucasus inscribed certain tensions between the sexes in Russia, I also analyze writers' tendencies to feminize and eroticize the territory. This was most evident in the literary invention of Georgia as an oriental woman but had a wider compass.

The book's organization is basically chronological. Chapter 2 examines the early nineteenth-century readership's dual quest for *dulce* and *utile* in the literary Caucasus. Next comes analysis of the alpine imaginative geography produced in Pushkin's "The Prisoner of the Caucasus" and secondary poetry of the era. "Sentimental pilgrims" (chapter 4) then investigates the yen for politically innocent alpine experience in travel literature, mainly from the 1820s and 1830s.

After thus taking the measure of the "Caucasian Alps" as a region often rhetorically depopulated, the book turns full attention to issues of oriental culture in chapter 5, "The national stake in Asia." This discussion probes the contradictory identities the Russian élite derived for itself *vis-à-vis* the orient during the romantic era. Chapters 6, 7 and 8 then investigate various lines of resistance to the ideology of the European civilizing mission in Pushkin's "The Prisoner of the Caucasus," Bestuzhev-Marlinsky's "Ammalat-Bek" and Lermontov's "Izmail-Bey." Contrast with the disruptive tendencies of these three works is provided in "Little orientalizers" (chapter 9), a discussion of secondary writers and hapless scribblers who fully underwrote war against the Caucasian tribes. Chapter 10 takes up the issue of feminization with special attention to Bestuzhev-Marlinsky's Caucasian travelogues. As the most artistically significant expression of the urge to read the territory as a woman, literature about Georgia is treated separately in chapter 11. Certain insights from this extended consideration of metaphorical femininity are also picked up in the concluding chapter on romantic literature, "The anguished poet in uniform," an analysis of late Lermontov's projection of spiritual turmoil about Russian aggression in the Caucasus.

The final chapters are dominated by Tolstoy, the writer who provides a certain all-encompassing focus on the big issues of literature, knowledge and imperialism which run throughout the book. At the outset of his career in the 1850s Tolstoy assumed an embattled stance towards romanticism and made literature address new problems: "What relation has the 'poetic' Caucasus to the empirical Caucasus?" and "What sort of impact has the 'poetic' Caucasus had on imperial Russia's readers?" In a discussion centered upon failed cross-cultural communication in *The Cossacks*, chapter 13 explores early Tolstoy's efforts to deflate Bestuzhev-Marlinsky and Lermontov. The next chapter keeps Tolstoy in focus by demonstrating how romantic discourse persisted despite him and even infused history in the latter part of the nineteenth century. *Hadji Murat* is then examined as old Tolstoy's confessional challenge to Russia's reigning mythology about the Caucasian conquest as a civilizing mission. No longer haunted by the romantic shades which had disturbed his literary apprenticeship in the 1850s, Tolstoy used some old "poetic" tricks himself to maneuver his envisioned readers into unflattering recognition of their (shared) history and present status as plundering beneficiaries of the empire. The book's final pages offer concluding observations partially concerned with ways the Caucasus' decolonized peoples might rewrite the history of their relations with Russia.

CHAPTER 2

The poet and terra incognita

Pushkin discovered the Caucasus.
Vissarion Belinsky

Belinsky's foreword to the epochal miscellany *The Physiology of Petersburg* (1845) offers a vital perspective on Russian imperial consciousness. In approving the book's aesthetic of descriptive naturalism as a new mode for exposing urban life's particularities, the critic naturally concentrated on Russia's capital cities. But in orienting his discussion, he looked much farther afield to urge Russian writers to clarify their national identity by investigating the whole, far-flung empire. Among other regions, he cited the Caucasus, the Crimea and Siberia as places whose geographical and cultural features were not yet sufficiently known to the Russian readership. Most of all, he thought "travelogues, accounts of trips, essays, stories and descriptions" should determine the affiliations and differences between all the various peoples: which ones were most "kindred" to the "purely Russian element," and which were "utterly alien?"[1] In casting a rhetorical eye over these vast expanses, Belinsky no doubt showed a "readiness to enjoy the experience of empire."[2] Without questioning the tsarist state's right to rule all the "other" nationalities, he looked forward to exploring the empire's "unknown" corners, observing exotic populations, defining them and assigning them cultural ranks in relation to his metropole.[3] Such an attitude surely was shared by many of Russia's armchair travelers who proved so receptive to the literary Caucasus.

However, the cultural texture of this reading experience was much richer than the imperial posture alone can sug-

15

gest. A great deal of the complexity lay in the belief that some of the empire's regions and ethnic groups were more kindred to Russians than others. Thanks primarily to young Pushkin, romantic literature's alpine Caucasus and Muslim mountaineers quickly won the most favored "Asian" slot in this hierarchy. But before delving into the way writers produced a Caucasian landscape and population so eminently suited to Russian national needs, it is worthwhile lingering on Belinsky's conviction that *literature* would contribute to knowledge. Although the introduction to *The Physiology of Petersburg* obviously pinned great hopes on non-fictional genres such as the "essay," imaginative writing held its own ("stories"), while the hybrid form "travelogue" appeared in two Russian variants (*puteshestvie* and *poezdka*). Belinsky thus endorsed fiction and semi-fiction as tools for unearthing reliable information.

The conviction that literature could help make any place *terra cognita* underlay Belinsky's well-known assessment of Pushkin as the "discoverer" of the Caucasus. Contained in the critic's sixth article on Pushkin (1844), this evaluation provides a good starting point for discussing poetry's special authoritativeness in the early nineteenth-century field of Russian reader response. Belinsky maintained that "Russian society became acquainted with the Caucasus for the first time" only in Pushkin's tale. In hailing the writer as a sort of literary Columbus, Belinsky specifically applauded verse as the chosen medium: in his opinion, Pushkin successfully slipped geographical and ethnographic information into a captivating story, instead of writing "too didactically and, perforce, too prosaically."[4] Of course, the very notion of "discovery" misconstrued Pushkin's *production* of a Caucasus, as we shall see. Nevertheless, Belinsky definitely had a point in declaring that readers of the 1820s looked to the poet partly for enlightenment about an intriguing foreign land. Enraptured by the verse but also keen for knowledge, the contemporary audience approached "The Prisoner of the Caucasus" as a work both *dulce* and *utile*. What textual and contextual factors encouraged this double demand?

THE PROBLEM OF GENRE

An investigation of the question must start with the problem of genre. Today's standard classification for "The Prisoner of the Caucasus" is the narrative poem (*poema*, a term to be further explicated shortly). Pushkin, however, did not set any particular store in the designation. He proposed a much wider range of generic labels for "The Prisoner of the Caucasus" in correspondence with Nikolai Gnedich, the friend and editor to whom he wrote from Kishinev to ask for assistance with publication. In a letter of April 29, 1822 the author gave Gnedich *carte blanche*: "Call this verse (*stikhotvorenie*) a fairy tale, a tale, a *poema* or whatever other name you want to give it."[5] Along with *poema*, Pushkin suggested "fairy tale" (*skazka*), an option which called attention to the element of pure invention in "The Prisoner of the Caucasus." The poet's third proposal was *povest'* ("tale"), a category nineteenth-century writers often allowed to overlap with *poema* or even "novel" (*roman*). To complete the list of generic labels employed by Pushkin, a draft of his letter to Gnedich called the poem's 121-line depiction of the Circassian warriors a "geographical article or traveler's account," embedded none too harmoniously in the fictive prisoner's story.[6] In a move never contested nor defended by the author, Gnedich published "The Prisoner of the Caucasus" as a *povest'*, no doubt in imitation of the subtitle "tale" used by Byron for "The Giaour," "The Bride of Abydos" and "The Corsair."[7]

As signaled by the profusion of terms Pushkin proposed, "The Prisoner of the Caucasus" exhibits varied authorial impulses. Its consequent resistance to neat classification was obscured, however, by Victor Zhirmunsky's influential definition of the "romantic *poema*" in the comparative study *Byron and Pushkin*.[8] Concerned with all of young Pushkin's "southern poems," Zhirmunsky characterized the romantic *poema* by thematic and compositional features such as a disillusioned hero, an exotic setting and fragmentariness. While preoccupied with textual properties, this analysis stressed Pushkin's historical role as an innovator in Russia. A major event in the rise of Russian romanticism, "The Prisoner of the Caucasus" abandoned the rigid classical norms predominant in eighteenth-century Russian literature. Proponents of the new romantic sensibility accordingly rallied around the tale, while conservative critics assailed it as a disorderly production because it fitted into none of the accepted genres defined by Boileau.[9] Zhirmunsky underlined Pushkin's discontinuity with Russia's established hierarchy of genres but did not perceive the new aesthetic freedom as an unruly force which undercut an ideal of textual unity. To the contrary, he took the "romantic *poema*" as a new genre whose discursive practices were all consistent. The "ethnographic catalogue" in "The Prisoner of the Caucasus" thus became just another "romantic" device in the service of "local color." More tellingly, Zhirmunsky said virtually nothing about Pushkin's footnotes, a significant non-fictional component of the text.

Like Zhirmunsky's Formalist rage for unity, a related line of criticism obscured the dual-purpose character of "The Prisoner of the Caucasus" by trying to pigeonhole the *poema* as strictly "high" literature for admiratory readers of the early nineteenth century. "*Poema*" had always encompassed the epic. In the 1820s, however, the proponents of romanticism largely appropriated the term to signify a long tale in verse in tune with their anti-classical artistic agenda. With this context in mind, some commentators have argued that "The Prisoner of the Caucasus" belonged to the loftiest literary echelon of the era, in distinction from satirical prose replete with details of everyday life.[10] Young Pushkin himself did indeed subscribe to a fundamentally eighteenth-century classical notion of poetry as the highest literary medium, set against "humble prose" in a stanza of *Eugene Onegin*.[11] However, the literary culture of his day was not marked by the rigid boundaries which this perspective might suggest. Versatility rather than specialization was upheld at the time as the norm for the typical gentleman poet who was expected to display competence in a variety of genres, just as he was required to assume a multifaceted, urbane social self. [12]

Disorderly to the taste of the era's conservatives but pleasingly versatile to his admirers, young Pushkin cut across generic boundaries in "The Prisoner of the Caucasus" to send diverse signals to the readership. Unlike Zhirmunsky, Boris Tomashevsky and Yuri Tynianov recognized the heterogeneity of Pushkin's tale.[13] But they too left Pushkin's readers largely outside their analyses. Bakhtin's concept of the "novelized poem" provides a corrective by shifting attention away from the literary polemics of the 1820s to focus instead on clashing discourses which may invite readers to seek varied satisfactions from a single text. As defined in a discussion focused on Byron's *Childe Harold's Pilgrimage* and *Don Juan*, the novelized poem has an unruly, "centrifugal" force: it revolts from an ideal of unified order and pushes verse into semi-fictional and extra-literary spheres by incorporating a diversity of discursive practices.[14] Although Bakhtin did not treat Pushkin here, the concept of novelization applies particularly well to "The Prisoner of the Caucasus," which was influenced in several respects by the much longer *Childe Harold's Pilgrimage*.

Pushkin's generically restless tale certainly won much popularity by providing escapist entertainment and aesthetic pleasure. As animatedly recollected by the orientalist Ilya Berezin, "The Prisoner of the Caucasus" filled readers with "rapture" and stimulated a pandemic daydream of the territory as a place of romantic adventure.[15] Narrative excitement abounded (a Russian's captivity in Circassia, a spectacular mountain *paysage*, savage warriors and a love affair with a native woman). Pushkin's mellifluous language immeasurably enhanced all these subjects, as many memoirs of the period affirm. In the opinion of Dmitri Mirsky, the "wonderful music" of the verse was quite simply the primary explanation for the extraordinary success of "The Prisoner of the Caucasus."[16] If exaggerated, Mirsky's discussion none the less pinpointed something extremely important: with its harmony of sounds, carefully selected diction and masterful adaptation of rhythm to intonation, Pushkin's language afforded a stunningly new aesthetic pleasure which outshone other literary works of the time.

But the romantic subject-matter and elegant versification did not prevent "The Prisoner of the Caucasus" from enjoying considerable extra-literary authority in its heyday. So important was the urge to read Pushkin for information that the literary historian Mikhail Alekseev once declared that consumers of the Caucasian tale were looking "not for make-believe nor captivating inventions and fantasies, but rather for facts and specifications."[17] As unsatisfactory as Mirsky's single-minded emphasis on Pushkin's "wonderful music" may have been, Alekseev's hasty generalization was in a sense no better: it erred on the opposite side by completely discounting the element of aesthetic, affective pleasures. The truth is that readers of the 1820s were enthralled by the thrilling adventure and musicality of "The Prisoner of the Caucasus" but simultaneously wanted geographical and ethnographic data to reassure them of the exotic land's real existence. This concurrent pursuit of *dulce* and *utile* was underlined aptly by Ivan Bessonov, an early editor of Pushkin who asserted in the 1840s that the Russian public had approached the writer's Caucasian and Crimean poems as "essays" written with brilliant artistry.[18]

The notion of an essay in verse provides an illuminating parallel with Chateaubriand's writings about America. In addition to the frequently noted thematic similarities to "The Prisoner of the Caucasus," Chateaubriand's semi-fictional works about a Frenchman's encounter with native Americans also invited reading for both entertainment and enlightenment. Chateaubriand took pride in the mixture (without admitting just how limited his journey in America had been). In a preface to *Atala* he described himself as a traveling author who had produced a text perceived by himself and his audience as "autre chose qu'un ouvrage de *pure imagination*."[19] With a similar evasion of the issue of actual exposure to the exotic region in question, Pushkin's brief preface to the second edition of his Circassian tale proudly directed readers to the "true, if barely etched, representation of the Caucasus and the *moeurs* of the mountaineers."

As regards "The Prisoner of the Caucasus," the big contextual factor which encouraged readers to seek something more than literary invention was the dearth of impressive nonfiction and semi-fiction about the territory. Prior to Pushkin, some explorers and travelers had dealt with the Caucasus but failed to fix its image in the public eye.[20] Furthermore, a Russian tradition of relevant journalism was also lacking. In other words, neither travelers' accounts, natural science, ethnography nor newspaper reports had assumed authority as the locus of true, real-life writing about the Caucasus.[21] In this situation, Pushkin's tale in verse performed functions of travel literature, geography, ethnography and even war correspondence. The poem intersected these fields to unequal degrees, however, as we shall see now in discussing the overlaps in turn.

PUSHKIN AND THE TRAVELOGUE TRADITION

In the eyes of the readership of the 1820s "The Prisoner of the Caucasus" coincided primarily with the travelogue, a semi-fictional genre which may be more or less informative. As argued in many studies, not always concerned with Russia, the boundaries between the *récit de voyage* and fiction are notoriously blurry.[22] The manner of producing travelogues and the motivations for consuming them are often difficult, if not impossible, to distinguish from the writing and reading of a piece of imaginative literature. The division between fact and fiction can also become imperceptible in the traveler's account itself. Since travel literature exists almost exclusively in prose, it is usually related to fiction alone. In seventeenth-century France and Poland, however, the *récit de voyage* was practiced by poets as well.[23]

Pushkin's poem shared travel literature's fundamental impulse to bring a foreign territory into a mutually illuminating relationship with the homeland. Like imaginative writing about a trip, a real-life traveler's narrative clarifies the character of the native realm by contrast to a different country. The pertinent Russian travelogue tradition stemmed from encounters with Europe, where civilization's attainments were incontrovertibly greater than the writer could find at home. Nikolai Karamzin set the immensely influential standard in *Letters of a Russian Traveler*, first issued serially in the *Moscow Journal* (*Moskovskii zhurnal*) in 1791–92. A great admirer of west European culture, Karamzin cast himself as a mediator between "our" sphere and "theirs."[24] The comparative dynamic naturally persisted in the great wave of *récits de voyage* in Europe which other Russians wrote under Karamzin's impact. Equally fruitful in imaginative literature about travel, the impulse to sharpen national self-definition by writing about foreigners operated in Pushkin's tale of Circassia, a "wild," Asian place whose imaginative geography and ethnography will occupy us in later chapters.

Along with the cross-cultural style of thought, Russia's travelogue tradition prefigured Pushkin's poetic foray abroad by serving the dual functions of entertainment and enlightenment. A typical example of the hybrid genre, Karamzin's *Letters of a Russian Traveler* combined factual *reportage* with literary invention. Although stimulated by an actual trip, the book was researched and written in the author's study after he returned to Russia. In a digressive manner patterned after his two major models Laurence Stern's *A Sentimental Journey* and Charles Dupaty's *Lettres sur l'Italie*, Karamzin discussed the geography, history, customs and politics of the various places he visited, while enlivening his account with literary citations, anecdotes and professions of intense, often tender feelings. In the arresting phrase of Yuri Lotman and Boris Uspensky, this semi-fictional mixture struck the Russian readership as a "Baedeker embellished by amusing tales."[25] Curious readers mined the travelogue for information about scenery, architecture and art, national monuments, politics and daily life in Europe. But at the same time, they were enchanted by Karamzin's new sentimental manner and path-breaking, elegant prose style. Literary merit accounted substantially for the popularity of *Letters of a Russian Traveler*, which appeared before the novel emerged in Russia and was consequently relished all the more for its diverting, story-telling proper-ties.[26]

As these remarks suggest, the sentimental mode of vicarious tourism obscured generic distinctions between a *récit de voyage* proper and a purely fictional story. The much cherished romances of Richardson, Rousseau and Karamzin himself ("Poor Liza," 1792) promoted a cult of emotionality and an enthusiasm for a life close to nature, both prominent themes in subjective travelogues.[27] Likewise, literature could offer the pleasure of surveying an interesting foreign landscape. Rousseau's immensely popular *Julie ou la Nouvelle Heloïse* was a major case in point with its depiction of St. Preux's rambles in the Alps. The themes and style of this text extensively infiltrated the section on Switzerland in Karamzin's *Letters of a Russian Traveler*. As illustrated by the interrelationship between Karamzin and Rousseau, the *récit de voyage* and works of fiction strongly reinforced one another in the age of senti-mentalism: the writing traveler made digressions from *paysage* in order to celebrate friendship and love, while the novelist provided touristic interludes. Readers could accordingly find the same sorts of satisfactions in both types of books without bothering to ask how empirically "true" the writing might be.

The reader's demand for entertainment and intellectual stimulation in a *récit de voyage* clearly coincided with the aims of much touristic travel itself, a condition which would persist in young Pushkin's time. As Michel Butor has underlined, "reading as traveling" can be observed in various places and historical periods.[28] However, a strong current of boredom in late eighteenth- and early nineteenth-century Russian society fostered an especially strong taste for armchair journeys. In 1785 the nobles reaffirmed their privilege not to render service to the state, and large numbers of them retired to country manors, deprived of amusements enjoyed by the leisured classes in the capitals. The placid routine of the landed gentry nurtured a great appetite for books of travel and romance, as Pushkin so memorably suggested in depicting the old-fashioned Madame Larin and young Tatiana in *Eugene Onegin*. To be sure, news of the French revolution and consequent upheavals in Europe galvanized many politically minded persons in Russia at the time. But despite such momentous events abroad, a sense of tedium plagued the Russian upper classes and fed their taste for *récits de voyage*, as well as tales of love and adventure. Karamzin acknowledged the situation when he launched the *Herald of Europe* (*Vestnik Evropy*) with an editorial promise that the periodical would provide reading material to "help while away the long evenings," especially for "our *belles*" of the *beau monde* and "provincial ladies."[29] While targeting women in particularly, this comment evoked two vast spheres of urban and rural boredom.

A BAEDEKER IN VERSE

Firmly rooted in the sentimental era prior to the conquest of the Caucasus, the zest for actual and armchair traveling was enormously intensified by Byronism in young Pushkin's time. By comparison to Karamzin's generation, more Russians of this period took long trips, often with the express purpose of relieving ennui. Never destined to receive the state's permission to go abroad, Pushkin expressed raging wanderlust in a letter to Prince Pyotr Viazemsky in 1820: "Petersburg is stifling for a poet. I long for foreign lands."[30] The yearning was ordinary among young, privileged Russians of the time, as illustrated by a visitor in the Caucasus who called travel an antidote for the "boredom of our monotonous life."[31]

The poetry of Byron both prompted Russians to go on journeys and served as a substitute for those who could not leave home. Initially known to Pushkin's generation as the author of tales of adventure in exotic lands, Byron acquired a Russian reputation as the traveling author *par excellence*. Translated excerpts from "The Corsair" appeared in the *Russian Museum* (*Russkii muzei*) in 1815; a few years later Konstantin Batiushkov translated the apostrophe to the sea from *Childe Harold's Pilgrimage*; and Vasily Zhukovsky's Russian version of "The Prisoner of Chillon" was published in 1821, just a year before the "The Prisoner of the Caucasus."[32] In the same period Byron's oriental poems, as well as the full text of *Childe Harold's Pilgrimage*, circulated widely in the French prose translations of Amédée Pichot, the imported versions read by the majority of Russians. All these works contributed to Russian perceptions of Byron as the "great wanderer," as the orientalist Berezin dubbed him in his *récit de voyage, Journey in Dagestan and Transcaucasia.*[33]

Childe Harold's Pilgrimage in particular had an autobiographical dimension which won it the reputation of a "Baedeker poem" inspired by the author's travels abroad.[34] In the preface to the first and second cantos, Byron called Childe Harold a "fictitious character" introduced "for the sake of giving some connexion to the piece."[35] He invested the hero with his own alienation and spleen, as in the celebrated apostrophe to the sea ("Adieu, adieu! my native shore," canto 1, xiii). But besides such elements of self-dramatization, the impact of *Childe Harold's Pilgrimage* as a reflection of actual travels was augmented by the copious prose commentary, largely devoted to Greece and the virtually unknown Albania. In the annotations Byron paraded his knowledge of history and geography, included long citations and constantly reminded readers that he himself had traveled the routes of the poem. Both chatty and full of insistence on the factual base of *Childe Harold's Pilgrimage*, the sometimes unreliable commentary seemed to hold a wealth of fascinating information and was published separately in certain British periodicals.[36]

A notable expression of Russian excitement over *Childe Harold's Pilgrimage* as a Baedeker poem appeared in the review of a travelogue in the *Moscow Telegraph* (*Moskovskii telegraf*) in the early 1830s.[37] The author demonstrated a readiness to shuttle back and forth between *récits de voyage* and imaginative literature in a twofold quest for entertainment and intellectual stimulation. He began by discussing the phenomenal popularity that travel literature had enjoyed in Russia for decades (and still heartily deserved, in his opinion, because the nation's novel remained so unimpressive). While praising the edifying features of *récits de voyage*, this discussion devalued fact-oriented, "scientific" accounts by contrast to the "poetic" kind. "Enjoyable and absorbing," the "poetic" travelogue covers the "misfortunes, dangers and difficulties" encountered during the voyage and exposes the reader to "fearful storms at sea and wonders of the world such as mountains much higher than the clouds." As if the allusions were not sufficiently clear, this devotee of "poetic" *récits de voyage* then summed up his sentiments by seconding the first line of the epigraph to *Childe Harold's Pilgrimage*: "L'univers est une espèce de livre, dont on n'a lu que la première page quand on n'a vu que son pays." Travelogues were thus situated along a continuum which shaded into verse itself: the author made "scientific" equivalent to turgid factuality and implied that versatile Byronic poets made the best guides, capable of simultaneously satisfying the armchair traveler's appetite for adventure and thirst for new knowledge.

Although written several years after the publication of "The Prisoner of the Caucasus," this testimony to a hunt for identical satisfactions in *récits de voyage* and poetry alike indicates a prevailing disposition of Pushkin's first readers. Exiled to the south of Russia because of writings deemed subversive by the government, Pushkin spent around two months in the Caucasus in the vicinity of Piatigorsk and the Kuban river basin.[38] His poem most directly evoked this personal experience in the dedication addressed to his traveling companion, Nikolai Raevsky. As illustrated in reviews of "The Prisoner of the Caucasus" in the Russian press, the author's status as a recent visitor of the outland invited viewing the work as an elaborate traveler's report. Viazemsky made the most interesting attempt to relate the text to the journey:

The author of the tale "The Prisoner of the Caucasus" wanted to transmit to the reader impressions which his trip made upon him (after the example of Byron in *Childe Harold*)...In contemplating the summits of the poetic Caucasus, Pushkin was struck by the poetry of wild, majestic nature, the poetry of the *moeurs* and customs of an unrefined but bold, martial, handsome people [ellipsis mine].[39]

A landmark in the revolt against classicism in Russia, Viazemsky's enthusiastic review of "The Prisoner of the Caucasus" showed a sensitive critic groping towards a new concept of romantic imagination as a transfiguring force. But in the quoted passage, Viazemsky strikingly suggested that "poetry" had been out there in the Caucasus *a priori*, waiting to be found and transmitted to readers in Russia. Instead of focusing on the artistic act of contriving images of the foreign land, this train of thought foregrounded travel as the requisite condition for sufficient inspiration. Pushkin thus acquired a certain stature as a tour guide.

In approaching "The Prisoner of the Caucasus" as the product of a trip, Viazemsky lavished special praise on the poet's artful transmission of purportedly authentic geographical and ethnographic detail. He marveled at the technical excellence of the verse and declared that – far from excluding accuracy – a polished poetic style was *more* veridical than "dead and, so to speak, literal representation." A new variant on the ancient call for literature which is both useful and pleasing, Viazemsky's evaluation of the wild landscape and exotic cultural content in "The Prisoner of the Caucasus" propounded a typically romantic belief in poetry as a realm of some higher realism, beyond the merely and drily factual.

THE POET'S RIVALRY WITH SCIENCE

As mentioned at the outset of this chapter, the very possibility of Pushkin's poem functioning as a traveler's report was greatly facilitated by the lack of competition from semi-fictional and non-fictional prose. Prior to the time of the poet's own exile, there were few Caucasian travelogues because the lack of border security blocked the development of tourism. Some pertinent *récits de voyage* had appeared in the Russian press, but they were undistinguished efforts which attracted no discernible attention.[40] The territory had simply not found its Karamzin, so that "The Prisoner of the Caucasus" was in a prime position to serve as a substitute for travel literature.

Even more strikingly, Pushkin challenged the existing corpus of natural science and ethnography. In the late 1760s Catherine II was reportedly perturbed to discover that her diverse maps located Georgia's capital Tiflis inland, on the Black Sea and on the Caspian coast.[41] To rectify the situation, the empress mounted scientific expeditions led by Johann Güldenstädt, Samuel Gmelin and Peter Pallas over the course of several years. Each of the explorers wrote lengthy studies full of data on the natural environment and indigenous peoples.[42] To judge by a Russian translation of his German, Pallas in particular was a felicitous author.[43] But like Güldenstädt and Gmelin, he too had fallen on deaf ears in Russia. The preface to Semyon Bronevsky's *A New Geography and History of the Caucasus* (1823) acknowledged debts to the eighteenth-century naturalists.[44] However, the tribute's whole point was to retrieve those writers from the oblivion into which they had sunk outside a tiny circle of readers.

Since "The Prisoner of the Caucasus" contains some reliable ethnographic detail, there has been much speculation about Pushkin's sources of information. His trip certainly afforded no opportunities for observing Circassian life. After visiting the area of Piatigorsk (known to Russians at the time as "Goriachye Vody" – "Hot Springs"), Pushkin and Raevsky headed for the southern shore of the Crimea with a convoy of sixty Cossacks. As the poet told his brother in a letter of September 1820, he had merely ridden "in view of hostile lands of the free mountain peoples."[45] His responsiveness was keen, though, as he stressed by adding, "You realize what appeal this specter of danger has for an active imagination." The mind's eye was presumably stimulated by readings, but nobody has been able to establish exactly what they may have been.[46] Conversation during Pushkin's travels in the south may also have shaped his ideas about Circassia. After leaving the Caucasus, the poet spent some time in the Crimea in the house of Bronevsky, an acquaintance of Raevsky. One might imagine them having lively talks about peoples treated in Bronevsky's book. However, the naturalist was definitely no mentor for Pushkin, who judged him well informed about the Crimea but "not an intelligent man."[47]

Whatever sources the poet may have consulted, he boldly crossed the boundary into contemporary science by footnoting "The Prisoner of the Caucasus." In sharp contrast to Byron's intrusive claims to truth in the massive commentary to *Childe Harold's Pilgrimage*, Pushkin's glosses were laconic and self-effacing, but they made a bid for extra-literary authority by introducing a line of scholarly discourse into the poem.[48] Among other things, Pushkin defined a linguistically mixed assortment of terms – *chikhir* (new red Georgian wine), *sakla* (house), *kunak* (consecrated friend) and *aul* (the word for tribal "village" already used in Zhukovsky's "To Voeikov"). A reference to Karamzin's *History of the Russian State* best illustrates the commentary's general presumption to go beyond the confines of imaginative literature. Pushkin cited Karamzin's second volume in order to substantiate the poem's mention of an ancient Russian prince who fought the Circassians' purported ancestors. By modern-day standards of historical research, Karamzin's own discussion of this distant epoch was heavily fueled by imagination, but it had won a considerable intellectual authority in its time.[49] Pushkin's note thus directed his audience to an outside, documented source where they might corroborate his own text.[50] In the same fashion, an annotation to Bestuzhev-Marlinsky's tale of thirteenth-century Novgorod, "Roman and Olga" (1823), would invite the audience to check the story against the documented treatment of the epoch in Karamzin's *History*.

Published neck in neck with Bronevsky's book and possibly influenced by its author in person, "The Prisoner of the Caucasus" was attended by signs of tension between the littérateur and the scientist. Bronevsky's preface to the second edition of *A New Geography and History of the Caucasus* presented the book as Humboldtian natural science meant to dispel the mythological aura of a territory most educated Russians associated with Prometheus, Medea and Jason.[51] The scientific protest was directed against the lingering power of ancient legends and did not declare war on contemporary

Russian poetry as a new mythology. All the same, Bronevsky's allegiance to facts instead of compelling stories held the seed of Russian culture's future argument about what constituted the "real" Caucasus.

Although the full-blown debate lay ahead, the regional specialist's big disadvantage to the poet was immediately apparent. Bronevsky's book was earnestly commended by reviewers, including Bestuzhev-Marlinsky in the *Polar Star* (*Poliarnaia zvezda*).[52] But even amidst the initial success, stylistic deficiences were noted. In the words of a commentator for the *Son of the Fatherland* (*Syn otechestva*), the book's content placed it among the best Russian publications of 1823, but "a purity of style cannot be counted as one of its merits."[53] Thus only a short while after the appearance of "The Prisoner of the Caucasus," the foremost exponent of scientific investigation of the territory was called to task for not writing with aesthetic flair. The demand for stylistic excellence in natural science and ethnography implied that the Caucasus deserved a Buffon, a man who enlightened while sounding well. Bronevsky was too pedestrian to fill the role, and in the meantime Pushkin's annotated tale in verse garnered authority as a Baedeker poem.

Young Pushkin's illimitable aesthetic ascendance over the natural scientist owed much to the extraordinary memorability of his "wonderful music." In the present era Russians still tend to know much Pushkin by heart and may even perform astounding feats of recollection. In the poet's own time, however, extensive memorization was more common. According to Belinsky, even into the 1840s most Russian readers could recite from memory the depiction of the mountains and the tribesmen in "The Prisoner of the Caucasus."[54] To judge from memoirs, some early nineteenth-century Russians accumulated much vaster mental records of verse.[55] During his trip to Erzerum ("Arzrum" to Russians) in 1829 Pushkin himself is said to have declaimed "The Prisoner of the Caucasus" by heart for a group of tsarist officers at a champagne fest.[56] In our age, when a poet's "reading" of his works is usually exactly that (especially if the verse was written several years earlier), Pushkin's bardic facility may seem astonishing. But today's text-oriented reader will no doubt be more struck by the performance of an admirer the poet encountered on that journey: Pushkin's military escort on the road to Vladikavkaz claimed that he recited the epilogue of "The Prisoner of the Caucasus," ran through "The Gypsies" and launched into the first chapter of *Eugene Onegin* before the poet finally called a halt.[57] While this soldier may have glorified himself a bit in his memoir, Pushkin's younger brother won recognition from other people for precisely such prodigious capacities: as Viazemsky once remarked, Lev Pushkin's mind was a veritable "printing press" where entire long poems by his brother were set (and occasionally released without the author's permission).[58]

A major factor in young Pushkin's triumph at the expense of Bronevsky, the "wonderful music" of his verse gave the newly romanticized Caucasus an inordinately potent, unverbalizable aesthetic resonance. "The Prisoner of the Caucasus" and secondary romantic verse of the 1820s would be eclipsed by prose in the next decade, when Bestuzhev-Marlinsky took the Russian reading public by storm. However, Lermontov's poetry subsequently reasserted the musical factor in the literary Caucasus, and young Pushkin's own tale of captivity in Circassia would come into a rebirth in late nineteenth-century Russia. In exhibiting a greater staying power than any other writers who treated the conquest, Pushkin and Lermontov provided much food for thought about a very special (if historically inconstant) Russian veneration for the works and lives of poets.

NO NEWS TO RIVAL THE MUSE

While no doubt intersecting the *récit de voyage* most extensively and also encroaching upon the turf of the geographer and ethnographer, the novelized "The Prisoner of the Caucasus" had a journalistic edge as well. The total lack of anything approaching war correspondence about the conquest was particularly pronounced in the 1820s when Russian journalism was such a literary activity and so closely overseen by the state censors. By contrast to today's American and European newspapers, the Russian periodical publications of the type prevalent in young Pushkin's era had no "news" in the sense of regular, continuous coverage of current events at home and abroad. Literary magazines such as the relatively long-lived *Herald of Europe* (1802–30) dominated the scene with offerings in poetry, fiction, travelogues, criticism and book reviews. In a category by itself was the four-sheet St. Petersburg broadside the *Northern Bee* (*Severnaia pchela*, 1825–64), edited by the infamous Faddei Bulgarin. As a reward for playing informer during the government's investigation of the Decembrist revolt, Bulgarin was allowed to publish political news, a privilege denied all other private periodicals. Interesting items could make their way into the *Northern Bee*. However, by 1827 Bulgarin's association with the secret police was common knowledge, and liberally minded persons held his "news" in contempt.

The journalistic context gave "The Prisoner of the Caucasus" a topical aspect. Embroiled in repeated conflicts with Turkey and Persia in the Caucasus since the late eighteenth century, the tsarist army also had gone to Chechnia in the 1780s to surpress the stirrings of Islamic holy war under the leadership of Sheikh Mansur. Such events were not exposed in the press, however. This left the Russian public in a very different position than nineteenth-century British readers barraged with newspaper articles about exploration in Africa or problems of the colonial administration in India at the same time that writers such as Kipling offered fiction about such experiences.[59] Russian readers knew vaguely of warfare occurring in the Caucasus, but for most of them young Pushkin provided the first specific evocation of tsarist armies in combat against the tribes. The brief monopoly of the poetic muse would be broken by the appearance of Alexander Yakubovich's campaign notes in 1825. Nevertheless, for a short period following the publication of "The Prisoner of the Caucasus" Russian readers could not even try to verify verse by comparison to writings by eyewitnesses at the theater of war.

Pushkin and his audience doubtlessly perceived a sharp boundary between verse and a newspaper report, and yet the role of a poet in a field of imperial conquest remained a little ill defined. In the epilogue of "The Prisoner of the Caucasus" the author struck the traditional stance of an odist rather than a reporter with a scoop, and he shared with other members of the literary élite of the early 1820s a low opinion of journalists as profit-minded scribblers. Furthermore, when in 1829 Pushkin detailed his observations of warfare along the Turkish-Caucasian border, he wrote *Journey to Arzrum* in prose. But interestingly enough, when a journalist from the *Tiflis Gazette* (*Tiflisskie vedomosti*) learned of Pushkin's presence in the area, he looked forward to reading a new poem born of travels, as he believed "The Prisoner of the Caucasus" and "The Fountain of Bakhchisarai" had been.[60] With enmity rather than admiration in his heart, Bulgarin also assumed that Pushkin would write inspiring poetry about the war against Turkey and accordingly vented his displeasure with *Journey to Arzrum*.[61] Somewhat equivocal about the proper sphere and function of verse, these commentators assumed that a talented poet at the front was duty-bound to share his impressions with homebound readers, perhaps to stimulate patriotism (as Bulgarin demanded) but also to artfully fill a gap in information, as the Tiflis journalist implied.

Despite obvious divergences between an ode and a correspondent's bulletin, the journalistic context of "The Prisoner of the Caucasus" indicates a major problem which would continue to face Russian audiences throughout the coming decades of battle against the Muslim tribesmen. Just where could a reader seek a stimulating exposure to the multifaceted process of empire-building in the territory, given the paucity of genuine "news" in the censored press? This question remained urgent in young Tolstoy's era of the 1850s, even though non-fiction about the Caucasus had proliferated monumentally by that time. As often observed, the conditions of censorship in nineteenth-century Russia increased the pertinence of literature (and literary criticism) as forums for discussing political, social and cultural issues not adequately aired elsewhere. This general rule applied to the literary Caucasus. During the entire period from the 1820s to the capture of Shamil in 1859, Russians never had any steady, uncontrolled newspaper coverage of the conquest, and this indubitably enhanced the literature's attractiveness.

POETRY AS ARTFUL FACT

In opening perspectives on "The Prisoner of the Caucasus" as a generically unruly work, this chapter has stressed the poem's power to convince readers it was a multipurpose text, at once artful and enlightening. Although not yet subject to much direct discussion in the 1820s, a belief in fine literature's informational capability was operating to ensure doubly keen responsiveness to Pushkin's Circassian tale. An incipient line of opposition to literature as a reliable branch of regional studies can be detected in Bronevsky's avowed aim to displace potent ancient myths with factual knowledge. However, at the inception of the literary Caucasus during the Golden Age of verse there was neither a Plato of the sciences nor a band of fact-oriented journalists degrading the poet as a liar and demanding that he yield his position of authority to a keeper of the truth. No dichotomous style of thought prevailed, declaring *either* literature *or* science, *either* imagination *or* verifiable data. To the contrary, writers and readers in the 1820s entertained notions of poetry's potential as artful fact rather than frivolous artifact. The outlook would thrive well into the next decade, as witnessed by Ivan Borozdna's annotated verses about his travels, *Poetic Essays on Ukraine, Odessa, and the Crimea* (1837).[62]

But the Bronevskian cry for more facts would eventually strengthen in Russia. After the Golden Age of poetry had passed, Bestuzhev-Marlinsky and Tolstoy would each defend his own distinctive brand of semi-fictional prose as the uniquely reliable narrative about the Caucasus. More combatively, historians, ethnographers and journalists committed to edification would degrade literature as a web of fantasies. To begin detailing this history of interplay between the affective and rationalistic ways of knowing the territory, the next chapter will explore the imaginative Caucasian geography founded by Pushkin.

CHAPTER 3

Imaginative geography

In gloomy Besh-Tau, the majestic hermit,
I found a new Parnassus.

Pushkin

In its treatment of landscape "The Prisoner of the Caucasus" approximated the territory to the Alps rather than the orient. The choice had its arbitrary element. Authors can read whatever they like into nature, and Russian literature would Islamize Caucasian peaks in the 1830s when war against the tribes had escalated. But if mountains themselves do not predetermine an alpine imaginative geography, their salience in Pushkin's experience undoubtedly contributed. The poet passed most of his time in the Caucasus around Besh-Tau ("five mountains" in Persian) and the other four peaks which gave Piatigorsk its name (a Russian calque of "Besh-Tau"). The most southerly point of Pushkin's trip, this area of mineral springs is situated in the central range, about 80 kilometers north of stupendous, twin-peaked Elbrus (5,633 meters, by comparison to Mt. Blanc, 4,807 meters). Had Pushkin ventured over the mountains into Georgia, he would have found a clime more readily assimilated to romanticism's conventional oriental *topoi*. To illustrate the possibilities, the minor belletrist Alexander Shishkov orientalized Georgia in a poem written in 1821 during military service in Tiflis: he cast the land as a gigantic pleasure garden with babbling "streams of Saadi" and maidens like "divine *peris*."[1] Balmy Georgia was excluded, however, from Pushkin's poem which started the "Caucasian epidemic" (as Zhirmunsky termed it).

36

Besides reflecting the limitations of Pushkin's itinerary, the concertedly alpine *paysage* of "The Prisoner of the Caucasus" expressed a romantic preoccupation with wilderness disjoined from its local population. As later chapters will substantiate, the poet certainly conceived the Caucasus as exotic Asia, but his imaginative geography effected a certain separation between the territory and the Asians who lived there.[2] For all its concern with the Circassians, "The Prisoner of the Caucasus" constructed the Russian encounter with nature as restorative tourism focused on the self: as a site of inspiration and rejuvenation, the land acquired meaning primarily in terms of its impact on the poet and his hero who falls captive and escapes.

Despite the poem's many intimations of Asiatic menace, a trope of Russian harmony with nature largely suspended the ongoing violence of tsarist imperialism. Captivity affords the prisoner both the erotic adventure with the tribeswoman and thrilling contact with mountain wilderness. Grounded in romantic rejection of the *beau monde*, both the love story and the communion with nature occur within a privileged sector removed from war.[3] Pushkin constructed a sheltered space for himself as well. His dedication to Raevsky alluded to his banishment to the south (the "song of an exiled lyre"). But instead of dwelling on the politically risky subject of exile, the poet staged his own encounter with the Caucasus as a voluntary ascent of a "new Parnassus."[4] More the gentleman traveler than the deportee, his authorial persona evoked an alpine trek which enabled a poem.

Although directly focused on battle, the tale's epilogue did not let the promise of pacific and enriching Russian contact with alpine wilderness completely slip away. Pushkin himself had required the protection of several dozen Cossacks at one stage of his journey. Nevertheless, he concluded his poem with the over-confident image of a traveler fearlessly riding alone through Caucasian canyons. A sort of invitation, these lines suggested that Russian readers might visit the invigorating mountains for themselves, as indeed they began to do in significant numbers after the publication of Pushkin's poem. An unwarranted confidence in the "pacification" program was more widely discernible in Russia at the time. As the military man, journalist and botanist Ilya Radozhitsky put it in 1823, the Caucasus seemed to have fallen "at the foot of the Russian throne."[5] Nothing could have been further from the truth. Instead of subjugating the tribes, General Ermolov's strategy of offensive warfare backfired to strengthen Muridism, a resistance movement with roots in Sufism.[6] Especially in light of Russian optimism of the moment, "The Prisoner of the Caucasus" cannot be faulted for failing to anticipate the formidable jihad about to erupt against tsarist power. What deserves analysis, however, is how the poem produced a captivating version of alpine experience shielded from the dangers and carnage of military conquest in Asia.

THE RISE OF MOUNTAIN GLOOM AND GLORY IN RUSSIA

Pushkin's contemporaries never sufficiently recognized that he invented rather than recorded Caucasian landscape. As remarked in the first chapter, reviewers of "The Prisoner of the Caucasus" in the 1820s hailed the poet as a traveler who offered an artistically heightened but veridical description of mountain vistas he had seen: according to Viazemsky's striking formulation, Pushkin had captured the true "poetry" of the place in a way impossible in dry prose. Two decades later, in essays vigorously endorsed in a Soviet Russian critical tradition about Pushkinian "realism," Belinsky insisted much more stridently upon the poet's powers of reflection rather than invention.[7] The critic's previously cited article of 1844 marveled at Pushkin's "life-like pictures" of mountain landscape, while disparaging the "prosaic" efforts of Gavrila Derzhavin's ode "On Count V. A. Zubov's Return from Persia" (1804) and Zhukovsky's address "To Voeikov" (1814). Belinsky knew that neither Derzhavin nor Zhukovsky had set foot in the Caucasus when they wrote these verses. "Prosaic" accordingly seemed to connote something uninspired and hopelessly inferior to what a writer might produce on the site itself.

Belinsky made this outlook explicit in the review of an edition of Derzhavin's works issued in 1845. Derzhavin's ode to Zubov had presented the Caucasus as a rugged mountain wilderness, complete with a thunderstorm, roaring waterfalls and a swarm of giant serpents biting one another. These snakes in particular aroused Belinsky's scorn as creatures wildly out of touch with the actual world:

In those days a poet had no concern with reality: he relied strictly on his imagination. What did he care that the Caucasus was not India and had no enormous snakes, or that *no* snakes have ever swarmed in stacks, that hay is the only thing piled in stacks, or that snakes have never amused themselves by giving each other transfusions of venom? [8]

Belinsky saw the serpents as Derzhavin's most flagrant lapse into fantasy, but he berated the poet more generally because the *real* Caucasus had not supplied his inspiration. Although "The Prisoner of the Caucasus" was not mentioned in this review, Belinsky's previous approval of the captivity tale's "life-like" scenery left no doubt that he considered Pushkin an antipode of Derzhavin: by contrast to the armchair traveler with his "prosaic" inner visions, young Pushkin struck Belinsky as a master of mimesis who caught the image of the actual "poetic land."

But instead of "discovering" an inherently "poetic" place, Pushkin *made* the Caucasus poetic by situating it squarely within long-standing traditions of European writing about the Alps. As Marjorie Nicolson showed in her study of the aesthetics of "gloom and glory" in England, attitudes of indifference or hostility toward mountain landscape predominated in European letters throughout the seventeenth century.[9] One of the most notable expressions of this negative orientation was John Donne's "An Anatomy of the World" (1611), where asymmetrical peaks and canyons appeared as "warts and pock-holes in the face of th' earth." But as part of preromanticism's new fondness for nature, British poets were responding enthusiastically to mountains by the 1720s, when tourism in the Alps was on the rise. This shift in sensibility expanded a traditional notion of the sublime, as compared to the beautiful. While beauty was identified with order, harmony and regularity on a relatively small scale, sublimity was marked by awe and veneration, traditionally associated with the contemplation of God and the heavens. In an extension of the concept, preromantic poets such as James Thomson invented the category of the "natural Sublime" to encompass mountains and other vast terrestrial phenomena. An experience of comingled delight and horror became the hallmark of this new, heady feeling for elemental forces of nature. Stark precipices, toppling boulders, avalanches, ferocious storms and raging waterfalls violated the standard notion of beauty as harmony and yet aroused an intense thrill in the observer. In the words of Thomson, the natural sublime swelled the soul with "pleasing dread," a formula whose variants in eighteenth-century Britain would include "delightful horror" and "enthusiastic terror."

Like France and other European countries, Russia recapitulated the British "discovery" of mountain gloom and glory, but only toward the end of the eighteenth century. Literary imports from the West naturally assumed a vital role. Thomson had Russian admirers, including Derzhavin and Karamzin who translated the British writer's "Autumn," a poem containing a catalogue of the world's great peaks. But the preeminent western transmitter of the *le goût de la montagne* in Russia was Rousseau. With its treatment of the Alps full of allusions to the *Nouvelle Heloïse*, Karamzin's *Letters of a Russian Traveler* greatly strengthened Rousseau's impact. Although Karamzin did not slight the Arcadian habitats of shepherds, he loudly voiced the "reverential dread" (*blagogoveinyi uzhas*) and strange exhilaration he felt at the sight of savage, violent features of rugged mountain country.[10] The first widely read Russian response to the Alps, Karamzin's *Letters* set *topoi* of the sentimental mountain trek which would migrate into Caucasian travel literature.

Unless one counts the Ural foothills, Russia itself possesses no mountains, so that the taste for alpine gloom and glory inevitably led to foreign lands. Derzhavin's ode to Zubov first set a stamp of sublimity on the Caucasus in two stanzas quoted in a footnote to "The Prisoner of the Caucasus." The passage situates the civilized protagonist amidst "nature's dread and glory" (*uzhasy, krasy prirody*).[11] Similar to the British formulas "pleasing dread" or "delightful horror," Derzhavin's terms conveyed a comingled feeling of awe and enthusiasm before the Caucasian range. The poet went on to present through Zubov's eyes "angry rivers in murky abysses," a "rumbling" avalanche, thunder and lightning in the "fearsome mountains." In stark contrast to this pervasive "gloom," the second stanza floods the scene in bright sunshine. Here Derzhavin displayed his talent for rendering the play of light and color: brilliant sun sparkles on water and ice, creating prism-like effects and turning rock masses to "bluish–gray amber." The "golden–crimson sun" gleams through trees of the dark pine forest, "delighting the gaze" and contributing to the generally "splendid" (*velikolepnyi*) vista.

Derzhavin's aesthetic of the sublime evolved in a section of Zhukovsky's "To Voeikov" written as a travelogue and also quoted in Pushkin's commentary on "The Prisoner of the Caucasus." Touches of "dread" figure in Zhukovsky's fifty-three-line description of the untamed territory: waterfalls roar "in the murk of chasms" in granite cliffs, and the light of day cannot penetrate the tenebrous thick of the forest.[12] But unlike Derzhavin's harmonious poise between gloom and splendor, Zhukovsky heavily accented the beauty of the stupendous terrain. Mountain rises upon mountain, "clad in blue mist," and Elbrus dramatically dominates the scene:

> And like a cloud above the rest,
> Elborus gleams in all his glory
> With dreadful majesty – a hoary
> Giant capped by a double crest.

Here Elbrus (in a variant spelling) functions as a metonym of the Caucasus' general magnificence – the "splendor of Creation" (*velikolepie tvoren'ia*) which meets the poet's eye at every turn.

ALPINE EXPERIENCE IN "THE PRISONER OF THE CAUCASUS"

As important as Derzhavin and Zhukovsky were as Pushkin's precursors, "The Prisoner of the Caucasus" made the mountainous territory an unforgettable place for Russian readers only by taking inspiration from Byron as well. The poems of Derzhavin and Zhukovsky could not fully satisfy the romantic era's demand for a lyric hero emotionally engaged with his surroundings. Written *in memoriam* to the man charged with executing Catherine's "oriental project" and then recalled to suffer disgrace under Paul I, Derzhavin's ode to Valerian Zubov solemnly extended the campaigner's journey into a metaphor of life's course. The somber allegorical undercurrent definitely frustrated a reader's yen for pleasurable armchair travel. Romantic zest was also lacking in Zhukovsky's "To Voeikov," which recounted a fellow littérateur's touristic jaunt through southern Russia and the Caucasus. Never clearly defined as a personality responding to the world, the addressee ("you") in this case was little more than a rhetorical pair of eyes used to register a succession of sights.

By contrast to Derzhavin and Zhukovsky, Pushkin employed Byronic formulas to integrate Caucasian *paysage* into a compelling traveler's tale for the first time in Russian literature. During his exile in the south Pushkin reread Byron in a particularly impressionable frame of mind and reached the height of a shortlived enthusiasm for him. The primary trace of this influence in "The Prisoner of the Caucasus" was the jaded hero in flight from the *beau monde* – the "renegade from society and friend of nature." Although having antecedents in figures such as Chateaubriand's René, Pushkin's unnamed traveler was most indebted to Byron's autobiographical creation Childe Harold. Alienated from his homeland, Childe Harold roams the Alps, Albania and other exotic places in search of something to cure his spleen. The special pertinence of mountain landscape in *Childe Harold's Pilgrimage* was epitomized by Byron's declaration, "to me high mountains are a feeling" (canto 3, lxxii). Remarkable as the stirring of a dulled, sated spirit, this "feeling" signals the traveler's capacity to be moved anew, once he has fled his familiar, stifling surroundings and come into contact with untamed nature. Like the famous apostrophe to the sea in *Childe Harold's Pilgrimage*, the response to the Alps establishes a standard romantic equation between the natural sublime and the traveler's intense inner life.

Although never given to Byron's emotive mode of self-projection, Pushkin expressed some identification with his hero as a social type. In a letter to Vladimir Gorchakov he explained that he wanted the captive to transmit "that indifference to life and its pleasures, that premature old age of the spirit which have become the distinguishing characteristics of nineteenth-century youth."[13] Reviewers of the time generally found the hero flat but clearly recognized his social significance. As Viazemsky observed, the prisoner's profound boredom reflected a *malaise* rampant among the Russian élite now enthralled by Byron.

A Byronic type with some of Pushkin's own emotional baggage, the prisoner discovers a kinship with the mountains during his captivity. Unconscious when first brought to the tribal village, the Russian awakens the next day to see the range looming as the walls of a fortress – the "enclosure of Circassian liberty." In this initial confrontation the mountains form an imprisoning space which isolates the hero from the civilized world. But during captivity the Russian's perception of the natural environment shifts in a manner conforming to the romantic construct of prison as a site of inner liberation.[14] Put to work tending the tribe's herds, the shackled prisoner expands emotionally under the impact of the elemental environment initially perceived as a foreboding Circassian citadel.

The long descriptive sequence which registers this experience uses borrowings from Derzhavin, Zhukovsky and Byron in a distinctive new blend. Like Derzhavin's ode to Zubov, Pushkin's text is organized by a principle of contrast between clement weather and a storm. In the opening lines of the passage the captive gazes upon the peaks on a clear morning:

> Trudging amidst the gloomy crags
> During the morning's early freshness,
> He marveled, staring at the view
> Of the remote, enormous faces
> Of mountains, hued gray, rose and blue.

Vistas of majesty resplendent!
The everlasting thrones of snow:
The summits look like clouds in steady
Lines to the viewer from below,
And rearing tall above the others,
Immense and stately, crowned with ice,
Elbrus – the double-peaked colossus –
Stands sparkling white 'gainst azure skies. (97)

Pushkin's attention to the effects of sunlight on the rock faces recalls one of the prominent features of the second stanza of Derzhavin's ode to Zubov. But in its particulars, this passage from "The Prisoner of the Caucasus" displays a larger debt to Zhukovsky. Like his predecessor in "To Voeikov," Pushkin placed the focus on Elbrus as the majestic twin-crested giant, looming above the other mountains and sparkling against the sky. As Pushkin remarked in a letter of March 1821, he had seen Elbrus and Kazbek only from a great distance during his trip.[15] Given these circumstances, it is not surprising that "The Prisoner of the Caucasus" virtually duplicated Zhukovsky's visual image of Elbrus and even appropriated one of his key rhymes, *dvuglavyi / velichavyi* ("two-headed" / "majestic").[16]

The same passage from "The Prisoner of the Caucasus" also illustrates how Pushkin translated into Russian certain descriptive motifs of *Childe Harold's Pilgrimage*. Byron's canto 3 contains the following lines:

Above me are the Alps,
The Palaces of nature, whose vast walls
Have pinnacled in clouds their snowy scalps,
And throned Eternity in icy halls
Of cold Sublimity, where forms and falls
The Avalanche – the thunderbolts of snow! (lxii)

In a paraphrase of Thomson's and Pope's formula "eternal snows," Byron presented snow and ice enthroned forever, a notion directly paralleled by Pushkin (*prestoly vechnye snegov*). Byron's association between snowy peaks and clouds was another trope which figured in Zhukovsky's projection of Elbrus and then resurfaced in Pushkin's text as well. In addition, Byron's metaphor of the Alps as "vast walls" was re-echoed when Pushkin's prisoner first feels entrapped in Circassia.

After celebrating the mountains in sunshine, "The Prisoner of the Caucasus" depicts a violent storm and expresses the heady Byronic "feeling" for untamed nature's violence:

> When thunder boomed – a storm's first presage –
> And turned into a rumbling peal,
> In mountains high above the village
> The captive frequently sat still.
> Below his feet the clouds grew somber,
> Dust swirled across the lowlands yonder,
> In fright the deer began to search
> For shelter in their rocky perch;
> From cliff-sides eagles took to flying,
> Filling the heavens with their crying;
> The sounds of horses, lowing cows
> Were muffled by the tempest's volume. . .
> Then lightning flashed, erupting clouds
> Sent rain and hail into the valleys,
> The torrents undermined the steeps,
> As flowing water surged in billows
> And dislocated age-old boulders,
> While lonely on a rugged peak
> The captive watched the heavy glower
> And waited 'til the sun returned,
> In shelter from the tempest's power,
> And with a certain joy he learned
> To hear the rainstorm's futile howling. (97, 99)

In this culmination of the poem's central descriptive sequence the socially disaffected hero feels his jaded spirit stir before the spectacle of savage nature: he is aroused by both the "glory" and the "gloom" of the Caucasian range and perceives in the tempest a correlative to his own troubled self.

While dramatizing the Byronic hero's kinship with untamed terrain, "The Prisoner of the Caucasus" also explicitly defines the territory as a source of inspiration for a traveling writer. More autobiographical than fictive, this feature of imaginative geography speaks of the poet himself rather than the captive, who has no authorial ambitions. The dedication to Raevsky calls Besh-Tau Pushkin's "new Parnassus" and hails the mountain country as the realm of "inspiration's wild genius." This notion of the Caucasus as Parnassus is reinforced in the epilogue, where the Muse enters as the writer's traveling companion. A site where imagination soars, Pushkin's rugged mountain land subscribes directly to Byron's romantic canon. In *Childe Harold's Pilgrimage*, for example, the Alps' inspirational power is opposed to the torturing "hum of human cities" (canto 3, lxxii).

THE SPREAD OF PUSHKIN'S GEOGRAPHY

When viewed strictly within Pushkin's own career, his Caucasian gloom and glory must be judged a minor byproduct of his brief Byronic phase. The poet's taste for savage alpine terrain proved quite limited. He wrote only a small number of texts devoted to mountain wilderness, and even in the highly romantic "The Prisoner of the Caucasus" the observer's "feeling" for rocky heights did not become so overwhelming as to interfere with clear visual images. In harmony with the prevailing tendencies of his poetry, Pushkin's correspondence did not emote about Caucasian landscape either. For instance, the long letter written to his brother in September 1820 proclaimed the mountain range "splendid" without going into a fit of rapture. This restraint set Pushkin apart from the sentimental mode of *récits de voyage* or private letters by romantics such as Byron, Bestuzhev-Marlinsky and the secondary Russian poets Stepan Nechaev and Vasily Grigoriev.

But if relatively minor in Pushkin's own œuvre, the poetic discourse of Caucasian sublimity took on a tenacious, emotionally heightened life of its own, beginning in secondary Russian verse of the 1820s. Pushkin had looked to precursors for models of description, and his successors extended the chain of intertextual representation by adopting the rhetoric and central tropes of "The Prisoner of the Caucasus." As illustrated by the verse of Thomson (or Derzhavin's ode to Zubov), an author can create vivid verse about peaks known only from reading.[17] But even after seeing the Caucasus during a stay in the spa country or a trip to Georgia, secondary Russian writers of the 1820s predictably produced works conditioned by previous texts, just as Pushkin had done. The rhetoric of gloom and glory ran as a unifying thread through this Russian literature. Time and again, the authors filled with "wonder" at the "dread and charm" of the "awesome," "splendid" Caucasus with its "eternal snows," violent downpours, "stormy," "mutinous" rivers and "raging" waterfalls.[18] Part of a broader Russian revolt against classicism, these expressions of admiration for alpine wilderness exemplified a radical shift in aesthetic sensibility generally affected by the early 1820s.[19] In treating mountains and waterfalls, previous writers like Derzhavin, Karamzin and Zhukovsky had laid important foundations for "The Prisoner of the Caucasus," as we have seen. None the less, it was Pushkin who attracted unprecedented attention to Russia's southern borderland as a new site for exercising the aesthetic of the sublime. With their freshly awakened awareness of the Caucasus, traveling Russian poets of the 1820s invoked Kabarda, Abkhazia and Dagestan, while representing all these various regions as generic mountain country clearly indebted to Pushkin.[20] The frontier territory quickly acquired a stylized character to become the "Caucasian Alps," the label attached to it in Nechaev's versified *récit de voyage*, "Recollections" (1823).[21]

In elaborating the "Caucasian Alps," secondary poets let their imaginations run to extremes of symbolism and emotion atypical of Pushkin. The Decembrist Kondraty Ryleev wrote an extended metaphor of Elbrus as a monumental embodiment of steadfast "Civic Courage" (1823).[22] While idiosyncratically aimed at promoting the Decembrists' foremost political virtue, this verse replicated the rhetoric and visual image of Zhukovsky and Pushkin: shining high above the clouds in a "hazy fog," Elbrus looms in "awesome beauty" – a "hoary giant" and the "glory of the Caucasian mountains." With no trace of Ryleev's aspiration to overthrow the tsarist state, Nechaev proclaimed his "reverence" before the "hoary

Caucasus" and "splendid" Elbrus, as though he had entered a church ("Recollections"). Somewhat later, the same rhetoric of sublimity served yet another end in Countess Evdokiia Rostopchina's "Elbrus and I," a lyric which confessed a secret passion for the peak conceived as a mighty man.[23]

Pushkin's trope of the "new Parnassus" proved extraordinarily productive, as other poets flocked to celebrate the Caucasus as a wild haunt of the Muse. In a verse written during naval service on the Black Sea, Efim Zaitsevsky invented Abkhazia as a "country of wild beauty." The observer's soul thrills to ice-capped peaks, rapid streams, forests and tribal villages: "ecstasy and pleasure" overwhelm him as he breathes the "fire of sacred poetry."[24] The same notes of spiritual exultation were struck in Grigoriev's "Besh-Tau" (written 1826) and Victor Tepliakov's "The Caucasus" (1829).[25] Aleksei Meisner's "A View of Kazbek at Noon" (1833) also contributed to the theme of loftiness and added an anthropomorphic touch by projecting the peak as an "inspired man, standing above the crowd."[26] This high-minded loner was a thinly disguised mutant of Pushkin's "majestic hermit," the Parnassian Besh-Tau.

All these poets evolved Pushkin's notion of the Parnassian refuge along quasi-religious lines. They presented Caucasian peaks not as the home of poetry alone but as the wider realm of "higher things," where a traveler experiences spiritual uplift and a sensation of escape from the vanity of the world. The thematic complex carried forward the "reverential dread" of Karamzin, Thomson, Rousseau and other celebrators of the Alps. But on beyond the eighteenth-century heritage of the soulful *goût de la montagne*, there were even remnants of the medieval idea of heaven's location on a sky-scraping peak. Bestuzhev-Marlinsky in particular would prove sensitive to this tradition, as indicated by his remarks on Dante's *Paradiso* in the journal he kept during military exile in the Caucasus.[27]

While predominant, the motifs of inspiration and spiritual exaltation overlapped with another emotive cluster centered around Caucasian power, combativeness and pride. A line of tension thus opened up between the self-reflective, enriching engagement with the "new Parnassus" and a confrontation with mountains fraught with potential antagonism to Russian outsiders. As both Byron and Zhukovsky ("Mountain Road," 1818) had done before him, Pushkin employed a metaphor of the mountain as monarch. The dedication to "The Prisoner of the Caucasus" casts Besh-Tau not only as a lofty "hermit" but also as the "five-headed tsar over fields and *auls*" (tribal "villages"). In an extension of the trope of the mountain as overlord of the land, Pushkin's epilogue addresses the territory as a collective embodiment of the tribes purportedly pacified by General Ermolov: "Submit and bow your snowy head, / Oh, Caucasus, Ermolov marches!" Here in the patriotic finale of the work the snow-capped peaks function as the head of a body politic. As a region supposedly subjugated by Russian arms, the landscape is suffused by the poet with indignation and injured pride. Without referring to warfare, Pushkin's "The Monastery on Kazbek" (1829) would also use some anthropomorphic symbolism. In this short verse the poet admiringly addresses the peak as a majestic presence looming over fellow mountains: "Kazbek, high above the family of mountains, your regal tent shines with eternal beams."

Like the construct of Parnassian heights, Pushkin's anthropomorphic tropes of native power found elaboration in subsequent Russian poetry. In "Recollections" Nechaev cast Elbrus as the "dreadful tsar" of the Caucasus, "surrounded by a retinue of servants," the lower peaks. Tepliakov developed the same metaphor of an enormous potentate in "The Caucasus," where Besh-Tau rises as the "five-headed tsar." A "gloomy ruler" bedecked in a "crown of sharp-pointed crags," the mountain monarch is encircled by lesser peaks standing "guard in granite armor." A metonymic variant on this motif of a sovereign and his sentries appeared in Grigoriev's "Evening in the Caucasus" (1826): snowy peaks loom as a glittery "row of hoary eyelids" (about to dim in the shadow of Russia's eagle, a traditional symbol of imperial might).[28] A trace of the figurative mountain king and his servitors would remain in Lermontov's "Hastening northward from afar" (written 1837), a well-known lyric which cast Kazbek as a "sentry of the Orient."[29]

Poets after Pushkin furthered expanded the possibilities of anthropomorphism by throwing their peaks into verbal combat. This artistic construct shaped Dmitri Oznobishin's "Mashuka [*sic*] and Kazbek" (c. 1828) and Liukan Yakubovich's "The Urals and the Caucasus" (1836).[30] In these verses the quarrelsome mountains advance claims to superiority on the basis of height, beauty, mineral wealth, or curative properties derived from local springs. The poetic conceit of debate between mountains would endure in Lermontov's politically charged verse "An Argument" (1841).[31] A brash self-confident type in a "cap" (a nearly permanent cloud cover), Lermontov's Kazbek has a dispute with Elbrus (alternatively called "Shat-gora"), a venerable "gray-haired" figure who fears an attack on the Caucasus. The oldster's apprehensions are realized as a massive army from the "North" advances on the territory at the poem's conclusion. In this anthropomorphic presentation the two peaks appear amidst their "tribe of mountains" (*plemia gor*), a trope subsequently reinforced by the adjective *soplemennyi* (which designates membership in the same tribe). Transformed into towering chieftains in a war counsel, Lermontov's allied mountains heatedly argue about their vulnerability to aggression from the tsarist state.

Like the Caucasian mountains, the Terek river also received anthropomorphic treatment in Russian literature under the impact of Pushkin. In the final stanza of "The Caucasus" as published in 1829 shortly after his second trip to the territory, Pushkin symbolized the Terek at the Darial Pass as a hungry "young beast," frolicking and howling at the sight of food outside his iron cage.[32] The trope of the constrained, raging animal took on a long life in Russian literature. Bestuzhev-Marlinsky's "Ammalat-Bek" (1832) called the river a "ferocious beast, black with wrath, roaring and pawing age-old rock masses;" and Vilgelm Kiukhelbeker's poem "The Orphan" (written 1833–34) less extravagantly evoked a similar creature.[33] While having clear antecedents in Ivan Dmitriev's "The Volga" (1794) and the German poet F. Shtolberg's "Mountain Stream," Lermontov's "Gifts from the Terek" (1840) also owed something to Pushkin's animate waterway.[34] In an anthropomorphic realization of the river's tributary relation to the Caspian, Lermontov's Terek is a "savage" vassal who serves an imperious white-haired "elder," the sea, by bringing him "gifts" from the war zone – boulders from Darial and dead bodies.

THE POETICS OF CAUCASIAN SPACE

As we have seen, young Pushkin's imaginative Caucasian geography was carried to new emotional and metaphorical extremes by other writers. Throughout the 1820s and 1830s, symbolism and subjectivity reigned in poetry about the territory. Pictorial images were relegated onto a secondary plane or eliminated entirely in favor of the writer's feelings. In this process relatively simple Pushkinian formulas such as "snowy head" or "family of mountains" blossomed into elaborate poetic conceits of peaks as sovereigns, sentries, inspired loners, tribes and combative debaters. Similarly, the Terek as "young beast" thrived and evolved into Bestuzhev-Marlinsky's glowering, ferocious animal and Lermontov's howling vassal to the Caspian Sea.

But despite the important differences which obtained between Pushkin and the later, full-blown romantic manner, "The Prisoner of the Caucasus" started the production of an imaginative geography which took a fierce hold on the readership. As observed in other literatures with reference to other regions of the world, a "poetics of space" fills a geographical location with powerful affective meanings generated by rhetoric, tropes, patterns of symbolism and the free violation of actual topographical relations.[35] Not necessarily dispelled in the popular mind by the accumulation of empirical data, these imaginary worlds may far outweigh the force of scientific description and can infuse or even override historical analysis and other fields of scholarly inquiry. In young Pushkin's era people drawn to science showed no great antagonism to poetic geography. Without impugning contemporary literature for non-factuality, Bronevsky's *A New Geography and History of the Caucasus* urged the public to forget the "fabled" land of Prometheus and Medea. In 1825 Pyotr Mukhanov made a similar call for more fact-oriented writing. Devoted largely to the eighteenth-century naturalist Güldenstädt, Mukhanov's article praised past efforts to explore the Caucasus but underscored how much remained to be done: in his view, the territory was still *terra incognita* for Russia – as unknown and uncharted as "deepest Africa."[36] Like Bronevsky, Mukhanov was defending natural science as the sphere of real knowledge, without noticing how contemporary poetry was fabling the Caucasus anew.

What these exponents of Humboldtian natural science failed to anticipate was how affectively irresistible and impervious to fact the romantic construct of alpine experience would prove to be in Russia. By rendering the Caucasus as the Alps of the homeland's own periphery, Pushkin invented a soul-stirring realm of the sublime, full of perils for citified travelers but ready to inspire and rejuvenate them. The territory was thus appropriated as a space for the therapeutic uses of the lyrical Russian self unhampered by native peoples. Thrilling nuances of Asiatic tribal menace certainly enlarged the Caucasian poetics of space, already laden with natural dangers like precipices, violent storms and avalanches, but local populations were not permitted to hinder Russian communion with alpine wilderness. This posture of "friendship" with nature transfigured the Caucasus into congenial meaning about the foreign writer's experience of artistic inspiration, spiritual uplift, civic courage and passionate love. Frequent references to the tribes certainly occurred, and even the economic objectives of tsarist imperialism noisily intruded in Nechaev's "Recollections" in a footnote on a potentially lucrative Caucasian silk industry. Nechaev's verse itself, however, conformed to the rule of staging a strictly pacific, uplifting encounter with nature, as if the Russian presence in the territory had no other rationale.

All the same, the self-absorbed dramas of these friends of wilderness, so preoccupied with "higher things," was significantly rocked by the intertextual landscape's second prominent cluster of symbolic motifs – the figures of local power, bellicosity and rebellion. Still subtle when the war was barely underway in the 1820s, the geographical imagery of Caucasian antagonism to Russia would become more pronounced and insistently oriental in the next decade when the jihad flared up. In young Pushkin's time, however, this symbolism represented the return of the repressed: romantic poetry's cherished theme of Russian communion with nature averted the eye from military conquest, but cross-cultural conflict lurked in the tropes of Caucasian sovereigns, their sentries and families. Often willfully blind to imperial Russian designs on the territory, the Caucasian lyric poetry of Pushkin's era betrayed the following, irresoluble dilemma. Enthusiasts of mountain gloom and glory professed a desire to profit from the Caucasus in a purely non-violent, aesthetic and spiritual way. But what about all those Asians who inhabited the restorative land and did not welcome Russia's incursion? The incoherence of the Russian quest for rejuvenative alpine experience in an oriental combat zone would haunt Caucasian travel literature, especially in Pushkin's time.

CHAPTER 4

Sentimental pilgrims

But where was that Caucasus?
Ilya Radozhitsky

Not long after young Pushkin's trip of 1820, the Caucasus began acquiring the status of a Russian tourist attraction. As implied by the lone traveler passing safely through canyons at the end of "The Prisoner of the Caucasus," Ermolov's campaigns in Chechnia and Dagestan seemed to have secured a new realm for pleasure trips. The perception was well conveyed in Ilya Radozhitsky's *récit de voyage* which provides the epigraph to this chapter. At the outset of his military service in the Caucasus, Radozhitsky declared that the territory was now firmly under the tsarist "scepter of art and science."[1] To his mind, steady Russian protection had transformed Georgia in particular into an "Italy" of peace and tranquillity. With the same beguiling promise of new opportunities for tourism, *National Annals* (*Otechestvennye zapiski*) in 1822 ran a guide for travel across the mountains.[2] This publication maintained that the Georgian Military Highway was now quite safe, despite pockets of "predatory" tribes.

But if even Georgia seemed newly accessible, Russian tourism was in fact concentrated at spas in the Piatigorsk area, suitably distant from battlefields. In the course of the 1820s and early 1830s the Caucasian cure became so fashionable among upper-class Russians that one of them likened the practice to a Muslim pilgrimage to Mecca.[3] Rudimentary facilities for using the mineral springs gradually gave way to well-appointed installations, as Pushkin would observe with evident dissatisfaction in 1829 when he passed through the

54

region a second time *en route* to Turkey.[4] By the early 1830s a landscaped hotel and bath houses, fountains, pavilions and shops greeted civilian visitors and the tsarist soldiers who were sent to the spas to recuperate from wounds or illness. The environs were not absolutely free from tribal "predators," but risky excursions were not really necessary for the alpine experience: as Pyotr Sumarokov remarked, the Piatigorsk mountains could be nicely appreciated through the window of one's quarters (frequently no more than a rented room in a local resident's house).[5] To vary their activities, vacationers might also watch the festivities of Bairam and sample exotic foods in nearby tribal villages allied to the tsarist state.[6] On the tamer side, there were outings to the German settlement of Karras, a community originally founded by Scottish missionaries in the early nineteenth century.[7]

The spas had a high reputation for physical therapy. A "medico-topographical" guide of the mid-1820s chemically analyzed the mineral springs and commended their curative properties.[8] These "amazing, salutary gifts of Nature" were meant to be good for just about everything. While attacking physical ailments, they purportedly lifted one's spirits, instilled a happy feeling and could instantly transfigure sickly faces. Especially prized in Russia (even in the Soviet era), sparkling Narzan was acclaimed as the spas' "champagne."[9] During a prescribed cure in the Caucasus in 1823, Stepan Nechaev took exception to such accolades in a short verse addressed to Grigory Rimsky-Korsakov, who had just left Russia for Paris, Italy and Vienna: now in unhealthy company, Nechaev looked forward to a reunion with his friend in Moscow over a bottle of Veuve Clicquot.[10] In a humorous vein, this poem highlighted Russia's new craze for Caucasian mineral water.

While the culture of the spa created a pervasive aura of therapy, travelers got a big dose of spiritual medicine by communing with nature, as so profusely attested in *récits de voyage* of Pushkin's era. Typically focused on the writer's emotions and short on pictorial detail, the travelogues of the 1820s were saturated with allusions which attest to literature's power as a guidebook. Reading put Russian travelers on the alert for Caucasian sublimity and gave them an appropriate discourse to imitate. As this chapter will illustrate, Rousseau and Karamzin remained very active models of a soulful *goût de la montagne* immeasurably more emotive than anything Pushkin ever wrote. It was young Pushkin, however, who activated the Caucasian literary pilgrimage and provided the readership with an enticing discursive bond between the Alps and Russia's "own" alternative. Lesser poets of the 1820s strengthened the connection by amplifying the mountains' putative powers for restituting tired spirits. Lured by the literary Caucasus, Russian travelers of the era sought their own encounters with the uplifting mountain land. When they chose to write about the experience, they usually produced emotive accounts which "corroborated" exactly what reading had led them to expect.

Although they were on the edge of a war zone, sentimental travelers greatly inflated contemporary poetry's fiction of an alpine space of "higher things" sheltered from military aggression. On apparently solitary treks, Russians with heads full of print meditated and prayed on the Asian frontier as if in Switzerland. Consciousness of continuing tribal hostility to tsardom sometimes invaded the quasi-religious idyll. However, despite acknowledgments that the conquest was by no means over, the sentimental journey erected a screen to the inhumanity of imperialism, as though the traveler's presence in the Caucasus owed nothing to military campaigns. Quite likely a source of moral solace, this strategy of high-mindedness obscured the pilgrim's complacence about Russia's assault on the territory.

The literary guidebooks which stimulated the travelers' quest for spiritual therapy in the Caucasus suffered notable but largely futile attacks from the early 1830s onward. Most famously, Pushkin challenged the romantic poetics of Caucasian space in *Journey to Arzrum*, the account of his unauthorized trip to the camp of the Russian army at war with Turkey in 1829. But as we shall see, this *récit de voyage* to Turkish battlefields stopped short of totally dismantling the discourse of

"The Prisoner of the Caucasus." Left partially intact in *Journey to Arzrum*, the soul-stirring alpine realm of Pushkin's youth was thoroughly demolished in Alexander Polezhaev's "Erpeli" (1832), a chauvinistic poem of war in Chechnia and Dagestan. Subsequent writers, including Lermontov and Tolstoy, also punctured old clichés of Caucasian gloom and glory right into the 1860s. Despite all the onslaughts, however, the genre of the sentimental pilgrimage survived throughout the Caucasian conquest (and even into the twentieth century).[11] For reasons to be summarized in this chapter's concluding section, the "Caucasian Alps" were apparently just too satisfying for most Russian travelers to relinquish.

THE EMPTY CHURCH

Operative as a poetic bridge between the Alps and the Caucasus, young Pushkin's popular tale of captivity in Circassia naturally topped the travelers' list of literary companions. Some visitors in the territory actually brought "The Prisoner of the Caucasus" with them.[12] Russians who left the poem at home might find a copy at a posting-station along the way, as Pushkin supposedly did *en route* to Erzerum.[13] But most significantly, even travelers without physical access to the text had Pushkin's verbal music imprinted on the brain. Belinsky attested to this condition of traveling under the spell of poetry memorized at home. When he went to Piatigorsk for his health in 1837, the sight of the mountains triggered his spontaneous declamation of the pertinent section of "The Prisoner of the Caucasus."[14] His previously cited article on Pushkin implied that such mental records were common: as Belinsky prepared to discuss the poem's scenery (and the conjoined "ethnographic" sequence), he skipped quotations on the assumption that most readers knew the whole extract by heart.

Literary pilgrims who chose to write *récits de voyage* typically assumed the posture of cultivated gentlemen prone to reverential meditations more Karamzinian than Pushkinian.[15] The characteristic blend of eighteenth-century sentimentality and the contemporary poetics of Caucasian space was definitively illustrated in Radozhitsky's *récit de voyage* to Georgievsk, published in 1823. In flatlands during an early stage of the journey, the traveler impatiently asked himself, "But where was that Caucasus?"[16] "That" Caucasus was quite simply young Pushkin's textual Caucasus, as affirmed by subsequent allusions. Once he caught sight of the mountains, Radozhitsky mimicked Pushkin (and Zhukovsky) by taking the snowy summits for "clouds massed on the horizon." As Elbrus loomed ever closer, the traveler ruminated about God in one of many passages which might have been lifted from Rousseau or *Letters of a Russian Traveler* ("majestic forces of the Creator and the insignificance of human existence.") But the religiosity could not guide a none-too-skilled pen through a pictorial description of the mountain. To tackle this weighty task, Radozhitsky simply cited "The Prisoner of the Caucasus" and seconded its rhetoric of "majesty and dread." While convinced that nothing more was needed to convey a proper understanding of the sublime place, Radozhitsky also paraphrased some lines from Zhukovsky's "To Voeikov," a text given new currency as a citation in Pushkin's captivity tale. All these features testified to the force of literature as a guidebook which prepared the traveler to find "that" Caucasus and gave him discursive tools to stage his own ego-centered encounter with it.

By comparison to other travelers of the 1820s, Radozhitsky endorsed Russian imperialism with unusual frankness (as though hitting his stride for the job of war correspondent he would assume later for the *Northern Bee*). His *récit de voyage* opened with the statement of pride in tsarist conquest conceived as a civilizing mission (the advent of "art and science"). The outlook served him in good stead when some Caucasian natives made an appearance much later in the travelogue. He encountered Kabardinian and Ossetian children among Russia's prisoners of war near Georgievsk and pronounced the little captives cute as supernumeraries in the "Asiatic ballets of Didelot."[17] Momentarily saddened at the thought of children wrenched from their parents and possibly orphaned, Radozhitsky quickly soothed his conscience by asserting that the adults were confirmed "savages" anyway, whereas their offspring would now evolve through schooling in Russia. Totally unconscious of his crushing condescension, he extolled the empire's power to transform each little "animal into a human being." The ideology of the civilizing mission was there to explain away the violence of imperialism which temporarily disturbed the traveler.

More fundamentally, however, the very rationale of the sentimental literary pilgrimage provided bigger blinders to the rapaciousness of the Russian presence in the Caucasus. Radozhitsky paid his opening tribute to the "scepter of art and science" but then focused his travelogue on lofty communion with the sublime. Alone with uplifting mountains in an area far from battlefields, he essentially fashioned himself as a cultivated venerator of nature. This sentimental posture rhetorically depopulated a territory which was in fact the homeland of peoples in the path of the expansionist Russian state.

The morally soothing construct of pacific Russian pilgrimage to unpopulated wilderness recurred repeatedly in subsequent travel literature. Like Radozhitsky, Nechaev knew that the tribes were there, but his *récit de voyage* marginalized them in order to appropriate nature as a private meditation chamber. An ethnographic excursus into a Circassian village allowed Nechaev to admire the women's "beautiful eyes" and the men's "intelligent, proud and martial" bearing. But in dealing with landscape, the traveler emptied the space of natives. Thoroughly familiar with the *Nouvelle Heloïse*, Nechaev first compared Caucasian and Swiss topography in order to insist upon the greater severity of Russia's borderland. He then staged this devotional moment:

As I admired this wondrous scene, I thought: Does man not thusly attain a solemn steadfastness of spirit only when he rises above the lowly sphere of earthly pleasures? And to do so, must he not traverse the primeval forest of passion and the thorny cliffs of misfortune? ... Highest and closest of all, two-headed Elbrus rises above the throng of hoary giants. The mountain's main face expresses a weighty calm, befitting a Tsar's majesty.[18]

Nechaev's next sentence noted tribal legends about the throne of a god on Elbrus but dismissed them as typical of "peoples living in perpetual childhood." Convinced of his intellectual superiority, the traveler failed to notice his own act of overlaying the mountain with affective meaning produced in the print culture of Orthodox Russia.

Just as easily, the high-minded posture permitted Nechaev to avert his eyes from Caucasian resistance to Russian imperialism. In a wistful moment he remarked that, "One would like to admire [the mountains] at closer range, one would like to penetrate their stony depths as far as possible, but their unwinking sentry never drops his weapon; and woe to the curious, bold person who penetrates the last refuge of unbridled freedom!"[19] With the hint of extracting ores from the "stony depths," this interesting comment signaled the economic goal of tapping a colony's natural resources. Nechaev also granted the natives' refusal to be dispossessed without a fight. However, the travelogue's prevailing strategy of sentimental tourism denied the political tensions admitted here. Mostly alone with mountains bucolic as the Alps, Nechaev professed that he had come primarily to "admire" the Caucasus, with no real designs to "penetrate" more deeply than the spas.

Sentimentality's efficacity as a blinder to imperialist appropriation of the Caucasus was demonstrated again in a *récit de voyage* to Georgia by Karl Reingardt, a doctor from Wilno. As in the other travelogues already considered, Reingardt produced landscape as a meditator's cell isolated from cross-cultural strife. He set a serene, moonlit scene near "glorious" Kazbek, capped with "eternal snow" and regnant as the range's "sovereign mistress" (a feminine variant of Pushkin's "tsar").[20] Reingardt admired the panorama beside the "hut of a mountaineer," but the native occupant was nowhere in evidence. With neither real nor metaphorical tribesmen to spoil the peaceful solitude, the traveler relished his "isolation among mountains which touch the sky," and plunged into speculations "about the succession of centuries and the changing course of human fate," the landing site of Noah's ark and the torments of Prometheus. The revery was broken by the admission that the Caucasian heights were still largely "inaccessible to man and enlightenment." Natives antagonistic to Russian bearers of "enlightenment" were thus acknowledged imperiously (as creatures inimical to "man"). But to keep hostile tribes from installing themselves in his text, Reingardt immediately redirected the reader's eye back to more tracts of rhetorically depopulated, sublime scenery, as he continued his trek.

As these cases illustrate, the sentimental journey recurrently had recourse to an implicit trope of the Caucasus as a church reserved for Russian worshipers. Two more, particularly undiluted examples may be cited to underline the point. In an attitude of awestruck solitude, a certain Gerakov reported this ecstatic experience: "Tears of emotion flow from the eyes of the enlightened traveler facing these massifs too immense to encompass at a glance. He kneels and exclaims: 'God exists and these are His wonders!' "[21] Another traveler, likewise alone in the Piatigorsk region, appeared to speak from a confession booth: "I bowed before the Almighty at the foot of the Besh-Tau mountains and equated myself to earth and dust. Indeed I am no more than dust set in motion by passions; and yet by taking wing, this animated dust can ascend to talk to the Creator of the magnificent Caucasus, the Creator of nature."[22] These travelers surely knew that the Asian frontier was not really so empty and churchlike, but they had to pretend that it was in order to replicate those sentimental prostrations of the soul initially performed in a very different political context in eighteenth-century writings about Switzerland.[23]

ATTACKS ON THE SENTIMENTAL JOURNEY

For all its prevalence, however, exalted communion with the wild did not suit absolutely every Russian's taste. In direct defiance of the Caucasian spa's therapeutic atmosphere, one traveler in the late 1820s symbolized the romantic enthusiasm for savage highlands as a disease.[24] Although definitely Byronic (a "British rage"), the malady was not merely "spleen" but rather a "mental obstruction" analogous to a blocked digestive tract. Appalled by the epidemic, the writer refused to follow his compatriots' special Caucasian "diet" of wild terrain. Although we cannot be certain, this cranky assessment may have represented the view of a wider circle of people tired of Caucasian gloom and glory but not motivated to denounce it in print.

In any case, by far the most celebrated assault on the sentimental *goût de la montagne* came from Pushkin's *Journey to Arzrum*, previewed for the *Literary Gazette* (*Literaturnaia gazeta*) in 1830 and then published in its entirety six years later. There is a long critical tradition of viewing this travelogue as a demystification of the romantic "The Prisoner of the Caucasus."[25] No rigid dichotomy can be drawn, however, because the Pushkin of the travelogue refused to deny completely "that" first Caucasus, the textual alpine realm of his youth.[26] The result was an ambivalent interplay between *Journey to Arzrum* and the imaginative geography of "The Prisoner of the Caucasus."

Without a doubt, *Journey to Arzrum* drastically deflated the pose of the gentleman traveler lost in lofty prayers to nature. First of all, the writing turns the eye from landscape by lingering on stopping points rather than Pushkin's passage along the Georgian Military Highway and subsidiary roads.[27] Tiflis receives extensive treatment when the author pauses there *en route* to the camp of the Russian army. In the reverse movement, home becomes the place to which he desires to return as fast as possible. Given the focus upon destinations, the intervening spaces become obstacles to overcome rather than captivating subject-matter. As he approaches Tiflis, for example, Pushkin proclaims sheer boredom with the scenery and emits one of his recurring cries of eagerness to reach Paskevich's army: "My impressions soon began to lose their keenness. Hardly one solid day had passed, and the roar of the Terek with its hideous waterfalls, the crags and precipices no longer attracted my attention. An impatience to reach Tiflis possessed me completely. I rode past Kazbek just as indifferently as I had once sailed past Chatyrdai" (in the Crimea).[28]

Besides minimizing landscape, Pushkin's *récit de voyage* punctured the sentimental bubble of alpine religiosity by confronting readers with carnage. After leaving Tiflis in search of the tsarist army, the writer spotted Ararat where Noah's ark supposedly landed. His response parodied the tradition of reading Caucasian peaks as promises of salvation: "I stared avidly at the Biblical mountain, I saw the ark moored on the summit, full of hope for a new beginning and life; and I saw the raven and the dove in flight, symbols of mortal punishment and reconciliation" (437). Out of context, these lines may seem free from irony. But Pushkin quickly shifted to the war in Turkey and provided dispassionate glimpses of corpses after a battle. Juxtaposed to a killing field, Ararat's religious mythology was vitiated.

War intruded again to challenge the tradition of spiritual uplift in the rugged heights in one of Pushkin's ambivalent allusions to "The Prisoner of the Caucasus." The writer let his imagination wander in a rare description of scenery: "The mountains stretched above us. On their summits a herd was creeping along like insects, barely visible. We could also make out a shepherd, perhaps a Russian taken prisoner at one time and grown old in captivity" (419). The remark evoked a human drama similar to the one which enthralled Russian readers of "The Prisoner of the Caucasus" several years before. However, *Journey to Arzrum* distanced itself from the youthful poem by raising the possibility of permanent captivity and offering no hint of amorous consolation with a Circassian tribeswoman. Indeed, the very next paragraph of Pushkin's travelogue cut the ground from under that type of fantasy, so central in "The Prisoner of the Caucasus": "The Circassians hate us. We have edged them out of their free pasture lands, their *auls* have been destroyed and entire tribes annihilated. With every passing day they move deeper into the mountains and make attacks against us from there" (420). No sheltered alpine space where a Russian was advised to seek spiritual renewal (and might even romance a wild woman), this Caucasus was a zone of hostilities with dispossessed natives.

While eschewing the soulful meditations about nature which might provide a rhetorical escape from these embattled Circassians, *Journey to Arzrum* also stripped glory from the tsarist conquest. In the continuation of the passage just cited, Pushkin voiced the hope that Russia would prove able to civilize the tribes by spreading Orthodoxy. But the travelogue's first chapter illustrated a brutality far removed from this pacific ideal of missionary activity. In an episode which seemed to parody Radozhitsky's evocation of extras in an "Asiatic ballet," Pushkin described the "grievous condition" of "half-naked and repulsively dirty" children among prisoners of war at Vladikavkaz (421). Held before the reader without further commentary, these little shackled victims of tsarist conquest were neither rationalized away by reference to a civilizing mission nor hidden from sight behind a curtain of homage to wilderness.

But although the anti-romantic strategies of *Journey of Arzrum* undermined sentimental travel literature's construct of the purely pacific Russian worshiper of nature, Pushkin none the less clung in certain ways to the restorative alpine Caucasus of his youth. At one point the travelogue featured mountain *paysage* as a "sanctuary" (422), a quasi-religious symbol in harmony with the author's youthful trope of the "new Parnassus." In the readership's intertextual field, this lingering promise of artistic empowerment was made good when Pushkin in fact wrote a poem about an experience related in *Journey to Arzrum* – the arresting sight of the monastery on Kazbek when the clouds suddenly parted.

In addition to this vestige of the "new Parnassus," the travelogue retained three other tropes of the romantic years. Pushkin engaged in interesting self-citation to record his first glimpse of the mountains: "I saw on the distant horizon the clouds which caught my eye exactly as they had done nine years before. They looked just the same there in the same place. It was the snowy summits of the Caucasian range" (417). Like poetry by Byron and Zhukovsky, "The Prisoner of the Caucasus" projected snow-caps as clouds, and the comparison had become a standard formula in *récits de voyage*. Instead of seeking an entirely different formulation, though, *Journey to Arzrum* upheld the cliché and even called attention to Pushkin's primary role in establishing it in Russian letters. Along with the irresistible clouds, the poet kept the overworked metaphor of the mountain as a potentate attended by a suite: *en route* to Tiflis he hails Besh-Tau as a majestic presence "surrounded by other mountains, his vassals" (418). In another case, Pushkin avoided the hackneyed formula "eternal snows" but conveyed the same idea by quoting Horace's line "stat glacies iners / Menses per omnes . . ." ("covered throughout the year with immobile ice," 442). In interplay with the other persisting clichés, it is not evident whether the rather tired Latin citation was offered tongue-in-cheek or rather with an approving nod, as though to show that hackneyed mountain gloom and glory could be made paradoxically "new" by placing a classical text in a Caucasian context. Along with the line of "clouds" and the mountain ruler with his "vassals," these latinized snows preserved "that" Caucasus produced by young Pushkin and made a place of pilgrimage by Russian travelers.

Some lesser poets and poetasters demystified the territory more unequivocally than Pushkin, who had a big personal stake, after all, in "that" romantic Caucasus. Pavel Katenin's "Caucasian Mountains" (1834) went so far as to call the range a "row of ugly walls" probably created by the devil rather than God.[29] Obviously sick of the sublime, Katenin disavowed the Parnassian connection to make the Caucasus the "plague of poetry." In a similar development as of the mid-1830s, certain other poets urged Russians to recognize that their homeland's plains and broad, navigable rivers were more beautiful than the Caucasus.[30]

But these protests were merely potshots by comparison to the demolition of sublime imaginative geography in

Polezhaev's "Erpeli." This poem of war in Chechnia and Dagestan had a notable biographical foundation. Outraged by Polezhaev's free-thinking burlesque "Sasha," Nicholas I conscripted the young author into the infantry in 1826.[31] Eventually the poet's regiment was sent to the Caucasus where he spent four taxing years (without any recuperative breaks in Piatigorsk).

Set entirely in the theater of war, "Erpeli" ridicules armchair travelers who take a fancy to savage nature while sitting cozily at home with a book. In the second of the poem's eight parts, Polezhaev imagines the arrival of a well-read recruit – a devotee of "scenes of wildness in all its primitive nakedness."[32] The verse then unfolds as a tour of sites the newcomer encountered in books before enlisting. Elbrus retains a modicum of traditional grandeur as an "old, hoary Titan" whose peak gleams through the clouds. Disillusionment mounts, however, when the celebrated Terek strikes the recent arrival as a "dirty swill." At the end of the excursion, Polezhaev unmasks the neophyte as none other than his own former self, now denounced as one of many "blockheads" who thought Pushkin's Elbrus properly typified the Caucasus.

The deprecatory reference to young Pushkin invites analysis of the overlap and divergence between "Erpeli" and *Journey to Arzrum*. The two works parted ways politically, while unequally sharing certain anti-romantic premises. *Journey to Arzrum* featured the Caucasus as a combat zone but withheld patriotic approval of the military onslaught by confronting the reader with dispossessed Circassians and miserable little prisoners of war. At the same time, Pushkin retained fondness for the romantic achievement of his youth. By contrast, Polezhaev unequivocally rejected romantic imaginative geography but endorsed the ideology of the civilizing mission: in displacing the tourist's alpine Caucasus with the ordeals of "Holy Russia's" battle against Muslim "savages," "Erpeli" totally subverted the sentimental literary pilgrimage and even blamed Pushkin for captivating "blockheads" with mountain gloom and glory in the first place.

The anti-sentimentalism of "Erpeli" far exceeded any disaffection from the alpine ethos in Russia's Caucasian travel literature. All the same, Pyotr Sumarokov's "Letters from the Caucasus" bears special mention as a significant retreat from heartfelt sublimity. Sumarokov vowed to escape the intertextual circle. Various Russian visitors already have "surveyed the sights," he remarked, "but I am not going to follow their method. I am not going to give extracts from old books and try to pass them off as something new."[33] In fact, Sumarokov did not prove wholly successful in his search for an untrod authorial path (he could not forgo Kazbek's "eternal snows," for example). But even if not completely free of literary echoes, "Letters from the Caucasus" struck a fresh note by eliminating quasi-religious sentiment and highflown rhetoric. Convinced that the scenery had "become all too familiar by now" to the Russian readership, Sumarokov indeed gave little attention to the mountains. He wrote instead about the spa's routine and recounted a visit to a Circassian village. This encounter with the natives betrayed an imperious thirst for oriental exoticism: the tourists all found the women less beautiful and the men less dashing than promised in Pushkin's "The Prisoner of the Caucasus."[34] The most disappointed member of the Russian party even faulted a certain tribesman for looking just like one of his serfs back home instead of having a suitably "Asian face."

THE PERSISTENCE OF SENTIMENTALITY

Despite the various efforts to demystify the territory, Russian travel literature remained largely sentimental in the 1830s. A few quick citations will suffice to illustrate the strength of the old *goût de la montagne*. The "eternal snows," the "splendid" and "dreadful" mountains like "proud giants," the "magnificent vistas," the "savage," roaring Terek were all reaffirmed by thrilled travelers.[35] Most strikingly of all, the thirst for spiritual therapy remained unabated. One Russian on a solitary trek in the highlands in 1833 cast off the "chains of the body" to fly "to the Creator of the universe."[36] At the end of the decade, another traveler reported the same exaltation and exhorted readers to make their own ascents of the Caucasus in order to flee the vanities of high society.[37] Already present in Tepliakov's poem "The Caucasus" (1829), this *topos* of exchanging the fool's gold of the *beau monde* for the spiritual bedrock of pristine mountains was notably promoted in Caucasian *récits de voyage* by Bestuzhev-Marlinsky, the decade's most popular writer (whose vigorous reassertion of the subjective mode will be assessed in a later chapter).[38]

The genre of sentimental pilgrimage to the "Caucasian Alps" would keep suffering attacks in Russia's literary market place. Ethnography, plans for colonial development of the Caucasus, and defenses of the civilizing mission began to steal more space from landscape in travelers' accounts of the 1830s. Furthermore, that decade brought the publication of campaign notes by Russian soldiers who sometimes debunked the aesthetic of the Caucasian sublime and the fantasy of erotic adventure in the wilderness.[39] In yet a different fashion, Lermontov's *A Hero of Our Time* (1841) would explode conventions of the floridly rhetorical Caucasian journey, as we shall see.

But instead of palling, the pleasures of the sentimental literary pilgrimage remained keen and were even amplified once travelers could add Bestuzhev-Marlinsky and Lermontov to their list of "guidebooks." The selective reading and outright misreading which this entailed were well illustrated by Evgeny Verderevsky's book *From the Trans-Urals to Transcaucasia: Humourous, Sentimental and Practical Letters from a Trip* (1857). In contemporaneous publications about Shamil, Verderevsky viewed the Caucasus solely as a war zone.[40] But unlike Verderevsky the publicist, Verderevsky the traveler suspended conquest in order to pursue a literary pilgrimage in the old, classically epistolary form. In addition to Pushkin, Bestuzhev-Marlinsky and Lermontov helped nudge his pen.[41] No matter what the "guide" was, however, the traveler invariably drew sentimental inspiration. *From the Trans-Urals to Transcaucasia* actually quoted *Journey to Arzrum*, for example, but only to profit from Pushkin's self-citation of the "clouds" which symbolized "that" Caucasus of the 1820s. Unfazed by the demystifications of *Journey to Arzrum*, Polezhaev's "Erpeli," anti-romantic campaign notes, or Lermontov's *A Hero of Our Time*, Verderevsky could not part with the sublime imaginative geography first produced in Russian poetry of the 1820s. As a tribute to the primacy of verse in young Pushkin's era, the sight of Elbrus prompted Verderevsky to switch to poetry to convey his "insuperable lyricism."[42] One line of this verse granted that the Caucasus was "bathed in blood." But this grievous knowledge never seeped into the traveler's prose account of his encounter with a romantic landscape he had set out to find. Thus even at this late date, the sentimental Caucasian journey was still thriving and ripe for the parodic attack which young Tolstoy's *The Cossacks* (1863) would mount against it.

As this chapter has shown, the sentimental literary pilgrimage to the Caucasus survived in Russian letters during the whole conquest. This remarkably persistent phenomenon provided two sorts of psychological and cultural satisfactions. The first was a form of compensation peculiar to Russia. By preserving the literary fiction of the "Caucasian Alps," travelers of the romantic era were in effect telling themselves that Piatigorsk was as good as Switzerland. This was valuable since many Russians, for one reason or another, could not actually go to Europe (Pushkin, for instance, was never allowed to travel abroad and was officially reprimanded for the unauthorized trip to Erzerum). Although he had never been to the West, Bestuzhev-Marlinsky defined the consolatory perspective in "Letter to Doctor Erman" (1831): "Anybody who has seen the Caucasus in storm and sunshine need have no regrets about not seeing Switzerland."[43] This proposition recurred in Russian travel literature, sometimes couched in rhetoric very likely borrowed from the increasingly famous Bestuzhev-Marlinsky himself.[44] On his first trip to Europe in 1857, Lev Tolstoy would express the same outlook less elegantly: in response to his relatives' delight with countryside near Geneva, he told them the place was "rotten by comparison to the Caucasus."[45]

But in addition to filling a need to believe that Russia's "own" mountains bettered Europe's, the fiction of the "Caucasian Alps" worked as a moral tonic by dissociating the sentimental traveler from imperialism's plundering designs. Throughout the conquest, Russian *récits de voyage* favored the posture of the sensitive soul content to aestheticize and worship the Caucasus. In harmony with nature in this sheltered space, the sentimental traveler could feel purehearted, disjoined from bloody warfare and not even implicated in plans for economic appropriation of the territory. After the tribes declared Holy War on Russia, travelers proved quicker to denounce Muslim "savages" and complain about Georgians or Armenians too "lazy" to exploit their bountiful countries properly.[46] Many who underwrote imperialism so directly, however, still liked to plunge back into peaceful contemplation of nature. As particularly well illustrated in Verderevsky's *From the Trans-Urals to Transcaucasia*, a Russian might express animosity towards "treacherous" tribesmen but then attempt to conceal political conflict by reassuming the role of the cultivated tourist with no plans to dispossess or exploit anyone. A reinforcer of the ideology of the civilizing mission, the sentimental journey's ruling *topos* of the reverent friend of nature insinuated that Russian intrusion in the territory was besmirching nobody's honor.

CHAPTER 5

The national stake in Asia

A two-faced Janus, ancient Russia simultaneously
looked toward Europe and Asia.
Bestuzhcv-Marlinsky

While physical geography inspired the alpine ethos just examined in poetry and travel literature, Russians considered the
Caucasus' native cultures strictly Asian. Ever since the mid-
eighteenth century, Russian map-makers had taken the Caucasian range as an outer limit of Europe.[1] No universal consensus on the matter reigned in popular imagination,
however. Instead of regarding the mountains as the vital
demarcation, certain travelers from Russia in young Pushkin's
era said farewell to "Europe" with apprehension and excitement when they crossed the Terek river.[2] The variability of
"Asia's" threshold and its capacity to stir irrational sentiments illustrates how arbitrary and affectively powerful such
delimitations can be. As Edward Said has stressed, the drawing of a boundary between "us" and "them" always carries
a plethora of "suppositions, associations and fictions" about
the foreign people.[3] In no way requiring the others' consent
about the character attributed to them, such structures of
thought basically convert the foreign into meaning about
"our" culture and mentality. An appropriation occurs, to
serve the needs of the observing writers and their compatriot
audiences.

As a preface to reading pertinent literary works of the
romantic era, the present chapter will explore the meanings
Russians deduced about themselves by rendering the Caucasus "Asian" or "oriental." We should note immediately

71

that these overlapping terms designated particularly broad cultural spheres for the élite of Pushkin's time. The Mongols loomed large in national consciousness as barbarians who had oppressed the homeland for some two hundred and fifty years. But in subsequent periods, the tsarist state had turned the tables to extend power over various Asian peoples. Ivan IV subjugated the Tatars of the Volga and Ural river regions. A push into Kazazh areas began in the 1730s. Catherine annexed the Crimea, advanced in the Caucasus and made new inroads into Central Asia. Conquered in the sixteenth and seventeenth centuries, Siberia also remained a very salient "Asia" for the Russian élite of the 1820s.[4] Beyond the confines of the multinational empire itself, Russia maintained long-standing contacts with China and other countries of the Far East at this time. India and the lands of the Bible also featured, of course, in the manifold Russian conception of the Asian world.

But if "Asia" encompassed many places, the Islamic East acquired special prominence in popular imagination. Beginning in the mid-eighteenth century, *The Thousand and One Nights* drew Russians into a pan-European "collective daydream" about sultans and seraglios.[5] Initially known in the French translations of Antoine Gallard, the fairy tales also became available in Russian translations issued in Moscow in a fairly steady stream between 1763 and 1826.[6] These collections enjoyed great popularity right into young Pushkin's heyday, when they were still regularly sold out at bookstores.[7] The exotic allure of *The Thousand and One Nights* was strengthened by many other western literary works. In addition to famous philosophical tales about "wise orientals" (Montesquieu's *Lettres persanes*, Voltaire's *Zaïre*), a massive, lowbrow French literature of harem intrigues began circulating in Russia in the early 1800s.[8] Around a decade later, the oriental poems of Byron immeasurably intensified the collective daydream of Muslim sensuality and violence which reigned in Europe and Russia alike. Another classic of western orientalism particularly well known in early nineteenth-century Russia was Thomas Moore's *Lalla Rookh* (1817), partially translated by Zhukovsky as "The *Peri* and the Angel."

During the period from 1810 to 1820 theatrical spectacles in Russia also encouraged rapturous musings about Islam: Mozart's *Abduction from the Seraglio* played a major role, along with the ballets of Charles Didelot, whose "Asiatic" productions (so admired by the traveler Radozhitsky) included a work based on "The Prisoner of the Caucasus."[9]

In drawing the Caucasus into Islam's exotic cultural orbit, the Russian upper classes of Pushkin's era postulated two, quite different identities for themselves. On the one hand, they assumed a western stance of superiority over the orient.[10] To build an empire in Asia was to behave as a European dedicated to the spread of Christian civilization and the realization of a colony's economic potential. This ideological pattern took shape in Catherine's era when Russia began advancing in the Caucasus at the expense of the Ottoman empire and Persia. Turkey ceded Kabarda to Russia by the Treaty of Kuchuk-Kainardzhi (1774) and entirely withdrew from the northwestern Black Sea coast after the war of 1787–92. Soon after the annexation of Georgia, Russia progressively drove Persia from its traditional spheres of influence in northern Azerbaijan, a region which the Shah finally ceded in its entirety by the Treaty of Gulistan (1813). The tsarist state also won nominal suzerainty over Dagestan at the same time. Further Russian campaigns against Persia and Turkey were mounted between 1826 and 1829, as we have gleaned in discussing Pushkin's *Journey to Arzrum*. Finally and most dramatically, the tribes of Chechnia and Dagestan arose in Holy War against Russia in the late 1820s under the leadership of the first Caucasian imam, Gazi-Muhammed. In light of the history of warfare and the exacerbation of conflict with the tribes, educated Russians of Pushkin's era tended to view the Caucasus as an enormous battlefield where the Orthodox state was locked in epochal combat with Islam.

Like the religious ambience, "European" economic objectives of expansion into "Asia" also dated from Catherine's reign. As most lavishly represented by the "oriental project," overlordship of the Caucasus was to bring Russia a chain of trading outposts all the way into India. In Russia in the 1820s the British Raj retained prominence as a colonial model to equal or even surpass. By the second decade of the nineteenth century, Russian journals were running articles about the wealth which England was amassing as the ruler of India.[11] In this period Russia's own colonial ambitions in the Caucasus were not widely aired in publications aimed at the general reading public, and even some high tsarist officials still viewed the territory as a perpetual battleground rather than a potentially valuable possession.[12] But in certain circles, the southerly Caucasus ("Transcaucasia") was gaining a reputation as a richly endowed but backward region, to be developed for the supposedly mutual benefit of the native population and Russia alike. Most notably, Alexander Griboedov coauthored a plan for a Russian–Transcaucasian Trading Company while employed as secretary to the tsarist legation in Tehran in 1827.[13] Although not enacted or even made widely known in its time, this proposal conveyed a significant perception of Georgia in particular as a tsarist colony awaiting transformation in the imperial British manner. Just a short while later, Russian journalists in Tiflis became fond of describing Transcaucasia as a "tropical India," with the implication that their homeland was going to reap lavish colonial benefits.[14]

Central to imperialist tsarist ideology, the imposition of oriental identity on the Caucasus undoubtedly allowed Russians to intensify their sense of Europeanness in religious, moral and economic terms. On the other hand, though, Russian romantics provided fascinating demonstrations of how futile it was to try to erect an ideological barrier between the native realm and Asia. As Vasily Nikitin once argued, Russia could not encompass itself in western civilization and declare the orient its Other because the orient comprised an "organic part of Russian history."[15] Medieval Russia had cultural and political roots in Asia, Asian peoples had comprised part of the tsarist empire since the sixteenth century, and the names of Tatar ancestry among the aristocracy of Pushkin's time attested vividly to the vast country's unique blend of East and West.[16] In the light of such considerations, a Russian could not believe in the alterity of the orient as readily and invariably as a European might. Most intriguingly of all, the native realm's cultural heterogeneity gave Russian romantics a stake in enhancing Asia rather than consistently acclaiming the western civilization in which they knew they did not fully belong. Of course, a good many European romantics too construed the orient as the cradle of marvelous poetry and philosophical doctrines which might regenerate spiritual life in the West.[17] But only in semi-Asian Russia did romantic constitutions of the East provide therapy for a profoundly ambivalent consciousness of national difference from Europe.

The contradictory patterns of meaning which Russia devised about Asia formed the literary Caucasus' cultural matrix to be explored now. When did Russian interest in the orient begin to evolve? To what extent did Russians mimic European attitudes, beliefs and ideas about the Islamic East? And in what respects did Russian discourse about Asia reveal tensions with the West? In examining these questions, this chapter will convey no Russian recognitions of a territory's right to independence from the tsarist state. However, the romantic enhancement of Asia revealed a Russian confusion about cultural frontiers which would manifest itself in ideologically significant disruptions of "civilized" identity in literary works about Caucasian mountaineers.

JOINING EUROPE'S *RENAISSANCE ORIENTALE*

Despite manifold contacts with Asians over the centuries, Russia rather curiously entered oriental studies only very late and then under European tutelage. As the eminent scholar Vasily Bartold observed, the study of eastern cultures and languages came to Russia as one of the western sciences and did not flourish until the state perceived a vested interest in the field.[18] In the first half of the eighteenth century isolated academicians in Russia attempted to persuade the government to establish programs in oriental languages and Islamic culture, but such proposals went unheeded or were even ridiculed as useless pedantry. The period of aggressive penetration of the Caucasus brought a radical shift in attitudes in high places. Catherine initiated some practical training of interpreters in eastern languages.[19] However, the big push toward establishing oriental studies came in the reign of Alexander I. The tsar's first directive on university education (1804) called for study of the languages of the Bible and the Muslim peoples.[20] Shortly after the annexation of Georgia, the Minister of Foreign Affairs, Count Kochubei, drew up a related plan to institute faculties of three different groups of languages in Kazan (Tatar, Arabic,Turkish), Tiflis (Persian, Georgian, Armenian) and Irkutsk (Japanese, Chinese, Manchurian).[21] Under the direction of S. Ya. Rumovsky, Kazan University emerged as the major center of oriental studies in Russia at this time. But significant developments would take place in the capital cities too. The Lazarev institute of oriental languages was founded in Moscow in 1815; and three years later St. Petersburg had an Asian Museum and a university program of Arabic and Persian studies initially manned by the Europeans Christian Frähn and two French disciples of the pioneering orientalist, Antoine Isaac Silvestre de Sacy.[22]

Perhaps the most politically and culturally eloquent expression of Russia's urge to take the East under scrutiny was Sergei Uvarov's "Projet d'une Académie Asiatique," written in collaboration with the German orientalist Heinrich-Julius Klaproth in 1810 and published the following year in Russian translation in the *Herald of Europe*. A future Minister of Education (1833–49), Uvarov voiced dismay about his country's isolation from the "renaissance of oriental studies" inaugurated in the West in the late 1750s by the French translators of Sanskrit, Arabic and Zendic texts.[23] He argued that an Asian academy would be not a scholarly luxury but rather a vital contributor to national interest and prestige:

Lying adjacent to Asia and exercising dominion over its entire northern part, Russia retains all the more a *political incentive* – an incentive so evident, so indisputable that the slightest glance at a map suffices to demonstrate the truth of the matter beyond any doubt. Russia, one might say, has gained its firm foundation in Asia.

An immensely long overland border serves as a point of contact with all the peoples of the Orient. So how can it be that among all the European nations Russia alone has paid no attention to Asia?[24]

As a child of the era of empire-building in the Caucasus, Uvarov stressed the "evident" political objectives which Russia could further by training orientalists. But even more strikingly, the proposal attributed value to an Asian academy as a cultural enterprise signifying membership in European enlightenment. Instead of acknowledging an oriental component *within* the tsarist homeland, Uvarov placed Russia among the "European nations" and defined "Asia" as the contiguous but utterly different place, to be approached for investigation from the outside. In short, the proposal gave the West's *renaissance orientale* the appeal of a cultural bandwagon on which every truly civilized country was obliged to find a seat.

Russian periodicals of young Pushkin's era recurrently proclaimed the Europeanness of subjecting Asia to intellectual scrutiny. By the second decade of the nineteenth century widely read journals drew upon French, British and German publications to provide regular coverage of oriental philology and translations of Arabic and Persian literature.[25] The Russian press also kept track of activities and publications of professional associations like the Royal Asiatic Society of London and France's Société asiatique.[26] In the same spirit of Europeanness, the work of Silvestre de Sacy was brought to general attention when *National Annals* published "On the Study of Arabic," the lecture Osip Senkovsky (Jozef Sękowski) delivered upon his accession to a chair of Arabic, Persian and Turkic languages at St. Petersburg University in 1822.[27] Only twenty-two at the time, this bright local star of oriental studies had begun his education in his native Wilno and then practiced Arabic for two years as a traveler in the Levant, decked in local dress right up to the turban. During the twenty-five years he held his academic post, he regularly published specialized studies. But as we shall see in subsequent chapters, Senkovsky also played a major role in the popular dissemination of hegemonic, Eurocentric discourse about Asia during

1834–47 when he edited the commercially unrivaled journal the *Library for Reading* (*Biblioteka dlia chteniia*).

Russians keen to leap on the bandwagon of oriental studies readily identified with Europe's self-image as the cultural caretaker of an Asia now hopelessly mired in barbarism and stagnation. Napoleon's invasion of Egypt had done much to promote the belief that the conservation of eastern cultures went hand in hand with military and political domination. With its contingent of scholars including the codecipherer of the Rosetta stone, Jean-François Champollion, the Egyptian campaign acquired a general reputation in Europe as a venture which enabled France to accelerate oriental studies and hold an impressive lead in the field.[28] This interpretation of the military inroad was readily employed in Russia to build an analogy with the possible cultural gains of tsarist conquest of the Caucasus. In an article "On the State of Oriental Philology in Russia" (1825) the Heidelburg-trained orientalist A. Richter hailed the Caucasian campaigns of Ermolov as a boon for specialists such as himself: the deeds of the army were going to assure entry into a Muslim realm formerly "inaccessible to scholars."[29] Perhaps aware that the Armenian specialist, A. M. Khudobashev, had accompanied Ermolov to Persia in 1817, Richter now linked arms with the general on the march in the Caucasus.[30]

A few years later the *Moscow Telegraph* (*Moskovskii telegraf*) also associated cultural research with the conquest of the territory by characterizing *la renaissance orientale* as an "intellectual Crusade."[31] This metaphor of Christian assault perfectly symbolized the army as a trail blazer for scholars. Cited here as "the masters of India" and the rulers of Algeria, the British and French were praised for seeking the source of the Ganges, studying the Bedouins and collecting relevant manuscripts and artifacts. But Russia too had won cultural "trophies" in the Crusade. At the conclusion of a war which eliminated Persian power in the Armenian khanates of Erevan and Nakhichevan (1826–28), the Turkmanchai treaty granted Russia a store of manuscripts, subsequently made available for study in St. Petersburg.[32] Such events sustained perceptions of the Caucasian conquest as a Napoleonic advancement of intellectual as well as political frontiers.

RUSSIAN PRIDE IN CULTURAL YOUTH

The Russian rush to join *la renaissance orientale* took place under famously judgmental western eyes. As vividly attested in western travel literature since the time of Ivan IV, Europeans had stigmatized Russia as a "rude and barbarous kingdom," a place of "infinite brutality."[33] During the romantic era the western charge of Asian backwardness and barbarism still resounded, as notably illustrated in *Voyage dans la Russie méridionale* (1826) by the French consul in Tiflis, Jacques-François Gamba.[34] Full of disdain for Russia's failure to transform the Caucasus into a viable colony since the annexation of Georgia in 1801, Gamba advised the French to move into the territory themselves. He also made an unfavorable comparison between *la Russie méridionale* and another "new country," the United States: America was far more congenial to a European, he claimed, because it originated from Britain, "where civilization had reached a high level." By contrast, Russia's southern colonies "are offshoots of Russia itself, where one habitually finds the habits and tastes of nomads." A firm believer in the Enlightenment conception of progress, Gamba assigned all Russia to a low, Asian rung on civilization's great ladder. The same outlook would be found in a book much better known today, the Marquis de Custine's *La Russie en 1839*. Writing at a time when anti-Russian sentiment was running particularly high in France, the marquis returned obsessively to the theme that Russians were not truly civilized but had merely acquired a thin veneer of occidental manners which failed to hide the "Oriental," the "Tatar," or simply the "bear" beneath the surface.[35] For the Marquis de Custine, as for Gamba before him, the Russians remained in essence an Asian people inferior in every way to cultivated Europeans.

However, instead of cowing romantic Russians into meek allegiance to western enlightenment, the traditional European aversion to shades of Tatary was flouted by embracement of

Asia as part of the national self. The Russian élite found support for its contradictory claims to European and non-European identity in an extremely influential product of *la renaissance orientale*, J. C. L. Simone de Sismondi's *De la littérature du midi de l'Europe* (1813). In an excerpt published in Russia in 1818 under the title "On the Arabs' Literature," Sismondi endorsed Europe as the caretaker of the decadent orient's cultural patrimony. Indeed to his mind, a complete collapse had left all the Arabs' finest literary products "in the hands of their enemies in Christian monasteries and the libraries of European states."[36] Seek not those glories in the East itself, cautioned Sismondi: today's entire Arab world is nothing but a desert of "tigers and tyrants," infested with "huge nests of bandits" and devoted to "ignorance, slavery, horrors and death."

But while charging the West with the task of preserving the cultural treasures of a fallen civilization, Sismondi showered praise on ancient oriental poetry as an achievement crucial to the rise of European romanticism. He opposed the ethnocentric theory of August and Friedrich Schlegel who insisted that romanticism derived essentially from the Normans and Germanic peoples (the "North").[37] Without entirely discounting the North as constituted by the Schlegels, Sismondi advanced his "southern" theory. He allotted a decisive role to the Moors' invasions of Spain and their subsequent influence on the literatures of the Romance peoples, and also attributed great importance to the cultural impact of the Crusades. With stress on the "magic," "enchantment" and "frenzied passion" of ancient oriental poetry, Sismondi constructed an engaging citadel of romanticism *avant la lettre*.

Although Russian romantics were a diversified group, many of them enlisted Sismondi to stake a worthy claim for themselves in the international literary arena. They were drawn into the South–North debate at a time when their tradition of imaginative literature paled by comparison to European achievements. As Lauren Leighton has shown, Russians' late entry into the European cultural domain and their pronounced literary subservience to France in particular gave them every reason to downgrade ultra-rational French tendencies and to assert instead that less developed nations have greater access to the wellsprings of imagination required to create an original (and thus truly national) literature.[38] The dynamic Hans Rogger termed "compensatory nationalism" clearly was operating in this romantic accreditation of simple, uncorrupted peoples.[39] Beginning in the latter third of the eighteenth century, the Russian élite's dread of national insufficiency *vis-à-vis* Europe stimulated a search for national pride and even led to assertions of superiority. The classical formulation appeared in Denis Fonvizin's letters from Europe written in the 1770s and 1780s. Fonvizin primarily targeted France as a cramped realm of cold calculation, the cash nexus, legalism, hypocrisy and stupidity masked by witty manners and *politesse*. In opposition to this construct of western alterity, he attributed to Russians a pleasing simplicity, generous feeling, authenticity in human relations, a richer spiritual life and truer sense of freedom despite all the lack of liberty and civil rights in tsarist society. A complex of inadequacy, focused on intellect and sophistication, thus engendered a complex of largely emotional superiority.[40]

RUSSIA'S ROMANTIC LINK TO THE ORIENT

Keen to assert national dignity *vis-à-vis* Europe, the Russian disciples of Sismondi's broad-based southern theory naturally took their distance from the Schlegels' Teutonic ethnocentricism. And yet in exhibiting this preference, Russians replicated a certain German strategy of the "young" nation's self-promotion *vis-à-vis* the orient.[41] In a compensatory reaction to the preponderance of Latin Christendom in the Renaissance, German orientalists such as Klaproth arrogated to themselves the preeminent place in the contemporary cultural flowering inspired by the East: they sought to persuade the rest of the world that they were the modern era's poetically superior race, most akin to ancient Persia's artful idiom.[42] Herder played a complementary role by glorifying German primitive poetry (*Volklieder*) as a product of anonymous, epic genius comparable to the Sanskrit *Vedas*.[43] In the German cultural field, "oriental" thus converged on "barbarous" in a manner which specifically devalued a French pride in reason and proclaimed the superiority of the "young" native land's *Sturm und Drang*.

Like the Germans, Russians upgraded themselves in relation to Asia during *la renaissance orientale* but with considerably greater ammunition, since they could boast much more genuine geographical, historical and cultural connections to the East. A Klaprothian logic informed Russian pretensions to special national capacities for oriental studies, for example. The first direct Russian translations of Arabic and Persian literature were published only in 1811 by A. V. Boldyrev, a Paris-trained orientalist also employed as a tsarist censor.[44] Toward the end of the next decade, however, the *Herald of Asia* (*Aziatskii vestnik*) anonymously ran the claim that Russians were bound to take the lead in translation because their native tongue was by far the most suitable medium: only the "noble soil" of Russian could permit the bright flowers of Arabic poetry to bloom again with all their brilliance and "natural perfume."[45] This theme of the "last shall be first" evolved over time. As a commentator in *Telescope* (*Teleskop*) would put it in 1833, Russia was now proudly holding her own in oriental studies, after apprenticing as the "little sister of the other European powers."[46] Although retaining the Eurocentric view of the field as an originally western science, a later journalist would brag of Russia's record as a nurturer of great specialists from within its own multinational confines: some of "our" Asians have become world-class orientalists, whereas neither the British nor French could point to similarly enlightened Indians or Algerians in their midst.[47] While thoroughly sanguine about centuries of tsarist subjugation of the borderlands, this assessment made a virtue of fluidity between "Russia" and "Asia."

The Russian literati's debate about nationally distinctive romanticism displayed a similarly favorable disposition toward the homeland's overlap with the East. Orest Somov, for instance, proclaimed Russian affiliation to poeticized

Islam in "On Romantic Poetry" (1823), an essay written under the influence of Mme. de Staël's *De l'Allemagne.*[48] An author of fiction and verse, Somov perceived a fruitful interplay between the eastern past and the romantic present in writings by Byron, Goethe and Thomas Moore, all wellknown Europeans inspired by the art and legends of the Moors, Indians, Persians and Turks. But Somov then featured semi-Asian Russia as romanticism's most favored breeding ground. With a sweeping glance from Finland to Siberia via the "enchanting" Crimea and the Caucasus' "wild terrors," he catalogued the "poetic riches" Russians could sample without venturing onto foreign soil. After rapidly sketching the empire's geographical and cultural diversity, Somov brought his rhetorical eye to rest on the "tribes who believe in Mahomet and serve in the sphere of imagination as a link connecting us to the Orient." To be sure, the author assumed an imperial posture. On the lookout for interesting subject-matter, he showed no sign of realizing that non-Russian nationalities swallowed up by the tsarist state might justly yearn for sovereignty, or have a word to utter about themselves. And yet it remains noteworthy that Somov singled out Asian Muslims as the empire's preeminently "poetic" group, most vital to Russians such as he. Monologic and politically complacent as it was, "On Romantic Poetry" clashed in this respect against Eurocentric imperialist rhetoric about civilizing alien "savages" of the Caucasus.

A similar perception of welcome interchange between Russia and Asia was advanced in other literary criticsm of the era, including Kiukhelbeker's. Although at odds with certain aspects of anti-classical sensibility, Kiukhelbeker joined the general romantic call for a literature imbued with national spirit. He accordingly warned his fellow writers not to exchange Russia's former tutelage to France for enslavement to German or British models. In his view, the future lay instead in the homeland's realizing its culturally mixed character: "By its geographical position alone, Russia might assimilate all the mental treasures of Europe and Asia" (as represented by Saadi, Hafiz and others).[49] Kiukhelbeker foresaw here not mere imitation but rather the emergence of "truly Russian" poetry which fused vital traditions of both East and West. Around the same time, in 1827, a book reviewer for the *Moscow Herald* (*Moskovskii vestnik*) articulated a similar vision with greater historical *élan* : "Located between the Orient and the West, our fatherland seems to have been designated by nature to serve as a link in the chain of humanity's universal development, to achieve a specific conjunction of European culture and Asia's enlightenment."[50]

While all these statements were significant antecedents, Bestuzhev-Marlinsky undertook an even more grandiose effort to make romantic capital of Russia's Asian roots. His essay on Nikolai Polevoy's historical novel *The Oath on the Tomb of the Lord* attempted to synthesize the contradictory theories of Sismondi and the Schlegels.[51] Carelessly galloping over centuries of comparative history, Bestuzhev-Marlinsky declared that the full blooming of romanticism in Europe in the present era was a result of a merger between "southern" forces (Moors, Crusaders, vivacious troubadours, unfettered imagination) and "northern" ones (Normans, Germanic tribes, severe legends, rationality). But where did Russia belong in this scheme which made "South" equivalent to "Orient" and let "North" double for "West?"

Bestuzhev-Marlinsky's answer evinced the Russian national need to convert semi-Asian identity from a liability into an asset. His argument was inconsistent and oblique. With consummate disregard for Catholic Christendom and the Renaissance, he argued that Russia's history had really been very similar to Europe's and that Russian writers were flowing in the general stream of romantic European culture. But then he went off on another tack to underline the homeland's split personality: "A two-faced Janus, ancient Russia simultaneously looked toward Europe and Asia. Its way of life comprised a link between the settled activity of the West and the nomadic indolence of the Orient." Whatever his inconsistencies, though, Bestuzhev-Marlinsky was clearly bent on declaring the Asian heritage a virtue. He accentuated the hardiness, bravery and chivalrous pride of Russian ancestors steeled by constant fights with nomadic tribes of the southern steppes. He evoked medieval Russian princes drinking fermented mare's milk with khans of the Golden Horde. Most boldly of all, he likened romanticism's own compelling power to the Tatars who conquered Russia. Through such details he outfitted Asia in dashing colors and fashioned a national past in which a romantic could take immense pride. In fact, the essay moved to the grand conclusion that it was Russia which was destined to reach the peak of unfettered romantic literary imagination akin to ancient Arabia: as cases in point, the author cited his own historical tales, as well as Polevoy's novel *The Oath on the Tomb of the Lord.* Bestuzhev-Marlinsky thus turned culturally mixed Russia into the vanguard of romanticism, indebted to western literature, to be sure, but now racing ahead into a glorious, distinctive future.

As in literary criticism of the romantic era, a sense of the national stake in Asia also stirred in Russian music. Particularly pertinent because of his Caucasian connections is Alexander Aliabev (1787–1851), a composer born in Tobolsk.[52] On the basis of dubious evidence Aliabev was exiled from Moscow to Siberia for murder in 1828. Four years later, failing health brought him permission to visit the Caucasian spa country, where he became acquainted with music of the Circassians, Georgians and other peoples. Soon afterwards, he made song-gathering expeditions into Central Asia and the Trans-Volga region as well. He published his collection *The Caucasian Singer* in 1834, authored an opera based on Bestuzhev-Marlinsky's "Ammalat-Bek" and wrote music for the "Circassian Song" of Lermontov's "Izmail-Bey." An influential forerunner of Balakirev and other composers now much better known in the West than he, Aliabev was a noteworthy, early exponent of Asia as the key to a "special destiny" for Russian music.

PUSHKIN THE AMBIVALENT INTERLOCUTOR

Young Pushkin's disclosure of Russia's national stake in Asia proved exceptionally important, but he functioned here strictly as a poet rather than essayist. Unlike the cases of Somov, Kiukhelbeker and Bestuzhev-Marlinsky, Pushkin never sought to constitute a privileged Russian relation to the orient in his expository writings. He fully shared his compatriots' general preference for Sismondi's theory, as shown in the unfinished essay "On Poetry Classical and Romantic" (1825). Indeed, Pushkin took a more extreme stand than his source by entirely disregarding the input of the Normans and ascribing exclusive importance to romanticism's oriental roots (the Moors, East–West cultural exchanges during the Crusades, troubadours).[53] At the same time, however, a comment on his verse cycle "Imitations of the Koran" held the "South" apart from the Russian self: Pushkin declared to Viazemsky that the oriental style could only be an adopted form for today's "Europeans," too "cold" to match the spontaneous frenzy of ancient Persia and Arabia.[54]

But for all the apparent rigidity of this dichotomy, the European posture was not Pushkin's steady state. One of his quips to Viazemsky demonstrates nicely his destabilizing skepticism about Russia's pretensions to western enlightenment. Delighted about a lucrative offer for publishing part of *Eugene Onegin*, Pushkin exclaimed, "Good old Russia! So it really does belong to Europe. And I'd always thought that was just a mistake of the geographers."[55] This little joke had psychological depth. It conveyed a will to believe that the homeland was still successfully engaged in occidentalization and modernization. At the same time, however, those erroneous mapmakers sprang from Pushkin's perception of Russia as more western Asia than eastern Europe.

Pushkin's consciousness of Russia's distance from the West was magnified by his personal identification with Africa in its real and figurative dimensions. As often remarked, throughout his career he cultivated contradictory self-images derived from his two genealogical strains – the occidentalized Russian aristocrat and the unruly blackamoor. One of his most famous permutations of this dualism appears in the lyric "The Poet" (1827). When the "holy lyre" falls silent, the poet is "perhaps the most worthless of all the world's worthless children," absorbed in trivial amusements of the *beau monde*. In the inspired state, however, he turns "wild and severe," estranged from society and drawn toward Apollo's haunts – the desolate seashore, the rustling grove. Andrei Siniavsky made a persuasive, if deliberately provocative case for "wild genius" as Pushkin's definitive posture. "Africa" in this reading became the poet's inner world of sacred play – a permanent resource of creative imagination aligned to "animals, wild tribes and the forest."[56] At war with Europeanized, aristocratic society, this generic "Africa" fathered a band of outlaws, rebels and primitives in Pushkin's literary works. Prominent among them was Pugachev of *The Captain's Daughter*, the romanticized peasant anarchist whom Marina Tsvetaeva defined as the incarnation of "every poet's passion for revolt."[57] As we shall see shortly, the encounter between the Russian and the Circassians in "The Prisoner of the Caucasus" was an early instance of the recurrent tension between tame European and wild non-European identities in Pushkin's writings.

While the author's own cultural allegiances were decidedly mixed in this poem, his romantic enhancement of the Muslim mountaineers allowed Russian readers to conceptualize an orient satisfying to the imperfectly westernized national self. As invented by Pushkin, the Circassians imparted to present-day Asia dashing machismo, engaging simplicity, emotional generosity and primitive poetry (rather than Sismondi's unrelieved "ignorance, slavery, horrors and death"). Despite the poet's ambivalence about the matter, this catalogue of "savage" virtues in "The Prisoner of the Caucasus" launched the Muslim mountaineers on a long literary career as the Asian "others" whom nineteenth-century Russians proved eager to embrace as surrogate selves. Indeed, so far as male personages were concerned, the tribesmen were the empire's *only* orientals so favored in Russian letters. Somov's essay "On Romantic Poetry" has already given us an inkling of this exceptional status: in all probability, this essay's warm words for Muslim tribes as Russia's direct liaison to the orient were inspired to a great extent by the recently published "The Prisoner of the Caucasus."

Through interaction with his immediate audience, young Pushkin thus disclosed Russia's national stake in a poeticized Caucasian tribal milieu. Unlike Somov, Kiukhelbeker, Bestuzhev-Marlinsky (and Lermontov, later on), Pushkin did not articulate pro-Asian sentiments in his criticism, correspondence or conversation. Indeed, he often averred staunch commitment to Europe. However, in blurring lines between "us" and "them," "The Prisoner of the Caucasus" inscribed a consciousness of the orient as an organic part of Russia.[58] Pushkin's institution of romantic Circassia as a field of national self-exploration made his performance paradigmatic for the Caucasus of the military exiles Bestuzhev-Marlinsky and Lermontov. In a crescendo of romantic anguish about imperialist assault on a beautiful land and impressive mountaineers, they too would inscribe the Europeanized Russian's incapacity to contemplate Asia without coming face to face with the self.

CHAPTER 6

The Pushkinian mountaineer

He loved their simple way of life.

Pushkin

The romantic era's intensified preoccupation with national identity gave "The Prisoner of the Caucasus" immense interest as a textual encounter with Asia. First awakened in the latter third of the eighteenth century, Russian national consciousness surged high on the wave of patriotism produced by victory over Napoleon.[1] In this context the westernized élite took a newly respectful view of the Russian peasantry as the key to a shared national spirit. The borderlands of the empire also attracted increased attention, as reflected in travelogues and ethnographic studies. Like the Caucasus in Bronevsky's book, the Crimea, Siberia, Central Asia, the Urals and Ukraine all came under scrutiny as geographically and culturally distinct areas which could clarify the relatively Europeanized life of the Russian capitals. The depiction of Circassian culture in "The Prisoner of the Caucasus" was absorbed into this wave of self-interested curiosity about indigenous peoples of the empire's periphery.

The romantic engagement with the national peasantry as well as primitive cultures gave special import to the mutually conditioned poles of "civilization" and "savagery" implied in Pushkin's poem. Labeled a "European" in relation to the Circassians, Pushkin's captive from the *beau monde* represented enlightenment understood as a western achievement in which the upper classes of nineteenth-century Russian society sought to participate. In the eyes of readers of the 1820s, civilization's benefits encompassed the arts and sciences, the rule of law,

89

amenities of daily life and the manners of polite society. But Russia's Europeanization had also spelled a twofold cultural dissociation. To recall Vasily Kliuchevsky's famous analysis, the occidentalized Russian nobles of Catherine's era remained foreigners abroad, yet felt increasingly like strangers at home. Alexander Griboedov strikingly conveyed the abiding, double alienation in his domestic *récit de voyage* "A Trip to the Country" (1826). A self-ascribed member of Russia's "injured class of semi-Europeans," the writer perceived the peasant village as the world of a "different tribe" – "wild," "incomprehensible" and "strange."[2] With resentful consciousness of westernization's cultural, spiritual costs, Griboedov indicated both the lack of full membership in Europe and the estrangement from Russia's own rural "tribe." The élite's concern with overcoming alienation by finding native roots would motivate much nineteenth-century Russian literature, in which the peasant features often as an exemplar of the distinctively national self.[3]

As suggested by Griboedov's notion of enlightenment as affliction, inquisitiveness about the folk as an enigma to probe in search of the Russian self operated in counterpoint to the literary Caucasus' engagement with foreign primitives. Pushkin was no avid admirer of Rousseau (whom he did pronounce, however, a "defender of freedom and rights").[4] All the same, "The Prisoner of the Caucasus" invited ruminations about human and social losses incurred in the civilizing process. The issue acquired special immediacy through Pushkin's transposition of certain Rousseauist motifs of eighteenth-century Russian treatments of the national peasantry (Alexander Radishchev's *Journey from Petersburg to Moscow*, Karamzin's "Poor Liza"). Bearers of a literary pedigree both rustic and wild, the Circassians of "The Prisoner of the Caucasus" fascinated an élite readership sensitive to occidentalization's negative impact on Russia. This peculiarly national dissatisfaction gave Russian enthusiasm for Pushkin's primitive mountaineers an edge of dissent from the Enlightenment hierarchy which placed western Europe at the pinnacle of world civilization.

In their readiness to turn to poetry for a cultural investigation pertinent to their own country's condition, Russian readers of the 1820s granted "The Prisoner of the Caucasus" much more ethnographic credence than it deserved (*pace* critics who have lauded Pushkin's anthropological "objectivity").[5] Never within close range of the "free mountain peoples" during his travels in the Caucasus, the young author produced a tribal milieu through the monologic power of uncontested imagination. He effectively silenced the Circassians, as Stephanie Sandler has recently stressed (in reading the poem as an act of rhetorical domination analogous to the tsarist state's drive to subjugate the tribes).[6] Completely mute, the Circassian warriors are indeed made knowable primarily through violent action. The unnamed Circassian heroine speaks at length, but as Zhirmunsky first observed, her conversations with the prisoner are a "false dialogue," a single discourse about love distributed between two speakers.[7] Although she has supposedly taught the prisoner some of the local language, the Circassian heroine speaks in the high poetic style of Pushkin's day, and when she realizes that her liaison with the Russian is doomed, she virtually parrots his earlier, Byronic formulations about the pain of unrequited passion.[8]

While uttering no culturally authentic word of their own, these Caucasian "natives" none the less reward investigation as Russian surrogates who disrupted imperialist ideology about a "European" mission to civilize Muslim "savages." As Russian commentators often have observed, Pushkin's vigorously free, stateless Circassia illuminated contemporary Decembrist aspirations for political change at home. But of more far-reaching interest, fluidities between "European" and "Asian" identity in Pushkin's poem threw certain issues of Russian self-definition into high relief in the context of imperialist conquest. In ennobling the Circassians, Pushkin's captivity tale inscribed the Russian need to accommodate Asia as a "young," energetic and poetic cultural force. The epilogue to "The Prisoner of the Caucasus" pursued a very different agenda, as we shall see. However, in launching literary

Circassia as the home of primitives affiliated to the Russian readership, Pushkin's romantic captivity tale opened a mental pathway of skepticism about the rectitude of the tsarist "pacification" program. Did Russia itself not deviate attractively from European standards of enlightenment? And if so, where was the glory in the tyrannical state's war to "civilize" the Caucasian mountaineers? Censorship made open discussion of such questions unthinkable, but they arose in personal papers of men who came of age in the Decembrist era.

THE MOUNTAIN WARRIOR

Spatial arrangements in "The Prisoner of the Caucasus" divide Russia from Asia. Like Pushkin's references to his own travels, the plot of the captivity tale draws a demarcation between Circassia and the readership's native realm. The poet presents himself as a man returned from the frontier with a story to tell (as in the epilogue's first two lines: "And so the Muse, Dream's careless friend, / Has had her flight to Asian countries"). In a parallel manner, the fictional hero's experience follows the trajectory of a round trip: he leaves Russia (in some undisclosed way), is confined in the *aul* and then makes his escape to retrieve familiar ground. Reinforced by Pushkin's own reputation as a recent visitor of the Caucasus, this pattern of action hinges on a Russian's crossing a border with the intention of going back home again.

In conformity with treatment of the Terek in some Russian travelogues of the era, Pushkin conceived the geographical divider as a river. Part two of "The Prisoner of the Caucasus" mentions the Kuban, but the author incongruously evokes the Terek as well, in the so-called "Circassian Song" about Chechen raiders.[9] As these details suggest, several associations seem to have fused in Pushkin's mind to make the poem's watery boundary a *topos* of cross-cultural encounter rather than an identifiable physical landmark.

Fraught with symbolic significance as the end of Russian space, the geographically imprecise river in "The Prisoner of the Caucasus" has the thrilling connotation of civilization's last outpost. High drama is staged on these banks. After the Circassian heroine frees the prisoner, they rush "toward the shore" together. The Russian jumps into the water and swims to the other side, while the despairing woman chooses to drown. The location of the lovers' farewell, the heroine's suicide and the Russian's triumphant end of his Asian adventure, the river bank is also a combat zone where Cossacks stand guard against the tribes from across the water. Although voiceless, Pushkin's Cossack frontiersmen are salient markers of the tsarist domain, as underscored in the captivity tale's last lines: the glint of the guards' "Russian bayonets" assures the hero that he has completed safely his passage from Asia.

But for all the tensions of the spatial arrangements, Circassian and Russian identities interpenetrate one another extensively in "The Prisoner of the Caucasus." The poem's mountain warriors have three major lines of affiliation with Russian national aspirations and values: liberty, heroic machismo and simple *moeurs*. The liberty of Pushkin's Circassians perpetuated certain features of a long tradition of social thought originated by Montesquieu in *De l'esprit des lois*.[10] Montesquieu's *théorie des climats* drew correspondences between environmental zones, the temperament of the inhabitants and their forms of sociopolitical organization. According to this scheme, severe mountain terrain fostered small, isolated societies with bellicose populations fiercely bent upon maintaining their liberty. Common currency in Russia by the time of Catherine II, Montesquieu's views about mountaineers were endorsed in the writings of the eighteenth-century explorers whom the empress sent to the Caucasus. Carried forward into Pushkin's era, the outlook was perpetuated in treatment of the Circassians and other tribes in Bronevsky's *A New Geography and History of the Caucasus*.[11]

Wild liberty held menace, as Zhukovsky's "To Voeikov" had insisted by depicting Caucasian tribes as vicious brutes with no redeeming features. Immediately after celebrating the beauty of mountains swathed in blue mist, Zhukovsky offered a catalogue of ethnic groups, including some names invented for rhymes.[12] These tribes live in the "cliffs of freedom," a key formula which conveys the idea of rocky heights as a realm beyond law. Constantly on the prowl for travelers, the mountaineers value their weapons as "their treasures and their gods" and prize a fine horse as a "fleet-footed comrade in arms." When not on the war path, they roam the *aul* "on the crutches of a sullen torpor," idly smoke a chibouk and talk about their murderous exploits, as they prepare for "new kills."

Although never designating the Circassians "savages" (*dikari*), "The Prisoner of the Caucasus" retained several of Zhukovsky's proximate formulations (the "treacherous predator" who is "born for war," the horse as "faithful comrade," weapons as "cherished" possessions). However, Pushkin simultaneously gave mountain liberty a positive ambience reminiscent of the Alpine realm of Schiller's *Wilhelm Tell*, the Scottish highlands of Walter Scott and the forests of James Fenimore Cooper's celebrated Indians. Once the captive is led into the *aul* at the beginning of "The Prisoner of the Caucasus," a multisemantic notion of the "free life" emerges as something possessed by the tribe and desired by the Russian. The shackled captive immediately laments his lost *svoboda* ("freedom"), a concept which covers the possibility of moving about as one wants.[13] But the same passage mentions Circassia's *vol'nost'* ("liberty"), a term which can connote anarchic license but also was used regularly in Russian writing since the eighteenth century to characterize the rights granted by a political system. "*Svoboda*" and "*vol'nost'*" come to overlap subversively in "The Prisoner of the Caucasus." The Russian "renegade from society" fled the *beau monde* and ventured into Circassia primarily in search of a freer world. However, the quest landed him in irons. This bitter twist of fate exemplifies the danger of the stateless man's total liberty. Unconstrained by law and the customs of civilized society, Pushkin's free Circassians capture the foreign hero, kill a Cossack border guard and behead slaves during the rambunctious festivities of Bairam. In short, the totally free mountaineer sometimes runs berserk, to transgress legal and moral bounds recognized in Russian society.

Such literary manifestations of lawlessness undoubtedly afforded readers a decidely lowbrow vicarious pleasure. Gogol's essay on Pushkin stressed the entertaining, illicit psychological satisfaction by drawing the following contrast between the shabby world of tsarist officialdom and the excitement of the wild frontier: even if the "savage tribesman. . .butchers his enemy while lurking in a canyon or burns down an entire village, all the same he makes a bigger impression and engages us more than our judge in a frayed frock-coat stained with tobacco."[14] Many homebodies in Pushkin's audience sought escape from humdrum existence by plunging into a tale of adventure, and violent action was no doubt particularly mesmerizing for them.

Of greater cultural interest, the vicarious pleasure entailed an eradication of difference between Circassian and Russian capacities for violence. The poet asserts that the tribesmen "feel proud" of their captive ("their booty") for the impassive, "careless courage" he displays before the fierce war games of Bairam and the decapitations. The mountaineers thus read the Russian's Byronic sang-froid as tough machismo like their own. The prisoner makes no direct response to the tribe's "bloody amusements." But as he sits in enigmatic silence, his thoughts turn to the Russian practice of dueling. He is preoccupied with "meeting the fatal lead" himself. Duelists, however, must be as prepared to kill as to die. By referring to this potentially lethal manner in which Russian gentlemen settled their accounts, "The Prisoner of the Caucasus" destabilizes "civilized" identity. Rather than provoking an outraged sense of moral superiority, Circassia's "bloody amusements" send the prisoner into a daydream (or perhaps a memory) about himself as a participant in a violent cultural ritual of the Russian *beau monde* of young Pushkin's day.[15] This ready transition between "their" violence and "ours" accentuates the Circassian's status as an underground Russian self, curious about how it would feel to run amuck – to "butcher" enemies wholesale or "burn down an entire village" (as Gogol put it), without suffering pangs of Christian guilt.

But along with the element of illicit psychological satisfaction, the free tribesman's existence outside an oppressive state structure appealed to the contemporary readership's more high-minded political aspirations. In this era of the Decembrist movement there were many members of the élite who had great hopes for Russia's liberalization. Relatively few were prepared to risk conspiring against the state, but a large number passively sympathized with the Decembrists' common goal of displacing tsarist autocracy in a more or less radical manner. Such readers were especially receptive to literature about the exercise of personal freedom and political liberties unknown in despotic tsardom.[16] Bestuzhev-Marlinsky, for example, played upon this chord in his tale of medieval Novgorod, a city which had enjoyed considerable independence from the Muscovite state. Pushkin's theme of "Circassian liberty" likewise had a subversive undercurrent about challenging tsarist tyranny. In "The Prisoner of the Caucasus" this political aspiration for *vol'nost'* coincides with the Byronic hero's curiosity about a "freer world" and blends with his wanderlust and joy at retrieving his precious freedom of movement when he escapes from captivity. Pushkin was very conscious of the provocative innuendoes of *vol'nost'* and *svoboda*. He had been exiled to the south largely for his anti-autocratic ode to liberty, and in a letter to Gnedich in September 1822 he expressed surprise that the censor's "fateful claws" had not deleted all references to a free life in "The Prisoner of the Caucasus."[17]

In this political context the violence inherent in "Circassian liberty" had double valency: it held menace for outsiders (the captive, the Cossack) but also reached into the readership to establish a dynamic of cross-cultural bonding, primarily but not exclusively with the men.[18] Circassia's freely expressed aggressivity reflected current Decembrist idealization of civic courage, which Ryleev would soon symbolize as Elbrus. In juxtaposition to the war games and decapitations of Bairam, Pushkin refers to the Russian duelist as a "captive to merciless honor" (a phrase used, minus the adjective, as an appellation for Pushkin himself in Lermontov's "The Death of a Poet").

These words aptly designate not only the duelist's code but also the virtue of a dedicated soldier or a conspirator with the good of his country at heart: like a fighter in a war deemed just, an armed insurrectionist must "mercilessly" steel himself to risk death and shed blood in the service of honorable ideals. Quite notably, some Decembrists, including Bestuzhev-Marlinsky, felt moral incertitude, as they contemplated taking up arms against the state.[19] The unflinching bravery and martial prowess required in such an undertaking points to the impressiveness of Pushkin's mountaineer as a resolute man of action, ready to resort to violence for an honorable cause. While apt to slip into excesses to set the "civilized" reader agog, the tribesman's formidable exercise of martial arts belonged inescapably to a configuration of soldier's virtues valued in Russia, where the victory over Napoleon was fresh in the collective memory, and a significant number of upper-class men were contemplating armed revolt against the state.

Besides liberty and the highly ambivalent ethos of martial heroism, Circassia's absence of luxury established another cross-cultural affiliation with Russia. A community of pastoral primitives, Pushkin's mountaineers are pillagers with an agricultural base. The shackled prisoner is left alone the first day, while the Circassians work the fields (*"Cherkesy v pole"*). Like peasants, the villagers return toward evening with scythes in hand (*"S polei narod idet v aul, / Sverkaia svetlymi kosami"*). Farming modulates the poem's preponderant theme of violence, to lend Circassia rusticity. Likewise, one section of Pushkin's central "ethnographic" sketch presents the tribesman as a pacific host accustomed to extend ritual hospitality to fellow Caucasians. The rustic dimension, spartan hut, meager fare and ready sharing with strangers illustrate the tribe's "simple way of life," so admired by the prisoner (whose means of witnessing the Circassian's nocturnal accommodation of a passing traveler are left unexplained, however). Contemporary Russian ethnography allotted favorable attention to the Caucasian mountaineers' ritual hospitality, which conformed to Marcel Mauss' classic study of the gift as a means of neutralizing an outsider's potential danger.[20] But regardless of how reliable Pushkin may or may not have been on this point, his constitution of a pleasingly simple Circassian style of life converged on the Fonvizinian catalogue of Russian claims to superiority over the capitals of western enlightenment (reciprocity instead of the cash nexus, generosity of spirit, disdain for luxury, impatience with ceremony).

THE MOUNTAIN MAID

While excluded from the rites of hospitality between native men in Pushkin's poem, the Russian captive benefits enormously from the generosity of the Circassian heroine, the "mountain maid." Like many a "savage" maiden in European literature stimulated by empire-building, the unnamed tribeswoman nurtures the prisoner with restorative foods and ultimately makes him a gift of herself.[21] The extension of hospitality to cover sex has an important antecedent in the story of Dido and Aeneas, as Peter Hulme has analyzed.[22] In the context of European expansion into the "New World," this old plot of the nurturing native woman and the traveler who loves and leaves acquired an ideological content manifest to us today. To quote Hulme's phrase, a myth of "cultural harmony through romance" came to surround the colonial encounter (between Pocahontas and John Smith, for example). In such narratives the primitive's spontaneous display of erotic affinities for the European interloper masked imperialism's drive to domination. Imagined ties of sentiments displaced the exploitative, often bloody realities of colonialist expansion. If only subconsciously, the comforting implications of cross-cultural romance were quite probably at work in the sympathy Pushkin's first readers expressed for the Circassian heroine of "The Prisoner of the Caucasus."

However, the recriminations which rained down on Pushkin's hard-hearted captive also evinced the Russians' fondness for counting emotional generosity among their own national virtues. With no compunction, the prisoner leaves the despondent tribeswoman to drown after she frees him and leads him to the river he swims to freedom. The poem's reviewers raised gallant objections to this denouement. In the most telling response, Mikhail Pogodin termed the Russian captive's harsh treatment of the "innocent" Circassian "inexcusable in every respect."[23] The phrase "in every respect" suggested both sexual and sociocultural abuse – the violation of a lover's trust combined with disregard for the many non-erotic gifts received as a passing stranger. Pogodin was in fact uncomfortable with the erotic content of Pushkin's tale: he found the rhetoric of flaming passion ("fiery kisses," etc.) so indecent that he scolded the poet for it.

This attitude revealed a strong preference for the Circassian heroine as an intensely friendly rather than specifically sexual creature. Viazemsky and other reviewers undoubtedly promoted the vulnerable tribeswoman as an incarnation of "natural" femininity (a conception which romantic Russian women writers such as Elizaveta Gan would endorse in orientalia of the 1830s).[24] But the lively Russian discussion of the rebuffed Circassian cut across the sexes. In siding with the generous primitive, readers were perceiving the "European" hero as a man emotionally diminished by westernization. He appeared as a walking admonition of the injuries enlightenment could inflict, while the tribeswoman exemplified a generous nature uncorrupted by the *beau monde*. The Circassian heroine thus transposed into a primitive key the Russian peasant theme as treated in Karamzin's "Poor Liza," the tale of a rural innocent who drowns herself after being seduced and abandoned by a Muscovite nobleman.[25]

In conformity with his Byronic posture of the time, young Pushkin shrugged off the sentimental recriminations of his hero. When Viazemsky called the prisoner a "son of a bitch" in a letter to Pushkin, the author replied that the Russian had not really loved the tribeswoman and had wisely refused to risk his neck in a rescue attempt in a treacherous Caucasian river.[26] This alliance between the author and hero may have evinced a Byronic emulation of the rough way Muslims purportedly dealt with their women. In a display of open admiration for behavior which Europeans were supposed to deplore, Byron once maintained that only "Turks" knew how to handle women – by treating them as property, locking them up and restricting their education to "agreeable arts."[27] Although Byron left it off his list, the murder of women for drastic disobedience was another feature of his orient, as illustrated in "The Giaour." In both this poem and Pushkin's "The Fountain of Bakhchisarai" wrathful lords execute harem beauties by drowning. Pushkin's was by far the more ambivalent text, but both works traded in a staple notion of the Muslim's absolute subjugation of women. Identification with brutal, "Asian" domination of women was even more evident in "The Prisoner of the Caucasus" and Pushkin's defense of its callous Russian hero.

In one significant respect, though, Pushkin deserted the hero of the poem to align himself with Circassian womanhood (just as he once admitted in a letter that the heroine was so much the more successful character that he should have named the tale after *her*). A rhetoric of temperatures in "The Prisoner of the Caucasus" pits unrestrained Circassian eros against cold "European" reserve. Invented as a hot-blooded figure with "burning desire," "fiery" feelings and "flaming kisses," the tribeswoman fails to enflame the cold hero: like a "corpse" with "dead lips," the "renegade from society" has a "sad chill" in his heart (less moved by love than mountains). Although this pattern equates erotic fire with Circassian femininity, Pushkin's treatment of tribal song blurs the lines of cultural and sexual difference. In part two of "The Prisoner of the Caucasus" a chorus of local women sings the thoroughly ersatz "Circassian Song" about Chechen raiders from "across the river." A participant in the same artistic activity, the heroine sings to the captive. On the other hand, however, the Russian hero "has grown cold to the lyre," as well as youthful dreams of love. Pushkin thus connected Circassia's erotic "heat" to the production, performance and appreciation of poetry. While isolating the cold "European" hero from a cross-cultural world of song, this thematic complex effects an intriguing alliance between the native female singers and the male poet himself who features the Caucasus as his "new Parnassus." So often conjoined in Pushkin's creative imagination, eros and poetry interconnect in "The Prisoner of the Caucasus" to forge another tie between Russian romantic sensibility and Circassia's primitive culture.[28]

THE SAVAGE VANQUISHED

If one accepts that the captivity tale converted the wild mountaineers into satisfying meanings about Russia, then one must contend with massive interference from the epilogue. Its opening sequence of autobiographical reminiscences preserves the Circassian warrior as a dashing figure who enchanted the Muse. But then comes commendation of tsarist campaigns against the tribes since the early nineteenth century:

> The glorious hour I will sing,
> When o'er the Caucasus, grown wrathful,
> Our double-headed eagle winged,
> Anticipating bloody battle;
> When o'er the Terek, steely-gray,
> The Russian drums began to play,
> Raising the roar of martial thunder,
> And boldly entering the fray,
> Came Tsitsianov, the commander.
> Oh Kotliarevsky, scourge of war!
> I'll sing your heroism in action,
> Across the Caucasus you tore
> Leaving a trail of black contagion
> To deal a death blow to the tribes.
> You later lost your taste for valor
> And laid your vengeful sword aside,
> Hankering after tranquil valleys,
> You sampled peacetime's idle round
> With honor as a wound still smarting.
> But from the East the howls rebound!
> Submit and bow your snowy head,
> Oh Caucasus, Ermolov marches![29]

Spoken in the poet's own voice, the epilogue applauds the assertion of Russian power over the tribes and conveys zest for the pageantry and bravado of war. Martially ferocious Ermolov had a special celebrity which deserves mention. His independent attitude toward the St. Petersburg authorities so endeared him to the Decembrists that they designated him head of the provisional government they meant to establish after their *coup d'état*. But as we shall see shortly, Decembrist aims could accommodate easily the sort of chauvinism to which Pushkin gave voice.

A generically distinct finale written about two months after the captivity tale, Pushkin's epilogue has invited speculations about its origins. It certainly does not envision an audience of liberal-minded readers eager to savor innuendoes about Circassian liberty. To the contrary, Pushkin was possibly making a conciliatory gesture toward government officials, in the hope of winning release from his exile. An alternative factor may have been the young poet's susceptibility to a bold political thinker of the day, the Decembrist conspirator Pavel Pestel (one of five men hanged after the insurrection of 1825). As laconically noted in his diary, Pushkin happened to meet Pestel in Kishinev in April 1821, the month before he added the epilogue to "The Prisoner of the Caucasus." In light of Pestel's views, this encounter may have been vital. But independently, a certain meeting of minds between Pushkin and Pestel was unmistakable, as Boris Tomashevsky has argued.[30] Like most, but not all the Decembrists, Pestel remained a Great Russian chauvinist, while aspiring to overthrow the tsarist state. His *Russian Law* advanced the view that border security compels any large power to dominate little ethnic groups on its periphery. A two-sided view of Russia's international standing made Asians particularly vulnerable in this scheme. Along with other Decembrist adherents to the Enlightenment idea of progress, Pestel regarded Russia as a backward, retrograde force *vis-à-vis* Europe. In relation to Asia, though, the semi-Europeanized homeland was granted the "western" role. This outlook made Russian imperialism in the orient fully compatible with a program for radical reform and modernization at home. Interestingly enough, a similar outlook was held by Alexis de Tocqueville, who endorsed American democracy while asserting France's right to beat Algeria into colonial submission.[31]

Pushkin's "The Prisoner of the Caucasus" exhibited the Pestelian readiness to deny small Asian tribes the right to national self-determination. The captivity tale gave expression to the yearning for liberty which was fueling the entire Decembrist movement in Russian society at the time. The epilogue, however, suggested that so far as international relations were concerned, the full exercise of political freedom was to be reserved for the privileged citizens of big, subjugating states.

THE NOBLE SAVAGE'S TENACITY

But for all its stridency, the epilogue did not close down "The Prisoner of the Caucasus" for the readership of the 1820s: it was by no means the "last word" about the tribes and Russia's relation to them. Some minor writers showed elements of continuity with Pushkin's celebration of imperial might (Grigoriev's "Evening in the Caucasus," Nechaev's "Recollections"). However, Pushkin's chauvinism struck no receptive chord in the readership at large. Most reviewers, for example, simply ignored the epilogue of "The Prisoner of the Caucasus" and focused instead on the captivity tale's unvanquished tribe (whom Viazemsky called an "unrefined but bold, martial, handsome people").[32] The dashing mountaineer's secure place in popular imagination is worth illustrating at some length, before we look more closely at public silence which surrounded the chauvinistic finale of "The Prisoner of the Caucasus."

By far the most famous part of the poem, Pushkin's 121-line sketch of Circassian culture was reprinted separately at least six times during his lifetime.[33] As noted earlier, Belinsky indicated in the early 1840s that most Russian readers still knew this section by heart, along with the description of the mountains which directly precedes it. Pushkin's captivity tale also inspired productions in other art forms: the "Circassian Song" was set to music in the 1820s and included in twenty different songbooks, while the amorous Circassian heroine became the focal point of Charles Didelot's ballet, "The Prisoner of the Caucasus" (1823).[34]

But the major legacy was, of course, literary. As seen earlier in discussion of imaginative geography, young Pushkin's stage of mountain gloom and glory was brief, but it initiated a vigorous tradition. Something similar happened with the poetic "ethnography" of "The Prisoner of the Caucasus." Pushkin himself would develop a much more sophisticated perspective on the civilized man's quest for the primitive in "The Gypsies" (written 1824), a poem about the Russian Aleko who joins a band of Bessarabian nomads, marries one of the women and ends by murdering her for infidelity. Unlike "The Prisoner of the Caucasus" which basically converted the Circassians into clarifiers of the Russian self, "The Gypsies" displayed genuine anthropological insight.[35] Written partly in dramatic form, it produced distinctive voices for the gypsies and suggested that a civilized outsider's intrusion into a primitive society merely sows discord and destruction.

While Pushkin came to recognize the problematic character of relations between primitive and civilized peoples, lesser Russian writers of the 1820s stuck to inventing the Caucasian tribesman as an Asian *Naturmensch* who sent back congenial reflections to the semi-Europeanized self. The precise, non-metaphorical language of Pushkin's central sketch of Circassian culture did not transform the mountaineer into a symbol of his natural environment. However, *la théorie des climats* was current in Russia, and Pushkin did directly juxtapose the rugged terrain and its inhabitants by having the captive examine both in a continuous textual sequence. Seemingly at one with the alpine landscape, the tribesman of "The Prisoner of the Caucasus" had a sublime, gloriously "wild" character. Minor authors such as Alexander Shishkov took the cue to formulate a direct metaphorical equation between environment and the mountaineer. As though engendered by the land itself, the tribesman became the "child of nature," the "severe offspring of the Caucasian mountains."[36] Like two mirrors face to face, landscape and inhabitants were mutually stamped with whatever attributes the Russian writer imposed on them (love of liberty, bellicosity, unbridled passions).[37] The rare Russian perception of nothing but hideous "dread" in rocky terrain in the 1820s predictably went along with a hostile notion of the mountaineers themselves as "revengeful, mean" marauders.[38] But on the other hand, since Byronic "friendship with nature" remained a common authorial posture throughout the romantic era, symbolic *paysage* sometimes quite strikingly confounded civilized and uncivilized identity. Bestuzhev-Marlinsky's "Ammalat-Bek" would exemplify the dualism by using the Terek river as a rhetorical emblem for both the author and his tribal hero.

In a more complex instance of young Pushkin's legacy, Nechaev's "Recollections" called attention to the mountaineer's bardic poetry. Rather than the feminine singers of "The Prisoner of the Caucasus," Nechaev imagined a Chechen rhapsodist commemorating the exploits of his land's "fallen heroes." Based on a slender thread of ethnographic knowledge, the mountain bard owed most to Homer and Ossian, the Russian readership's two major referents for "primitive poetry" at the time.[39] As we shall see, the Homeric enhancement of the Caucasian tribesman would persist in Russian writing during the jihad (when many a mountain "hero" had clearly not "fallen"). The military exile Bestuzhev-Marlinsky, for example, proclaimed the "majestic" Circassian warrior the very "model of Ajax or Achilles."[40] By the early 1850s the accumulated force of Homeric allusions in the literary Caucasus no doubt helped elicit one Russian ethnographer's assertion that the Circassians would have loved the *Odyssey* and recognized themselves in it.[41]

Although particularly prevalent in verse of the 1820s, young Pushkin's impact was also evident in Alexander Yakubovich's campaign notes "Fragments about the Caucasus."[42] Yakubovich had some solid ethnographic information to ply, including the self-ascribed name "Adyghe" rather than "Circassian" (*"Cherkessy"* in Russian). But "Fragments about the Caucasus" was couched largely in romantic discourse. Yakubovich employed the rhetoric of the sublime (nature's "dread and glory"), promoted the idea of the tribes as children of their rugged environment and injected excitement by depicting his narrow escape from an ambush. Last but not least, he presented the Caucasian warrior as a chivalrous figure reminiscent of the Middle Ages, a veritable "knight" of the mountains. As a writer in the tsarist army, Yakubovich was a particularly interesting exponent of tribal grandeur. Despite his status as a soldier, his campaign notes poeticized the mountaineers, while remaining conspicuously silent about the tsarist military effort. This equivocation about the rectitude of the conquest quite probably kept politically obsequious Bulgarin from printing a projected second installment of "Fragments about the Caucasus" in the *Northern Bee*.

While all these cases illustrate the tenacity of young Pushkin's heroic tribesman, a bucolic strain in the "Caucasian epidemic" also merits note. As presented in the anonymous prose work "The Circassian," published in the *Nevsky Almanac* of 1829, the Caucasian hero was a pastoral highlander rather than a Homeric fighter.[43] A prisoner of war incarcerated in Finland and interviewed by the Russian narrator, the tribesman is homesick, sorry he took up his sword and afraid he will never see his fiancée again. An interesting confusion of traditions occurred here: the bold warrior of "The Prisoner of the Caucasus" was transmuted into a masculine version of Pushkin's emotionally vulnerable "mountain maid" (whose literary sisters would proliferate only in the 1830s). Virtually indistinguishable from the gentle shepherds of eighteenth-century Russian literature, the Circassian captive in Finland was tearfully embraced by the narrator as a kindred spirit. In the unfinished poem "Tazit" (written 1829–30) Pushkin too imagined a pacific Caucasian tribesman alienated from the local ethos of war and the vendetta. While far outnumbered by the literature's warriors, such sensitive tribal souls illustrated an interesting Russian uncertainty about just what constituted Asian wildness.

QUESTIONING THE RECTITUDE OF THE CONQUEST

The 1820s' obsessive concern with noble Caucasian savagery bespoke the Russian national stake in Asia. Apt to feel touchy about western perceptions of the tsarist homeland as a barbarous country, the semi-occidentalized élite had a vested cultural interest in keeping the Caucasian mountaineer a kindred personage who provided a clear alternative to Europe perceived as an *overly* civilized, cramped and moribund realm. Questions of Russia's national character and status in the world of nations, mixed feelings of inferiority and superiority *vis-à-vis* the West, hopes for a freer society, and differing opinions about the relevance of Europe as a model for Russia's future evolution found a resonance in the literary Caucasus. Romanticized in various ways, the mountain tribes sent back flattering signals to their culturally heterogeneous receivers.

Yet it should be recognized as well that the romantic appropriation of the tribes as satisfying clarifiers of Russia was accompanied by some expression of moral misgivings about the conquest. The most famous instance was Viazemsky's private protest against the Great Russian chauvinism of the epilogue of "The Prisoner of the Caucasus." In a letter to Alexander Turgenev in September 1822, Viazemsky characterized this section of the poem as an "anachronistic" ode of the sort Mikhail Lomonosov wrote to please eighteenth-century empresses:

I am sorry that Pushkin bloodied the last lines of his tale. What kind of a hero is Kotliarevsky or Ermolov? What is so good about his "leaving a trail of black contagion to deal a death blow to the tribes"? That sort of notoriety makes your blood run cold and your hair stand on end. If we were bringing enlightenment to the tribes, then there would be something to sing about. Poetry is not the ally of butchers. The political life may need them, and then history must judge whether their acts were justified or not. But a poet's anthems should never glorify slaughter.[44]

Most vexing of all, continued Viazemsky, he did not dare scold Pushkin in his review, lest he fall afoul of censors, ready to pounce on unacceptable opinions about the Russian mission to civilize the Caucasus. Viazemsky was no radical prepared to risk speaking his mind publicly, and he even allowed that "history" might absolve the iron-fisted subjugation of the tribes. But in this letter to a friend, he withheld approval of the conquest, punctured the state's self-image as an agent of enlightenment and conveyed revulsion for the "pacifiers'" blood-curdling deeds. A similar fear of official reprisals might have compelled other commentators to refrain from expressing their reservations about the war in reviews of "The Prisoner of the Caucasus."

Viazemsky's refusal to condone the Russian conquest as a civilizing mission has parallels in the writings of two little-known Decembrists. Even that staunch advocate of imperial expansion, Mikhail Orlov saw both futility and irony in Russia's war against the Muslim tribes: "It is just as hard to subjugate the Chechens and other peoples of this region as to level the Caucasian range. This is something to achieve not with bayonets but with time and enlightenment, in such short supply in our country."[45] Much more in line with Viazemsky's sentiments, Nikolai Lorer bluntly questioned imperialism's moral rectitude and even asserted the tribes' right to sovereignty. In memoirs partially published in the late nineteenth century, Lorer recalled his military exile on a Black Sea front in the 1830s. At one point he referred to the Caucasus' "divine sites" and wondered if "forces of enlightenment" might eventually possess them. He then distanced himself from the conquest in ethical, as well as strategic terms: "Fire and the sword will yield no good; and besides, who gave us the right to use such means to try to impose education on people now perfectly satisfied with their own freedom and property?"[46] Lorer thus recognized national self-determination as a global birthright, by contrast to Pestel's doctrine of a big state's prerogative over bothersome little ethnic groups on its periphery. Military exile greatly contributed to Lorer's misgivings by acquainting him with horrific manifestations of bestiality in the tsarist general Grigory Zass. In eerie anticipation of Kurtz in Joseph Conrad's *Heart of Darkness*, Zass collected tribesmen's heads, impaled them on stakes around his house and occasionally sent specimens to anatomists in Russia and Berlin.[47]

The varied reservations about tsarist pursuit of a European "civilizing mission" suggest that the Russian élite of Pushkin's era had not arrived at a consensus about its relation to the

Caucasian tribes. The national stake in Asia largely explained the thriving fortunes of the noble savages who illuminated Russian cultural values, emotional ideals and liberal political aspirations. However as best illustrated by Viazemsky's private outcry against Pushkin's textual alliance with butchers, the readership's romantic engagement with the Caucasian mountaineers also apparently betrayed skepticism about Russia's credibility as the agent of western enlightenment and evinced some qualms about war as any civilizer's tool. Ermolov's campaigns were generally thought to have widened the southern border's zone of security. But did the future hold a recurrently embattled frontier, a program of educating the tribesmen or a war of extermination? Should a European power be allowed to eradicate the admirable features of Asian primitivity, especially by means of the sword? And was Russia sufficiently occidentalized to arrogate this task to itself in all good conscience? The Caucasian œuvre of the military exile Bestuzhev-Marlinsky would anxiously inscribe such questions about the rectitude of bloody conquest in the name of European civilization.

CHAPTER 7

Bestuzhev-Marlinsky's interchange with the tribesman

A dagger in experienced hands is as good as an axe, a
bayonet or a sword.

Bestuzhev-Marlinsky

After being exiled for participation in the Decembrist revolt,
the belletrist and critic Alexander Bestuzhev embarked on a
second literary career as Marlinsky, the pseudonym under
which he gained fame as a writer in the Caucasus. No longer
widely read today even in Russia, he enjoyed phenomenal
popularity in his lifetime. To be sure, he had detractors. In
a review of 1840 Belinsky castigated his romantic excesses
and declined to plow through a new edition of his collected
works.[1] Discriminating men of letters such as Ivan Turgenev,
Ivan Goncharov and Tolstoy also came to judge Bestuzhev-
Marlinsky unreadable: they associated him with puerile
adventure stories, while granting, however, that they had
loved him during boyhood and adolescence.[2] But the derogatory judgments of Belinsky and the literati in their maturity
represented a minority opinion.

Mikhail Semevsky evoked the prevailing, less sophisticated
climate in an article in *National Annals* in 1860. Semevsky
recalled the time when the public at large did not know the
identity masked by Bestuzhev's *nom de plume*:

Marlinsky! Marlinsky! Thirty years ago that name was being
repeated with enthusiasm by virtually all the men and women readers of Russia's books and journals. As a person of the period put it:
"They saw in him the Pushkin of prose. One of his novellas was
the most reliable lure to attract subscribers for a journal or pur-
chasers for an almanac." Who at the time did not read Marlinsky's

110

brilliant stories, novellas and novels? Who did not find them enrapturing and thoroughly engrossing? His similes were learned by heart, he was copied, his works sold like hotcakes, and his biography – his life – attracted the interest of the mass of men and women readers. Often not knowing Marlinsky's real name, the women made up fabulous stories about him, he was elevated to heroic stature, and the charming admirers of the talent of the author of "Ammalat-Bek," "The Frigate *Hope*," "The Test," and so forth, fell in love with him via the printed page.[3]

While making many interesting observations, Semevsky raised two major points to be explored in the present chapter. First of all, he dwelled on the readers' intensely emotional responses and suggested that women were affected differently than men. More fundamentally, he evoked a vast mystery of identity particularly germane to Bestuzhev-Marlinsky's writings about the Caucasian conquest.

Part of the intriguing mystery resided in the generic diversity of the author's Caucasian corpus. Arrested and deported after the Decembrist revolt, Alexander Bestuzhev spent several years in Siberia before being transferred to the Caucasus as a soldier. He arrived in the territory in 1829 when Russia was battling Chechen and Dagestani tribes led by the first Caucasian imam, Gazi-Muhammed. While average readers remained ignorant of "Marlinsky's" personal history, they had no doubt that he was in the thick of action. He cultivated his identity as a soldier especially strongly in "Letters from Dagestan" (1830), campaign notes which conveyed an impression of escalating war. Besides characterizing Gazi-Muhammed as a "tireless fanatic, brandishing new heads from every canyon like a hydra," this essay spoke of the "Asian instinct for hatred" and compared the jihad to colonies of swarming ants, an overflowing river and flooding mountain streams.[4] At the same time, though, Bestuzhev-Marlinsky characteristically blurred the "Asian" profile by repeating hearsay that Gazi-Muhammed was the grandson of a Russian turncoat – the offspring of anti-tsarist sentiment in the readership's own country.[5] If ascendant in the campaign notes, the military persona conversant with danger asserted himself more subtly in other genres as well. Little bits of war correspondence entered the semi-fictional historical tale "Ammalat-Bek." *Récits de voyage* featured the military traveler between battles; and in "The Red Veil" the Russian narrator on campaign near Erzerum recounts how a Turkish beauty was murdered by a compatriot for loving a tsarist officer.

The soldier's merger with the ethnographer proved especially productive in Bestuzhev-Marlinsky's Caucasian output.[6] As explained at length in his "Story of an Officer Held Prisoner by Mountain Tribesmen (1834)," he took military service as an opportunity to learn about the Caucasus' indigenous cultures. The first part of this hybrid narrative is indeed a reliable ethnographic essay about a small Dagestani tribe. Moreover, a bracing current of cultural relativism rippled through the text. In underlining the existence of distinctive traditions, *moeurs* and levels of material development among the Caucasian tribes, the author warned his readers not to dismiss these peoples as "savages."[7] Moreover, he reminded his compatriots how the "English peer, the French wit and the German professor" have so often derided Russia for backwardness (42). But after exhibiting sensitivity to the world's multiplicity of cultures and challenging Eurocentric standards of "civilization," Bestuzhev-Marlinsky switched generic gears to move from the ethnographic essay into the second part of his work – a mock-utopia heavily reliant on a fantasy of the mountain women's sexual availability.

The introduction of the two-part "Story of an Officer Held Prisoner by Mountain Tribesmen" tellingly announced both the ethnographic and fanciful impulses. Bestuzhev-Marlinsky lamented Russian readers' ignorance of the Caucasus and prepared them to receive new data. But he disdained dry factuality: convinced that people prefer to learn from a teacher "without a pointer in hand," he promised to dress his "useful" piece of writing in the "pleasant coat" of lively novelistic form.

This earnest aspiration to combine edification with entertainment underlay "Ammalat-Bek" (1832), the writer's most famous semi-fictional work about the Caucasus. Set during 1819–28, the tale sprang from a historical incident in Dagestan: after nearly four years of apparent friendship between them, Ammalat-Bek killed Evstafy Verkhovsky, the tsarist colonel who had intervened to persuade General Ermolov not to execute the tribesman for raids into Russian territory. Violent action superabounds in Bestuzhev-Marlinsky's narrative (the slaughter of animals, combat, murder, grave-robbing and decapitation). But the sensationalism coexists with the author's effort to assure readers that he is telling a "true story," as proclaimed in the subtitle (*byl'*) and argued in the afterword, the "Note." While in the Caucasus, Bestuzhev-Marlinsky encountered various tribes and studied Azeri, designated the "Tatar" tongue by Russians of the epoch. Linguistically adept, he was known to pass as a Dagestani and sometimes disappeared into the mountains for several days at a time, feeding speculations about his political allegiances.[8] Without a doubt, this colorful writer had knowledge to impart, and long sections of "Ammalat-Bek" purvey reliable information about language, local customs, religion, history and so forth. In notable contrast to Pushkin's phony "Circassian Song," Bestuzhev-Marlinsky's tale includes authentic folklore – the tribal "death songs" expertly rendered in Russian verse by the author and discussed in one of his thirty-nine footnotes. Significant as an openly didactic apparatus, the annotations also deal with Islam, recent battles, tribal clothing, horsemanship and weapons.

However, even if we grant that "Ammalat-Bek" commands a considerable amount of factual knowledge, this still leaves open the big issue of the way meaning is created in a literary text. Despite the work's ethnographic excursuses, the quasi-scholarly practice of footnoting, and the protest to truth in the afterword, "Ammalat-Bek" is dominated by an exceedingly affective discourse which bedazzled the author's devotees, as recollections from the period attest. Indeed as we shall see, the flashy oriental "coat" in which the "true story" was bedecked seems to have totally monopolized most readers' attention.

In sweeping Russians off their feet, "Ammalat-Bek" refused to deliver a coherent political message. An exemplary case of destabilized cultural identity, the tale made a muddle of the civilizing mission by inventing the Dagestani hero as both the Islamic other and a surrogate self. On the one hand, Bestuzhev-Marlinsky often seemed to retain allegiance to Russia as the "European" power destined to expand into backward Asia. But on the other hand, his romantic sensibility and embattled relation to the tsarist state produced drastic confusion about the rectitude of the war against the tribes. Exiled for insurgency and placed under police surveillance in the Caucasus, Bestuzhev-Marlinsky suffered tsarist political harassment until his death. He was a romantic rebel, and the production of dashing Asian outlaws evidently afforded him psychological satisfaction. A riveting surrogate of the Russian self, Ammalat-Bek delighted readers and stimulated their daydreams of the writer as a renegade enlisted in the jihad. As a rule, however, the enraptured consumers missed the demoralizing intimations of Russian violence in "Ammalat-Bek": in his interchange with the tribesman, the military exile Bestuzhev-Marlinsky disclosed a punishing anxiety about the war purportedly undertaken for the benefit of Christian civilization.

THE DUALITY OF THE ORIENT

Major contradictions of "Ammalat-Bek" are distilled in dualistic projection of the orient. The tale's opening pages situate Dagestan in seductive Islamic terrain not previously associated with Caucasian tribes. In a deviation from literature of the 1820s, Bestuzhev-Marlinsky excludes mountains, to evoke instead a balmy clime reminiscent of the Turkish coast in works by Byron, or the Crimea in the Russian poetic tradition represented by Pushkin's "The Fountain of Bakhchisarai." An exquisite place in springtime, Ammalat-Bek's homeland is full of fragrant roses, nightingales and plane trees like "Muslim minarets."[9] In another instance of the prettified orient so admired by romantics, the hero and his friend Safir-Ali loll on a colorful carpet, absorbed in a discussion of the Persian poets Saadi and Hafiz (232).

In tension with the intimations of eastern enchantment, "Ammalat-Bek" also conjures the menace of Islamic fanaticism. The story is set in the context of the jihad fired by agents from Istanbul and sustained by local bigots who preach hatred of Russians (152, 160). However, a footnote maintains that most Caucasian tribesmen are "bad Muslims" who do not actually practice their religion (162). The varying force of Islamic antagonism to giaours is indeed borne out in the tale. Bestuzhev-Marlinsky invents Ammalat-Bek as a chieftain open to gestures of friendship from Russians, while Akhmet-Khan is the wicked bigot who incites the hero to murder by demanding Colonel Verkhovsky's head as the brideprice for his irresistible daughter Seltaneta.[10]

While waffling about the significance of Islam in Ammalat-Bek's primitive make-up, Bestuzhev-Marlinsky offers stock notions of oriental slave trade .and despotism. Shortly after Russia's siege of Anapa in 1828, Bulgarin declared the event a victory for "European culture."[11] "Ammalat-Bek" concurs by featuring Anapa as a weapons-supply center for "mountain bandits" and a "bazaar where the tears, sweat and blood of Christian captives were put on sale" by the Turks (261). With a selectivity which would characterize many of his compatriots' later obsession with the "barbarous" Ottoman slave trade, Bestuzhev-Marlinsky waxes indignant here, while repressing Russian serfdom, an institution which made the vast mass of the population the property of the upper classes. Of course, as a Decembrist exile, he wrote under terrible constraints and could make no indictment of Russia. Was he blind to the parallel with serfdom? Or did he expect readers to catch the subversive drift of his rhetoric about "our" victory over merchants of human beings? A similar streak of ambiguity runs through his discussion of cruel tyranny as the tribes' legacy from Persian and Turkish overlords. As in the case of slavery, on this point too Russia was fenced off from oriental evil, although home-grown despotism was something which had led the author himself to participate in armed insurrection against the state. But perhaps Bestuzhev-Marlinsky conceived a hierarchy of despotisms in which Nicholas I, for all his viciousness, fared better than a Persian shah or Turkish pasha.

In the definitive assertion of divided feelings about Asia, "Ammalat-Bek" deprecates the Caucasus for backwardness, while capturing its allure as a lush garden. Contained in one of Colonel Verkhovsky's fabricated letters to his Russian fiancée, this passage articulates a standard European view of the whole East's cultural and personal retardation:

I am very glad that I will be leaving Asia, that cradle of mankind, where the mind still remains in swaddling clothes. The static character of life in Asia over the course of centuries is astounding. All efforts at amelioration and education have been smashed to smithereens against Asia: it belongs most assuredly to space rather than time. The Indian Brahman, the Chinese mandarin, the Persian bek and the Caucasian mountain chieftain are now just the same as they have been for two thousand years. What a sad truth! . . . The sword and knout of conquerors have left them unmarked as water; the books and models provided by missionaries have not had the slightest impact. Sometimes they change their prophets but never acquire the knowledge or virtues of outsiders. I am leaving the land of fruit to be borne back to the land of work – that great inventor of everything useful, that animator of everything lofty, that alarm clock of the human soul, which has fallen into a voluptuous sleep here in the bosom of that charmer, nature (245; ellipsis mine).

In this assessment the Caucasus is drawn into a stereotypical orient where the natives are sunk in sensual indolence, oblivious to time and impervious to European schemes to transform them.

The clash between the oriental "land of fruit" and the European "land of work" coincides quite strikingly with the Freudian opposition between eros and civilization. A believer in a Russian civilizing mission in the Caucasus, Verkhovsky upholds the value of industriousness, discipline and efficiency, while professing disdain for the urge to loll about in a blissful stupor of creature comfort. In this avowed rejection of Asian sloth and pleasure-seeking, we see a defense of the Freudian reality principle which is directed toward repressing the id and redirecting, or sublimating, erotic desire toward the pursuit of socially valuable goals. But the trope of the "land of fruit," outside the flux of time, injects much tension into the passage. This symbolic notion conjures a pastoral or Arcadian world of natural abundance where no great effort is required to obtain the necessities of life and a high level of instinctual gratification prevails. As a later chapter will show, Bestuzhev-Marlinsky's *récits de voyage* would explicitly call the Caucasus an "Eden," beautifully pristine but ripe for economic exploitation by industrious men. The "land of fruit" in "Ammalat-Bek" crystalizes the same range of divided feelings about the territory as a backward but seductive part of the globe.

ELIMINATING THE SAVAGE

In his vacillations about wild Asia, Bestuzhev-Marlinsky both underwrites and disrupts Eurocentric ideology about the tribes. A loyal son of the "land of work," Verkhovsky espouses the civilizing mission understood as an educational program rather than General Ermolov's strategy of military subjugation. To judge by Bestuzhev-Marlinsky's *récit de voyage* "The Caucasian Wall (A Letter from Dagestan)," the benevolent imperialist Verkhovsky conveys the exiled author's own will to believe in the rectitude of the conquest in which he was participating. Like the writer in real life, Verkhovsky visits the remains of an ancient Persian fortification near Derbent, one of the towns seized by Peter I in an invasion of 1722. Verkhovsky's assessment of Peter exactly matches the opinion expressed in Bestuzhev-Marlinsky's own voice in "The Caucasian Wall."[12] In both texts, the Russian military traveler proclaims the tsar the "Demigod of the North," imagines him at the site of the wall and hails him as the visionary westernizer who "wrenched Russia from the sphere of Asia's decrepit kingdoms and trundled it into Europe with his mighty hand" (216).

The ideology of the civilizing mission is likewise served by Ammalat-Bek's private journal. In an act of authorial ventriloquism, the Caucasian hero "corroborates" Verkhovsky's view of oriental backwardness. The tribesman's diary thanks the colonel for ending his long sleep and inducting him into the "new world" of enlightenment. Similarly, as an echo of Verkhovsky's characterization of Asians as babes in intellectual swaddling clothes, Ammalat-Bek expresses a belittling conception of himself as a child compared to Europeans. Along with motifs of cultural slumber and infancy, the journal also features two of the tale's numerous tropes of animality: Ammalat-Bek likens his former self to a falcon who cannot fathom his hood, or a horse who knows not why humans shoe him.

But most comprehensively of all, "Ammalat-Bek" underwrites the ideology of the civilizing mission by shaping a plot which culminates in the wild man's apparently preordained elimination. The ethnographic excursuses and the highest concentration of annotations come at the very beginning, in chapter one. The quasi-scholarly business of footnoting is abandoned entirely by chapter ten, after which ghastly thrills are amassed. First Ammalat-Bek shoots Verkhovsky on a lonely road and makes his escape. Like a "jackal," the murderer sneaks back to the Russian camp at night, digs up the colonel's grave, reels at the stench of the corpse and hacks off the head with repeated blows of his dagger. Ammalat-Bek then rushes hellbent to Akhmet-Khan to exchange the head for Seltaneta. But now on his deathbed, the Khan is revolted by the bloody offering, curses Ammalat-Bek and deprives him of Seltaneta forever. Ill judged for the murder by other local people as well, Ammalat-Bek becomes a renegade warrior, still enhanced, however, by tragic grandeur: explicitly accused of "fratricide" by Safir-Ali, Bestuzhev-Marlinsky's hero converges on Cain, the primal murderer so compelling to romantic imagination.[13] In the story's last line Ammalat-Bek dies fighting the Russians at Anapa (chapter fourteen). As though by the hand of fate, his killer is Verkhovsky's brother, a major piece of undeclared poetic license on Bestuzhev-Marlinsky's part. In a typically imperialist "solution" to conflict between the savage and civilization, "Ammalat-Bek" thus exterminates the Caucasian hero in action presented as unplanned Russian retribution for the death of one of "our" own.[14]

A dramatization of savagery running amuck and ultimately eliminated, this denouement harmonizes perfectly with the endorsements of civilization in Verkhovsky's letters and Ammalat-Bek's journal. Bestuzhev-Marlinsky provides a gripping fictive demonstration of the view that wildness is destined to be eradicated, if not properly mastered and contained: just as the animal in man must be tamed through book-learning, the acquisition of Christian ethics and good manners, so too shall the Russian soldier shoot the Muslim bandit who refuses to be reconstructed. Savagery meets its demise, with the implication that a fraternity of Europeans is fated to prevail.

SURROGATE EROS

But the very refusal to kill Ammalat-Bek until virtually the last stroke of the pen inscribes a fierce authorial attachment to the oriental surrogate (whose initials Alexander Bestuzhev happened to share). Perhaps with the censor and police in mind, the exiled writer in certain respects legitimized the Caucasian conquest as the march of European progress. "Ammalat-Bek" continually subverts itself, however, by allowing civilized Russia and savage Dagestan to collapse into one another. Belinsky once complained that Bestuzhev-Marlinsky's handsome Muslim tribesmen looked and talked all too much like the tempestuous Novgorodians and Livonians in two of the author's other historical writings. To carry the logic of this astute observation further, Ammalat-Bek not only resembles these characters of very distant eras but even more intriguingly emerges as the underground self of Bestuzhev-Marlinsky and his enthralled readers in the period of imperialist war in the Caucasus.

The interchange between Ammalat-Bek and the author is strikingly signaled in the Terek's treatment as their shared symbolic emblem. The story draws Ammalat-Bek into semantic alignment with the river by describing both as bestial, savage, raging and rebellious. Furthermore, the waterway's course to the Caspian Sea is described in anthropomorphic language in a long passage near the beginning of chapter four. In this sequence the Terek first enters as a bandit, rejoicing in his liberty and stealing boulders as he storms through the Darial Pass. In making a turn through eastern lowlands, the river becomes a "Muslim" and then a stolid "worker" at a mill. This passage seems to recapitulate the civilizer's goal of transforming wild tribesmen into enlightened, cooperative subjects of the tsarist empire. But Bestuzhev-Marlinsky sets up interference by introducing a rhetorical line of self-identification with the Terek. In a traditional flight of enthusiasm for the sublime "dread" of Darial (cliffs, toppling boulders and torrential storms), chapter four ushers in the river as a "ferocious beast." The conclusion of this first paragraph intensifies the thrilled ambivalence: illuminated by lightning, the Terek fulminates with "fiery foam," its choppy waves "like spirits of Hell stabbed by the archangels' sword." The motif of Satanic revolt is compounded by a trope of the river as a "genius, struggling with nature," his force derived "from the heavens." At once a sublime beast, the supreme fallen angel and an embattled genius, the Terek conjoins Ammalat-Bek with Bestuzhev-Marlinsky's romantic ideal of himself.

This symptomatic interchange between the writing subject and the Muslim tribesman reflected a conception of *homo sapiens* which expanded "Asia" into a space in the human psyche, something on the order of the Freudian id. In a letter to his brother Pavel in 1828 Bestuzhev-Marlinsky maintained that "passions are the same everywhere, although they differ in their object and expression."[15] Emotions are "naked" in savage people, he continued, while in civilized societies they acquire a "genteel cover." Largely on the basis of this notion of layered personality observable throughout the world, the author fashioned a literary biography of Ammalat-Bek, a man about whom he had no written sources. More preoccupied with psychology than anthropology, Bestuzhev-Marlinsky presumed to lay bare the mind of the Caucasian hero in order to explain his act of murder.

The writer's conviction about humanity's shared passions produces two inordinately unstable cultural dichotomies about love in "Ammalat-Bek." A pivotal assessment of erotic fire appears in Verkhovsky's second letter to his fiancée:

Ammalat is in love, and what a love it is! Never in all my youthful ardor did I experience a love so frenzied. I burned like a censer, kindled by sunlight; he blazes as a ship set afire by lightning in a stormy sea. You and I, Maria, have read Shakespeare's *Othello* several times, and only the raging Othello can give you some idea of Ammalat's tropical passion (243).

The imagery of fire furthers the same poetic purpose as the tale's ruling trope of the orient as a balmy garden (where the stupendous mountains of "eternal snows" are excluded). Suffused with a "tropical" atmosphere, Asia is conjured in "Ammalat-Bek" as one big torrid expanse, encompassing Othello as readily as Dagestanis. Similarly, at other points in the story the Caucasian hero is likened to the sun, dispelling the snow which falls on Seltaneta's heart in his absence. This symbolic pattern of wintry feeling and blazing passion is endorsed predictably from "inside" Ammalat-Bek: after reading some Russian literature provided by Verkhovsky, the tribesman remarks in his journal, "How sluggish and cold their love is, like a moonbeam shining on ice." But for all the protestations to difference, the very imagery of frigidity and heat conforms to Bestuzhev-Marlinsky's belief that "passions are the same everywhere." The tribesman's erotic energy is a raging, elemental force, while the metaphor of an incense-burner safely contains the Orthodox Russian's little "flame," associates it with church and thus intimates holy matrimony. Both the "European" and Asian lovers partake in the same fiery substance, even though it assumes different forms.

The cross-cultural similarity of erotic experience is insinuated likewise in a wobbly dichotomy about the sex drive as a beast within. Verkhovsky articulates the notion in another letter to his fiancée: "Our passions are domestic animals or, if they be wild, beasts which have been tamed and made docile, trained to dance on the rope of decorum with a ring through the nose and claws clipped. In the Orient they are tigers and lions running free" (201–2). As the emblem of "our" side, Verkhovsky immediately proposes a domestic animal but then evokes a dancing bear. This trope puts a heavy accent upon training and repression. For Russians and orientals alike, however, erotic desire is presented as a beast – and potentially even a savage beast – which is merely subdued and leashed in the civilized world. As in the case of symbolic "fire," Ammalat-Bek's ferocious passion for Seltaneta thus converges toward "our" experience, instead of attesting to irreconcilable difference.

Far from denying the concept of raging, fiery eros as something too threatening to accommodate in "European" identity, Bestuzhev-Marlinsky cultivates it with obvious relish. He even lifts Ammalat-Bek to tragic Shakespearean stature by likening him to Othello, a prototype of the erotically intense non-European whose love for a woman was manipulated by a vicious schemer, leading him to commit murder. Linked to such phenomena as the sun, the garden, and the Terek, Ammalat-Bek is a *Naturmensch* who lives by depths of the heart, instinct and spontaneous feeling, as opposed to reason, social etiquette and the conventional moral codes of the Russian reader's world.[16] Clearly absorbed by "Asia" as a realm of illicit sex, Bestuzhev-Marlinsky projects onto the Dagestani primitive a daydream of utterly uninhibited erotic desire, just as the imaginary part two of the "Story of an Officer Held Prisoner by Mountain Tribesmen" depicts a neverland where beautiful local women are routinely made available as bedmates for visitors, including the Russian captive. As exemplified most straightforwardly in the latter case, Bestuzhev-Marlinsky had no qualms about identifying with oriental eros.

THE VIOLENT SURROGATE

But if openly romanticizing the tribesman's conflagrative, tigerish libido, the author identifies with Ammalat-Bek's murderous aggressivity in a largely unconscious, covert manner. Of course, this line of affinity between the writing subject and his Caucasian hero utterly undermines the moral foundation of the tsarist civilizing mission in "barbarous" Asia. As we have seen, the tale of passion and murder in Dagestan imputes a good deal of bloodlust to the Islamic killer, by contrast to principles of Christian kindness and forgiveness incarnated in the victim Verkhovsky.[17] However, the center does not hold in this clash between "oriental" aggression and Russian mercifulness.

The apparently unconscious nature of the destabilizing treatment of violence comes to light in the representation of the tsarist military man as decapitator. In his first letter from the front Verkhovsky recounts how his fellow soldiers cut off the heads of bullocks with swords and even daggers in order to exhibit their expertise with the weapons (chapter five). Within a tale in which so many words are expended in defining oppositions between Dagestanis and Russians, a reader contemplating the whole story may well start wondering just what the difference is between the tsarist military men, mindlessly decapitating animals in a display of martial arts, and Ammalat-Bek's purportedly "Asian" proclivity to violence and the particularly grisly business of beheading. Yet Bestuzhev-Marlinsky shows himself unaware of the extent to which he dismantles "civilized" identity by introducing the tsarist soldier as a killer, relishing senseless slaughter. The episode is relayed through the eyes of the spectator Verkhovsky in a tone of boisterous camaraderie and amazement at the physical prowess, as though a sporting event were taking place. The Russian soldiers vie with one another with gusto; and in a scene which sprang strictly from the author's imagination, General Ermolov is shown decapitating a bullock with one blow of his sword. Furthermore, as he begins the act, the Russian commander-in-chief assumes formidably heroic proportions in a comparison with Odysseus, preparing to kill Penelope's suitors.[18]

Irony is oddly absent in this episode in which Verkhovsky marvels at acts of decapitation (with no inkling that a dagger will behead *him* by the end of the story). Indeed, the colonel's perceptions thoroughly fuse with authorial speech. Bestuzhev-Marlinsky's footnote to the scene of sportive slaughter assures the untraveled members of the "European" audience that such astounding feats are commonplace in Asia: "A dagger in experienced hands is as good as an axe, a bayonet or a sword." Far from ironizing, this psychologically interesting annotation invites the Russian reader to experience an amazement which the author himself seems to have felt personally and then projected onto Verkhovsky as a newcomer at the oriental front. Furthermore, the reference to the *Odyssey* in "Ammalat-Bek" conveys the identical outlook Bestuzhev-Marlinsky expressed in personal correspondence about his regiment's "Homeric skirmishes" with Gazi-Muhammed.[19] All these features of the text – Verkhovsky's merger with the author, the annotation about the force of a dagger "in experienced hands," and the Homeric allusion – proclaim Bestuzhev-Marlinsky's obliviousness to the link established between Ammalat-Bek and the Russian military men as killers and decapitators.

The passage about killing animals discloses Bestuzhev-Marlinsky's troubled alliance with Ammalat-Bek as his violent underground self. In an evidently involuntary manner, the comment about the "experienced" wielding of a dagger conjoins the Asian weapon of choice with standard tsarist military equipment – the bayonet and the sword. This triad opens a breach in "civilization's" camp by intimating the "savagery" of killing on the battlefield. The detail illustrates the more sweeping operation of a projective mechanism identified in Dominique Mannoni's classic study of the psychology of colonization: in a manifestation of "obscurities of the unconscious," the "civilized" man attributes to the "savage" dastardly impulses which reside in himself.[20] In essence, the tale of Ammalat-Bek's treacherous murder of Verkhovsky proclaims lethal aggression a quintessentially oriental proclivity but simultaneously endorses as virile, martial action the facility for killing which Russian soldiers themselves had to possess, as Bestuzhev-Marlinsky knew well from his personal experience in combat against the tribes.

These disclosures of profoundly divided feelings about bloodshed have a clear connection to the author's history as a Decembrist. In the Novgorod tale "Roman and Olga" written prior to the insurrection of 1825, Alexander Bestuzhev had revealed anxiousness about his capacity for heroic martial action.[21] Perplexity about violence in the name of a political ideal would also find release in "The Frigate *Hope*" (1833).[22] So too is "Ammalat-Bek" obscurely invaded by psychic turmoil about participating in military carnage. When Bestuzhev-Marlinsky's Caucasian tale dwells upon the Russian soldier as a proficient butcher comparable to Odysseus, the victims are animals rather than Muslim guerrillas. But in parallel to an old horse which Ammalat-Bek beats to death in a fit of fury early in the story (as a foreshadowing of his equally pitiless murder of Verkhovsky), the decapitated bullocks stand in for men – the tribesmen whom Bestuzhev-Marlinsky was helping to slaughter in the service of the Russian state. Although survival in combat requires killing without remorse, this capacity cannot be promoted with relish by a Christian, even in wartime. However, by displacing the Russians' exercise of martial arts onto animals, Bestuzhev-Marlinsky could openly admire violence as a "Homeric" virtue. The Dagestani shadow of Odysseus, the romanticized killer Ammalat-Bek embodied the author's illicit ideal of the skilled man of arms totally outside Christian morality.

ASIA IN THE READER

The contemporary readership registered the seductive interchange between Bestuzhev-Marlinsky and Ammalat-Bek in ways conditioned by gender. Women were not entirely immune to the tale's militarized wanderlust. Primarily restricted to the domestic scene, they sometimes envied a man's opportunity to escape tedium by going to war in the sublime Caucasus. Rostopchina conveyed such sentiments in a verse addressed to her brother Serozha, about to embark on a tour of duty in the territory.[23] A desire to experience the martial life would surface more elaborately in a late nineteenth-century story by the nonentity Vera Zhelikhova, whose heroine at a Caucasian fort learns to ride like a mountain brave (*dzhigit*) and defies her husband by taking risky horseback excursions disguised as a man.[24] Such literary works by and about women expressed a wish to participate in the rugged, dangerous life of campaigners in the Asian wilderness.

However, instead of identifying with valiant men in fiction, the typically homebound women readers of "Ammalat-Bek" were more prone to embrace the tale's oriental eroticism. According to Semevsky's article cited at the beginning of this chapter, women "fell in love with [Marlinsky] via the printed page." But daydreams about the author himself blended together with thrilled curiosity about the dashing savage, Ammalat-Bek. In the estimation of the nineteenth-century Caucasian regional specialist E. G. Veidenbaum, all Russia's "sentimental ladies and girls were enraptured by Seltaneta's ardent lover."[25] Not in the least repelled by the tribesman's murder of benevolent Verkhovsky, these readers were cultivating a secret ideal of the wild man's "tigerish" erotic powers. Ammalat-Bek represented a wish-fulfilling alternative especially for women of romantic temperament who found themselves in dismal marriages in Orthodox Russia. Writings by secondary authors of the period again prove illuminating. Rostopchina, who was unhappily wed to a somewhat younger *habitué* of the *beau monde*, imagined a civilized woman's affair with a Caucasian tribesman in a poem beginning, "In the mountains I met a Circassian and swore an everlasting love."[26] Set to music in the 1840s, this song became popular in Russian salons and encouraged women to keep swooning over torrid erotic gratification. In a more lurid key, Elizaveta Gan's story "A Recollection of Zheleznovodsk" also revealed Ammalat-Bek's force as a Russian woman's repressed ideal of savage eros.[27] As the next chapter will detail, this work recounts the adventures of a lady taken prisoner by tribesmen and nearly raped by a local "prince." Like Rostopchina, Gan had a miserable marriage (to a boorish general much older than she), and a yearning for some erotic charge in life overflowed into her literary activity. Completely in accord with a traditional discourse about spontaneous, "natural" passion, Rostopchina's poem and Gan's story illustrated the self-involved erotic daydreams which Russian women readers, and readers turned writers, were wont to spin around the passionate tribesman Ammalat-Bek.

While Russian women took to Ammalat-Bek as an illicit erotic ideal, men in the readership followed Bestuzhev-Marlinsky's own route of emulating the Asian killer as an underground self. Most of these readers, though, betrayed no anxiety about exercising violence against the tribes in combat. On the contrary, Bestuzhev-Marlinsky's Caucasian œuvre prompted many Russian men to enlist in the army in the 1830s and 1840s. As recollected in several memoirs, the author instilled eagerness to see the spectacular Caucasian wilderness, experience the thrills of battle and make a brilliant military career in the hottest theater of war then available. Arnold Zisserman's *Twenty-Five Years in the Caucasus* best expressed the collective syndrome. Zisserman recalled how he rushed to the nearest recruiting station after falling under the sway of "Ammalat-Bek" at the age of seventeen. He stressed the pleasures of the text by defining it as a "seductive" work, full of an "ardent fantasy" which "sent gullible young souls into ecstasy and lured them to the Caucasus."[28] In a rather common experience, however, young Zisserman found the soldier's life much duller than literature had promised. None the less, he continued to perceive a rousing "poetry of warfare" in battle. The same sort of experience was conveyed in a memoir by I. von der Hoven, a soldier who actually met Bestuzhev-Marlinsky in the Caucasus.[29] Von der Hoven asked for a transfer from Petersburg to the southern front after reading Bestuzhev-Marlinsky's "wonderful descriptions of nature," especially in "Mulla-Nur," a well-known work about a Caucasian bandit similar to Robin Hood. Comparable testimony was provided by other veterans who recollected how they joined the Caucasian army in search of the landscape and the rousing martial action they had discovered reading Bestuzhev-Marlinsky (as well as Lermontov).[30]

This interesting body of memoirs transmitted no ostensible sense of commitment to a civilizing mission. Instead, these Russians spoke a romantic nineteenth-century idiom about war as courageous action. They did not count patriotism among their motivations for becoming soldiers, nor directly express an urge to exterminate "savages." A touristic rather than jingoistic sentiment ran through the recollections, as the themes of wild nature and the "poetry of warfare" recurred. However, the very act of enlistment brought these excited male readers onto the battlefield to test their martial prowess against the legendary tribesmen. Only slightly represssed in the memoirs, Bestuzhev-Marlinsky's own sort of secret attraction to Ammalat-Bek's violence ran just beneath the surface of the enlistees' expressions of enthusiasm for wilderness and the bravura of campaigns. If overtly preoccupied with the Caucasian war as an event affording opportunities for travel and a prestigious military career, the readers knew they were not embarking on a pleasure trip by joining the army. Their memoirs also made it clear that they did not enlist in order to have desk jobs. They longed instead to enter a world of machismo and experience themselves as heroes in combat. This desire put Bestuzhev-Marlinsky's male devotees upon a course of action which supplanted the vicarious experience of *reading* about slaughter with the reality of war, giving release to violence. For all the talk of valor and the "poetry" of nature, joining the Russian army meant getting a license to kill. In the theater of war the morality of the civilized Christian world was set aside, so that acts punishable as crimes at home in peacetime would win admiration and medals for the soldier. The recruit would have to prepare himself to be effective in the killing fields, acquiring the "Homeric" skill with weapons which "Ammalat-Bek" celebrated most forthrightly in the episode about beheading bullocks.

These readers acted out identification with Ammalat-Bek, the tale's primary, riveting model of the dashing killer. The Russian practitioners of martial arts, including General Ermolov, appear only in cameo roles, while the victimized Verkhovsky is never shown doing anything violent: the exponent of enlightened behavior and Christian virtue, he certainly could not have been emulated too enthusiastically by the young recruit (unless we posit a death-wish as a guiding element in a soldier's psyche).[31] By contrast, the Asian outlaw Ammalat-Bek set the compelling, illicit standard of what a successful soldier must be, precisely by dramatically flouting Christian society's moral and legal strictures against killing. In legitimizing murder, war in effect set loose the "orient" within. One Russian veteran of Caucasian campaigns recalled the experience in these telling terms: "Not blood but lava ran in my veins," he declared, claiming that his brother-in-law even called him " 'Ammalat' – and 'Vesuvievich,' to boot!" (i.e., a patronymic based on the name of the volcano).[32] Untroubled by the moral and ideological implications, this tsarist soldier had taken pride in releasing his "savagery" on the Asian battlefield.

All the testimony to Ammalat-Bek's status as an illicit ideal of unleashed eroticism and violence can be underlined by remembering how Bestuzhev-Marlinsky merged with his Caucasian heroes in the minds of his devoted readers of both sexes. The colorful machismo of tribesmen like Ammalat-Bek and Mulla-Nur was so intense that the author's death in combat in 1837 became surrounded with fabulous stories about his defection to the enemy. As news of his demise gradually reached the Caucasian spa country and the Russian heartland, rumors arose that he was still alive, fighting with the Muslim tribesmen and living in the mountains with five native wives.[33] Of course, this fantasy captured the very essence of the oriental existence of uninhibited erotic gratification and freely expressed aggressivity which the author's semi-fiction had produced. When Arnold Zisserman was on mission from the Caucasus in the late 1840s, a St. Petersburg civilian actually asked him "if it were true that Shamil was Marlinsky, turned renegade and made leader of the tribesmen after arranging to feign death in combat."[34] Enthralled by Bestuzhev-Marlinsky's noble primitives, this Russian man conceived Shamil himself as a compatriot who had turned his gun against the tsar.

As the query about Shamil so perfectly illustrates, Bestuzhev-Marlinsky's Caucasian œuvre generated a prolonged mystery of authorial identity which was at once the semi-Europeanized readers' unresolved question about who *they* really were in relation to the tribes. Ammalat-Bek's popularity certainly conforms to the general rule that most readers everywhere prefer a sublime villain to a good, bland hero. But the annals of European literature inspired by imperialism offer no case quite like the production and reception of this Caucasian tale. Could the British, for example, have ever been so enraptured by a Friday who shot and decapitated Robinson Crusoe? The unlikelihood of such a response in the British context points back to semi-Europeanized Russia's national stake in Asia (while undoubtedly also testifying to the enormous importance of racial difference in European writing about Africa and the Caribbean). Bestuzhev-Marlinsky's dashing tribal outlaws quite possibly afforded vicarious political satisfaction to Russians repelled by Nicholas I.[35] The cultural pay-off was more evident, however. As a *Naturmensch* akin to Othello (but none the less a member of the readership's own "white, Caucasian" race), Ammalat-Bek served Russian national esteem by equating the orient with emotional intensity, macho vigor and inspired primitive poetry.[36]

There was indubitably another dimension, which had its own complications. Given the profound ambivalence of Bestuzhev-Marlinsky's tale, some contemporary readers quite likely took vicarious pleasure in Dagestani eroticism and violence without renouncing belief in Russia's "European" stature and the consequent legitimacy of war against the tribes. The Russian men whom Bestuzhev-Marlinsky drew into the Caucasian killing fields even turned the martial lessons of Ammalat-Bek against his tribal brothers in real life. On the other hand, however, at least one of these enthralled male readers shared Bestuzhev-Marlinsky's own anguished confusion about war as the means to a supposedly benevolent end. Unlike the Russian soldier who lauded the ferocious "lava" in his veins, Zisserman wrote with shame about the "bestial instincts" he had discovered in himself and his comrades on the Caucasian battle-ground.[37] Although generally well repressed by the "poetry of warfare" in Zisserman's recollections, even this momentary recognition of appalling savagery in "us" was significant. More than any of his other Caucasian writings, Bestuzhev-Marlinsky's "Ammalat-Bek" attempted to negotiate the terrible gap between the romance of an empire in the orient (the "poetry") and the stark brutality of imperialist war in action (the "bestiality"). In military exile the author was serving Nicholas I as an exterminator of Asian peoples with whom he identified to a great extent. The circumstances of Bestuzhev-Marlinsky's death suggest that the ethical strain ultimately proved unbearable: in an act often judged as deliberate suicide, the writer made a foolhardy charge during pitched battle at Cape Adler.[38] After being wounded severely in the chest, he was dragged aside by comrades while fighting continued. His body was never recovered and presumably was hacked to pieces. Whatever may have prompted it, this violent end tragically harmonized with the ideal of stalwart heroism celebrated in the tribal death songs of "Ammalat-Bek.'

Both a fortifier and subverter of imperialist ideology, the schizoid "Ammalat-Bek" predictably produced a double-sided legacy in Russian literature. On the one hand, more than any previous writer, Bestuzhev-Marlinsky encouraged readers to approach the Caucasus as a Muslim field where they might feel a confident kinship to Europe. In praising Peter the Great, "Ammalat-Bek" even defined the goals of tsarist imperialism in Asia as the defeat of "barbarism" and the pursuit of the "good of mankind." This was a hegemonic line of thought pursued in the 1830s and 1840s in Russian pulp which reduced the tribesman to a subhuman creature fated to be wiped from the globe. But while Bestuzhev-Marlinsky may have given some inspiration to these little orientalizers, he himself was clearly plagued by grave doubts about the imperialist view of war as regenerative violence necessary to build a better world. His unresolved conflicts about the tsarist conquest of the Caucasus would re-echo in late writings of Lermontov, the military exile who attained a frankly self-reproachful recognition of bestiality in Russia's war against the tribes.

CHAPTER 8

Early Lermontov and oriental machismo

"With oriental languor in his eyes,
He was a poison to our women!"
Lermontov

By contrast to the tremendous public impact of "The Prisoner of the Caucasus" and "Ammalat-Bek," "Izmail-Bey" provoked hardly any reaction from its immediate readership. A product of Lermontov's adolescence, the poem was first published with the censor's deletions in 1843. The posthumous appearance conformed to a peculiarity of the author's career. Although a precocious talent who began writing in his teens, Lermontov published little verse before dying at the age of twenty-six in a duel in the Caucasus in 1841. He made his first big mark on the Russian literary scene when the novel *A Hero of Our Time* appeared the year before his death. The sole edition of verse prepared in his lifetime also came out in 1840. Marred by traits of juvenilia, "Izmail-Bey" was just one of many works never revised to meet mature Lermontov's high standards for publication.

The poem none the less rewards attention as Lermontov's earliest disavowal of Eurocentric ideology about civilizing the Caucasian Muslim tribes. "Izmail-Bey" does not grapple with the era's vexed questions of Russian national identity. However, Lermontov's awareness of Islamic culture was awakened by the study of oriental literature and philosophy in 1830–32 at Moscow University, where one of his professors was the Russian Arabist, Boldyrev.[1] This exposure to the thought of ancient Arabia and Persia left the writer with a life-long affinity to eastern responses to the mystery of fate,

133

as *A Hero of Our Time* would demonstrate. Even more significantly, like earlier romantics such as Somov and Kiukhelbeker, Lermontov developed a view of privileged Russian relation to the Islamic East's storehouse of cultural treasures. In 1841 he remarked to an acquaintance that Russia should stop "trying to match Europe and the French" and draw instead upon Asia's insufficiently understood "cache of riches."[2] While perhaps not free of the condescending hint that orientals had not fully fathomed their own philosophical heritage, this recorded conversation shows Lermontov's alignment with other writers and intellectuals of the romantic era who thought Russia would realize its national identity in a synthesis of European and Asian cultural forces.[3] No outright denial of the enduring value of certain western achievements, the synthetic viewpoint nevertheless was inimical to the Eurocentrism which underlay justifications of the Caucasian conquest as a civilizing mission.

Lermontov's disaffection from ideological premises of Russia's war against the tribes was already expressed in "Izmail-Bey," but with a lurid stamp of approval for oriental machismo in its martial and sexual manifestations. Not yet the commissioned officer trained at a St. Petersburg military academy in 1832–34, the poet unequivocally identified with Izmail-Bey, the Muslim who slaughters tsarist soldiers on Caucasian battlefields and steals their women in the erotic combat zone of Russia's *beau monde*. Wild libido and violence imbued all six Caucasian tales young Lermontov wrote in the late 1820s and early 1830s. In "Izmail-Bey," however, the sensational material was harnessed to a denunciation of Russia as an empire of slavery and genocidal warfare. Of course, the censor expunged many pertinent lines in 1843; but even so, Lermontov's alliance with his tribal hero was unmistakable.[4]

As the story of a Muslim Don Giovanni who reigns supreme over Russians in war, "Izmail-Bey" brings fascinating issues of gender to bear on imperialism. The performance of an *enfant terrible*, the poem envisions a "crowd" of Russian readers open to shock. But the most readily disconcerted reader was a

Europeanized Russian male with a double-barreled anxiety about orientals' outmanning him in war and love. Young Lermontov confirmed this reader's worst fears by stressing Izmail-Bey's erotic success with Russian women: there was a gender division in the imperial ranks. The women readers who swooned over Ammalat-Bek must have already put Russian manhood on guard. Bestuzhev-Marlinsky, however, had kept his Dagestani Othello erotically confined to Asia, whereas Lermontov turned Izmail-Bey loose in the North. To judge by the reticence of the first readers, the conjunction of martial and sexual force seems to have made "Izmail-Bey" virtually taboo. The year of publication had proved propitious indeed for the poem's *enfant terrible*: by 1843, Shamil was alarming Russia with his military prowess *and* had absconded with one of "our" women, the Armenian Anna Ulykhanova who became his favorite wife. By definition a thing not to be spoken, the "taboo" of oriental machismo's double threat shall be inferred in this chapter largely by listening to Belinsky, an extensive commentator on the literary Caucasus who pointedly evaded "Izmail-Bey."[5]

SEEKING A HOME IN THE SOUTH

All of Lermontov's early Caucasian tales prominently feature violence and carnality. "The Circassians" details bloody battle between Russians and tribesmen. In Lermontov's "The Prisoner of the Caucasus" the Russian protagonist is shot dead by the father of the enamored Circassian heroine, who conforms to her Pushkinian prototype by drowning herself in a river. "Kally" ("bloody" in Ossetian), "The *Aul* Bastundzhi" and "Hadji Abrek" have lurid denouements in which ravishing tribeswomen (a lightly clad sleeper, a bather, a bosomy dancer) are butchered by local men driven by a vendetta or crazed by unrequited passion. Exceptionally published in the poet's lifetime, "Hadji Abrek" (1835) appeared without his permission (and to his immense vexation) in Senkovsky's *Library for Reading*, a regular haven for tawdry orientalia.

But unlike the era's common lot of orientalizers, Lermontov overlaid the Caucasus with a quest for home apparently related to his unhappy family life. Three years old when his mother died, he was taken in hand by his wealthy maternal grandmother Arsenieva (née Stolypina) who notoriously doted on him and isolated him from his father, her social inferior.[6] An anguish about lost parents surfaced in Lermontov's adolescent verse in the form of orphans, outcasts and brooding criminals (including men accused of killing their mothers in childbirth). The Caucasus, though, was an especially favored site in these writings.

With an emotional pitch previously unsounded in Russian literature, Lermontov invented himself as a child of the southern territory, where Arsenieva took him at the ages of three, five and ten. The writer seemed primarily in search of a surrogate male parent. Most tellingly, the dedication to "The *Aul* Bastundzhi" asks the Caucasus to bless the poem as a "son." No gentle maternal presence, this land is a "severe tsar of the world" who is addressed, however, as an adored but stony male parent: "At heart I am yours, forever and everywhere yours!" cries the poet, even "in the North, a country alien to you." "Hadji Abrek" and "Izmail-Bey" construct similar affective bonds between the writer and a mountain habitat whose traditionally rugged, masculine character is mirrored by the heroes' brutal energy. Indeed one might wonder if the tales' violent machismo, conjoined with sublime landscape, was not providing the author a good deal of psychological compensation for a father overruled by a possessive grandmother.

Cast in filial relation to the Caucasus in its conventionally sublime guise, Lermontov took a notable interest in the tsarist conquest as a maker of orphans, resembling himself. Passion-crazed Selim ("The *Aul* Bastundzhi") has lost his father in battle, and his mother has died in childbirth. Izmail-Bey also lacks parents. Again, the mother has died in childbirth (the infant's "crime"), while a vendetta forced the father into hiding. In an extension of the bereft personal condition, Lermontov likewise featured the tsarist army's destruction of tribal villages, after seeing such a site as a boy. Victims of expansionist Russia, these dispossessed Caucasians embody homelessness on a communal scale ("The *Aul* Bastundzhi," "Izmail-Bey").

While eclipsed by the masculine union of the poet, rugged country and orphans who grow into macho heroes, a search for the mother also figured in Lermontov's Caucasian juvenilia. The short lyric "The Caucasus" (1830) conveys the poet's sense of discovering at last the place where he belongs. After equating the "southern mountains" with the "sweet song of a fatherland" (*otchina*, etymologically related to *otets*, "father"), he refers to his mother's death and basks in her gaze as he stands on the "summits of the cliffs." The last stanza recalls a "pair of divine eyes," a phrase generally thought to evoke the precocious romantic love which Lermontov in an autobiographical jotting of 1830 claimed to have experienced for a little girl whom he met during childhood in the Caucasus. This combination of the lost mother and the unforgettable girl imparts tender feminine character to the highlands where the orphaned male speaker finds comfort.

THE POET'S IDENTIFICATION WITH IZMAIL-BEY

Lermontov's deep-seated emotional engagement with the Caucasus *in loco parentis* gave him an incomparably unabashed zest for tribal surrogacy uncomplicated by pretensions to extra-literary authority. Certain Russian critics have argued otherwise. With a sideswipe at "bourgeois comparativism" in thrall to Byron and Hugo, A. N. Sokolov in the Stalinist era contended that Lermontov's entire Caucasian corpus arose from reliable ethnographic and historical knowledge stockpiled by the author since childhood.[7] Less vociferously, other critics of the 1940s and 1950s detected echoes of tribal folklore in Lermontov's early tales.[8] But as U. R. Fokht argued nearly twenty years ago, the "psychological aspect of the mountain tribesmen" always held Lermontov's greatest interest.[9] Frankly offered as products of the Muse, the poet's Caucasian surrogates have ethnographically appropriate decor but virtually no didactic paraphenalia (footnotes, the subtitle a "true story," an explanatory preface or afterward).

"Izmail-Bey" is an exemplary illustration of Lermontov's general withdrawal from the extra-literary enterprise best represented by Bestuzhev-Marlinsky but founded by footnoting poets of the 1820s. The most widely accepted historical prototype of Lermontov's hero was Izmail-Bey Atazhukov, a Kabardinian taken captive as a boy in the 1780s and educated in Russia.[10] The author was familiar with the political history of this man who won a tsarist Cross of St. George in combat against Turkey, then went back home and joined the war against Russia. But "Izmail-Bey" drastically tampered with Atazhukov's biography in order to suit one of the poet's recurrent romantic preoccupations – the clash between an extraordinary individual and the common herd. Lermontov's lack of concern with historical reconstruction was matched by a nonchalance about cultural authenticity, as exemplified by the "Circassian Song" of "Izmail-Bey." With a refrain advising a young man to buy a good horse instead of getting married, this rhythmically catchy production was largely derived from an eighteenth-century collection of Russian folk songs and would be recycled for Kazbich, the Chechen bandit in *A Hero of Our Time.* [11]

Offered as an "oriental tale" with epigraphs from Byron ("The Giaour," "Lara") and Walter Scott (*Marmion*), "Izmail-Bey" is emplotted not as political history but rather as a revelation of the hero's secret erotic passion. The tale's framing stanzas place an omniscient author in monologic relation to Izmail-Bey. The Russian poet is a "traveler" in the Caucasus with a silenced Chechen guide who is the putative source of the story. The narrator vows to transmit the tale to "the distant North," in order to keep it from perishing "as a secret unknown to the crowd" (1: 5).[12] He thus knows the whole story from the outset but likes to tease readers with questions. Did the "wrath of Mahomet" drive the Circassians into the mountains? he asks, for instance, before immediately revealing the true culprit, the Russian state (1: 8). The rhetorical questions typify the narrative's overall strategy of deferring the ultimate revelation. A work of 2289 lines, "Izmail-Bey" delivers its big secret only in the epilogue after the hero is shot by Roslambek, the "cruel brother" who envied his local popularity and resented his insistence on fighting Russia openly, instead of engaging in sneaky tactics. When the villagers prepare Izmail-Bey's body for burial, they misread signs of his fourteen-year sojourn in Russia. They take his St. George award as the Christian cross of an "accursed giaour" and are puzzled by a golden curl in his locket. The (uncensored) poem's audience, however, has been prepared to interpret the lock of hair as a talisman from a Russian Orthodox woman loved by the Muslim hero but abandoned because religious differences made their marriage impossible.[13] Privy to the golden curl's meaning, the reader fully understands at last why Izmail-Bey back home in the Caucasus spurns the love of the beautiful tribeswoman Zara (who disguises herself as a male retainer in order to watch over him).

The strategy of sharing a "secret" with the audience amounts to little more than producing Izmail-Bey as the poet's *alter ego* in Circassian garb. While supplying touches of local color here and there, Lermontov shapes his hero so thoroughly in his own Byronic image as to deprive him of separate identity. Like the wandering narrator, the tribal hero first appears as a "traveler" and remains a displaced person throughout the story. The poet also calls attention to the "cold glint" in the tribesman's dark eyes, likened to those of "our young men" (I: 13). A motif which would be central in the depiction of Pechorin in *A Hero of Our Time*, the icy gaze like "ours" functions in "Izmail-Bey" to brand the Circassian with contemporary Russia's Byronism – estrangement, traumatic disappointment in love, and a cold reserve masking a sensitive core. The Caucasian hero himself, however, lacks the very habit of self-reflection and has no consciousness of his Byronic qualities. He is simultaneously denied even the semblance of a national culture. As a baby, for example, he hears the "raging howl of a storm" rather than lullabies (II: 4). When he returns to the Caucasus to find his village razed, he vows to take revenge against Russia but has no sense of *patrie* or religious commitment. As the military showdown draws near, in fact, the poet asserts that Izmail-Bey resists tsarist power not for the sake of his "fatherland" nor even his local *aul* but simply for his "native cliffs" (III: 4).

But for all the inauthenticity of this *Naturmensch* in Byronic cloak, the *enfant terrible* interestingly employs him as a mask to taunt readers rather than stroke their imperial egos. Like Izmail-Bey, stupidly reviled by locals as an "accursed giaour" after his death, the poet stands in tension with his own "crowd," his addressees in the North. A word already freighted with philistinism in Pushkin's writings, "crowd" in Lermontov's work also signified Russian high society's vulgar self-importance and snobbery, lethally inimical to the poet. Scorn for the *beau monde* first erupted publically in the work which brought Lermontov fame and his first exile to the Caucasus, "The Death of a Poet" (1837), written *in memoriam* to Pushkin as a victim of intriguers at Nicholas' court. "Izmail-Bey" was beginning to cultivate this alienation in private. A self-styled "singer" with a "proud heart," Lermontov's persona disdains glittering society with its worldly rewards ("a crown"). The sensibility bonds him to the "proud" tribal "singer" who performs the "Circassian Song" and has no interest in "gold." After locating himself in a cross-cultural brotherhood of poets, the Russian writer emulates the "primitive" bard by fashioning a Homeric simile of tribesmen going into battle like a flock of cranes (III: 16).

In embracing Izmail-Bey's milieu as his spiritual home ("my splendid Caucasus"), the *enfant terrible* challenges Russian readers convinced of their superiority to "savages." The poem conjures a Golden Age of freedom when Circassians coexisted happily with the tsarist state (I: 6). But the "dangerous enemy" to the north upset the balance by encroaching upon the tribes' "beloved homeland" and forcing them into "voluntary exile." Russian aggression against the primitive community is then writ small in the Circassian hero in a manner casting aspersion on the poem's envisioned readers (I: 12). Upon introducing Izmail-Bey, the narrator strikes one of his recurrent interrogative poses to wonder how the tribes-man has fared during his long absence from home: perhaps he has been "infected in stifling Europe by debauchery and the poison of enlightenment." Stated for the first time in the literary Caucasus, this Rousseauist proposition made the reader's country the tribesman's corrupter rather than his civilizer.[14] By eliminating these lines about Russia's evil, the censor sheltered the envisioned "crowd" from the full brunt of Lermontov's Rousseauist attack on civilization. With the cut restored, however, one sees how the poem aimed to inculpate self-satisfied consumers complicit in imperialism.

THE INTERCHANGE BETWEEN MILITARY AND SEXUAL PROWESS

As inhabitants of the land made "foreign" and "alien" through the eyes of Lermontov's tribal surrogate, the Euro-peanized readers are situated in an ideological field victori-ously assaulted by interrelated martial and erotic weaponry. Shortly after Izmail-Bey's entry in the poem, his brush with a spokesman for tsarist conquest leads to murder by the sword. Unlike Ammalat-Bek who kills a benefactor committed to educating him, Izmail-Bey slaughters a "sneering Cossack" who happens to be hunting in the area where his *aul* used to stand (1: 15). When the hero seeks information about the pile of rubble he has just seen, the Cossack treats him as a paltry alien: the place was laid waste five years ago when "your intrepid people got scared of the Russians!" A brash advocate of the dispossession, the Cossack boasts that the villagers went into hiding from "us." Izmail-Bey cuts him down with his sword, his cold eyes now flashing like the blade's "bloody steel" and his cheeks aflame "like Etna's lava." Entirely elim-inated by the censor in 1843, this volcanic episode has a sharp political edge. Like the duelist's code of "merciless honor" which blurs into Circassian violence in Pushkin's "The Pris-oner of the Caucasus," Izmail-Bey's instinctive slaughter of the Cossack is revenge for dire insult. In this case, however, the unflinching attack takes place cross-culturally, and for the first time in the literary Caucasus the man who gets his just deserts is bragging about imperial Russian might.

"Izmail-Bey" treats war in a politically similar way. The opening stanzas of part three depict Russia as a "new Rome" brutally expanding its dominion through assault on the Circassians:

> Where are the mountains, steppes and oceans
> Unconquered by the Slavs in war?
> And where have enmity and treason
> Not bowed to Russia's mighty tsar?
> Circassian, fight no more! Likely as not,
> Both East and West will share your lot.
> The time will come: you'll say, quite bold,
> "I am a slave, but my tsar rules the world."
> The time will come: the North will be graced
> By an awesome new Rome, a second Augustus.
>
> *Auls* are burning, their defenders mastered,
> The homeland's sons have fallen in battle.
> Like steady comets, fearful to the eyes,
> A glow is playing 'cross the skies,
> A beast of prey with bayonet, the victor
> Charges into a quiet dwelling.
> He kills the children and the old folks,
> And with his bloody hands he strokes
> The unmarried girls and young mothers.
> But woman's heart can match her brother's!
> After those kisses, a dagger's drawn,
> A Russian cowers, gasps – he's gone!
> "Avenge me, comrade!" And in just a breath
> (A fine revenge for a murderer's death)
> The little house, delighting their gaze,
> Now burns: Circassian freedom set ablaze!

A deflation of contemporary cant about Holy Russia's civilizing mission, this passage casts the readership's troops as predatory "beasts" (*khishchnyi zver*) and "murderers" whose targets are children, women and the elderly. Interestingly enough, the censor of 1843 left the raid intact but deleted the first stanza about "Augustan" Nicholas' "new Rome." The selective excision suggests that readers who brought jingoistic passions to the poem could take "delight" in the razed village, just like the textual soldiers. However, this pleasure could be had only by donning astoundingly large blinkers to Lermontov's excoriation of the tsarist army. The Russian raid with its atrocities against civilians sets the scene for defensive action from Izmail-Bey's side. The dynamic of rightful retaliation is intensified by an echo of the hero's murder of the "sneering Cossack." When the tsarist army attacks Izmail-Bey's home territory, fearless Cossacks lead the charge and immediately kill several Circassians (III: 19). But then the hero cuts a "bloody path" into the fray and "mercilessly" annihilates enemies right and left, like a "young lion" protected by the "Prophet" (III: 20). Lermontov lets Izmail-Bey "hack his way" through the tsarist army with impunity (whereas Ammalat-Bek was ultimately felled by a Russian). Wounded but not eliminated by a foreign hand, Izmail-Bey resists for two more years, only to be murdered by Roslambek, his ignoble brother who incarnates the universality of malice. At the end of the story the poet's tribal *alter ego* is gone, but his "merciless," Homeric rage to kill the imperialist dispossessors is never contained by the Russian side.

In identifying with Izmail-Bey as an annihilator of soldiers who serve the "new Rome," Lermontov unifies the warrior with the lover whose "secret" is laid bare after death. The *enfant terrible* thus enlarges his performance to provoke readers with a professed horror of Asia's excessive libido. The relevant cultural horizon lies not in the Othellan passions of Ammalat-Bek but rather in a standard Eurocentric conviction about Muslims' gross sensuality. A perfect example of the outlook appeared in the Russian press during Lermontov's adolescence in Ilya Radozhitsky's retelling of "Kyz-Brun" ("maiden's promontory"), a Circassian legend about a young wife falsely accused of adultery and thrown from a cliff. Radozhitsky turned the tale to the same ideological ends he served by applauding tsarist conquest in his travelogue "The Road from the Don River to Georgievsk." To characterize the victim's husband in "Kyz-Brun," Radozhitsky digressed on the Muslim tribesmen's erotic sensibility in a dreadfully written passage:

For them, buying a wife means acquiring a piece of necessary property. There a man is rarely aroused to the feeling of noble passion, let alone mutual attraction. Nothing but a thirst for pleasure, as non-specific as the need to eat and drink, makes him obtain this source of delight, for which she is strictly kept in a harem like fruit secreted in a greenhouse.[15]

With these infelicitous words Radozhitsky invited his readers to join him in the ranks of "noble" Christians appalled by oriental lust.

A like-minded vision of Izmail-Bey as an Asian sex maniac is written into Lermontov's poem in the personage of a Russian military man once engaged to marry a blonde woman seduced by the Circassian hero. The jilted fiancé holds forth as a secondary narrator, the source of a tale within the tale (II: 22–27). Bent on revenge, he roams the wilderness near his Caucasian military encampment and encounters Izmail-Bey at night. The Russian fails to recognize his prey and pours out his story to him. Left fully intact in the censored text of 1843, this recollection reduces the hero to aggressive sexuality.[16] When first introduced in the poem, Izmail-Bey has the glacial eyes of "our young men." According to the soldier, however, the ocular ice melted to "oriental languor" in the presence of Russian women. He claims that "voluptuous and cunning" Izmail-Bey displayed an insatiable urge to erotic conquest in Petersburg, where "not a single" targeted woman could "escape his art." More than personally affronted, the would-be avenger regards the Circassian's indefatigable pursuit of Russian women as a cultural and political offense – an outsider's "contempt for the laws of a foreign land." Within the story constructed by the omniscient narrator, the curl in Izmail-Bey's locket implies an enduring attachment to the blonde woman. None the less, through the word of the soldier, who asserts that Izmail-Bey had numberless conquests, the poem offers an outraged masculine view of womanizing as an act of aggression against Orthodox Russia.

As practiced by the Circassian Don Giovanni, sexual conquest becomes an extension of the jihad. In a realization of the metaphorical notion of the ladykiller, the poem builds a parallel between scoring on the battlefield and in the boudoir. When recalling Izmail-Bey's strategems to ensnare the *belles* of Petersburg, the fiancé laments, "He was a poison to our women!" The "poisoner" accumulated his female "victims," caught the blonde maiden in a "fatal net" and acted as "her killer."

The phallic connotations of Izmail-Bey's sword condense the parallel between his victories in the Caucasian killing field and the North's erotic combat zone. During the battle scenes of part three the jilted Russian fiancé wrathfully charges his enemy (III: 19–23). As usual, however, Izmail-Bey wins the cross-cultural duel: his trusty sword swiftly decapitates the hapless challenger (in a clear throwback to Ammalat-Bek). The head of Lermontov's tsarist soldier falls from his "shuddering body" like "ripe fruit from a young branch." Although a singularly inept figure of speech for beheading a horseman, the severing of pendulous fruit from a branch evokes another form of mutilation – castration. As Freud cautioned, "sometimes a cigar is just a cigar," but the phallic import of Izmail-Bey's blade can be substantiated by other nineteenth-century Russian material. For example, in M. Liventsov's piece of pulp "Memoirs of a Lady Held Prisoner by Mountain Tribesmen" the captors strip the Russian heroine and her maid to their underwear and sell them at a local slave market.[17] As he ogles them during the bidding, the handsome tribesman who purchases them keeps convulsively squeezing the handle of the dagger on his belt. More pertinent to "Izmail-Bey," however, is the phallic symbolism of blades in other verse by Lermontov, including the trope of the knife in the seduction scene of "The Demon."[18] Last but not least, we may recall how the poet provoked his fatal duel with N. S. Martynov by making him a laughing stock at Piatigorsk. According to numerous memoirs, the bantering which most infuriated Martynov concerned the tribal dagger he was fond of wearing.[19]

Saddled with Lermontov's appellations such as "*l'homme du gros poignard*," Martynov found the apparently *risqué* jokes most intolerable in the presence of women.

BELINSKY AS THE DISCONCERTED READER

In the final years of Lermontov's life, history began assembling for "Izmail-Bey" an unsurpassable readership for an *enfant terrible* – the Russian contemporaries of the Caucasian imam martially ascendant and newly married to a converted Armenian. Under Shamil's leadership in the latter half of the 1830s, the Murid resistance movement assumed daunting proportions in the eyes of high-ranking tsarist military men. General Evgeny Golovin called the imam the "most savage and dangerous" enemy Russia had ever faced in the Caucasus: "His power has acquired a religious–military character of the sort Mahomet used to shake three-quarters of the globe at the dawn of Islam."[20] The conditions of guerrilla warfare disadvantaged the Russians, provoked their frustration and scuttled their morale. Nicholas' displeasure with the army's performance led him to change the commander-in-chief several times during the decade and to visit the theater of war himself in 1837. The tsar ultimately concluded that a bigger army held the key to victory. In a dispatch of November 1843 he promised his generals "more troops than the Caucasus ever dreamed of," so that Russia might annihilate the tribes and "take the mountains" at last.[21] The Muslim "bandits" were certainly far from capitulating. That very summer, Shamil had attacked several Russian forts and allied towns in Dagestan, inflicting an unprecedented number of casualties. As recollected by Arnold Zisserman, the imam's military prowess shook the confidence of the tsarist high command and the rank and file alike.[22] It no longer seemed out of the question that Shamil might prevail. Indeed, according to Nikolai Dobroliubov's assessment published just after Shamil's surrender, the imam gave the "terrifying impression" of being "invincible" in 1843.[23]

But besides putting the fear of Allah into Russia with the jihad, Shamil scored his *coup* on the erotic front with Anna Ulykhanova. From a family of Armenian merchants in Mozdok, Ulykhanova was abducted by the Murid chieftain Akhverdi Mahoma in the early 1840s.[24] Approximately sixteen at the time, she was taken to the imam, roughly twenty-five years her senior. Despite her brothers' repeated efforts to ransom her, Ulykhanova stayed with Shamil and became his wife after converting to Islam. Subsequently called "Shuanet" and destined to be Shamil's favorite, she remained with him the rest of his life, to share his exile in Kaluga after his surrender.

The cultural and personal shock of Shuanet's behavior was registered in Prince Iliko Orbeliani's official military report about his captivity in Dargo, Shamil's home base in Dagestan. Held for ransom for several months in 1842, the Georgian officer recalled conversations with Shuanet in which he "reproached her for evidently having forgotten her religious faith, her family and country, and abandoning herself whole-heartedly to an enemy of Christianity."[25] The response he got was a profession of love. Forced to confront the fact of erotic charisma, Orbeliani clearly sought to fathom the mysterious workings of emotion which had made Ulykhanova forsake Christendom, kin and country. He also tried to comprehend the renowned "enemy of Christianity" as a lady's man. Amazed to discover that Shamil was not the "staid imam we usually picture," Orbeliani described the leader of the jihad playfully leaping about the room with Shuanet and showering her with endearments.

Although Lermontov would call Shamil a "rascal" during his military service in 1840, it is not clear to what extent Russian civilians were apprised of the reputation the imam held in the tsarist army.[26] The Russian press certainly was not publicizing the homeland's military setbacks. In one way or another, though, officers on leave at the Piatigorsk spas and in Russian cities presumably carried word of the army's defeats, frustrations and flagging morale. Similarly, Shamil's union with Ulykhanova did not immediately become a *cause célèbre* among Russian readers. As shown by Orbeliani's report, however, this development in the imam's personal life was noted with interest by the tsarist high command. Like Shamil's military successes, his marriage too probably gained a certain notoriety within the civilian Russian readership, especially in the frontier area.

Since the real, historical readers had so little to say about "Izmail-Bey" (or Shamil, for that matter), we cannot document how well they realized the ideal of the gender-divided audience envisioned in the poem.[27] But by turning now to Belinsky, we can plumb this silence about Lermontov's macho oriental hero. The sensitivity of the subject was quite amusingly disclosed in the critic's treatment of Elizaveta Gan's oriental tales. Gan's story "A Recollection of Zheleznovodsk" is a fantasy of the Caucasian tribesman as a sublime rapist. Narrated in the first-person, the fictional memoir opens with the heroine's celebration of horseback-riding alone amidst "wild nature" near Piatigorsk. Two solicitous Russian officers insist on accompanying her one day in order to protect her from Circassian "bandits." Tribesmen ambush the party, and the lady faints. When she regains consciousness to find herself bound and slung across a horse, she experiences a thrilled apprehension about her situation: "So my dream had come true: fate was casting me into that country which I had desired to see for such a long time – into the canyons, the refuge of the wild sons of nature. I was going to see the Caucasus in all its charm and terror."[28] Put to the service of feminine desire, the traditional rhetoric of sublimity expresses an ambivalent "dream" to venture deeper into dangerous territory. Wilderness begins functioning here as a metaphor for more intimate knowledge of the savage "sons of nature" themselves.

Caucasian "charm and terror" are personified in the tribesman who tries to rape the captive woman. The appearance of the sublime sexual aggressor is forestalled by preliminaries which stress the tsarist officers' unmanliness. Timid with their captors, the Russian men ungallantly permit the heroine to be ushered away, even though she begs for protection. After several days of solitary confinement, a sympathetic tribeswoman passes the heroine a note from the officers, outlining a plan for escape. But that very night a "dark figure" suddenly enters the captive woman's quarters and prevents her from joining her compatriots whom she hears galloping away to freedom. The intruder participates in stormy nature and the local nobility (although not a word about the tribe's class structure is uttered elsewhere): "Lightning flashed. I saw the prince, and his eyes gleamed more dreadfully than all the sky's lightning." This image of the elemental rapist–prince sustains the mixed feelings articulated in the heroine's first intimation of terrifying charm.

With its ruling spatial metaphor of dangerous *terra incognita* which Russian men forbid the heroine to enter alone, the story allowed Gan to flirt with erotic experience declared off-limits by her society – the same realm of oriental machismo conjured in "Izmail-Bey." However, unlike Lermontov with his Byronic relish for womanizing, Gan retreated at the crucial moment instead of crossing the boundary: the accosted captive seizes the prince's dagger and cuts her throat to preserve her virtue. "A Recollection of Zheleznovodsk" none the less leads readers away from the conclusion that sex with a tribesman would be worse than death. Instead of dying, the heroine awakens safe in her bedroom with the adventure revealed as a dream. But the author refuses to apologize for her tale or draw a cautionary moral from it. To the contrary, she betrays a phallic preoccupation as she brags about her heavily charged imagination, ignited and firing like an "overloaded cannon" (61). Convinced that readers with little "powder" in their hearts will dislike her story, she swears to "keep having such dreams every night and describe them in even greater detail." With this final jeer at polite society, Gan allotted the lustful tribesman a continuing place in her erotic fantasy life (but wrote, as usual, under her pseudonym Zeneida R–va). The dream's expression of the illicit desire to be ravished by a savage in all his "charm and terror" was thus fully sustained in the "prisoner's" waking hours.

In pertinent, interrelated responses to the literary Caucasus, Belinsky donned the uniform of one of Gan's tsarist soldiers, keen to chart the boundaries of proper erotic terrain for Russian ladies, and ready to warn *all* civilized folk to steer clear of the orient. Although he admired Gan as the most remarkable Russian-woman writer of the period, the critic curtly dismissed "A Recollection of Zheleznovodsk" as a silly imitation of Bestuzhev-Marlinsky.[29] Today's reader will no doubt concur. And yet Belinsky's response bespoke some nineteenth-century Russian masculine discomfort over a lustful Asian prince contrasted to unheroic tsarist officers. This becomes clear in reading Belinsky's warm appraisal of Gan's "Dzhelaleddin," the story of a love triangle between the eponymous Crimean Tatar prince, a fickle Russian seductress, and the Crimean woman Emina, passionately devoted to the hero. Belinsky disliked certain "strong echoes of the Marlinskian manner" in "Dzhelaleddin" but valued the heroine who loved her man "with all the ardor of oriental passion."[30] The critic focused on the denouement to make his point. Dzhelaleddin commits suicide after the "cold" foreigner abandons him, but Emina is there to drive away the ravens and tenderly beshroud his corpse. After the prince's burial, she goes insane, burrows into his grave and dies, her mouth chock-full of dirt. Touched rather than amused, Belinsky endorsed this incarnation of the oriental love slave and flowed with Gan's drift about the model's pertinence to Russian women: "More than a man," wrote the critic, "a woman is created by nature for love," even though she should not be consigned to the "exclusive service of love," as in Asia's harems. Considered together, Belinsky's responses to Gan's two oriental tales suggest that Russian masculine pride assumed a big role in his readings. The critic found Emina a satisfying incarnation of elemental femininity, the orient at its best. On the other hand, "A Recollection of Zheleznovodsk" dealt a blow to the national male ego by accrediting the Russian horsewoman's dream of ravishment by a sublime tribesman, pitted against pesky, lily-livered tsarist officers.

As illustrated in the article on Gan, Belinsky's commentaries on the literary Caucasus regularly marshaled a discourse of oriental alterity. A preeminent Westernizer, he equated Asia with barbarism and consistently sought inspiration in

Europe for Russian reform.[31] The outlook made him sanguine about the tsarist conquest of the Caucasus. His major article on *A Hero of Our Time*, for example, condoned the victimization of Bela, the Circassian tribeswoman whose abduction by the Russian aristocrat, Pechorin, eventually causes her death. In Belinsky's view, poor Bela had suffered but was doomed from the outset: this "semi-savage daughter of wild canyons" wanted only love, whereas the Europeanized Pechorin had more complicated intellectual and cultural needs.[32]

Belinsky took a different Eurocentric tack in an article on Polezhaev in 1842. Without noticing how he might have applied the admonition to Pechorin (or perhaps subconsciously *inspired* by him), the critic now warned Russians to stay out of Asia for their own moral well-being. The discussion revealed a conception of the orient as the global seat of sexual depravity. Although Belinsky praised Polezhaev in many respects, he faulted his stress on eros, particularly in the long poem "The Harem." Also known as "The Renegade," this work features a Russian hero eager to exchange his Christian cross for the Koran in order to romp in a seraglio with gorgeous concubines. With an endless horizon of oriental lust in mind, Belinsky assumed that the censor's many cuts had removed unspeakable indecencies (although today we know the official target was blasphemy rather than sex).[33] In culminating his argument, the critic blamed the Caucasus for depraving Polezhaev. Conscripted and sent to the territory at a tender age "when Europe had but momentarily stirred in his soul," the young poet was unable to cope with Asia. The wicked id of the Caucasus had dug its clutches into a Russian and set him on a path which invariably leads to the "death of soul and body, shame and destruction during one's lifetime and beyond the grave."[34] This conclusion evoked not only spiritual corruption but a sexual athlete's physical deterioration, the threat of venereal disease and reputations ruined forever. A champion of social justice now enthroned as the founding father of the nineteenth-century Russian intelligentsia, Belinsky lived a brief life of political passions. While giving him all due respect on that score, however, one senses that his orient was a tortured projection of everything he felt he had missed in the erotic life.[35]

Belinsky's various responses to the literary Caucasus declared him the perfectly vulnerable masculine reader envisioned in "Izmail-Bey." He could not be accused of the social snobbery of Lermontov's targeted "crowd," but he had their political convictions about "European" superiority to the tribes. Of equal importance, Belinsky's related notion of Asia as the id of the world and his readiness to delineate the Russian woman's proper sentimental territory left him hypersensitive to the erotic component of Lermontov's anti-imperialist performance. The critic had constructed "his" Lermontov in reading *A Hero of Our Time* and was apparently too disconcerted for words by the *enfant terrible* who jeered in "Izmail-Bey," "I *am* the savage, invincible in battle and lethal to 'your' women!"

The political convictions and sexual anxieties inferable from Belinsky's evasion of "Izmail-Bey" can be more sharply captured by comparing Friedrich Bodenstedt's enthusiastic appraisal of the poem. A German writer brought to Russia in the early 1840s as a tutor in the Golitsyn family, Bodenstedt ranked "Izmail-Bey" above Lermontov's "Mtsyri" ("novice" in Georgian), a late Caucasian tale in verse now solidly established in curricular and critical canons. As seen in *Die Völker des Kaukasus und ihre Freiheitskämpfe gegen die Russen*, Bodenstedt was one of Europe's main advocates of the tribesmen. He romanticized them as intrepid fighters for freedom and ecstatically pronounced their death songs Homeric.[36] It is perhaps not by chance that Bodenstedt also considered Russia's upper classes ravaged by pederasty.[37] Though he did not openly speculate about the sexual behavior of Shamil and his warriors, Bodenstedt apparently regarded them as the Caucasian war's "real" men in every respect.

This lonely German voice from the past implies much about the relative neglect "Izmail-Bey" suffered in Russian commentary of its era. The tale's publication in 1843 invested Lermontov's hero with the awesomeness of Shamil, the leader of the jihad with an Armenian apostate among his wives.

Unforeseeable by the poet, the convergence was revealed only posthumously, when the imam's martial power reached a peak. As long as Shamil posed a real military threat, Izmail-Bey's formidable performance in combat seems to have hit too close to home for the Russian censor to tolerate. Furthermore, the prominence of sexual conquest in "Izmail-Bey" made the tribal hero a shadow of Shamil as a real-life Dagestani Othello who had outdone Ammalat-Bek by finding an Armenian Desdemona. In this context Russian men must have preferred to forget Izmail-Bey and quite likely pressured curious women of Gan's ilk to keep illicit daydreams about the tribesman's erotic secret to themselves.

THE TABOO ABOLISHED

But if history momentarily established a taboo of Izmail-Bey as the specter of Shamil, the course of events ultimately brought Lermontov's poem into the cultural mainstream. While not fully available to the readership during Shamil's phase of stunning military victories in the early 1840s, the battle scenes of "Izmail-Bey" were ranked among the "highest glories" of Lermontov's verse by a Russian critic four decades later.[38] Of greater import, in the mid-1850s, when Shamil's defeat was clearly just a matter of time, Russian readers began to vent their repressed but evidently burning curiosity about the Caucasian tribal way with women. In dealing with this subject, Russian women sounded very different from Russian men.

The colloquy between a masculine and feminine viewpoint started in Evgeny Verderevsky's *Shamil's Prisoners* (1856), one of the most avidly read books in Russia at the time. Based on interviews, this work recounted the experiences of the Georgian princesses Chavchavadze and Orbeliani who spent over eight months of 1854 to 1855 as captives in Shamil's household along with some of their children and a French governess. Verderevsky's preface promised "bloody horrors" to equal the worst deeds of James Fenimore Cooper's Indians.[39] In fact, however, no bloodshed nor molestations were forthcoming (although an infant daughter fell from Orbeliani's arms and was trampled by horses during the flight from Georgia). Once installed at Dargo, the princesses expressed nothing but respect for Shamil as a humane jailer and devoted father (who had abducted them, after all, to exchange for his son spirited off to Russia as a boy, some twelve years earlier). Shamil's qualities as an adored husband also featured prominently in the princesses' account. They remembered (Russian-speaking) Shuanet as a consoling presence during their captivity and relayed her love for Shamil in passages of direct discourse. But whose words were these really? The verbatim ascription is dubious given the passage of time (and the absence of note-taking at Dargo). However, Shuanet's Shamil evidently made an impression on the Georgian princesses. As quoted by Verderevsky, the women thus captured the imam's allure as a Dagestani Othello, while the book's preface recoiled from him as the perpetrator of "bloody horrors."

Later expressions of Russian interest in the tribesman's erotic life bear complementary testimony to the gender division in the envisioned audience of "Izmail-Bey." Attitudes similar to those of the Georgian princesses were transmitted in memoirs by M. Chichagova, the wife of one of Shamil's Russian overseers in Kaluga. Chichagova exuded fond memories of Shamil and professed great friendship with Shuanet. Among her recollections of heart-to-heart talks with the "Armenian apostate," Chichagova shed a tender glow on bonds of sentiment between the renowned polygamist and his patently favorite wife.[40] On the other side of the gender gap, a Russian veteran of the Caucasian war ruminated about Shamil's private life strictly in terms of virile domination: Shuanet's "man and master" from the first, the imam had never lost his capacity "to enchain the beauty's heart."[41] Even more tellingly, another Russian veteran opined that the tribal warriors' mind-boggling capacity to fight the tsarist state for more than thirty years resided somehow in their "unlimited power over woman."[42] This haunting suspicion totally exposed the Europeanized Russian man's soft spot targeted in "Izmail-Bey": was the oriental's daunting military power not matched by enslaving virility in the erotic life?

The historical material suggests that the ideal, gender-divided readership of "Izmail-Bey" finally got in touch with itself. When the war was over, Russian men could speak their formerly anxious envy of the oriental way with women. On the other side of the division, Russian women could more freely indulge their curiosity about "abandoning oneself wholeheartedly" to a dashing tribesman. Lermontov had not allowed any of Izmail-Bey's erotic conquests to utter a single word. However, in constructing a Circassian incarnation of oriental machismo in its martial and sexual dimensions, the poem left open a space where Russian women could slip into sentimental reveries, while their male compatriots had nightmares about being outmanned in love and war.

CHAPTER 9

Little orientalizers

Looming in a swirl of fog,
Shah-dakh stands in steely armor,
Cast from granite through a wonder
Worked by Allah in his forge.
Dmitri Minaev

The varied disruptions of imperialist ideology in "The Prisoner of the Caucasus," "Ammalat-Bek" and "Izmail-Bey" can be appreciated all the more through contrast with largely obscure Russian littérateurs who unreservedly underwrote war against the tribes. Concentrated in the 1830s, these little orientalizers discursively coincided with Pushkin, Bestuzhev-Marlinsky and Lermontov in many respects (cross-cultural encounters, the rhetoric of dread and glory, the preoccupation with wild liberty, violence and eros). But this body of second-rate and purely hack literature entertained no doubts about boundaries between Russia and Asia. Intent upon demonstrating the Caucasus' savage alterity, the little orientalizers administered *une thérapeutique du Différent*: by reducing the tribesman to barbarism and depravity, they sought to assert what Russians were *not* in order to lend the conquest "European" legitimacy.[1] The romantics' noble primitives with their Homeric machismo, emotional authenticity, ritual hospitality and native songs were thus expelled by the Asian wild man conceived as a repellent animal. In the meantime, though, the Caucasian tribeswoman held her ground as an erotic ideal.

Literary apologetics for imperialism in this period were surely encouraged by the steady rise of the Murid resistance movement under the three imams, Gazi-Muhammed,

156

Hamzat-Beg and Shamil. Like the famous Bestuzhev-Marlinsky, lesser Russian writers in uniform produced literature in this context of intensifying warfare. Alexander Polezhaev and Pyotr Kamensky, for example, were campaigners who conveyed ill will toward the enemy. The ferocity of the fight, the degeneracy of the Muslim warriors and the justness of Russia's cause became standbys in this literature. A lack of biographical information makes it impossible to say if certain authors served in the army. But whether on the basis of personal experience or merely hearsay about the war, the little orientalizers transmitted hostility toward the backward "bandits" who refused to bow to the mighty Russian state.

During the 1830s the conquest also acquired a new economic ambience conducive to denigration of the tribesman as a bloodthirsty, lustful animal. As the next chapter will detail, the territory's economic potential as a Russian colony gained wide public recognition in this decade. Literature rarely broached the subject directly. Writers trafficked instead in the tribal warrior's wickedness, a Russian's risk of falling captive and the possibility of romance with a gorgeous "daughter of Mohammed."[2] But if only covert, a growing awareness of the war's economic implications very likely helped generate the literature's rigid dichotomy between vicious Asians and enlightened Russians: more hideous "savagery" was projected onto the wild mountain men, and fiercer commitments to "civilization" were made as economic stakes of the Caucasian conquest were increasingly advertised in Russia.

OUR ALGERIA

Pyotr Kamensky was one of the era's most popular apologists for escalating warfare. The author of potboilers such as *Dead Men's Heads, or Russians in Chechnia*, Kamensky specialized in sensational tales of oriental sex and violence, graced with footnotes on Islamic culture and the politics of imperial expansion. He won a considerable following in Russia and was even dubbed "our Cervantes" by Andrei Kraevsky, the founder of the well-known *National Annals* (*Otechestvennye zapiski*, 1839–84).[3] Aesthetically alarmed by Kamensky's ascendence, Belinsky tried to set indiscriminant readers straight by belittling him as a hapless imitator of Bestuzhev-Marlinsky.

Kamensky's Caucasian œuvre is definitively illustrated in the harem drama, "Kelish-Bey."[4] Set in Muslim Abkhazia in the 1770s, the tale recounts the tensions of an erotic triangle composed of the old eponymous hero, his Georgian concubine Fatma, and her secret lover Aslan, Kelish's son. In an echo of Bestuzhev-Marlinsky, Kamensky uses a rhetoric of heat to represent the illicit passion of Fatma and Aslan. Likewise, elemental nature rages through "Kelish-Bey," to reach a frenzied pitch in the denouement when Aslan kills his father by stabbing him and then shooting him for good measure ("Oh tribesman, capable of crimes which would make cannibals shudder!" cries the author). Mistakenly convinced that Aslan has forsaken her, Fatma commits suicide by leaping into the Black Sea. As an accompaniment to the murder and suicide, fiery streaks of lightning flash in the sky, a hurricane shakes the forests, and a blizzard roars in the mountains.

Immediately after the tumultuous denouement Kamensky enters to sanction Russian conquest of the Caucasus. In an abrupt shift from the eighteenth century to the present, he introduces the calm, purposeful voices of tsarist military men. The very precision of the date ("August 31, 1831") contributes to a semblance of order, stability and control, as opposed to old Abkhazia's chaos and depravity. With no awareness of the oriental tale just told, the soldiers simply function as conduits for an authorial message: Russia must persevere in the effort to tame the Caucasus by displacing the "dagger and sword" with the "cultivator's plow and sickle," the manufacturer's tools, the tradesman's scales and money. Through these metonymic symbols of a future era of agriculture, industrial development and commerce, "Kelish-Bey" signals the economic objectives inextricably bound to the avowed moral and religious objectives of the Caucasian war.

In a quintessential expression of imperialism's treasured myth of regenerative violence, Kamensky's conclusion calls for mass extermination of the tribes as a measure necessary for eradicating "savagery" from the globe. "Kelish-Bey" builds an analogy between the Caucasus and Algeria where the colonial ventures of the French led to conflict with the Bedouins under the leadership of Abd al-Qadir in the 1830s. In the words of one of Kamensky's officers, the French "travel a hard road, shedding blood every step of the way, but they keep moving forward and do not abandon their effort to conquer the Algerian and transform him." Kamensky's mouthpieces then argue that the Caucasus' Muslim regions have an unusually "wild soil of savagery" because they never attained the level of ancient Arabic civilization in Algeria. "Kelish-Bey" thus implies that Russia must pursue its bloody fight even more relentlessly than the French in Algeria. A means of transfiguring military aggression into *une mission civilisatrice*, the Algerian analogy popularized by Kamensky was taking shape around this time in official reports of the tsarist Minister of War, Alexander Chernyshev.[5] Such views of the Caucasus as another Algeria would become commonplace in Russia, as well as France.[6]

Kamensky's justification of war in the name of civilization gave popular literary expression to the era's upsurge of jingoism. In 1829 in a letter to General Ivan Paskevich, Nicholas I summarized Russia's possible courses of action toward the tribesmen as "pacification or extermination," two terms which ominously coalesced.[7] The tsar's formulation captured in a nutshell a more widely circulating belief that the backward Caucasian natives understood nothing but force and could not be civilized through peaceable means such as the development of trading companies or educational efforts (captured in literature by Verkhovsky's benevolent plan to enlighten Ammalat-Bek). Jingoism was aired freely in "A Trip to Georgia," for example. A diatribe against pacific approaches, this unsigned article by a Russian functionary in Tiflis advocated crushing the Muslim tribesmen in "bloody battle" as swiftly as possible.[8] Convinced that "Asians" interpret reconciliatory gestures as signs of cowardice, the author singled out Chechens for special abuse: in his words, the tribesman was a "wild animal" with "only the outward form of a human being," a "vile, fearful enemy" with "all the cruelty of a bloodthirsty beast." An open release of "contempt and loathing" for the tribal enemies, "A Trip to Georgia" offended Bestuzhev-Marlinsky's brother, Pavel, and provoked him to decry its crude formulations in a piece published in *Son of the Fatherland*.[9]

However, protestations of belief in noble Caucasian savages became all but non-existent in Russian periodicals of the era. In an article of 1837 M. Vedeniktov [*sic*] retained hope in the possibility of peacefully civilizing the Muslim tribes (even as he degraded them as "wild animals" and "children").[10] But the tide of "contempt and loathing" was running high. Fully in harmony with "A Trip to Georgia," Ya. Saburov's *récit de voyage* "The Caucasus" (1835) asserted that Russia would surely have to exterminate the tribes since they were too hopelessly immersed in barbarism to be transformed through enlightenment.[11] Members of the Russian élite in Tiflis continued to speak of the war in similar terms twelve years later: upon meeting an American visitor, they assured him that the Muslim tribesmen were just like "your Indians" and could be "quieted" only through "extermination, owing to their natural energy of character."[12]

POETRY ABOUT WAR

The conduct of war in the Caucasus found its major singer in Alexander Polezhaev, a poet of some enduring reputation who heartily served his era's Muse of lurid orientalia. Thanks largely to his treatment of the hard lot of the common soldier, Polezhaev figures among the "realists" in Soviet Russian criticism.[13] However, this label disregards the large arsenal of rhetorical devices which heighten his depiction of campaigns to quell the jihad. Polezhaev's characteristic technique can be best sampled in "Erpeli," the more artistically ambitious of his two long poems of battle. Through symbolism contained in several of its eight sections, "Erpeli" renders Russia's fight against Gazi-Muhammed as a clash between light and darkness. This typically imperialist symbolism sprang very readily to mind in Russia in an era when "enlightenment" was a common synonym for the civilizing mission, encoded by writers through such tropes as a tsarist "lamp" piercing a "curtain of ignorance."[14] But as we shall see, Polezhaev's dichotomy of Orthodox light and infidel darkness had much deeper roots in Russian culture. It figured already in the great medieval epic *The Lay of Igor's Campaign*. Of greater historical immediacy, "Erpeli" replicated the symbolic dynamics of Lomonosov's famous ode on the tsarist seizure of the Turkish fortress Khotin in Moldavia (1739).[15]

Polezhaev's ruling metaphor of war against Gazi-Muhammed is the "light of day in struggle against a shroud of fog."[16] On one side of the epic battle stands "Holy Russia" with a resplendent army of "knights" (the *bogatyri* of national legend). The "god of golden light" – the sun – flashes on the soldiers' weapons and Christian crosses. Dawn arrives momentously for the tsarist troops, and brilliant moonlight illuminates their military camp stretched out like a "white giant" at night. In opposition to bright Orthodox Russia, the Muslim forces are rendered as godless barbarians lost in the dark of religious obfuscation. Polezhaev calls the tribesmen the collective "new Satan," a "throng of exiled demons," and an army of "devils and thieves" led by Gazi-Muhammed and "Magogs" (local feudal lords) in the service of "invisible Allah." These figures of exclusion from Christendom are compounded by motifs of Muslims as "children of darkness" akin to night, fog, rain and murk. Their mountain habitat is a gloomy "mythological kingdom of subterranean shades and spirits," whereas the Russian sons of light are attracted solely to the Caucasus' sunny, pastoral world of "Elysian valleys." Animal imagery further heightens the clash between light and dark (exactly as in Lomonosov's ode on Khotin): Polezhaev's Muslims are flocks of "ferocious wolves," while Holy Russia's soldiers fight as "eagles" for the "house of Romanov."

In a jingoistic extension of cultural monologism, "Erpeli" places a violent military agenda in Gazi-Muhammed's mouth. As an illustration of "senseless prophesizing," the imam vows to send Russia "back across the Don." Although presented as an insane military objective, this threat makes a lot of sense poetically by echoing a well-known motif of *The Lay of Igor's Campaign*, where the Don lies deep in the territory of the enemy, the Polovtsians. Polezhaev's refrain about the Don thus enhances the Caucasian campaign with the legendary splendor of Christian Kiev's skirmishes with nomadic pagan tribes of the southern steppes. In additional passages of direct discourse Gazi-Muhammed announces his plan to raze Russian fortresses, attack Cossack *stanitsy* (border settlements) and wreak the worst vengeance upon the Christians' "children, wives and maidens." The threat against women and children was particularly inflammatory in wartime. But the violent exhortation which Polezhaev put in Gazi-Muhammed's mouth more generally invited readers to view the Caucasian war as defensive Russian action against the brutal jihad.

Several short poems of the era also contrived voices for tribal enemies. Like "Erpeli" itself, these minor exercises in cross-cultural ventriloquism had a certain precedent in Griboedov's "Predators at the Chegem" (a title possibly imposed by Bulgarin for publication in the *Northern Bee* in 1826).[17] Also known as "Sharing the Booty," this verse is written as a tribal cry of victory and probably was inspired by a recent devastating attack by a force of Kabardinians and Circassians against a Cossack *stanitsa*. Although exultant crowing predominates, Griboedov's "native" voice asks Russia why it makes war against the Caucasus. This stance of the provoked victim cast the readership's country as the *originator* of a cruel conflict (an unsettling insinuation glossed over in Bulgarin's jingoistic commentary on the poem).

Unlike Griboedov's song of successful pillage against bellicose Russia, later ventriloquistic verse invented strictly wicked "native" speakers, like Polezhaev's Gazi-Muhammed. The central protagonist of Liukan Yakubovich's "The Circassian" (1838) rallies local youths to join a raid against the Russians in order to enjoy "a little shooting and hacking."[18] After the speaker is killed, his heartless comrades are plunged in interior monologues about competition for possession of his weapons, horse and wife. In Prince Dmitri Kropotkin's "Lezgin Song" (1837) a tribeswoman bids farewell to a departing local warrior and begs him to bring her back a Russian's head.[19] M. Venediktov did yet another variation on the politically potent technique of direct discourse in "Song of the Trans-Kuban Tribesmen" (1835).[20] Written as a prayer asking Allah for assistance against the campaigns of General Zass, this poem announces a Caucasian cutthroat's intention to avenge tsarist military victories in his native realm. In a vicious circle Venediktov's incensed Muslim serves as a rationale for Russia's continuing bloody warfare.

THE MOUNTAINS OF ALLAH

Besides singing the heroism of Holy Russia's war, little orientalizers also used landscape to constitute the Muslim tribesman as a loathsome, bellicose beast. This entailed suppression of the 1820s' theme of the Caucasus as a Parnassian site of spiritual uplift for the civilized traveler. Pushkin's *Journey to Arzrum* still called the untamed terrritory a "sanctuary" of pristine nature. But literature governed by *la thérapeutique du Différent* completely disavowed such notions of an attractive wild refuge and turned Russia's Alps into the hostile range of Allah.

This shift in imaginative geography possibly had origins in "View of the Mountains from the Kozlov Steppes," one of Adam Mickiewicz's *Crimean Sonnets* first translated into Russian in the 1820s. In Mickiewicz's dialogue between the pilgrim and the mirza, the Crimean range emerged as Allah's creation where the faithful move into exalting proximity to Him. A line of creative evolution seems to have passed from Mickiewicz's poem to Lermontov's "Hastening northward from afar," a lyric composed when the poet was returning to Russia from his first exile in the Caucasus in 1837.[21] Lermontov personified Kazbek as a white-turbaned "sentry of the Orient," but he also described the mountain as "Allah's eternal throne." As in Mickiewicz's sonnet, Lermontov's Islamized peak evoked a spiritual aspiration to make contact with the starry heavens.

Unlike Lermontov's perception of powerful, soaring beauty in Kazbek, lesser Russian versifiers of the era infused antagonism into orientalized mountains. Dmitri Oznobishin's "Caucasian Morning" conjures a sensuous valley menaced by looming peaks.[22] Most likely inspired by Georgia, the site is characterized initially by rustling foliage, roses, a pearly river, gentle animals and low-lying mountains crowned by a "golden diadem" of sun. Erotic promise imbues the scene, as the poet feminizes a blossom and a fruit tree, desirous of loving attention from the masculinized sun and breeze. The last third of the poem then shifts abruptly from the garden to rugged mountains perceived as bastions of Islamic power. The green forest lands of Mashuk become a "shah's emerald saddle-cloth." Elbrus' two peaks (only one of which is snow-capped) appear as a "padishah's tent" and the "lord of a hivernal land" in a "silver turban," with his "hips" curved across the clouds "like a Circassian saber." Finally, Besh-Tau and Piatigorsk's four other peaks are symbolized as creatures from Persian demonology, "terrible Divi on sentry duty."[23] Laden with emblems of the Islamic East, the mountains of "Caucasian Morning" radiate hostility to Christendom and the terrestrial paradise summoned in the first two-thirds of the poem.

While Oznobishin used varied tropes of orientalization (including the mountain as a turbaned warrior), anthropomorphism totally dominated Dmitri Minaev's "Reproach against the Caucasus," the verse which provides the epigraph of the present chapter. As befitted the widespread allegorical notion of Islamic "darkness," Minaev imagined the Caucasian range at night. In nocturnal gloom Mt. Shah-dakh towers as a giant in chain mail, a spiked helmet and granite armor forged by Allah. After establishing this bellicose monster as a personification of the Muslim tribes, Minaev censured the Caucasus as a "criminal predator" guilty of murdering a "divine nightingale," a "bard" who sang the territory's praises to "us" in the North. Written too early to refer to

Lermontov, the poem no doubt alluded to Bestuzhev-Marlinsky. The popular author of "Ammalat-Bek" had mentioned Azerbaijan's Shah-dakh in a travelogue and was remembered with reverence by other Russian poetasters in the late 1830s, relatively soon after news of his death in battle had spread.[24] A self-styled advocate of romantic Russian sensibility, Minaev "reproached" the Islamized Caucasus for viciously executing the Koran's death sentence against infidels.

By making the orientalized territory the enemy of poetry, Minaev challenged the old literary traditions about the Caucasus as Parnassus and the home of native song. This aspect of the work interacted with contemporaneous Russian debate about the poetry of primitive cultures. During the era of the jihad an epic conception of the Caucasian tribes continued to find an important spokesman in Bestuzhev-Marlinsky, as indicated by the death songs in "Ammalat-Bek." As articulated at length in his essay on Polevoy's *The Oath on the Tomb of the Lord*, Bestuzhev-Marlinsky subscribed to a romantic belief in the primitive's natural gift for poetry, as manifested in cases so diverse as the Caucasian tribes, the ancient Arabs and Scandinavians of the fjord country.[25] Baron Ekshtein's article "Ancient Poetry of the Arabs prior to Muhammed" (1831) had likewise drawn a bardic affiliation between fjords and desert sands.[26] But as implied in Ekshtein's title, the heyday of primitive Arab song was situated in the distant past, before the advent of Islam. Left largely implicit in this discussion, an indictment of Islam moved into the foreground in Senkovsky's "Poetry of the Desert," published in the *Library for Reading* in 1835.[27] A respected orientalist of the time, Senkovsky praised the Bedouins' talent for excellent verse but maintained that Islam had sent artistic activity into sharp decline throughout the Arab world: the teachings of "Mahomet" were utterly inimical to poetry, he argued, because they squelched "freedom of imagination" and compelled the faithful to concentrate their energies on war against the infidel.

Fraught with implications about the Caucasian tribesmen, the recriminations against Islam in Senkovsky's "Poetry of the Desert" showed the editorial bias which favored Minaev's "reproach" for the *Library for Reading*. When Senkovsky pitted "Mahomet" against artistic creativity, he implicitly withdrew the Caucasian warrior from the Homeric–Ossianic brotherhood promoted in Russian literature in the 1820s, in "Ammalat-Bek" and various theoretical discussions of primitive bards. If the consolidation of Islam spelled decline for Arab poetry, so too might Muridism be accused of annulling the Caucasian mountaineers' capacity for song. Minaev's "reproach" advanced just such a proposition in literary form by projecting the southern territory as a monstrous poetry-killer outfitted in Allah's armor and unconditionally inimical to Russians.

ROMANCING THE WILD WOMAN

While reviling the tribesmen in assorted ways, little orientalizers fabricated sensational stories of love between the Caucasus' Muslim women and Russian men. Not overtly concerned with empire-building, these tales underwrote tsarist conquest by implying that chivalrous, valiant Russians were needed to rescue the women from their homeland's barbarism. A sharp division by gender thus split the literary population of savages. On the one side stood irredeemable brutes driven by fanaticism, lust and greed for profits of the slave trade. On the other side were captivating tribeswomen readily romanced by Russians and often murdered by kinsmen for loving giaours. A testimony to a persistent obsession with the oriental love slave, these Caucasian heroines belonged to the period's larger literary gallery of geographically diverse Asian enchantresses (odalisques, harem queens, Arabs and the Turkish beauty in Bestuzhev-Marlinsky's popular story "The Red Veil").[28]

The general syndrome of vilifying the tribesmen while idealizing their sisters was first manifested in Alexander Shidlovsky's extensively annotated poem "The Grebensk Cossack" (1831).[29] The Lezgin heroine Zara exemplifies a standard fantasy of "savage" sex. As this "mountain maid" sits alone in the wilderness, a handsome Cossack comes riding by, and they make love without exchanging a word. Shortly after this fiery encounter, they marry. A fierce exponent of liberty, Zara sets free a tribesman whom her husband has taken captive. But the prisoner turns out to be her brother, who kills her for marrying a giaour and depriving the family of the money she would have fetched from an Ottoman slave trader. Like Pushkin's prototypal "mountain maid," Shidlovsky's erotically vibrant, nurturing tribeswoman is annihilated. However, by contrast to the Circassian in "The Prisoner of the Caucasus," Zara dies by the hand of her own Muslim kin. A man of the remote past not yet regularized as a border guard, Zara's husband is a freebooter engaged primarily in hunting and fighting. But if quasi-savage himself, Shidlovsky's Grebensk Cossack hero assumes a relatively more civilized stature *vis-à-vis* the vicious Muslim men of the tale. The woman has chosen the giaour as her mate, and he avenges his wife's death by killing her brother and incurring a mortal wound himself in the process.

The Cossack would reappear as an Orthodox soldier in Nikolai Gnedich's "A True Story of the Caucasus," a poem set in the reader's own period of the jihad.[30] "Blinded by passion," the love-struck hero has proposed marriage to the tribeswoman Fati and even promised to convert to the "law of Mahomet." But he temporizes, unable to renounce Christianity. Fati's brother finally comes to the Russian camp and tosses his "dishonored" sister's head at the Cossack's feet. The stunned hero falls to his knees and kisses his fiancée's head. When his comrades come looking for him the next morning, he apparently has vanished into the wilderness, perhaps to take revenge against the savage. In this case the Orthodox man contributes to the demise of the beautiful oriental because he cannnot live up to his promise to convert to Islam. The tribeswoman is thus sacrificed to her lover's act of cultural heroism: by holding fast to the religion so central to his national identity, the Cossack asserts belief in Christianity's superiority to the competing creed.

Another member of this valiant breed appeared in P. Markov's poem "Zlomilla and Dobronrava – Two Mountain Maids, or Meeting a Cossack" (1834).[31] The tale is narrated by the Cossack hero. In the wilderness he comes upon a "bestial Chechen" with his sword ready to strike Zlomilla, a half-naked Circassian beauty crouched at his feet. The Cossack immediately dispatches the aggressor with his rifle and begins kissing the semi-conscious woman ("That maid was my reward!"). However, even though Zlomilla deliriously strips off all her clothes, the hero is too gallant to take further advantage of her. She explains that her aggressor was her lover, who murdered her parents when she refused to run away with him. Zlomilla develops affection for the kindly Cossack, but loyalty to her own people eventually prevails. She betrays him, he is taken captive and marked for execution. Overcome by guilt, the tribeswoman then drowns herself.

"Zlomilla" is a coinage suggesting "mean but nice," and it epitomizes the heroine's flawed but basically positive character in interaction with the outsider. Although Zlomilla behaves nastily to the Cossack, she repents by committing suicide. Markov accordingly declares the oriental beauty's capacity to rise above the viciousness of her native realm and opt for Christian values. Moreover, readers know from the outset that the Cossack narrator lived to tell his tale. Exactly how that happened remained untold because the second part of "Zlomilla and Dobronrava" never appeared. The title, though, promised to introduce another "mountain maid," Dobronrava, a name connoting "good ways." One can only speculate about the turn the plot was to take. Dobronrava surely freed the captive. But did she flee with the Cossack, or was she destined to join literature's ranks of Caucasian women who die for loving tsarist military men?

The plot of cross-cultural romance would reach an apogee in N. Zriakhov's *The Russians' Battle with the Kabardinians, or the Beautiful Mohammedan Dying on the Grave of Her Husband.* Initially published as a chapbook in 1843, the work was reissued subsequently many times, sometimes in anonymous versions.[32] The wounded Cossack hero Andrei is taken prisoner by a Kabardinian prince and held for ransom. The prince's daughter Selima nurses Andrei back to health, and during the convalescence he rapidly persuades her that Orthodox Russia is superior in every way to Muslim tribal culture. Selima renounces her homeland, flees to join Andrei after he is released, and marries him. The happily wedded couple settles in the spa country where a baby is born. But the Russian husband never recovers from his old wounds (or else, in a variant version, is killed by an avenging Muslim tribesman). The bereft Selima then dies of grief in the cemetery. Although both parents expire, their offspring endures as a potent incarnation of the myth of empire-building as a realization of elective emotional affinities.[33] Destined to become one of Russia's best known pieces of literature about the conquest, this tale of cross-cultural marriage would run into nine editions by 1850, to reach the phenomenal circulation of 50,000 copies.[34]

Cossacks were especially effective carriers of these stories' message that tribeswomen were a good, assimilable population for the Russian empire, even if their male relatives deserved extermination. As Tolstoy's *The Cossacks* would illustrate definitively, the technically Orthodox but completely non-Europeanized Cossack communities along the Terek comprised a fascinating cultural buffer zone for the westernized Russian élite.[35] The Grebensk Cossacks' rebellious history and cultural distinctiveness were indicated in some footnotes to Shidlovsky's poem. But for the most part, the literary Caucasus prior to Tolstoy underplayed these frontiersmen's differences from Russia. Instead of focusing on former days of freebooting, writers emphasized the Cossacks' present service as border guards and tsarist soldiers (as seen in Pushkin's "The Prisoner of the Caucasus," Nechaev's "Recollections," much of Shidlovsky's commentary to "The Grebensk Cossack," Lermontov's "Izmail-Bey" and the cross-cultural love stories of Gnedich, Markov and Zriakhov). Loaded with a history of assimilation into Christian tsardom, the gallant Cossack romancer of the Muslim tribeswoman readily functioned as a bridge between occidentalized Russia and the wild but civilizable Caucasus.

A related Russian poem of cross-cultural erotic alliance dispensed with the Cossack but retained the symbolic notion of "marrying" the beauty of the wilderness (symbolized by wild women) with the hardy masculine force of Russian civilization. Written partly in dramatic form, V. Zotov's "The Last of the Kheaks" (1842) has no Russian among the dramatis personae.[36] However, the author intrudes to assume the masculine civilizer's role. A slave to the mountain chieftain Eli-Egrukh, Zotov's Kheak tribesman falls in love with his master's fiancée after saving her from drowning and lasciviously administering mouth-to-mouth resuscitation. To go along with the geographical vagueness and scarcity of names, no steady plot-construction or delineation of character occurs in the tale. Prior to the violent denouement, the Kheak hardly sees the woman again. However, he seizes upon her as a tool of revenge when his fugitive father is tracked down in his mountain hide-out and killed by a mob loyal to Eli-Egrukh. Shortly after the old man's death, the Kheak abducts Eli-Egrukh's fiancée from her bed, drags her to a cave in the cliffs and gloats as she lies before him naked to the waist. Despite her assumption that she is going to be raped, the woman boldly warns the Kheak that the chieftain will punish him. But the abductor explains that revenge, rather than lust, is motivating him. At the end of the poem he knifes the woman and decapitates her, before Eli-Egrukh's rescue-party arrives.

As the voice from outside the "savage" realm, Zotov injects "our" (strictly masculine) view of the Caucasus as a dualistic territory divided along lines of gender. In the first section of a long passage beginning "we have a region in the South," the poet contrives a "Hell" of rugged mountains, "mean" streams and tribal guerrillas who thirst for blood like "tigers." Thoroughly inimical to "us," this "dreadful" place is immediately contrasted to "Heaven," dear to "us." Zotov repeats the line "we have a region in the South" but now evokes a pacific realm peopled by voluptuous beauties. With pastoral motifs Russian writers associated primarily with Georgia, he summons a terrestrial paradise of roses, grapes, myrtle, olive trees, laurel and silvery waters. The local women's nationality is not specified, however: they are just generic orientals with pearly teeth, coral lips, raven locks and generous bosoms. All the promise of an Asian Eden is associated here with women, pitted against barren, infernal terrain and the masculine menace of the jihad.

In championing the Caucasian woman while damning her kinsmen, all these tales underwrote imperialism by ennobling the Russian as enemy of barbarous Islam. To judge by the memoirs of a military man, even Nicholas I was not immune to this fiction. In a conversation of 1838 the tsar remarked that the Caucasian war might end more quickly if mass marriages were arranged between his soldiers and tribeswomen rescued from the ships of Ottoman slave traders: the Muslim relatives of these Christianized wives would feel prohibited from killing their new in-laws, and combat would gradually grind to a halt.[37] The memoirist said that he tactfully reminded Nicholas that many of those women would rather "die than marry giaours." This anecdote and the rejoinder about cultural values on "their" side illustrate the blinding power of literature's mythology of romancing the tribeswoman into civilization. Quite interestingly, the pivotal fiction of the chivalrous Orthodox soldier would be exploded in Ivan Golovin's hybrid book *The Caucasus* written in emigration in the 1850s. Without referring to literature in this context, Golovin maintained that women whom tsarist forces retrieved from slave ships were frequently transported to Russian forts "to be violated by the soldiers."[38] Golovin was a notorious character, universally despised by the Russian émigré community in Paris, but on the whole his book has an unsensational, believable tone.

Besides endorsing the ideology of the civilizing mission, literature's mythology of the tsarist soldier as the seductive protector of abused oriental women quite possibly earned a psychological dividend on the domestic front by assuaging Russian guilt about serfdom. This is suggested by the fixation on the Ottoman slave trade in writings about the Caucasian tribes, as well as Georgia. Abolished only in 1861, serfdom entailed the regular sale and purchase of peasants, with some markets specializing in women. How removed from the base "Asian" could the Russian buyer or vendor of human property feel? Little orientalizers buried this question by insisting that the Islamic East monopolized a contemptible traffic in human beings and the treatment of women in particular as marketable property. Like the more sensational depictions of violence against Caucasian beauties (especially for loving giaours), the prominent theme of tribesmen in cahoots with slave traders, or merely hungry for the local brideprice, dissociated Russia from the use of people as commodities and, more specifically, from the exploitation of women.

EPHEMERAL ORIENTALIA'S IMPACT

As this chapter has shown, little orientalizers imposed a system of alien, fearsome cultural references on a territory which the Pushkinian poetics of space had constituted as alpine wilderness, cherished for its rejuvenative, inspirational power. Although the traditional rhetoric of dread and splendor still thrived in Russian literature and travelogues of the 1830s, the old imaginative geography was modified by the symbolism of Allah's mountains hostile to enlightened Orthodox Russia. Increasingly obsessed by Islam, poets such as Oznobishin retained from young Pushkin's era the giant, sovereign and sentry as favorite tropes for peaks. But with the escalation of the jihad, these figures of speech acquired a newly menacing character, as epitomized by Minaev's "Reproach against the Caucasus." To a limited extent, landscape was similarly orientalized in travel literature in this period. In Saburov's "The Caucasus," for example, Besh-Tau wears a "multicolored Muslim turban," a sparkling river is a "Lezgin saber," and Elbrus is personified as a gigantic "lion of the desert," an inept trope associating Caucasian mountaineers with Arabs of the hot sands.[39]

The displacement of Parnassian heights by Allah's mountains existed in mutually reinforcing relationship with the 1830s' newly simplistic invention of the Caucasian Muslim tribesman as a vicious, lustful beast excluded from civilization just as adamantly as the compliant oriental woman was invited in. The savage braves thus lost their ambivalent romantic aura as free *Naturmenschen* and become unidimensional sons of Allah – "children of darkness," "animals" and "fanatics." Reduced to the oriental other, the tribesman proclaimed Russia's Europeanness and consequent right to subjugate the Caucasus in the name of civilization.

But how persuasive was the little orientalizers' propagation of savage Muslim alterity? Two kinds of criteria are pertinent to this question – the aesthetic and the political. Zotov's "The Last of the Kheaks" strikes us now as pure doggerel in the service of empire-building, but the poem was published by Russia's Imperial Academy of Sciences. The imprint of this prestigious institution gave Zotov's lurid tale the status of high culture and exemplified how pulp about the tribes could satisfy both the literary and ideological demands of people in high places. By contrast, Belinsky's responses to the literary Caucasus often showed an interesting divergence between aesthetics and ideology. The critic sought to guide readers away from cheap sensationalism but regularly promoted fictions of Asian alterity in his own writing. This made him a strange bedfellow of Kamensky and like-minded hacks of the period. Belinsky deplored the horrid style of Kamensky (and Zotov) without noticing that he himself participated in the invention of "Asia" as inner bestiality which the "European" spirit must control.[40] Likewise, Belinsky's ideal of self-abnegating, oriental femininity coincided completely with the model Kamensky and his ilk recommended to Russian women, in opposition to cold-hearted, Balzacian *femmes fatales* of the *beau monde*.[41]

For all his own lack of sophistication about the "Orient," Belinsky sensed that the least aesthetically discriminating readers were probably most vulnerable to political influence from the little orientalizers. In the estimation of the Soviet Russian critic Gadzhiev, these "reactionary" writers warped quite a few minds.[42] Necessarily the fruit of speculation, this judgment rings true to common sense. The shortage of news in the Russian press encouraged readers to formulate ideas about the Caucasian war on the basis of literature, as well as conversations with military men on leave in the spa country or capital cities. Thanks to belles-lettres' high profile, little orientalizers' stories of Muslim wickedness, brutality and fanaticism conceivably persuaded many gullible Russians that the tribesmen would have to be killed *en masse* so that Christian civilization might expand.

And yet despite the heavy hand of *la thérapeutique du Différent* in Russian writing, the ambivalent œuvre of Bestuzhev-Marlinsky still reigned supreme in the literary Caucasus in this period (as Gadzhiev was quick to note). "Ammalat-Bek" undoubtedly provided Eurocentric hacks with an important narrative model which proclaimed that recalcitrant tribesmen risked extermination. However, in expanding "Asia" to encompass the id, Bestuzhev-Marlinsky teased Russians into ruminating about how much "oriental" eros and violence lay beneath their own "genteel coats" of civilization. An intriguing eradicator of firm boundaries between "us" and "them," he stimulated the readership's extraordinary fantasies of him as Shamil or at least a defector, now fighting the tyrant Nicholas I. In the cultural field of the 1830s these politically disruptive dynamics coexisted with the little orientalizers' jingoistic convictions and with Bestuzhev-Marlinsky's own equivocal critique of Asian backwardness. A subversive romantic discourse about the tribesmen still lived, to nurture any skepticism a Russian reader harbored about the ideology of the European civilizing mission.

CHAPTER 10

Feminizing the Caucasus

Oh my darling! How enchanting you are now!

Bestuzhev-Marlinsky

European authors have often portrayed imperial power as male dominance over the feminized colonial realm.[1] Writers in Russia during the reign of Nicholas I showed the same rhetorical bent. Rostopchina's poem "The Forced Marriage" (1847) allegorized tsarist repression of Poland as an "old Baron's" abuse of his rebellious young wife, wed against her will.[2] The preeminent Ukrainian poet Taras Shevchenko repeatedly depicted his homeland as a woman ravaged by masculinized Russia, Poland or her own politically dislocated native sons.[3] While preserving the same gender relations, Alexander Odoevsky contrived a contrary myth of powerful masculine seduction in "The Marriage of Georgia and the Russian Kingdom" (1838).[4]

Although Georgia received such treatment more consistently than other regions of the Caucasus, the whole territory was drawn into a rhetoric of feminization and erotic interaction in Bestuzhev-Marlinsky's cycle of *récits de voyage* which were published separately between 1834 and 1836 and then collected among his "Caucasian Essays." The Russian word *Kavkaz* (Caucasus) has masculine gender, but the territory was perceived at the time as the realm of untamed *priroda* (nature), a feminine noun. Since gender is imbedded in the language, *priroda* to the Russian ear does not automatically conjure a female personage. To underscore the point we need only to remember how Russian poets usually disregarded the feminine gender of *gora* (mountain) to favor tropes of

175

masculinization for peaks (tsars, sovereigns, sentries, warriors and giants). Bestuzhev-Marlinsky, however, took feminine *priroda* as an invitation to personify the Caucasus as a woman, while repressing the grammatical femininity of *Rossiia* (Russia) itself. "Ammalat-Bek" dropped a hint of things to come by featuring Dagestan as a "land of fruit" where the natives "nestle in the bosom of that charmer, nature." Partly inspired by Dagestan, Bestuzhev-Marlinsky's *récits de voyage* relate a largely solitary trek from Derbent to the Alazani valley in Georgia. The itinerary thus unfolds in the southerly region which nineteenth-century Russians commonly called "Transcaucasia." But Bestuzhev-Marlinsky mapped a larger country of the mind by consistently writing about the "Caucasus," *Kavkaz*. Indicative of broader tendencies at work in the period, these travelogues gave voice to a newly heightened perception of the entire Asian terrain as "virgin" terrain ripe for Russian exploitation.

THE PASTORAL AMBIENCE

The Russian readership's awareness of the Caucasus' potential as a colony began intensifying dramatically in the 1830s. A major publicizer of the economic stakes of the war against the tribes was Platon Zubov (an architect of the "oriental project" under Catherine II).[5] The frontispiece of Zubov's *Picture of the Caucasian Region* (1835) showed towering mountains beneath the Romanov double-headed eagle topped with a crown over an "N" for Nicholas. Worth a thousand words, this image of tsarist supremacy set the tone of the discussion. Zubov argued that Russia had to take the Caucasus' "lazy" natives in hand to effect a "colonial transformation." His catalogue of the territory's natural wealth included oil and minerals, tea, coffee, cotton and sugar cane, silk production and fishing. But in Zubov's estimation, "fear of the tribesmen" prevented Russia from tapping these "luxuriant gifts of nature." He hoped the tribes might convert to Christianity, renounce their life of brigandage and become willing subjects of the tsarist empire. Behind this stated wish, though, lay the sinister threat that recalcitrants would have to be eliminated, lest they block the influx of hard-working Russian settlers needed to achieve colonial transformation. Exactly the same outlook was expressed in 1837 in the *Library for Reading* in the anonymous review of another book which outlined an imperial Russian agenda in the Caucasus.[6] In reiterating the theme of "generously endowed nature," the commentator claimed that the Asian territory promised Russia even greater wealth than India brought the British. But like Zubov's book, this article too blamed bellicose Muslim tribesmen for thwarting the march of economic progress.

In addition to such wide-ranging discussions of empire, the Russian press from the 1830s onward provided many specifications of the Caucasus' natural resources. This occurred both in periodicals with a general readership and in publications with specialized audiences, such as the *Journal of Mining*.[7] Although not necessarily invoking the claims of civilization or even mentioning the Muslim tribes, the various Russian authors who wrote about minerals, silk production, salt deposits and the like were obviously indicating potential profits for the tsarist empire. Such reporting helped establish an image of the Caucasus as the source of phenomenal booty for the Russians in the ongoing war.

The evolving notion of natural plenitude gave the territory a new pastoral ambience, at odds with the rocky sphere of mountain gloom and glory. By the end of the 1820s, a passion for grassy hills and valleys erupted in *récits de voyage* about Georgia (as well as in imaginative literature). In common with Rousseau's writing about the Alps, Russian travelers of the era perceived Georgia's lowlands as inviting, hospitable terrain nestled amid stark, barren mountains.[8] Bestuzhev-Marlinsky's travelogues participated in the trend by lavishing rapt attention on valleys in present-day Azerbaijan, as well as Georgia. In the same spirit, another traveler of the era celebrated fertile Gelendzhik on the northern coast of the Black Sea.[9]

Perhaps especially acute in natives of Russia's wintry clime, the pastoralism conveyed a longing for a realm of natural abundance. The opening sentence of Griboedov's proposal for a Russian–Transcaucasian trading company articulated the wish by attributing unlimited plenitude to the Caucasus' southerly regions: "nature has prepared everything, but people have not yet taken advantage of nature."[10] Without displaying Griboedov's hope of achieving mutual rewards for the colonizer and the colonized, a staunchly chauvinistic Russian official in Tiflis similarly maintained in the early 1830s that just a few enlightened entrepreneurs would suffice to make nature yield its bounty in Georgia (as long as the "bloodthirsty" tribes of neighboring areas were checked).[11] Although not actually proclaiming the place "paradise," both Griboedov and this tsarist functionary conveyed a conception of a realm so richly endowed that man might derive benefits from it with a minimum of work. A Russian traveler of the late 1820s had made the inferences explicit by christening the pristine Caucasus "Eden."[12] The imagery of the great garden recurred repeatedly in Bestuzhev-Marlinsky's writings, as already illustrated by the trope of Dagestan as the "land of fruit" in "Ammalat-Bek." Contemplated at length in this figurative light, the Caucasus in the author's travelogues became "paradise on Earth" where the civilized interloper stood entranced "like Adam . . . on the first evening of his life" (201).[13]

The ideal of Edenic abundance was readily loaded with erotic overtones connoted by "virgin land." A terrestrial paradise assures a good life with relatively little effort. As Annette Kolodny has argued in her study of American writers, this pastoral yearning often bespeaks a desire to experience the land as a nurturing female who creates a warmly satisfying, comforting environment for the individual.[14] Early American colonists, for example, fashioned metaphors of their country as a great mother but also gendered her as a loving maiden whose fertility begged to be exploited. Nineteenth-century Russian writing about the Caucasus exhibited the same urge to feminization, with the spotlight squarely centered on the passive virgin ready to satisfy male desire and indeed just waiting for man to take advantage of her.[15] Competing tropes like the priestess, sister and mother occasionally featured in Bestuzhev-Marlinsky's travelogue cycle and related writings by some of his contemporaries. But objects of erotic yearning were the leading ladies in the figurative drama we shall now begin exploring.

THE RAPE OF THE TERRITORY

Bestuzhev-Marlinsky's role as a feminizer of Caucasian wilderness must be assessed within the general stylistic texture of his *récits de voyage*. Soviet Russian criticism gave his travel cycle the "realist" seal of approval by pouncing upon infrequent passages of concrete description.[16] For the most part, however, Bestuzhev-Marlinsky's accounts are sentimental and extravagantly rhetorical. Intently centered on his inner experience, he ignores his balmy surroundings for long stretches at a time, as illustrated by an extended evocation of wintry Siberia, his first place of exile (184–87). More typically, Caucasian landscape holds his attention but sends him into flights of rapture, short on pictorial detail. In a cogent response to the sentimental style, the historian Nikolai Dubrovin once remarked that Bestuzhev-Marlinsky's travelogues might have been penned in Switzerland as readily as the Caucasus.[17]

Although Bestuzhev-Marlinsky announces didactic aims elsewhere (as in the introduction to "The Story of an Officer Held Prisoner by Mountain Tribesmen"), his *récits de voyage* defend writing as creative distortion. The section entitled "The Road to the Town of Kuba" flatly tells readers not to expect objective description: "Anybody who imagines that my essays are acquainting him with the Caucasus, rather than with me myself, is sadly mistaken" (130). Here a principle of self-expression completely overrides the didactic impulse. Unconcerned about the potential educational value of a text, the travelogue promises to invent rather than transmit *realia*: "That is why it is absurd to demand that a poet do life-like portraiture of a place: he would cease being a poet if he went about such a task. His compass is his mind, his palette – his heart, and his brush – imagination" (122–23). With this strong defense of the primacy of inner vision, Bestuzhev-Marlinsky places himself among the "poetic" writers, fully licensed to create imaginative geography rather than provide a pictorial record of the road.

The aesthetic of distortion transfigures the Caucasus into a sign system to be deciphered by the writer. Perhaps mindful of Byron's epigraph about the big book of nature (*Childe Harold's Pilgrimage*), Bestuzhev-Marlinsky employs a telling series of semiotic metaphors. He refers to the outskirts of Kuba as a "nice preface" which whets the appetite for a disappointing "book," the town itself (139). Steeped in imaginative Caucasian geography of the 1820s, he views mountains as the "originals" of literary "copies" he "read" back home (152–53). The stars participate too in this series of tropes: gazing at the heavens on a clear night, the author reads the celestial bodies as letters spelling the big, glorious "word – GOD!" (172). Along the same lines, his journal of the period decodes the mountains' snowy crest as a "hieroglyph" promising pure souls eternal life in heaven (263).

As these notes of spiritual uplift would suggest, Bestuzhev-Marlinsky often assumes a reverent posture toward the wilderness. At twilight in the mountains in "The Last Post on the Way to Staraya Shamakha," the traveler bows his head, exclaims "Thy will be done!" and voices the following "prayer":

Fate has guided my life along a path of thorns and stones, through night and clouds, but stars shone upon me at times, and I learned to be grateful for every ray of light that reached me. Sparks of divine grace flew down upon me most often and most purely when I wandered to the summits of mountains. Then my soul understood the hymn of praise, "Glory to God in the highest, peace on Earth!" (171)

Typical of many passages in the travelogue cycle, this "prayer" cultivates the soulful *goût de la montagne* made fashionable in Russia by Rousseau's and Karamzin's Alpine writings and then reproduced in the 1820s by secondary Russian poets of the literary Caucasus such as Tepliakov.

To judge by Bestuzhev-Marlinsky's jottings on the *Paradiso*, Dante also fed his notion of mountains as the realm of "higher" things.

As illustrated by the writings of two of Bestuzhev-Marlinsky's compatriots, the tradition of moral exaltation was by no means inherently incompatible with symbolizations of the territory as a woman. In the anonymous "Recollections of the Caucasus," the Russian traveler reverently beholds Gelendzhik as a "beauty" (or "*belle*," *krasavitsa*) whose moral purity enhances her physical attractiveness: "Which of us has not fallen in love with her? In whose soul has she not aroused lofty feelings and ideas? She always nourishes the soul, as faith nourishes Christians! She is the world's temple, where God is praised!"[18] Religiously exalted without a hint of carnal desire, the beautiful land is invested with the holiness of a priestess revered from afar. In similar evasion of the erotic, the minor belletrist Count Vladimir Sollogub would call Georgia Russia's "sister" (whereas most writers tended to symbolize the Caucasian land as an object of Russian male desire).[19] A functionary in the ministry of foreign affairs, Sollogub brooked no hint of incest: in compliance with grammatical gender, he symbolized Orthodox Russia as a protective woman with little Georgia under her wing in a religious sorority. Again, a note of piety and lofty intentions accompanied the trope of feminization, as in the travelogue about Gelendzhik. Indeed, Sollogub solemnly declared that tsarist objectives in the Caucasus were "purely religious."

But by telling contrast to those symbols of inviolate femininity, Bestuzhev-Marlinsky's personifications of the Caucasus as a woman appear in arenas of erotic combat. His reverent urge to pray to the territory thus proves unsteady, as betrayed by his very choice of Biblical allusions. While Edenizing the land, Bestuzhev-Marlinsky seeks to repress the Fall by envisioning Adam "on the first evening of his life" – newly created and all alone like a perpetual child. However, a loss of innocent relation to the Caucasian garden is symbolically inscribed in the travelogues' rhetorical patterns of erotic desire.

One of Bestuzhev-Marlinsky's principal metaphorical plots advertises the erotic enticement of the feminized Caucasus and foresees her loss of virginity. Nature initially touches the traveling narrator like a "beloved woman's gentle hand" (134–35). The land itself is subsequently gendered as a woman who "spoils" her "happy lover" (168). Under the lover's admiring gaze, the wilderness assumes the guise of a beautiful "bride-to-be" (*nevesta*), "fresh with the charm of spring, full of desire and promise" (187). This maiden is coupled first with a local admirer, the sun: "The enamored sun drinks in [nature's] aromatic breath, caresses her with warmth, kisses her with rays, imprinting new beauty upon her smiling face with every kiss. Oh my darling! How enchanting you are now!" The minor poet Aleksei Meisner had already symbolized Caucasian *paysage* as a woman passionately embraced by the sun ("The Sun Parting from Elbrus," 1833).[20] But Bestuzhev-Marlinsky's projection of erotic love onto the land has an extravagant, primordial quality: it evokes ancient myths of union between a female Earth and a masculine force of the sky, while conforming to the poetics of primitive, oriental "heat" exemplified in "Ammalat-Bek."

In the midst of the travelogue's torrid encounter between the sun and the land, Bestuzhev-Marlinsky fashions a trope of Russian rape of the Caucasus. The exclamation, "Oh my darling! How enchanting you are now!" springs from the military traveler's own lips, as he addresses the land to declare rivalry with the sun:

With all due respect for somebody else's property, I am ready to fling myself from the saddle onto your breast, to embrace you and cover you with kisses. Yes! The electric flame of springtime in the Orient pours a boiling stream of youth into the chest and casts treacherous sparks of whimsy into the tinder box of imagination. In the air one hears a voice, the rustle of a satiny dress, and troubled breath, sweetly wafting (187–88).

This amusing purple passage conveys a man's yearning to take erotic possession of the beautiful foreign maiden, rather than worship her or embrace her with brotherly affection. A forthrightly imperialist dynamic operates here as the Russian outsider challenges a local male for possession of the oriental "property" (the "bride-to-be") and articulates his desire to ravish her. The sensuous female's "satiny dress" conjures a St. Petersburg society *belle*, but this incongruous detail does not alter the passage's political thrust: through a symbolic love triangle centered on feminized terrain, Bestuzhev-Marlinsky eroticizes the Russian drive to gain supremacy over the Caucasus.

The author's central construct of fierce erotic desire encompasses economic exploitation in the entry entitled "The Mountain Road from Dagestan to Shrivan via Kunakenty." His vision of purportedly inevitable industrial conquest starts with a typically rapturous evocation of an unpopulated, "virgin" place where "no man has ever been before." Then the sexual innuendo rings out violently in an apostrophe to nature addressed by the familiar form of "you" (*ty*):

the time will come when people will descend on you, and their sweat will intoxicate you, as the heavenly dew does now. They will settle into your secret canyons and gorges, cover you with social life's dusty siftings, pollute you, tread down your very tiptop, drill mines and stone quarries through your heart, extract your innards, turn you inside out, pervert you and crop you. They will adorn you with trinkets of their own paltry being, force you to work to satisfy their greed, make you a hireling to their fancies (159–60).

While immediately followed by a playful notion of making ice-cream from the mountains' "virgin snows," this passage is dominated by an unrelenting symbolism of strenuous sexual assault – the violation of "secret" places, gigantesque acts of penetration and brutish manhandling. In this forecast of the future, the Caucasus is the victim of a gang rape, ultimately transformed into a whore and compelled to serve her debauchers.

Bestuzhev-Marlinsky very characteristically displays mixed feelings toward the rape of the land, and we can begin to measure the depth of his ambivalence by drawing a contrast with a much later Russian perception of economic development as sexual violation of the Caucasus. The populist and socialist thinker Gleb Uspensky visited a Black Sea coastal area in the 1880s, prior to industrialization. Thoughts of despoliation disgusted him: his *récit de voyage* imagines "Mr. Capital" as a "lecher" who "voluptuously smacks his chops over the fresh tender flesh" of the "naive, virgin" terrain, as he prepares to trample its hidden places, drive railroads through it and clutter it with trash.[21] To judge by this rhetoric, tropes of debauchery and sexual degradation seemed more apt than ever to an observer of late nineteenth-century industrial "progress." A witness to real capitalist ventures in Russia, Uspensky expressed nothing but revulsion for "lecherous" entrepreneurs, so eager to defile a pristine region.

By contrast to Uspensky in the 1880s, Bestuzhev-Marlinsky in the era of conquest both dreaded and relished the future industrial rape of the Caucasus. As a romantic writer who drew much inspiration from wilderness, he fully recognized that capitalist transformation of virgin nature would spell a "loss for the poet" (159). Nevertheless, he could not suppress his sense that the exploitation of Caucasian paradise posed exciting challenges to human ingenuity and efficiency. In keeping with his awed vision of the Edenic garden, his travelogue's despoilers are greedy and crass (while still falling far short of Uspensky's drooling voluptuary). However, in Bestuzhev-Marlinsky's eyes, the figurative sexual assaulters also epitomized technical know-how, initiative and the "European" work ethic so memorably extolled in "Ammalat-Bek" as the "alarm clock of the human soul." An admirer of stunning feats of engineering in the Alps like the construction of tunnels and the enlargement of the Simplon Pass road undertaken at Napoleon's demand, Bestuzhev-Marlinsky participated in a Promethean enthusiasm for industrial progress widely spread in Europe and Russia at the time.[22]

It is important to note in this connection that Russia's military strategy in the Caucasus evinced a Promethean drive to triumph over nature. The ordeal of combat in the mountains aroused in tsarist commanders something of the alpinist's urge to reach an awesome summit just to prove that he can. From the days of Ermolov to the monumentally disastrous

Dargo campaign led by Viceroy Mikhail Vorontsov in 1845, Russian regiments marched into the rugged heights of the Caucasus to attack tribal villages.[23] The high command attributed tremendous psychological significance to these expeditions, even though they rarely brought new territorial gains. Affronted by Kazbek as an enemy who did not "respect" him, Ermolov urged his troops to "raise our banners on the peaks."[24] As he himself explained, he undertook mountain campaigns primarily to show the tribes that Russians could overcome "obstacles posed by the lay of the land itself" and get to places where no outsiders had ever been.[25] Successive commanders-in-chief voiced the same sentiments about wilderness as a tribal ally which had to be beaten appropriately.[26] The challenges of fighting mountain guerrillas were formidably real, but they were met with something in addition to rational planning: the drive to plant the Russian flag on the heights betrayed a streak of irrational Prometheanism, not unlike the Nazi mystique of alpine conquest celebrated in Arnold Fanck's films starring Leni Riefenstahl.

The Promethean urge to experience oneself as master of the wilderness also dictated despoilment of Caucasian forests. In a prelude to "pacification," Ermolov began this assault in 1817 when he widened roads and started constructing Russian forts in Chechnia. But after the Dargo campaign completely discredited the goal of seizing the mountains, Russia undertook to clear forests on a massive scale (as exemplified in young Tolstoy's story "The Wood-felling"). Pursued right to the end of the war, the tsarist army's program of deforestation was wanton destruction of nature of the sort encompassed in today's ecologically conscious notion of "raping the land."

THE ANGEL OF DEATH IN PARADISE

Bestuzhev-Marlinsky's scenario of erotic designs and sexual assault on the Caucasus suggestively symbolized the whole range of military, political, economic and even Promethean factors at work in the Russian conquest. But his imagination was not yet exhausted. In a demonstration of the unlimited prerogatives of artistic license defended so vigorously in the *récits de voyage*, he supplemented the tale of despoilment with intimations of Russian failure to win a seductive heartbreaker. As in a contemporaneous *récit de voyage* by a Russian on campaign in Chechnia, Bestuzhev-Marlinsky's Caucasus could be just "as cheating as a coquette's heart," even though she beckoned as a "smiling maiden" – "sweet to the eye."[27]

The final installment of Bestuzhev-Marlinsky's travelogue cycle crazily alternates between soulful daydreams and the brutal reality of military conquest. Erotic promise once again suffuses the air when the traveler reaches the frontier of Georgia at the end of his recorded trek. The Alazani river appears as a "bashful but ardent bride-to-be" who yields to her native banks, after giving the author the impression she was running to *him* (199–200). Once the river has spurned him in this manner, Bestuzhev-Marlinsky strikes back with aggressive rhetoric about the inevitability of tsarist domination of the Caucasus. He likens himself to Adam in paradise but then focuses upon his Lezgin fellow travelers and mentally recalls their country's bellicose history (201–2). The "Russian bayonet" has now intimidated them, he gloats. In a mounting frenzy, he approves the "angel of death" and "spirit of war" as constructive forces: lethal conflict lays a path for the "angel of peace," "enlightenment" will triumph in the Caucasus, Russia will win – so hooray for "Nicholas and victory!" (204). Given its bombastic exaggerations and hysterical pitch, this long utterance about the conquest's regenerative capacity cannot be taken at face value. The author's cheer for imperialism is thrown into a parodic register and gives the impression of a man desperately attempting to convince himself that he is indeed a worthy "lover" of the Caucasus, rather than a vile aggressor.

A sense of inevitable loss then creeps into his writing. He flees the specter of war to focus once again on his Edenic surroundings. Precisely at this point, though, he strikes the pose of a man unlucky in love. The peaceful wilderness provokes a confession of worldly dreams, as presumptuous as his paradisiac reveries:

But I had earthly dreams too – splendid, fresh and sweet, sprinkled with the dew of hope, dreams to make the heart leap like a noble steed at the sound of a battle horn. I had such dreams, but I will not let the *beau monde* have them either. They are not for sale nor free for the taking: they are secret. Oh my beauty, do not ask me what the cherished secret is! With that fire of betrayal in your eyes you have grown used to burning the vows made to you by others, but you will sooner reduce my heart to ashes, than steal its mystery. (208)

Bestuzhev-Marlinsky does not clearly identify his addressee. This "beauty" (*krasavitsa*) may be merely a reprise of the theme of unrequited love often treated in his stories. But in invoking such a personage during his soulful encounter with pristine wilderness, Bestuzhev-Marlinsky lends the Caucasus itself the character of a *femme fatale* likely to injure her admirer. The figure of the horse aroused by a battle horn suggests a certain readiness for the war between the sexes, but feminine victory is a foregone conclusion. This *femme fatale* who springs into Bestuzhev-Marlinsky's head annuls his previous incarnations of himself as the Caucasus' "happy lover," prospective bridegroom or debaucher. A formidable actor in the erotic wars, the "beauty" with "betrayal" in her eyes intimates that Russian "dreams" to achieve a thoroughly satisfying mastery over the enticing territory are going to be frustrated.

The travelogue's final pages strengthen the metaphorical resonance of lost hopes, while betraying the author's guilt about serving the "angel of death" who symbolizes the tsarist conquest. After his revery about the *femme fatale*, Bestuzhev-Marlinsky is jolted back into the real world – a dirty, mice-infested posting station where he passes the night. The grubby place occupies his pen for nearly ten pages, until another feminine symbolization of Caucasian beauty finally appears in the account's last scene: rosy dawn in the wilderness appears as a "goddess" who tiptoes into his quarters, rouses him with a kiss and frolics ahead of him while he mounts his horse. As he climbs into the saddle, the author cries, "A horse! A horse! A kingdom for a horse!" (as translated in his footnote, with Shakespeare's "my" displaced). Bestuzhev-Marlinsky thus identifies himself with Richard III, the deformed usurper who murders everybody in his path to power. Most strikingly of all, of course, the Russian military exile chooses the famous words uttered by the evil king just before he is dispatched.

The Shakespearean allusion stunningly illuminates Bestuzhev-Marlinsky's self-conception as a soldier in the imperial army. He is mounted and ready to gallop after the Caucasian "goddess." But in echoing the defeated Richard, the author proclaims himself a consummate political villain, acknowledges the justice of killing bloody usurpers and bespeaks anxiety about the *moral* price Russia may pay in gaining military victory in the Caucasus. The "angel of death" is here unmasked as a purely usurpatory, murderous force rather than the cruel means to a glorious political end. Gruesome Shakespearean tragedy has eclipsed the ethos of Homeric heroism in "Ammalat-Bek" and the author's correspondence from the Caucasian front.

By identifying himself with Richard III, Bestuzhev-Marlinsky exposes the nagging doubt about imperialism allegorized in the travelogue's erotic symbolism: How can bloody acts of dispossession possibly make Russia the happy sovereign of the Edenic territory? In featuring the Caucasus by turns as an enticing virgin, a bride-to-be, a subjugated whore, a *femme fatale* and a teasing goddess, the author inscribes his suffering over the contradiction between experiencing pastoral attraction to Caucasian "paradise" and attacking it as a soldier in Nicholas' army. No matter which way he contrives the figurative tale of relations between imperial Russian man and the feminized territory, he cannot escape presentiments of loss and frustration. In the scenario of rape and debauchery, the male despoils what he found beautiful and becomes a pimp; the *femme fatale* may prove conquerable but promises to devastate the military traveler, while the goddess speeds forever beyond his reach. All these cases demonstrate Bestuzhev-Marlinsky's incapacity to conceive a mutually happy union between the Russian Adam and the Caucasian Garden. The rape story overtly admits Russian violation of the pastoral ideal; the goddess is simply not to be had; and the perceptions of wilderness as a flirtatious victimizer project knowledge of tsarist despoilment back onto the victim (perhaps with the implication that the "cheat" deserves to be "paid back").

To no surprise, Bestuzhev-Marlinsky's tormented inscription of Russian aggression proved incompatible with a vision of the Caucasus as Mother Nature. On the one occasion when he maternalized the territory, she was utterly inaccessible to human children: in "Ammalat-Bek" the metaphor of nature as a "charmer" was conjoined with a perception of Asia's sky as the "unembraceable breast" of a "loving mother." This notion of the great mother who promises to comfort but remains unreachable anticipated the lost paradise of Bestuzhev-Marlinsky's wartime cycle of *récits de voyage*. Unable to drive the "angel of death" and the "land of work" entirely from his mind, the military traveler could not invent himself as an innocent child passively cuddled in the bosom of nature: he took Adam as his emblem but incriminated himself in the multifaceted Russian rape of the territory. At some level his imagination told him it was best to stick to nubile "beauties" and exclude "mother," lest he commit figurative incest.

The "loving mother's" problematic character for Bestuzhev-Marlinsky can be underlined by comparison with erotic tensions in Liukan Yakubovich's "Cliffs" (1837), a short lyric set in unnamed mountain country.[28] In the embrace of "Mother Nature" the poet experiences a sense of spiritual renewal in the highlands. Rendered fresh and pristine as his surroundings, he perceives all life as a "virgin, full of the force of love." While developing a standard theme of moral uplift in the mountains, Yakubovich's combination of metaphors illogically characterizes nature as both maternal and sexually inexperienced. Moreover, he uses the word for a male virgin (*devstvennik*), even though "life" in Russian is feminine. An expression of the pastoral yearning to be at one with nature, this rhetorical transsexuality tears down the grammatical categories of gender to effect a merger between the male self and the beloved wilderness.

But at the same time the definition of the male persona as a "virgin" introduces incestuous import by implying the potential of sexual awakening and the loss of a tender, filial relation to Mother Nature. The final lines signal the instability of prelapsarian innocence by employing Biblical diction for primal "dust" (*perst'*), a "creature" (*tvar'*) and a "serpent" viewed as an "emblem of eternity." In coexistence with the serpent, a "wide-winged eagle" crosses the sky "free as the play of thought." With these two symbols from the animal kingdom the conclusion of "Cliffs" suggests contradictory human potential – either to ascend toward the ethereal heavens associated with the mind, or else heed the serpent and sink to the dust. In parallel to Bestuzhev-Marlinsky's Caucasian writings, Yakubovich thus implies the untenability of prelapsarian relation to the Edenic wilderness: by introducing the "eternal" capacity for sin symbolized traditionally by the serpent, his "virgin" who is both the self and the world threatens the putative child's idyll with Mother Nature.

FEMININE ALTERITY

Without negating the old aesthetic of the sublime, Bestuzhev-Marlinsky gave expression to an ideologically significant battery of erotic desires by imposing femininity on Caucasian *priroda*. He never had a plethora of little feminizers in his wake. Under his impact several amateur authors of Caucasian travelogues perpetuated clichés of the sentimental journey and indulged the quasi-religious *goût de la montagne* without ever symbolizing the territory as a woman. But if having a much more limited sway in Russian letters than the *topoi* of mountain gloom and glory, the feminization of the embattled Caucasus is noteworthy material to add to the comparative study of imperialism's cultural manifestations.

With the exception of Count Sollogub's Georgian "sister," the male authors' rhetorical figures all established a sexual boundary between Russia and the Caucasus. In a realization of the era's preoccupation with "virgin" land, Bestuzhev-Marlinsky read the territory primarily as a tantalizing maiden ready for the taking; but he also symbolized places in Azerbaijan, Georgia and Dagestan as a fiancée, a *femme fatale*, a goddess and an infinitely distanced mother. Other travelers of the time proposed tropes of a purely spiritual woman or the cheating coquette disguised as a sweet maiden, while Alexander Odoevsky presented Georgia as tsardom's happy bride (in the mainline of imaginative literature we are about to explore now). This diversified range of symbols attested to irreconcilable psychological conflicts in Russian efforts to define a self-satisfying attitude toward the pristine Caucasus earmarked for colonial exploitation. In every case, however, the evocations of women exhibited imperialist discourse's fundamental tendency to marginalize and to augment the alterity of the desired colony or the subject nation of an empire. Rostopchina and Shevchenko turned feminization to anti-tsarist ends in poetry about Poland and Ukraine, but nobody made a similar effort in writing about the Caucasus.[29]

There was, all the same, significant torment in Bestuzhev-Marlinsky's contradictory metaphorical scenarios of raping and debauching the Caucasus, or else falling victim to her coquetry and rejection. At a time when the jihad was raging in Chechnia and Dagestan, and Georgian noblemen had recently planned an aborted revolt against Russian power in their homeland, Bestuzhev-Marlinsky in military exile translated the pursuit of empire into mutually spiteful sexual relations. He could not repress war and the abuses of imperial rule via myths of perpetual Eden, a blissful marriage, supportive sisterhood or passive worship of a wild priestess or goddess. Full of erotic tensions, his interrelated feminizations of the Caucasus radiated a self-implicating knowledge of masculine imperialist aggression which would resurface in late Lermontov's writing about lands of the Muslim tribes under attack by Russia.

CHAPTER 11

Georgia as an oriental woman

Many suitors paid you court,
You selected a colossus.
Alexander Odoevsky

The Russian urge to feminize the Caucasus found most remarkable literary expression in the symbolization of Georgia as an oriental woman. This body of writing provides a fascinating counterpoint to the intensely ambivalent treatment of Circassians, Dagestanis and Chechens in works of Pushkin, Bestuzhev-Marlinsky and Lermontov. The three principal producers of the romantic Caucasus invented Muslim tribesmen as shadow selves endowed with heroic machismo, a love of liberty, instinctual authenticity, simplicity and an aura of Homeric song. These literary creations channeled authorial rebelliousness against the tsarist state and gave sustenance to a cultural ideal of semi-Asian Russia as an enviably youthful, ascendant nation rather than a hapless laggard seeking identity by tagging after Europe.

But while romantic appropriation of the tribesmen thus inscribed Russia's superiority complex toward western enlightenment, Georgia bore the brunt of the coexistent inferiority complex which led Russians to protest how European they already were. Pushkin, Bestuzhev-Marlinsky and Lermontov contributed unequally to the invention of Georgia as an oriental other. Lermontov was by far the most important, followed by Pushkin, while Bestuzhev-Marlinsky left only the brief but significant symbolization of the Alazani valley as a nubile bride-to-be. In each case, however, the three prominent members of the nineteenth-century canon contributed to

192

a rigidly dichotomous cultural mythology. Concentrated in the period from 1820 to 1850, this subdivision of the literary Caucasus has three striking features. First of all, despite Georgia's long participation in Christendom, authors insisted on the country's Asian, quasi-Islamic character. The second peculiarity is the exclusion of native heroes. By stark contrast to the literary Caucasus' gallery of memorable tribesmen such as Pushkin's Circassians, Ammalat-Bek, Izmail-Bey, Kazbich, Hadji Murat and Shamil, Georgian male protagonists are very scarce in Russian works. Moreover, when they do appear, they are usually denigrated. The third major feature of literary Georgia throws gender relations into high relief. As in much European writing about the orient and other exotic regions of the world, the male producers of these Russian texts foreground the Georgian woman, the native whose alterity is at once national and sexual.[1]

The literature about Georgia is distinguished further by the systematic advancement of a metaphorical proposition about the land as a woman who must be protected *and* dominated by men stronger than those of her own country. The proposition relies to a great extent upon a dualistic construct of woman as an intensely good figure (the innocent virgin, the devoted mother) liable to metamorphose into a fiend (the murderess, the sorceress, the temptress). This view strongly implies the necessity of keeping such treacherous creatures under control, and the issue of authority turns primarily upon nationality, while taking male supremacy for granted. Thus, within the context of the orient and in the absence of the Georgian hero, Russian writers created an erotically charged cultural mythology about themselves as the powerful and rational European agents, uniquely capable of both protecting Georgia and keeping her wickedness in check.

Literature's interplay between sexual and imperial domination laid bare a central tension in the Russian ideology of the civilizing mission. Tsarist officials moralized the annexation of Georgia as a measure to defend Christianity and European cultural values against the barbarism of Islam in Persia, Turkey and Dagestan. Threatened by imminent aggression from the Persians, Georgia may well have perished, had it not been incorporated into the tsarist empire under Alexander I. A heavy price was paid for survival, however.[2] The first two decades following the take-over of eastern and then western Georgia brought little but strife and turmoil in relations between the subject people and the new overlords. From the time when Russian military men started marching through the Darial Pass, recurrent revolts took place, involving every class of Georgian society at one time or another. Corruption was rife among tsarist officials, no respect was paid to local laws and traditions, native women were raped by Russian functionaries and soldiers, and in 1820 Cossacks killed a Georgian archbishop who was making the church a rallying point for nationalist sentiment. A big gap thus opened between the annexation's religious rationale and the brutality of empire-building in action.

Russian literature's orientalization and feminization of Georgia shed interesting light on this discrepancy. Imperialist ideology made pious protests of Christian kinship with Georgia even as the land was being thrashed into submission. But in a hunger for exoticism, Russian men of letters virtually filtered Christianity out of the imaginative field and asserted instead the primacy of Islam and savage paganism.[3] By relegating Georgia to the orient in this manner, the writers disclosed precisely the kinds of convictions about alien "Asians" which underlay Russia's cruel exercise of power over the former protectorate.

GEORGIA AS THE ORIENT

A stormy religious and cultural history made Georgia's relegation to the orient particularly problematic. The land had an ancient Christian culture, whereas Kievan Rus was Christianized only in 988. Proselytized by Syrians in the third century, Georgia adopted Christianity as the state religion around 330 under King Mirian of Kartli-Iberia.[4] However, the land subsequently suffered many assaults from Islam. The Arabs dominated the Caucasus for approximately two hundred years from around 640, and their rule left indelible cultural traces upon Georgia without eradicating Christianity. In a second major onslaught of militant forces of Islam, Georgia from the mid-sixteenth to mid-eighteenth century became a fragmented battleground where the Turks and Persians recurrently fought to expand their spheres of influence. During this period some Georgian nobles suffered for refusing to renounce their Christian faith, but for the most part the princes became at least nominal converts to Islam and ruled at the discretion of their Muslim overlords. In Tiflis in eastern Georgia the interaction with Persia was particularly extensive, and by the mid-seventeenth century a blend of Christian and Muslim elements came to characterize cultural and political life there.[5] A picturesque admixture of the European and Asian persisted in the capital city into the early nineteenth century, when significant numbers of Russians started going to Georgia.

Despite the cultural heterogeneity, Georgia's Christian heritage had naturally been accentuated in Russian political ideology since the time of Catherine II. But in the romantic era with its mania for visting the East, persons desiring exotic experience clearly found it much more satisfying to orientalize Georgia rather than to contemplate its similarity to Orthodox Russia or its antagonism to Islam. This outlook was exemplified by the secondary poet and civil servant Vasily Grigoriev who was sent to Tiflis in the late 1820s to gather statistics. Upon learning of his new assignment he expressed great pleasure at the opportunity to leave his dull routine in St. Petersburg and fulfill a "cherished desire to travel."[6] But most interestingly, his anticipation about Georgia was couched in terms appropriate to Persia or any number of other places: "A new realm of professional activity, a new land has begun opening before me. The Orient – land of everything wondrous, where I have already flown so often in imagination, the land which I shall now see in all the poetic charm of its natural setting and the *moeurs* of its inhabitants." To no great surprise, once he arrived in Georgia, Grigoriev imposed oriental categories upon *realia*. The sight of women in colorful skirts dancing on a flat roof on a starry night in Tiflis struck him as "a scene straight out of *The Thousand and One Nights.*" Duly inspired, he then wrote "The Georgian Woman," a verse about an enticing local maiden who dances with great abandon but is destined to become the unhappy slave of her husband.[7] Georgia's status as a Christian country obviously made no appeal to Grigoriev's imagination. It was totally eclipsed by obsession with the orient as a refuge from Russia's boredom.

Grigoriev's responses typify a Russian tendency to perceive Georgia as a Muslim rather than age-old Christian culture. In the literature produced by such visitors, a standard figure was the beauty in a *chadra*, the long veil customarily worn in public by the women of Tiflis.[8] This recurrent motif illustrates how Russian writers spun an atmosphere of exoticism around Georgia by picking out its most indisputably Islamic features. Another means of orientalization was to remove the Georgian woman from her contemporary social context and place her in the Islamic past or in a harem in another land. The most famous example is Zarema, the concubine of Khan Girei in Pushkin's Crimean poem "The Fountain of Bakhchisarai." Lermontov's short poem "A Georgian Song" (1829) shows a Georgian love slave kept by a repulsive old Armenian, and the heroine of Kamensky's harem drama in old Abkhazia ("Kelish-Bey") is a Georgian abducted in childhood by Lezgin slave traders.

THE VICTIM TURNED MURDERESS

The impulse to tell stories about harems sprang from early nineteenth-century Russians' morbid interest in the Ottoman slave trade, an activity through which some Georgian women were in fact transported to seraglios in Turkey. Kamensky's "Kelish-Bey" painted this commerce in females in the most lurid colors and left the suicidal Georgian concubine an unavenged casualty of oriental bestiality. In Lermontov's "A Georgian Song" as well, the captive heroine is summarily eliminated – executed this time by her master when he learns that she has a lover.

But in addition to such plots about utterly powerless, abused heroines, Russian literature offered the much more interesting, dualistic image of the Georgian woman as a victim with the capacity to kill. Pushkin's Zarema possesses this double identity. "The Fountain of Bakhchisarai" turns upon Zarema's jealousy provoked by Girei's infatuation with his new captive, the Polish Catholic princess Maria. Pushkin's two heroines call into service a standard opposition between the Asian libertine and the erotically restrained, more spiritually developed European Christian.[9] Dark and sensual, the Muslim convert Zarema appears as a thriving concubine determined to preserve her place of preeminence in the seraglio. By contrast, the blonde Maria is represented as a virginal figure who feels nothing but haughty indifference toward Girei and induces him to allow her to sleep unmolested in a private chamber with a cross at her bedside.

Although Pushkin builds an opposition between the Georgian libertine and the virginal European, he also stresses the fact that the fiery queen of the seraglio was a victim of slave traders. Zarema recalls her childhood in a long monologue addressed to Maria. She was abducted as a girl, at a time when her mother had begun instructing her in the Christian religion. As she herself recognizes, this brief exposure to Christianity during her childhood constitutes a point of similarity between herself and Maria. Indeed, these two women turn out to have much in common so that a more general blurring of cultural boundaries occurs in the poem.[10] In certain ways, confinement in an Asian harem resembles the restricted life Maria led in her father's household in patriarchal Poland. Similarly, the European princess' present situation as a terrified "innocent virgin," far from home, replays the events of Zarema's girlhood. The Georgian converges on Maria as an inculpable Christian victim swept into the world of the seraglio, albeit at a different time of her life.

But if once a helpless abducted female, Zarema also has the much more gripping role of the murderess. In a denouement not actually represented, the Georgian kills Maria (and then is executed by drowning). After creating intriguing lines of affinity between the two heroines, "The Fountain of Bakh-chisarai" in its resolution of plot suggests that a ferocious jealousy, to the point of murder, is distinctively Asian. In threatening to kill Maria, Zarema says, "I can wield a knife, I was born near the Caucasus," meaning in Georgia, adjacent to the rugged mountain range. Zarema's violent proclivities are presented as innate and due to her very birth in a non-European part of the world, wilder than Maria's Catholic Poland. Maria and Zarema share violent death at the end of Pushkin's poem, but they clash in an important respect. Throughout "The Fountain of Bakhchisarai" the European appears strictly as a figure of passive innocence. She has been controlled and constrained by her father, her Crimean captors and Girei, and she is finally eliminated by enraged Zarema, apparently with no contest. By contrast, the Georgian woman assumes important functions in Pushkin's poem as both victim and killer.

Another heroine with a dual role features in Griboedov's "Georgian Night," a tragedy in verse known in manuscript to some of the author's contemporaries in the 1820s, but extant today only as a fragment.[11] Rather than creating a violated maiden, the play presents a devoted mother and introduces pagan rather than Muslim motifs. But despite these obvious differences between Griboedov's tragedy and "The Fountain of Bakhchisarai," both works show the Georgian woman as a victim transfigured into a murderess.

Griboedov's play centers on the conflict between a Georgian prince (identified only by the initial "K.") and a servant ("T.") who was his wet nurse and then his daughter's nanny. In order to ransom a favorite horse rustled by a neighbor, the prince sells one of his serfs, T.'s adolescent son. The woman pleads with him to bring back her son. The prince calls her a "Fury" and begrudgingly promises to ransom the serf but then fails to keep his word. Oblivious to the power of maternal bonds, he forgets his own filial relation to T. and feels no real concern with the woman's love for her son. In the denouement of the play, now lost, the all-nurturing mother turns hellhag to take revenge with the aid of the *ali*, malicious female spirits of Georgian paganism. Bewitched by the *ali*, the prince's daughter falls in love with a Russian officer and runs away with him. The outraged prince tracks the lovers to a mountain summit and tries to shoot the Russian, but the evil spirits have the daughter killed instead. T. then shoots her own son (whose presence in the scene is not explained in the available material). Fatally stunned by this irrational act, the prince finally comprehends how horribly he himself violated the sacred tie between parent and child. Thus in Griboedov's play the Georgian heroine's vindictiveness is so extreme that she destroys her child, killing what she loves most in the world in order to drive the prince to death.

Just as "The Fountain of Bakhchisarai" grounds Zarema's aggression in her national origins, "Georgian Night" also insinuates that T.'s crazed thirst for vengeance springs from something quintessentially Asian. With typical disregard for Georgia's status as a Christian land, Griboedov gravitates toward the exoticism of local pagan belief. The victimized mother T. might have been a pious Christian, taking consolation in prayer. Instead, she emerges as a heathen priestess who casts wicked spells and grossly offends the envisioned audience's standards of civilized behavior.

In localizing Asian danger and ferocity specifically in women, Griboedov's tragedy broaches the legend of Medea. "Colchis" was an ancient name of a western part of Georgia, and eighteenth-century Russian poetry had exhibited a fascination with this fabled domain of Medea, Jason and the Golden Fleece.[12] In continuity with this traditional interest, Griboedov endows T. with the awesome vengefulness of Greek mythology's most famous Asian sorceress and murderess of children. Like Medea, the heroine of "Georgian Night" is conversant with black magic and murders her offspring in order to devastate a man by whom she feels brutally betrayed. Of course, the parallel with the story of Medea and Jason is far from perfect because Griboedov's T. stands in maternal relation to the prince, instead of being his wife. Quite interestingly though, in "Georgian Night" the absence of the erotic in the history of the relations between the two main protagonists finds some compensation in the *ali*. In Georgian demonology, these spirits of the wilderness were generally conceived as beautiful females, crafty and cruel. According to one major tradition, they appeared naked before men to lure them to doom and reported their conquests to a hideously ugly, long-fanged Mother of Vice at an annual bacchanalia on a mountain peak.[13] By provoking the old "Fury" T. to forge an alliance with the treacherously gorgeous *ali*, Griboedov's Georgian prince is undone by a full battalion of female Asian sorcery, just as Jason in the course of his lifetime had to contend with the dangerous magic of Medea in all her guises, young and middle-aged.

LERMONTOV AND GEORGIA'S PASTORAL ALLURE

Of all the Russian writers who wrote about Georgia, Griboedov was probably most knowledgeable about the culture and history of the country, and he forged especially close personal ties with it by marrying a Georgian woman, Nina Chavchavadze. However, it was Lermontov who left the greatest number of enduring literary works about this territory, which he visited in 1837. His corpus of writings stands in continuity with Pushkin and Griboedov by sustaining the Georgian woman's dualism. However, Lermontov placed a new accent on the native maiden's attractive purity and the interrelated pristine beauty of her homeland.

Both of Lermontov's most famous Georgian heroines are named "Tamara," and one incarnates her country's pastoral allure, while the other personifies Asian danger. The latter character is the beautiful sorceress–queen depicted in the twelve-stanza poem "Tamara" (1841). She lives in a tower by Darial and exemplifies the site's dreadfulness. "Treacherous and mean as a demon," Tamara is a siren who lures men with her sweet voice, seduces them and then has them murdered. Lermontov presents this combination of debauchery and violence as a definitively oriental blend. Tamara is a *"peri"* with chambers like a seraglio, guarded by a eunuch and furnished with a "downy soft bed" and luxurious fabrics. Very much like Pushkin's Cleopatra, who in the fragment "Egyptian Nights" allows a man to sleep with her at the price of his life, Lermontov's Tamara holds noisy orgies at night and has the decapitated bodies of her lovers thrown into the Terek in the morning. With her total dedication to fornication and killing, the ravishing Georgian queen of Lermontov's imagination transmitted a typically Eurocentric nightmare of Asian licentiousness and violence.

No simple fabrication on the part of a foreigner, Lermontov's "Tamara" tapped a vein of Georgian legend. During its most glorious era in the twelfth century, Georgia was ruled by Queen Tamar, and two diametrically opposed bodies of lore came to be associated with her name. The stronger tradition, belonging to a pagan cult which survived into the nineteenth century, took Tamar as a miraculous healer, the queen–physician, onto whom attributes of the Christian Virgin were sometimes projected.[14] However, "Tamar" also was one of the names featured in traditional stories about a sexually depraved, man-killing sorceress who lived by the Terek.[15] The *récit de voyage* of the French consul in Tiflis, Jacques-François Gamba, had definitely acquainted Lermontov with such a story in which the woman was called "Daria." Perhaps the poet even knew the tradition naming the wicked temptress "Tamar."[16]

However versed in Georgian legend, Lermontov displayed a personal conviction about woman's treacherous dualism by inventing a second Tamara, the fallen virgin of "The Demon." This Tamara cuts the figure of the good *alter ego* of the wicked temptress who lurks at the Darial Pass. Again, the poet probably took some inspiration from Georgian lore.[17] However, none of the relevant material, concerning the love of a mountain god for a beautiful mortal, anticipated Lermontov's story about the erotic conquest of a helpless maiden.

While charged with tragic import as a mighty rebel from God, the Demon indubitably behaves as an incubus bent on sexual possession.[18] Lermontov's supernatural hero is a daunting winged figure who can view the whole world as he cruises the skies.[19] He activates the plot, haunts Tamara's bedroom at will and displays a dazzling eloquence when he openly confronts her. On the other hand, the heroine is dominated in a patriarchal world – a "sad slave" whose father intends to marry her to a rich man. In a process of silencing, Lermontov largely deprives Tamara of a voice in the seduction scene. Her Christian defenses are steadily eroded by the Demon's bewitchment until she is reduced to quivering vulnerability, ready to be ravished. Lermontov euphemistically attributes Tamara's death to the "fatal poison" of the Demon's kiss. But an incubus' more ambitious erotic designs are etched in a rhetoric of phallic assault: "Alas! the evil spirit triumphed!" in action "irresistible as a knife."

Tamara's sexual awakening tarnishes her, but she never completely loses her aura of moral purity. Even before the seduction scene, she becomes a "sinner" by hearing the Demon's voice and experiencing erotic desire. Likewise, Lermontov twice attributes a "sinner's soul" to the dead woman. This introduces a shade of moral dissolution; and yet in the end, a guardian angel triumphs over the Demon and flies away with Tamara's soul, absolved of sin and accepted in the realm of the blessed. The emissary from God asserts that the heroine was not evil: she loved, he says, and "Heaven has opened for love!"

Lermontov correlates Tamara's dominant quality of goodness to her homeland's compelling beauty. Beginning with Griboedov's verse celebrating the Alazani valley with its "gift of purple grapes," Russian lyric poets represented Georgia as a warm, fruitful country and often associated it with sensuous local maids.[20] In a culmination of this pastoral tradition, the Georgian maidens of Lermontov's "The Demon" and "Mtsyri" became emblems of their land in lines of verse memorized by generations of Russian readers.[21] The Earth is "God's world" in "The Demon," and Tamara is its crowning glory. She is conjoined with grassy valleys, sparkling brooks, flowers, ivy and almond trees. The union between the land and the woman is emphasized by the exclusion of male characters from the poem's Arcadian spaces. Similarly, in "Mtsyri" a young Georgian woman "svelte as a poplar" is observed alone in a lush landscape, as though she is the most definitive human inhabitant of the place. This latter text takes a step toward gendering the land through a reference to the Aragva and Kura rivers as "two sisters."[22] If not so emphatic as Bestuzhev-Marlinsky's symbol of the Alazani river as a bride-to-be, this detail none the less illustrates how the pristine Georgian countryside tends to assumes a feminine character by mirroring local maidens in Lermontov's poetry.

The pastoral urge to invent Georgia as an erotically enticing female was exemplified most elaborately in one of the era's least artful pieces of literature, Alexander Shishkov's *Ketevana*.[23] This unfinished novel deals with events in Kakhetia in 1812 when local peasants spontaneously revolted against the imperial regime and annihilated some detachments of tsarist soldiers. In conformity with the general norm of literature about Georgia, Shishkov focuses upon a native maiden, the gorgeous and clever Ketevana, who falls in love at first sight with the hero Lonskoy, a Russian military man of unblemished honor. The foils to these two major protagonists are upper-class Georgian men – an assortment of emasculated fools and contemptible conspirators, intent upon manipulating the hot-headed peasantry for their own selfish ends and conjoined to Persia in their resistance to Russian rule.

In an autobiographical digression in the novel Shishkov recalled his first trip to Georgia. When he saw the sunny, verdant country for the first time, the place assumed in his eyes the delightful form of a "beautiful woman, lying luxuriantly on a multicolored carpet, her head resting on the snowy Caucasus as on a white pillow, while the fragrant roses of Gilan bloom at her feet!"[24] Used in Russian travel literature as well, this metaphor endows the land with gender as an amply contoured odalisque, reclining before the admiring eye of the foreign male observer.[25] Shishkov's hero Lonskoy likewise perceives Georgia in an enticing womanly guise: upon his arrival, after an arduous journey on horseback over the mountains, he finds the salubrious air "sweet as the kiss of a bride-to-be for her fiancé, home from a campaign" (432). These rhetorical figures of a passive odalisque and a passionate fiancée are paralleled in the plot by the bosomy, sultry Ketevana (and to a lesser extent, by a secondary Georgian character, Nina, a more subdued lovely woman who is married to a decrepit local prince). Ketevana is fiercely attracted to Lonskoy as a man from a more refined, advanced civilization, and she refuses to wed the Georgian suitor her father has selected for her. However, "Asian" excesses put the cool-headed Russian hero on guard: the heroine's "black eyes were too fiery: a flame burned in them but did not warm the heart" (445).

Shishkov's novel clearly constructs an elaborate pattern of meaning about Georgia as a smoldering oriental woman, unpossessed by local men and voluptuously languishing. In various incarnations (Ketevana, Nina, the country itself) the feminine entity waits to be taken by Russia, represented exclusively as male (Lonskoy, the author as traveler, and the apparatus of tsarist functionaries, including a man who abducts Nina). The metaphor of erotic promise functions as an invitation to exert imperial domination over the territory: in this novel about revolt from the tsarist administration the sexual dynamics are harnessed to a belief in Russia's right to subjugate all elements of the Georgian population, from the deposed royal family to the mutinous peasantry. At the same time, Shishkov's rhetoric about the country as a generously endowed, unravished beauty points to the economic goals of Russian imperialism in the "virgin" Caucasus.

THE ABSENT GEORGIAN BRIDEGROOM

With its depiction of a heroine who rejects a local man in favor of a tsarist officer, *Ketevana* is but one illustration of Russian literature's tendency to make the Georgian male strictly a non-contender in the erotic realm. Men from Russia score the greatest success with Georgian women ("Georgian Night," Lermontov's "Rendez-vous," 1841), although an occasional Armenian (Kamensky's "Maiko") or even a "Tatar" rival is allowed into the picture ("Rendez-vous").[26] Sometimes the Russian male writer presumed to create the voice of the foreign female, pining for a lover of his nationality.[27] This rhetorical move is particularly striking, for example, in Yakov Polonsky's "Nina Griboedova," a poem which fashions the young Georgian widow into a veritable icon of undying fidelity to the memory of her Russian husband. With respect to the exercise of erotic power, "The Demon," of course, has a special stature, since it deals with a hero not of this world. But it is highly relevant that Lermontov did not discourage his contemporaries from taking the mighty "spirit of evil" as his *alter ego*.[28] In Russian literature, no Georgian man ever wins a woman's heart, and Lermontov's poem conforms to the rule with its forceful hero who ravishes Tamara, after easily defeating her fiancé in a duel on a cliff.

The pattern of cross-cultural erotic alliance reached its apotheosis in Alexander Odoevsky's "The Marriage of Georgia and the Russian Kingdom" (quoted in this chapter's epigraph). The allegory personifies Georgia as a fiery dark "maiden," while Russia is a bold, light brown-haired giant who guides the axis of the world with an iron hand. Afire with passion for her bridegroom, the woman has refused all "other suitors." By referring to defeated rivals who failed to win Georgia, Odoevsky no doubt alluded primarily, if not exclusively, to Persia and Turkey. However, this poem's bridegroom clearly has bettered the woman's *local* suitors, in addition to the two Muslim contenders. The allegory does not depict Georgia's male population, but the implicit lack of a good match at home lies behind the feminized territory's surrender to the Russian colossus.

The absent Georgian bridegroom is the most telling index of the generally wretched status which men of the native realm are allotted in Russian literature. Not a single work by a Russian writer has a Georgian hero, although Caucasian Muslim tribesmen won this honor, as witnessed most saliently by Bestuzhev-Marlinsky's "Ammalat-Bek," Lermontov's "Izmail-Bey" and Tolstoy's *Hadji Murat*. Instead of central, heroic roles for native men, the general norm in writing about Georgia is the unappealing bit part. The drunkard, the rash fool, the coward, the evil bandit, the incarnation of impotence – these are the major roles in which the Georgian man briefly struts across the stage.

Russians' standard idea of Georgia as a place full of vineyards naturally produced many heavy drinkers in the literature. Lermontov's catalogue of orientals in the poem "An Argument," typifies the Georgian man as an imbiber of sweet wine, indolently sprawled under a shady tree. A jollier enthusiasm for the grape as part of the good, easy life is attributed to the upper classes in Polonsky's verse "To a Kakhetian." In a more sensational key, Kamensky's "Maiko" presents a picnic near Gori as the occasion for "one of those Georgian drinking bouts, next to which all the orgies of the ancient and modern worlds seem child's play."[29] Likewise, in another piece of pulp, entitled "A Feast in the Caucasus," local Georgian men run to "Asian" excesses and become wildly drunk at a picnic, while the visiting Russian narrator styles himself a "European" who takes part in the festivities with relative restraint.[30]

Along with the drunkard, Lermontov also shaped images of the Georgian as a rash, timorous, thievish or impotent man. Tamara's fiancé in "The Demon" represents the first type. When the Demon starts blinking his unearthly lights at night on a dangerous stretch of the mountain road, the imprudent fiancé charges with his sword and is lured over a precipice to his death. In this dramatic scene Lermontov calls the fiancé's entourage a band of "timid Georgians," scurrying away in terror. To turn from cowardice to thievery, a few lines in "The Demon" scornfully characterize one of Tamara's paternal ancestors as a robber of travelers and pillager of villages – an "evil man," in short, who in his old age had a chapel constructed high in the mountains as an act of repentance. Finally, in Tamara's gray-haired father Gudal we have a figure of impotence who fails to protect his daughter from sexual aggression and death.

Although Gudal receives little attention in "The Demon," his ineffectuality at protecting the virgin makes him a literary cousin of the Georgian man as presented in "The Imeretian," a frank apology for imperialism written by Polonsky during his service in the governor general's office in Tiflis. The poem unfolds as a Georgian's expression of gratitude for the benefits of Russian domination over his homeland. Before a "people of the same faith" came to the rescue, Georgia was at war constantly but ineffectually. After reviewing this history of increasing desolation, the Georgian speaker condemns himself for failing to safeguard his country's beautiful women from the degradation of the Ottoman slave trade. In this characterization, the Imeretian men suffer from an impotence which is at once political, military and erotic, all summed up in the loss of local women to barbarous Muslims. By contrast, the mighty Russian saviors are credited not only with halting the shameful traffic in love slaves but also with initiating Georgia's economic development.[31]

INVENTIONS IN THE SERVICE OF EMPIRE

As in all cases of cultural myth-making, Russian literature about Georgia involved interesting repressions and distortions. Why the adamant refusal to grant heroic attributes to Georgian men? It is as though the early nineteenth-century Russian writers identified Georgian manhood exclusively with the last king of Kartli-Kakheti, Giorgi XII (d. 1800), who did indeed cut an impotent figure. He was an overweight gourmand of long standing, known for eating and drinking instead of military exploits; and in the end he was bed-ridden, dying of gout and begging the tsar to protect his country. But no matter how large this ailing monarch might have loomed in Russian minds, what makes literature's exclusion of the heroic Georgian male especially striking is that history presented so many other possibilities to the imagination. For instance, Russian writers might have drawn inspiration from Georgia's chivalric tradition of the Middle Ages, exemplified by Shota Rustaveli's *The Man in the Panther Skin* (and indeed Russians were struck by such material, but they transferred it onto Caucasian tribal heroes, like Ammalat-Bek).[32]

Aside from such fabulous feats as wrestling with wild beasts and donning their pelts, contemporary reality provided abundant evidence of Georgian courage and military prowess. After the annexation, many men of this nation served as officers in the tsarist army. They participated in the Napoleonic wars and fought alongside Russians in combat against Turkey, Persia and the Caucasian Muslim tribes. Finally, without broaching warfare, the literature might at the very least have reflected the wide range of mutually rewarding professional and personal relationships which developed between Russian and Georgian men beginning in the late 1820s. Along with the contacts made in the army or the imperial administration, the homes of Prince Grigol Orbeliani and Griboedov's father-in-law Prince Alexander Chavchavadze left many a Russian sojourner in Georgia with memories of warm hospitality and evenings of stimulating talk, often focused on literature.[33] Yet with the small exception of the Russified Pavel Tsitsianov, cited as an effective military commander in the epilogue of Pushkin's "The Prisoner of the Caucasus," none of this varied experience – on the battlefield, in the office and in the salon – yielded any positive images of Georgians in Russian literature.

The consistent denial of power, courage, vigor, intellectual gifts and erotic appeal to Georgian men required active repression on the part of Russian writers, a fact that did not go entirely unobserved in the nineteenth century. In response to the dismissive characterization of the fiancé's entourage in "The Demon," a relative of Lermontov protested that the poet's service as an officer in the Caucasian army had undeniably shown him that "Georgians are not timid."[34] So why, asked the memoirist, did Lermontov cast them in this mold? The question could be extended to the pervasive disparagement of Georgian men in Russian literature; and the answer seems to be that depreciating Georgian manhood afforded Russian males a gratifying self-image as members of the vast, empire-building nation which they thought destined to assume "European" suzerainty over a somnolent little territory in Asia. Although in various writings Lermontov expressed profound doubt about the rectitude of Russia's war against the rebellious Muslim mountaineers, in the introductory section of "Mtsyri" he called tsarist domination of Georgia a providential occurrence – an act of "divine grace" which allowed the small country to prosper in peace, behind a "barrier of its friend's bayonets."

While romantic Russian writings about the Muslim tribes included plenty of oriental love slaves, literary Georgia interlaced sexual and national subjugation in a peculiar fashion. In the treatment of the Georgian male, Russian literature underwrote the imperialist designs of the tsarist state by inventing a quintessentially impotent Asian other (whose historical prototype was Giorgi XII). Authors sometimes implicated Georgian men in wild behavior (drunken carousing, contemptible banditry, connivance with the barbarous Persians), but enervation was the primary sign of their membership in a primitive, stagnant orient of the imagination. The Georgian never figured in the literature as a valiant comrade in arms of Russians, combatting forces of Islam for the sake of Christian civilization. He seemed to have a permanent hangover, and this definitive lack of energy conspicuously entailed sexual impotence (by stark contrast to erotically strenuous Muslim tribesmen such as Ammalat-Bek and Izmail-Bey).

Although the invention of the impotent native male served a crucial role in the cultural mythology, the quest for a satisfying European identity *vis-à-vis* Georgia relied primarily upon the *topos* of the land as a double-sided oriental woman. In the corpus of writings created exclusively by male Russian authors, the alterity of the Caucasian country was rendered mainly as sexual difference. Women held center stage as the major representatives and the incarnations of Georgia; tales of love abounded in which they succumbed to passion for Russian men (or else that relentlessly forceful and *therefore* "non-Asian" seducer, the Demon); and happy marital union became the ruling metaphor for imperial domination. This mythology of elective erotic affinities repressed all of history's conflicts and found a vital point of historical reference in Griboedov's marriage to Nina Chavchavadze.

However, no doubt precisely because they knew that the annexation entailed strife and aggression, Russian writers needed to invent Georgia not merely as an enticing, passive

creature but also as a violent woman who could provide justification for the brutalities of empire-building. For this role
too history supplied a prototype, the deposed and humiliated
Georgian queen Miriam who killed the tsarist general I. P.
Lazarev with a dagger when he came to her quarters with
orders to deport her in 1803.[35] Almost entirely repressed by
Russian writers, the death-dealing queen nevertheless had her
revenge: she haunted the literary imagination to produce murderous daughters (Pushkin's Zarema, Griboedov's surrogate
Medea and Lermontov's hellish Tamara).[36] But the plot of a
Georgian woman's hostility to a Russian man was strictly
taboo in literature. To the contrary, writers insisted on cross-
cultural erotic alliance and thus could have Georgia both
ways – loving Russia but needing to be tamed.

The psychosexual dynamics of Russia's embattled protectoral relations with Georgia evidently did much to foster this
imperial mythology's relentless Eurocentrism. During an era
when the French in particular repeatedly berated them as a
nation of barbarians, Russian writers used the literary Caucasus to resolve a complex cultural anxiety about being insufficiently European. But while little orientalizers like Kamensky consistently assumed a Eurocentric posture toward all the
Caucasian peoples, Pushkin, Bestuzhev-Marlinsky and Lermontov inscribed Russia's entire gamut of mixed feelings
about difference from the West. They achieved a gratifying
reconciliation between the Russian self and the orient by
fashioning macho Muslim heroes as their Asians of choice.
Georgia, on the other hand, was thoroughly marginalized and
excluded from this strategy of compensation for Russia's
undeniable distance from Europe. To all appearances, the
psychology of sexual domination assumed an enormous role
in Russian literary imagination. Giorgi XII acquired mythic
stature as the impotent king, in a real sense outmanned by
the equally unforgettable Miriam, the queen who wielded a
phallic weapon to strike a blow for her nation's honor. Contempt for the helpless Georgian man and a will to break the
resistance of the potentially dangerous Georgian woman pervaded this subdivision of the literary Caucasus. Set outside

the privileged circle of a manly, tribal Asia packed with authorial surrogates, Georgia was emasculated and feminized as the orient which declared Russian empire-builders equal to the British in India.

CHAPTER 12

The anguished poet in uniform

Two hours in the flowing water
The battle raged. In vicious slaughter,
Not speaking, face-to-face like beasts,
Men killed, and bodies dammed the river.

Lermontov

Unlike his writings inspired by Georgia, late Lermontov's works dealing with the Muslim tribes conveyed a suspicion that the conquest was a spiritually losing proposition for Russia. Bestuzhev-Marlinsky's vision of the "angel of death" in Eden hinted as much about the war. It was Lermontov, however, who most memorably illuminated the Caucasus' contradictory character as a redemptive space and a killing field. The autobiographical foundation was compelling. During his relatively brief exile in 1837 Lermontov did not see action. But after a duel with the son of the French ambassador in St. Petersburg in 1840, he was sent to a perilous area of the front by express orders from Nicholas I.[1] A commissioned officer, the poet participated in combat and twice won recommendations for awards for bravery, which the government refused to approve, however, so that he could not demand a discharge for distinguished service. During his first exile Lermontov had decided to request retirement from the army in order to devote himself exclusively to writing. The wish to remain a civilian poet was already symptomatic of tensions inscribed in late works.

Lermontov's letters often struck notes of heroic adventure in the Caucasus. On the eve of his first exile, for example, the writer mused about his prospects with a self-mocking reference to Napoleon's claim: "Les grands noms se font a l'Orient."[2] While heavily ironic, the comment none the less indicated the author's real interest in Napoleon's Egyptian campaign as an imperial venture with avowed scientific, as well as military objectives.[3] The preeminent empire-builder of modern times, Napoleon would remain in Lermontov's eyes an unforgettable incarnation of the self-willed individual ascendant over the common herd (as seen in the poem "The Last Housewarming," 1841). War's enhancement as courageous action was a vital part of Napoleon's aura. To judge by the letter Lermontov wrote to Aleksei Lopukhin two months after a gory battle at the Valerik river in Chechnia in July 1840, he was by no means immune to this martial contagion: he claimed that he had "developed a taste for war" as an addictive form of gambling next to which society's pleasures seemed sham.[4]

However, despite the Napoleon connection and the avowed relish for war as a deadly game of chance, both *A Hero of Our Time* and "Valerik" disclosed Lermontov's anguish about committing aggression against the Caucasus, while valuing it as a redemptive, Parnassian retreat. For all his heroic posturing, Lermontov never renounced his view of Russia as a brutal "Roman" state bent on subjugating a primitive world of harmonious relation to nature ("Izmail-Bey"). Quite strikingly, his empathy with the orphaned tribal hero of the late poem "Mtsyri" sustained his early fixation on expansionist Russia's destruction of families and entire communities in the Caucasus. Lermontov had imagined war in "Izmail-Bey" and other tales of adolescence, but during military service the carnage of battle, the "punitive" ruination of crop lands and destruction of livestock became stark realities of the conquest in which he was taking part. He consequently had to contend with his culpability as a member of the rapacious imperial army in the Edenic Caucasus.

GOING "NATIVE"

Lermontov's confused identity as a campaigner in the orient reverberates in Pechorin in *A Hero of Our Time*. As critics have repeatedly observed, the relationship between the author and his hero is particularly complex.[5] Through the novel's multi-voiced narration, the disruption of chronology and the accumulation of a variety of incidents, Pechorin acquires an enigmatic, contradictory character. He is indubitably endowed with some of the author's own attitudes, beliefs and ideas about Asia and wilderness alike. However, Pechorin remains something of the Byronic *poseur* without ever fully recognizing this about himself. Lermontov stands furthest from him in that regard and manipulates him to parodic ends.

In regard to Asian culture, the author and hero are tightly bonded by a preoccupation with kismet. As noted earlier, Lermontov near the end of his life averred to Andrei Kraevsky that Russia should draw upon the East's "cache of riches" instead of continually "trying to match Europe and the French." Pechorin's meditations on personal destiny reflect the author's own engagement with Islam's philosophical treasures.[6] This theme reaches a culmination in the novel's concluding episode, "The Fatalist," a tale set in a Cossack *stanitsa* along the Terek where Pechorin goes for two weeks on a mission. Is fate stamped on one's forehead and the hour of death foreordained, as the the idea of "Mohameddan predestination" maintains? Or do free will and the power of reason play a decisive role in controlling the course of one's life? Pechorin repeatedly changes his mind about this philosophical matter. As far as the action of the novel is concerned, the scale tips in favor of free will, malevolent as it may be. Pechorin's scheming behavior proclaims his confidence in being master of his destiny, and some of his references to "fate" simply shield him from facing his own responsibility for demolishing people.[7] Pechorin shows no awareness of self-deception on this matter, however, and Lermontov leaves the thorny issue of determinism unresolved.

Although Lermontov may have been groping toward a new formulation about Russia's distinctive third path somewhere between eastern and western cultures, *A Hero of Our Time* achieves no positive synthesis. To the contrary, Pechorin precipitates violent strife in Chechnia (and Russian society too, as represented at Piatigorsk in the episode "Princess Mary"). In arranging the abduction of the Circassian Bela in the novel's opening story, Pechorin brings ruin to all the principal tribal protagonists.[8] Bela is hopelessly degraded by the standards of her native culture and finally murdered by Kazbich as revenge for the horse Pechorin stole to use as the illicit brideprice. The heroine's family falls apart when her brother delivers her to Pechorin and absconds with the prized horse. Her father is then killed by Kazbich, inconsolable over the loss of his splendid steed. While never perceived by Pechorin as an analogue of imperialist conquest, his careless destructiveness parallels the tsarist state's onslaught against the tribes. His lethal domination of Bela in particular certainly seems to predicate a Eurocentric view of the Caucasus as an inferior realm destined to come under Russian rule.[9]

But while the story has political undercurrents, the degree of Lermontov's complicity in Pechorin's behavior is devilishly hard to define. The master of "wicked irony," the author maintains throughout the novel varying degrees of distance from his protagonists.[10] Commentators have shed much light on Lermontov's ironic stances in various parts of *A Hero of Our Time*, but "Bela" has a special parodic thrust all its own. The work extensively reproduces a genre of violent oriental tale often featured in the *Library for Reading* at the time. First issued separately in 1839, "Bela" mounts an attack against one particular case, the semi-anonymous "The Bedouin Woman" published the previous year.[11] A tale of a cross-cultural love affair during the French conquest of Algeria, "The Bedouin Woman" hypocritical offers readers the vicarious pleasure of illicit sex in wild Asia. Concubinage with native women is rampant in this story's Foreign Legion, and soldiers are prone to gang rape during their raids on Bedouin villages. However, the high-minded German hero (Franz) preserves the heroine (Ambra) from such a fate, hides her in his tent, moralistically declines her invitations to sex and tries to marry her after military authorities have forced her to go home to her father, a powerful sheik. After constructing the Bedouin woman as an erotically unbridled, self-styled "slave" of love, the author reports her brutal death on the story's last page: following Franz's death in combat, a comrade reads his diary, to learn that the sheik and his sons knifed Ambra to punish her for loving a giaour.

As these remarks make evident, "The Bedouin Woman" offered a two-sided pleasure to the historical audience, newly aware of the Caucasus as "Russia's Algeria." On the one hand, consumers of this oriental tale could relish illicit sex and violence by running with the dissolute pack of secondary male characters (including the French commander-in-chief). But at the same time, the reader could recover moral high ground by identifying with atypical Franz – the protective, virtuous hero with marriage on his mind.

"Bela" parodically reproduces much of the oriental genre's discourse, only to deny readers a hero who towers as a pillar of European refinement in barbarous Asia. Although a sensitive man with an exceptional mind, Pechorin is depicted as a degenerate who goes "native" in the orient. Given the viciousness of intrigues at the Russian spa in Piatigorsk, *A Hero of Our Time* extensively blurs boundaries between "civilized" and "uncivilized" behavior at the societal level.[12] But Pechorin, of course, is the primary case of the Russian who acts like a Caucasian bandit. He no doubt transmits some of Lermontov's own emulation of oriental machismo. However, when viewed alongside pulp like "The Bedouin Woman" and the literary Caucasus' related tradition of cross-cultural love stories, "Bela" reads as a parody of plots about chivalrous Christian soldiers intent on delivering Muslim women from barbarism. Like literature's little orientalizers, Russian journalists too asserted the religious commitment of tsarist campaigners in the Caucasus.[13] "Bela" thoroughly travesties this sanctimonious fiction of gallant Orthodox designs on the Muslim beauty. In fact, the tale turns the Eurocentric cultural mythology completely on its head: with no aspiration to induct the tribeswoman into Christian civilization via marriage, Pechorin yields to predatory urges which engineer her extermination.

Lermontov never expressed a concept of layered personality, comparable to Bestuzhev-Marlinsky's notion of the "genteel coat" of civilization covering the wild beast within. Nevertheless, a pattern of degeneration into savagery is etched in *A Hero of Our Time* in the chronological rather than narrative sequence of Pechorin's adventures with women. The novel covers a period of approximately seven years in episodes arranged in the following order: "Bela," "Maksim Maksimych," "Taman," "Princess Mary" and "The Fatalist." But the flashback structure forces the reader to unscramble the thread of events to arrive at a conventionally ordered biography of Pechorin, who has already died returning from a trip to Persia when the novel starts. "Taman" begins the chronological sequence and is followed around two years later by "Princess Mary." Next come "The Fatalist" and "Bela" within a few months of one another (although it is debatable which of the two occurs first).[14] The chronological conclusion is "Maksim Maksimych" when Pechorin is encountered briefly on his way to Persia, a few years after the events of "Bela."

The three episodes featuring women chart a spatial progression which is at once the evolution of Pechorin's psychosexual character as he goes deeper into the Caucasus. In "Taman" on the Black Sea he is a greenhorn outwitted and fleeced by a ring of smugglers, including a young woman who nearly drowns him. Two years later (perhaps after experiencing combat), he operates with cynical self-assurance among the French-speaking Russians of the spa in "Princess Mary."[15] Now a daunting intriguer, he teases the proud young princess into falling in love with him, ruins her reputation, provokes a duel with her rejected admirer Grushnitsky and kills him. Finally, in the wilds of Chechnia, Pechorin assumes the guise of a local bandit. The furthest reaches of Asia depicted in the novel, Chechnia is a world where violence and commerce in women are the norms, and Pechorin conforms to them just as readily as he wears tribal garb, learns to ride like a *dzhigit* and drops the French so inappropriate to the frontier milieu.

By readily adhering to savage standards, Pechorin degenerates to release the "Asia" within him, that realm of depravity which Belinsky's essay on Polezhaev would proclaim a monstrous part of everybody. The violent denouement of "Bela" most overtly underscores the hero's interchangeability with an oriental. As recollected by Maksim Maksimych, the sight of Kazbich galloping away with Bela thrown across his saddle provoked Pechorin to let out a "yell no worse than any Chechen's."[16] During the story Maksim Maksimych voices unambiguous convictions about the tribes' cultural inferiority; and if we could press him on the point, we could well imagine his saying that he never meant to equate Pechorin to a Chechen. But the unsophisticated old campaigner is not Lermontov. Totally ignorant of the Byronic literature in which Pechorin is steeped, Maksim Maksimych is an obviously limited interpreter of his demonical young comrade from St. Petersburg. The comparison with a Chechen might be a slip of the tongue which he would like to qualify. It is unlikely, however, that Lermontov's pen slipped. The novel's pattern of degeneration makes Pechorin converge on Caucasian savagery in a far-reaching manner, and the phrase "no worse than any Chechen" is but a pithy summation of the whole experience of going "native."

Pechorin's degeneracy torpedoed the fiction of oriental otherness at the heart of tsarist ideology about the Caucasus. Although possibly sensed earlier, the demolition was openly remarked in Russia only in the 1850s. Soon after the publication of Lermontov's novel, confirmed believers in the civilizing mission closed their eyes to Pechorin's simulation of oriental banditry. As remarked earlier in connection with "Izmail-Bey," Belinsky found much to deplore in Pechorin but never questioned his cultural superiority over the tribesmen or Bela – that wild "daughter of the canyons," just too limited for a St. Petersburg aristocrat with a solid education. However, as we have seen, Belinsky's essay on Polezhaev expressed an acute anxiety about "European" man's backsliding into "Asia." It appears telling that Belinsky penned this assessment of the orient's corruptive power shortly after reading *A Hero of Our Time*: he seems to have registered the subversive pattern of going "native" in "Bela" but repressed it with protestations of Pechorin's firmly civilized status.

Without the interesting shade of doubt detectable in Belinsky's utterances about "Asia," Stepan Shevyrev expressed moral outrage at Pechorin but none the less saw in *A Hero of Our Time* an irrefutable demonstration that the savage Caucasus was "completely different" from "our" world.[17] These men of Lermontov's immediate time denied the dynamic of going "native," perhaps because the war against the tribes was far from won, and they had to maintain their faith in its rectitude. In 1858, however, the critic A. Galakhov would open a very different perspective. After proclaiming Pechorin's escapades "bestial," Galakhov declared that Lermontov had made it impossible to distinguish the "civilized barbarians" from the "uncivilized" ones.[18] As this deft formulation made clear, *A Hero of Our Time* dismantled the therapeutic fiction of oriental alterity (although not so openly as to frustrate Belinsky's and Shevyrev's wish to keep Pechorin securely inside enlightenment's camp).

WILDERNESS AS A WOMAN

Pechorin's capacity to play the Chechen wild man in no way interferes with his romantic cult of the Caucasus' natural beauty, the second indisputable bond between him and the author. One of the novel's most remarkable stylistic achievements, the depiction of scenery has multiple functions. In the travelogue frame of "Bela," for example, the master narrator's evocations of nature build suspense by retarding Maksim Maksimych's story of Pechorin and his Circassian concubine. On the other hand, the passages of landscape description in Pechorin's private journal ("Taman" and "Princess Mary") contribute enormously to his characterization, as we shall see. But while turned to different uses, the natural setting is consistently rendered in a precise, pictorial language antithetical to Bestuzhev-Marlinsky's famous, extravagant rhetoric.[19]

Mature Lermontov's dislike of grandiloquence ran counter to tendencies of his adolescent verse. As we saw in chapter 8, the budding poet associated the Caucasus with both rugged men and his lost mother. In the feminine sphere, nubile mountain maids nudged aside the maternal presence in two other lyrics of the same period. A pastoral promise of spiritual renewal and redemption surrounds the heroine of "The Circassian Woman" (1829). Equally enraptured by the "glories of savage nature" and the local "maiden," the poet likens love at first sight to the flight of a repentant spirit aroused by "sounds from paradise" and determined to gaze upon heaven itself. Here the Circassian beauty appears as the natural woman who can lead the adoring traveler into the earthly "paradise" of the pristine wilderness. Lermontov's "Morning in the Caucasus" (1830) accentuates erotic rather than spiritual appeal. After describing the gradual spread of rosy light across the mountains at sunrise, the poem ends by comparing the scene to "girls blushing all over" when they catch sight of a man watching them bathe in a shady pool.[20] An ambiguous figure, the tribal Peeping Tom is described as an attractive admirer whom the women resist with difficulty. The voyeurism makes the tribesman the vehicle of the male poet's own eroticized yearning to derive instinctual gratification from virgin wilderness.

While disdaining such tropes so reminiscent of nature as the sun-kissed "beauty" ogled in Bestuzhev-Marlinsky's travelogues, *A Hero of Our Time* retains significant vestiges of adolescent Lermontov's pastoral associations between the territory and a mother or maiden. The notion of the land as a surrogate mistress figures in Pechorin's journal in "Princess Mary." A coquettish quality is projected onto the cherry trees which "look into" his open window at Piatigorsk, spread their perfume around the room and strew blossoms across his desk as he writes (62). These sensory details suggest the gestures of a flirtatious *belle*, coaxing him to come outside. Likewise, when Pechorin recollects riding to the duel with Grushnitsky, he says that the beauty of the morning made him feel "in love with nature more than ever" (120). The verb (*liubil*) could arguably be rendered simply as "loved," but the passage conveys an emotional vibrancy and heightened feeling which justifies "in love" (as Vladimir Nabokov has it in his translation). In a third pertinent passage, Pechorin indirectly eroticizes nature while trying to deny and repress the very impulse: "There is no woman's gaze that I would not forget at the sight of mountains covered with curly vegetation and illumined by the southern sky, at the sight of the blue sky, or at the sound of a torrent falling from crag to crag" (81). This defiant assertion puts untamed nature and erotically compelling women on the same plane. Pechorin imposes a system of rivalry between them and in so doing, suggests that he seeks the same sort of instinctual gratification from both. Chronologically anterior to his adventure with Bela, these musings about wilderness communicate his subsequently expressed hope that a beautiful Circassian "angel" might revive his jaded spirit and bring him into harmony with the natural life.

The undercurrent of erotic longing coexists with the novel's more prominent motif of childlike relation to nature. In this mode Pechorin denies the surrogate mistress and projects wilderness as a consoling maternal presence. Most strikingly, he characterizes the pure air as a caressive force, the "kiss of a child" which in turn renders him "childlike," purified of "passions, desires, regrets" (62). The master narrator in "Bela" expresses an identical notion of recovering a state of childlike innocence under the impact of the pristine Caucasian environment (27). *A Hero of Our Time* thus imbues nature with maternity by attributing filial love to the *observer* (even though wilderness itself is the source of the childlike kiss).

This rhetorical interchange is most evident in an episode immediately after the duel with Grushnitsky. In a moment of despair, Pechorin falls to the ground and weeps "like a child" (only to coolly analyze his overwrought state a short while later, 130). He flings himself onto the earth, as though seeking comfort. The force of the action is such that critics generally detect a hidden metaphor of filial relation to the land. A classic statement of 1914 concluded that Pechorin's love for the magnificent Caucasian environment was a love for "Mother Nature who gathers her prodigal sons into a compassionate embrace."[21] Later readers expressed similar opinions about nature's consoling power, without invoking the figure of the great mother.[22] One should not forget that

Pechorin sometimes perceives a decidely unmaternal, ominous quality in the wilderness, as when he likens clouds to snakes coiled around a mountain peak. But even a recent commentator who acknowledges such complexities in Lermontov's treatment of landscape insists that the hero is fundamentally a "child of nature" who shares "her" (the metaphorical parent's) inconsistencies and amorality.[23] In this reading, Mother Nature prevails, ready to console Pechorin but maddeningly indifferent to human values.

THE SADO-MASOCHISM OF WAR

Pechorin's incapacity to retrieve a lost state of innocent harmony with nature expressed Lermontov's sense of a human proclivity to evil which may take its toll on the perpetrator as well as the victim. *A Hero of Our Time* often presents the Caucasus through Pechorin's eyes as an unsullied space with the restorative properties of a garden, but the serpentine clouds have a sinister ring. The figurative snakes give nature itself a multiple character. More importantly, however, the trope evokes original sin to suggest that humanity is a fallen race incapable of recovering the prelapsarian condition of the wondrous garden which is nature at its best. This intimation of evil seeds in the human soul enriched Lermontov's recurrent theme of human disharmony with beauteous nature, as in "Three Palms" (1839), a verse about a desert oasis wantonly destroyed by an Arab caravan.

The violation of nature's pastoral promise assumes self-inculpatory shape in "Valerik," Lermontov's definitive poem of war in the Caucasus. Based on personal experience, the work deploys a rhetoric of confession which uncovers psychic division in the poet in uniform. "Valerik" is framed as a letter to a woman of the Russian *beau monde*, and the opening words signal a mode of "interior dialogization" defined in Bakhtin's work on Dostoevsky.[24] Lermonov starts with the phrase, "I am writing to you randomly." The pronouns announce a first-person narrative addressed to a chosen party. But a curious note is struck by the adverb "randomly" (*sluchaino*, which might also be translated "by chance" or "accidentally"). This beginning establishes a contradictory, combative relation to the addressee: the writer feels compelled to send a confessional word to the woman; but by declaring the act a random occurrence, he seeks to deny her significance as the interlocutor and declares himself indifferent to her reaction to his revelations. Wary of the silent addressee's anticipated responses, he is on guard against her from the outset.

Impelled to confess and yet on the defensive, the poet assumes a sado-masochistic stance toward the woman. He first stresses his injury as the loser in their love affair of years ago: he is the adoring admirer who was rejected but never forgot the beloved. However, a lexicon of quasi-religious guilt quickly complicates this simple picture of a victim and his victimizer. As recalled by the writer, "days of bliss" were "paid for" in years of "fruitless repentance." The failed affair is the "cross" he bears, the "punishment" he still endures. Ironic as it may be, the rhetoric of sin and retribution conveys guilt about the break-up and gives the impression that the narrator may have provoked the woman to leave him by taking his turns as the victimizer.

The letter's overall thrust communicates the full extent of the writer's sado-masochistic sentiments toward his addressee. The frame starts with elegiac recollection of lost bliss, but then the poem's narrative section confronts the society *belle* with military massacre. The letter from the Caucasian front thus operates simultaneously as an officer's confession of private anguish and a rejected lover's act of revenge: instead of gallantly sheltering a lady from the horrors of war, the poet divulges his active participation in a blood bath and rubs her face in gore.

Signaled in the opening lines, the sado-masochism bespeaks a double-sided identity confirmed by subsequent features of the frame. When describing his daily routine at the front, the poet slips into addressing himself as "you" (familiar *ty*, as opposed to the formal *vy* for her): "you slumber in thick grass / In the broad shade of a plane tree or bunches of grapes." The departure from first-person narration articulates a colloquy within a divided psyche. Rhetorically outside his own skin, the writer visualizes himself in a somnolent state, while knowing full well that he will soon be propelled into violent action. Two selves coexist in his consciousness – the drowser peacefully nestled in the lap of nature, and the blood-shedding warrior.

Like the switch from "I" to "you" for the self, a trope of war as theater reveals a bipartite mind both repelled by war and aroused by its Napoleonic challenge. Just before launching into the account of the battle at the Valerik, the poet concludes the frame by recalling an earlier skirmish he watched from afar with other officers. He characterizes combat as a "tragic ballet," a metaphor which vividly conjures a psyche split in two.[25] Situated in the figurative audience but about to depict himself in the thick of combat, the writer accentuates his dualism. He features himself as a spectator passively witnessing battle. At the same moment, though, he is poised to assume the role of the actor, the poet in uniform who mounted the figurative stage to make war by the Valerik.

These various signals of double identity and psychic distress may seem contradicted by the writer's apparently successful integration into the army. Removed from his addressee's *beau monde*, he is aswim in the rugged, masculine world of the Caucasian front. In the recollection of a battle in the frame, he conveys an electric excitement when the shooting starts. He also advertises his comradeship with the army's allied tribesmen (rendered as pleasingly distinct people with "tawny skin," "dark furtive eyes" and guttural language). A valiant Cossack also wins the poet's admiration. Given these expressions of camaraderie, some commentators have argued that Lermontov's persona achieves a satisfying identity in the military milieu and even grows wiser through combat: warfare supposedly matures him by putting him in touch with tragedy and exposing the utter vapidness of his addressee, the society *belle*.[26]

But such readings do not contend with the element of fierce self-condemnation in Lermontov's confessional epistle. Rather than attesting to the poet's mental health as a tsarist officer, the principal narrative sequence of "Valerik" confirms the sado-masochism evinced in the frame. The military persona's dual status as the punished and the punisher *vis-à-vis* his female addressee is paralleled by recognition of himself as a self-destructive murderer. In an account which corresponds to actual records about Lermontov's participation in the engagement, the poet in "Valerik" leads his troops into the fray. In the ensuing battle men methodically slaughter each other at close range for two solid hours "like beasts." The poet leaves the field in an agonized state of shell shock. While others mourn dead comrades, he can find neither "pity nor grief" in his heart. He impassively notes the piles of corpses, the pervasive smell of blood and red rivulets on the stony ground. Then he articulates his "anguish," his "deep and secret sorrow" rooted in the disjunction he perceives between slaughter and the serene beauty of the mountains against the sunny sky. Before making a detailed analysis of the poet's projection of nature, let us pause on the implications of the secrecy of his feelings. He confesses his anguish solely to this feminine addressee, even though he might have presumably revealed his depression to his Chechen *kunak* or another army comrade without calling his manhood into question. The ethos of war in "Valerik" definitely accommodates lapses from machismo, as shown by men crying over the death of a young captain shortly after the battle ends.

But the big difference is that these soldiers cry about a victim of the tribesmen, while the narrator is tormented by an isolating sense of his own criminality. In a demonstration of the way all great writers create their predecessors, "Valerik" transmits a Dostoevskian state of drastic alienation produced by killing: Lermontov's lyric persona comprehends war as murder rather than invigorating machismo only when he has blood on his hands; and as a result of combat, he becomes disconnected from his own comrades. In killing the enemy, he kills emotional capacities which bonded him to the men on his side.

To compound his self-inflicted psychic injury, the poet's slaughter of his fellow men entails aggression against nature. Although "Valerik" contains very few metaphors, Lermontov's pictorially exact representation of combat in the shallow stream acquires much symbolic power. The poem summons water's traditional associations with purification and restoration, only to show these properties destroyed by war. In the early description of army life, a Muslim tribesman performs his ablutions at a stream. Water serves a religious ritual here and calls to mind the Christian rites of baptism and purification (sometimes actually practiced in rivers). Along with spiritual cleansing, "Valerik" stresses the water's physically restorative property. During the battle the fatigued narrator wants to slake his thirst, but the water runs red and tepid with blood. As translated by the narrator's Chechen *kunak* near the end of the poem, "Valerik" means "stream of death." Although its origin is not explained, the name becomes a reality through the carnage in which the poet participates: both a literal blood bath and a figurative baptism of blood, combat perverts and annuls water's purative, restorative uses.

While "Valerik" never genders the land, the soldiers' despoliation of restorative nature conjures the maltreatment of a primal maternal being of the sort evoked in *A Hero of Our Time*. The poem of war presents wilderness as a microcosm of the Earth, ample and bountiful enough for humanity to live together in peace. As the narrator says in his anguished state: "the sky is clear, / And beneath the sky there is room for all." These lines convey an unstated notion of a human family united in relation to the planet as a figurative mother. The poet very notably accents the land's fertility, as in the image of himself dozing in thick grass shaded by grapevines.

In addition to lush vegetation, the centrality of water in "Valerik" contributes to the intimation of Earth as a great mother violated by human children. Besides its associations with purification, restoration and rebirth, water is traditionally linked with the beginnings of life itself, in the form of amniotic fluids. Although "Valerik" has no symbols of giving birth, Lermontov's "Gifts from the Terek" draws a pertinent link between maternity and life-giving water. This anthropomorphic verse depicts the Caucasian river as a male child "born" on a mountain peak and "suckled at the breast of clouds." The Terek itself is masculine but has his source and sustenance in a watery maternal element, the rain which feeds the mountain streams. An elaborate extended metaphor, "Gifts from the Terek" conjoins mother and son in a liquid flow reminiscent of nursing and birth itself.[27] "Valerik" retains a subliminal trace of the symbolism of water as a great mother, giving and sustaining life. Like the land's fertility, the river in its natural state concretizes the abstract notion of Earth as mankind's plentiful home. The ravages of war thus acquire symbolic overtones of matricide or incestuous rape.

The intimations of heinous crime against Mother Nature reveal the full force of the poem's dialogism. Burdened by a deeply "secret" sense of violating maternal Earth, the officer's thoughts range back to Russia's erotic combat zone – back to a woman already familiar with his capacity for transgression, repentance and punishment. The confessional epistle indeed maps the comprehensive sado-masochism of a man who lacerates himself in a syndrome of crime and punishment in every sphere of his existence. Both the victim and tormenter of his addressee, he has no gratifying erotic life. By degenerating into the animality of combat, he kills his inner spark of empathy and loses communion with his comrades. As a leading, acutely self-conscious actor in the massacre, he also snaps his restorative tie to the natural world. Face to face with himself as a vicious "beast" in the Caucasian garden, the military persona of "Valerik" is a stunning embodiment of what Joseph Brodsky called Lermontov's "thoroughly corrosive, bilious self-knowledge."[28]

As an epistle never meant to be sent, "Valerik" is a self-directed confession which inscribes violent conflict about committing murder in the Caucasus in the service of the tsarist state. Engaged from the start in an intense interior polemic and a process of self-discovery, the confessor appropriately ends by spitefully writing off his addressee. In reasserting the frame, he apologizes for "boring" the woman and derides her as a social butterfly untroubled by death. "I will be happy," he says, if this "artless story" amuses you; but if it does not, simply take it as an eccentric "prank" and forget it. With these derogatory, self-mocking words, the poet slips through a well-prepared escape hatch to avoid the censure of his chosen listener. He had emotionally overwhelming reasons for selecting his addressee, he has shown his vulnerability and inculpated himself in beastly carnage. But he was never ready to hear *her* affirm the worst about him. With this conclusion the sado-masochistic despoiler is left with only himself to talk to.

The intense solipsism of interior dialogization in "Valerik" was a prophecy of the poem's failure to find sensitive interlocutors upon publication in 1843. A jump ahead of his readers, Lermontov strikingly predicted the absence of proper listeners in a letter written to Aleksei Lopukhin from Fort Grozny in October 1840. Quite possibly working on "Valerik" at the time, the poet imagined himself orally recounting his wartime experiences to Russian friends in the future. As the Caucasian campaigner tells his tale, his audience disappears: the lady of the house falls asleep, while her husband is called aside on domestic business. The poet's one remaining hearer is a baby (who "does a pooh" on his knee).[29] Containing a typically Lermontovian touch of self-derision, this anxiety about a non-existent audience was borne out in the reception of "Valerik." Nineteenth-century readers with faith in the tsarist civilizing mission were completely tone-deaf to Lermontov's song of self-destructive Russian bestiality in the Edenic Caucasus. Belinsky, for example, simply praised "Valerik" as artful embellishment of grim realities of war.[30] More tellingly, Russian veterans of the conquest admired the pictorial exactitude of Lermontov's depiction of combat, while extolling the pleasures of his poetic language.[31] Like the vanishing audience envisioned in the poet's letter from Fort Grozny, these real readers left the anguished narrator of "Valerik" isolated by not listening to everything he had to say. Young Tolstoy, however, caught more of Lermontov's tragic timbre and would copy it in "The Raid" (1853), a story also misread in the era of empire-building as a transmission of the "poetry of warfare."[32]

DEATH IN THE SANCTUARY

But if "Valerik" fell on largely deaf ears in the nineteenth century, Lermontov's fate none the less raised its own voice to inject an unforgettable romantic agony into Russia's cultural mythology of the Caucasus. Prior to the writer's duel in Piatigorsk, other Russian men of letters had died as an outcome of their contact with the "southern Siberia."[33] However, Lermontov's death struck the imagination more profoundly for several reasons. Only twenty-six, he evidently had not exhausted his creative potential. Belinsky, for example, once remarked that if Lermontov had lived, he would have surpassed Pushkin. Lermontov's reckless streak intensified the poignancy of the premature annihilation of artistic genius. He had a career as a duelist, which finally proved his undoing. Furthermore, a sense of imminent death pervades one of his most famous Caucasian lyrics, "A Dream." As the poem's speaker lies alone dying of a bullet wound in Dagestan, he imagines a woman back in Russia engrossed in a vision of his final agony the moment he expires. Written just a few months before Martynov shot Lermontov, the poem gives the eerie impression of predicting the author's death.

But besides the poignancy of a poet's dying young, the *élan* of a duel in the Caucasus and the haunting premonition of death in "A Dream," there was another aspect of Lermontov's career which probably affected nineteenth-century Russians subconsciously, even though they lacked the historical perspective to recognize it. Lermontov's life and death as the poet in uniform replicated the contradictions of Russia's own relation to the Caucasus. Beginning with Pushkin, the territory acquired a dualistic image as a Parnassian sanctuary and a bloody battlefield. When Bestuzhev-Marlinsky wrote of the "angel of death" in paradise, he pinpointed the incoherence of the cultural mythology's two strains and suggested that a

Russian national tragedy was underway. He seemed to be asking: "Can we murder our way into the restorative garden? Can we secure Eden by exterminating the natives?"

To a greater extent than any other Russian writer, Lermontov went to the heart of this paradox of genocidal warfare as the route to terrestrial paradise. The Caucasus was his Parnassian refuge from the contemptible *beau monde* and the whole repressive realm of "unwashed Russia" with its omnipresent police and slavish masses.[34] Fully alive to the wilderness' restorative, inspirational power, he told a Russian friend in 1838 that a trip to the territory would make him forget political economy and turn *him* into a poet too.[35] Lermontov saw his forays into the Caucasus not as permanent escape from his native land but rather as a time of communion with the Muse, a period to conceive and produce works through which to make a name for himself among his compatriots. Thus his lyric "Hastening northward from afar" confesses to Kazbek the fear that he may have been forgotten at home during his exile. But while Lermontov's poetry associated the Caucasus with creativity, spiritual renewal and celebrity through literature, it also conveyed the degeneracy of war, forebodings of death and a dread of oblivion.

The affective power of Lermontov's invention of the Caucasus as both a redemptive space and a killing field was amplified by Russian interpretations of his fate. Belinsky's major review of *A Hero of Our Time* set this dynamic into play in 1840. The article identified the territory as Lermontov's artistic birthplace: "The Caucasus was the cradle of his poetry, just as it was the cradle of Pushkin's."[36] The metaphor of the "cradle" very strikingly presented the Caucasus as a strictly beneficent, nurturing environment for creators of Russian literature. Belinsky knew about war and exile but denied them with the symbol of a happy nursery.

It is interesting to compare Belinsky's formulation with two contemporaneous observations, only one of which directly concerned Lermontov. The first appeared in Edmund Spencer's *Travels in Circassia* (1837). With no comments about Russian literature, Spencer viewed the Caucasus exclusively as a battleground where the tsarist state was wasting the blood of its subjects with a "wanton prodigality" inconceivable in the conduct of "any other Christian power."[37] Moreover, the casualties of combat were augmented annually by thousands of deaths from malnutrition, typhus and other diseases. The ghastly toll prompted Spencer to term the Caucasus Russia's "grave," an arresting antipode of Belinsky's "cradle."

These two figures of speech which distilled Russia's incoherent relation to the Caucasus were both implicit in Nikolai Grech's assessment of Lermontov. True to his character as a political toady who collaborated in journalistic ventures with Bulgarin and Senkovsky, Grech wrote an indignant pamphlet in response to Custine's *La Russie en 1839*. In briefly treating Lermontov, Grech asserted that the Russian government should be absolved of charges of cruelty toward the writer because military exile made his poetry flower: "Only in the Caucasus did [his talent] unfurl to its full extent."[38] This interpretation merged the Belinskian "cradle" with the poet's grave. Grech confronted Lermontov's exile and death in the Caucasus; but as an apologist for the tsarist regime, he justified the state's persecution of the poet. Lermontov's punishment became his salvation. Extermination became his route to poetic immortality.

Without noticing it, Grech displaced onto Lermontov the fundamental paradox of Russia's pursuing the Caucasian "civilizing mission" through genocidal warfare. Tsarist bloodshed took its ideological justification as a step toward enlightening the orient, so that killing the natives became in a sense the way of saving them (at least the "redeemable" survivors). In Russian national experience a similar contradiction between redemption and annihilation rebounded back against the conquerors themselves. Under the impact of Bestuzhev-Marlinsky and Lermontov, Russian men enlisted in the Caucasian army in quest of sublime, restorative wilderness. As Tolstoy would write in his story "The Wood-felling," the Caucasus in the romantic era was perceived as a "promised land" where an upper-class Russian might escape his meaningless existence and find spiritual renewal.[39] In the

Tolstoy story the Russian enlistee's anticipations about redemptive nature merely dissipate in a dull routine of cutting down a pristine forest. But more dramatically in the life of the nation, the quest for salvation and spiritual revitalization in the Caucasus ended in bloodshed. Instead of winning redemption, the Russian campaigner degenerated into bestiality during combat and desecrated the "promised land" with carnage (as Arnold Zisserman painfully acknowledged in his memoirs). These were fundamental paradoxes of imperial Russia's war in the Caucasus which Lermontov acted out as the poet in uniform. In monumentalizing his tragic fate, his nineteenth-century Russian admirers appear to have had subliminal intimations of his status as a microcosm of the nation itself at war in Edenic Asia.

CHAPTER 13

Tolstoy's revolt against romanticism

Olenin was about to speak to him, to ask what *aul* he
came from, but the Chechen spat contemptuously and
turned away after scarcely looking at him.
Tolstoy

When Tolstoy first began writing in the early 1850s while
with the Russian army in a Cossack *stanitsa* along the Terek,
he faced the tremendous challenge of finding a new word to
say about the Caucasus. The works of Bestuzhev-Marlinsky
and Lermontov were a big thorn in his side. As Tolstoy
recalled in the unfinished essay "Notes on the Caucasus. A
Trip to Mamakai-Yurt," he had embraced these two writers
as his principal sources of knowledge about the territory
during his adolescence.[1] By the time he reached his twenties,
however, he rebelled from Bestuzhev-Marlinsky and Lermontov in a quest for greater realism. Up in arms against the
literary heritage, young Tolstoy felt convinced that people did
not swoon over mountains, nor have tumultuous love affairs
with savages, nor conduct war, nor even die in combat in the
ways previously depicted.[2] His first stories about the Caucasus
accordingly sought to replace romantic modes with a more
hardheaded, fact-oriented outlook. This same general objective governed his short novel *The Cossacks*, which was tentatively begun in verse in 1852, written mainly in the latter part
of the decade and published in 1863.

As an adversary of romantic inventions, Tolstoy certainly
had his work cut out for him. By the 1850s, studies of Caucasian geography, ethnography and history had proliferated
massively in Russia. The readership could now consult an

233

enormous body of non-fiction (not all of which met the most rigorous intellectual standards, of course).[3] Moreover, a major new dispenser of information about the territory had appeared on the scene – the *Caucasus* (*Kavkaz*), a newspaper founded by the Viceroy Mikhail Vorontsov in Tiflis in 1846.[4] But despite the steady accumulation of non-fictional material, the Russian readership remained captivated by romantic literary mythology. The low success of writers bent upon edification was tellingly attested in Arnold Zisserman's memoirs. When Zisserman went to St. Petersburg on mission from the Caucasus in 1848, he encountered a civilian population complacently ignorant about the territory. One man was astonished that Zisserman had never come across his brother, another officer in the Caucasian army. "But you're all stationed together down there, aren't you?" asked the Petersburger.[5] In commenting on the conversation Zisserman sarcastically observed that like so many other members of Russia's "so-called educated class," this gentleman "imagined the Caucasus as virtually one big fortress surrounded by Circassians with whom our troops exchanged fire day after day." Although Zisserman did not say so, romantic Russian literature was glaringly implicated in the muddled outlook of the "so-called educated class." Only minds steeped in the exciting poetics of space could conjure and sustain the utterly irrational but affectively engaging notion of the Caucasus as a "big fortress" located somewhere beyond a southern cordon line and besieged by ubiquitous "Circassians."

Zisserman's experience suggests that even littérateurs who incorporated solid data into their entertaining writings had failed to achieve didactic goals. Bestuzhev-Marlinsky in particular packed a lot of creditable ethnography into "Ammalat-Bek." But how many readers simply skipped it in haste to enjoy the plot of passion and murder (as students today so frequently neglect the essays on history in *War and Peace*, in order to see how Tolstoy's fictional characters are faring)? Quite interestingly, mature Lermontov's continuing avoidance of the semi-fictional mode reflected a belief that the educative effort was futile. At the outset of "Maksim Maksimych" in *A Hero of Our Time* the master narrator announces that he intends to spare the audience "statistical remarks" about the Caucasus, being convinced that "nobody would read them anyway." Belinsky too provided complementary testimony to the readership's low toleration for the strictly *utile*. He was bored by factual but prosaic travelogues about Russia's periphery and yearned instead for novels which would divulge the exotic regions' "secret life of nature" in the fashion of James Fenimore Cooper.[6] As though to illustrate what he meant by nature's "secret life," Belinsky in another essay declared Lermontov's extravagantly anthropomorphic "Gifts from the Terek" the "apotheosis of the Caucasus."[7] Devoid of critical content, this phrase stemmed from an overwhelmingly emotional transaction with the text: Belinsky's formulation was simply the cheer of a reader enthralled by the poet's vigorously musical invention of the wild Asian frontier where a savage river delivers tributes to the imperious Caspian – the corpses of a Cossack woman shot in the breast and a Kabardinian warrior in arm plates engraved with verses from the Koran.

Young Tolstoy was not alone in resisting the readership's well entrenched taste for the literary Caucasus' irrational, aesthetic pleasures. In 1850 the leading Russian journal, the *Contemporary*, lauded Yakov Kostenetsky's military memoirs, *Notes on the Avarian Expedition in the Caucasus, 1837*.[8] The reviewer welcomed the book for providing a "wealth of facts" instead of "flowers of eloquence" and discommended literature for dealing "more with fantasy than with the Caucasus in actuality." In this attack on the textual Caucasus fathered by Pushkin, the journalist admitted that the campaign notes were not stylistically accomplished. But instead of faulting the book on those grounds, he claimed that Kostenetsky's "goodhearted directness" and "lack of artifice" were better than literature for people who truly wanted to study the Caucasus. Tolstoy regularly read the *Contemporary* at the *stanitsa* Starogladkovskaya and seems to have consciously adopted its editorial bias against literary "fantasy" in "The Raid," a story published by the journal in 1853.[9]

But while compatible with the outlook of the *Contemporary*, Tolstoy's rejection of romantic tradition evinced a considerably more complicated search for authorial identity. His early stories and *The Cossacks* display the impulse to educate readers by using footnotes. Moreover, the novel contains an entire chapter in the form of an ethnographic essay about the Grebensk community. At the same time, however, Tolstoy was bent upon finding his own brand of literary power, different from the romantics' and capable of supplanting them. In open combat with Bestuzhev-Marlinsky and Lermontov, young Tolstoy definitely seems to have suffered from what Harold Bloom effectively labeled the "anxiety of influence," a literary novice's embattled revolt from a powerful precursor who threatens to leave him overshadowed.[10] Tolstoy's combative search for an imposing voice of his own made parody a favorite weapon in his arsenal and often led him to assert himself in largely negative terms – as not-Marlinsky, not-Lermontov. All the same, *The Cossacks* not only dismantled the old poetics of Caucasian space through parody but also opened an entirely new perspective on the question of Russian relation to the oriental. The Grebensk Cossacks naturally dominate this novel, but the little Tolstoy had to say about the Muslim tribesmen marked an interesting break with romantic modes of inscribing the self in the savage.

While seeking his own literary voice, Tolstoy was also groping for self-definition in the political sphere. Unlike the exiled romantics, Pushkin, Bestuzhev-Marlinsky and Lermontov, the young count had no particular bones of contention with the state. Fed up with his dissolute life in Moscow, Tolstoy impulsively went to the Caucasus in the spring of 1851, where his brother Nikolai was serving in the army. As a *junker* (a volunteer of noble birth with a private's rank), Tolstoy had relatively comfortable quarters and plenty of time for hunting, reading and writing. Less than a month after his arrival at Starogladkovskaya, he joined a military operation as an onlooker (as depicted in "The Raid.") The thrills of the campaigner's life and a yen for military prestige led him to seek a commission.[11] However, after participating in a little fighting, he wrote in his diary in January 1853 that war was "so ugly and unjust that anybody who wages it has to stifle the voice of his conscience."[12] With the contradiction between prestigious machismo and hideous injustice unresolved, Tolstoy received his officer's commission in 1854 and asked for a transfer to join the war against Turkey, first in Wallachia and then the Crimea. A veteran of the siege of Sevastopol, he retired from the army in 1856.

As his military career would indicate, young Tolstoy reserved judgment about the rectitude of the Russian conquest of the Caucasus. In a letter to his brother Sergei and sister-in-law Maria in December 1851, he made this promise as he anticipated having a hand in a raid on a tribal village: "I'll be doing my best with the help of a cannon to facilitate the extermination of *treacherous predators and recalcitrant Asians.*"[13] Tolstoy's diction and underlining poked fun at official rhetoric about preserving Holy Russia from Muslim savages. However, a draft for "The Raid" conveyed authorial sympathy with the empire's objectives: "Who can doubt that in Russia's war against the tribesmen, justice stands on our side, stemming from a desire for self-preservation? If it were not for the war, what would protect the diversified, rich, enlightened lands of Russia from pillage, murder and raids by savage, bellicose peoples?"[14] By contrast, a different draft of Tolstoy's story granted the possibility that the tribes were also motivated by the instinct for self-preservation and a just desire to safeguard their homeland. Neither of these two contradictory evaluations was retained in the final version of "The Raid," as though the newcomer to both war and literature could not make up his mind. Even *The Cossacks* remained non-committal about the morality of the conquest, while none the less acknowledging tsarist atrocities of the sort young Tolstoy may have had in mind when he pronounced war so "ugly and unjust."

THE ASSAULT ON CAUCASIAN POETRY

More concerned with aesthetics than political ethics, "The Raid" blamed Lermontov and Bestuzhev-Marlinsky for inciting Russian military men to imitate romantic literature. The story pinpoints this phenomenon in the person of Lt. Rosen-krantz, characterized as "one of our young officers styled into dashing *dzhigity* after the works of Marlinsky and Lermon-tov. These people regard the Caucasus exclusively through the prism of the heroes of our time, the Mulla-Nurs and so forth; and they take these images as a guide for all their actions, rather than following their own inclinations."[15] A draft for "The Raid" more reproachfully opposed the literary "prism" to "reality."[16] There Tolstoy also listed Ammalat-Bek and Bela alongside Mulla-Nur and capitalized "Heroes of Our Time." An emulator of Pechorin, Rosenkrantz in the final version of "The Raid" is used to deflate Lermontov's famous plot of going "native" in "Bela." Tolstoy's character installs his Circassian mistress at the Russian fort but is a simple-hearted man in a prosaic domestic arrangement. Bent upon imitating a story, Rosenkrantz comically fails to live up to the demonic model of Pechorin in the wilds of the orient.

In elaborating the theme of life refracted through literature, Tolstoy's handsome young ensign Alanin serves as Rosen-krantz's tragic counterpoint. "The Raid" depicts the stalwart, unpretentious old campaigner Captain Khlopov as an embodi-ment of a "Russian form of courage." As articulated by Pecho-rin in *A Hero of Our Time*, this phrase defined the antithesis of Grushnitsky's foolhardy bravado shortly before the duel. With parodic thrust, Tolstoy borrows Lermontov's words only to turn them against him. Near the end of "The Raid" Alanin charges into battle in a vainglorious manner typified by the nar-rator as an "outmoded French sort of chivalry." A crusty old soldier of the Russian folk also pronounces Alanin's action stupid. By plotting Alanin's fate as an antipode of prudent, unassuming Russian courage, Tolstoy carries forward the cri-tique of the Grushnitsky type advanced in *A Hero of Our Time*. But the narrative pattern of "The Raid" contends that Lermon-tov's own novel has now assumed an invidious role in promot-ing romanticism among the readership: bedazzled by litera-ture's distortive "prism," young military travelers like Alanin have developed a bookish derring-do and are foolishly offering themselves up for slaughter.

Tolstoy's "The Wood-felling" continued to attack the literary Caucasus as the obfuscator of reality. Recounted from the same autobiographical standpoint as "The Raid," the story features a conversation between the narrator and Bolkhov, a thoroughly disillusioned officer. Bolkhov speaks of civilian Russia's "bizarre legend" of the Caucasian "promised land," where a wastrel or unhappy lover might renew his life amidst the "eternal virgin snows and stormy torrents."[17] When they actually embark on military service, the dreamers discover they have made "terrible miscalculations." Among other things, they learn that the Caucasus is divided into ordinary administrative units, the *gubernii*. Focused upon prosaic fact, this knowledge clashes mightily against the old traditions of alpine imaginative geography. In resisting the romantic poetics of space, Tolstoy insists on the superiority of actuality. Bolkhov wishes that the Caucasus had lived up to his romantic expectations, but the narrator vigorously argues that the real place is better, albeit "in a different way" than literature had led him to expect.

In this context "The Wood-felling" likens dreamy, armchair travels to the mental state induced by "verse in a language which one does not know very well." The essay "Notes on the Caucasus" had explicated this notion fully when Tolstoy recollected his boyhood and adolescent enthusiasm for Bestuzhev-Marlinsky and Lermontov:

it happened so long ago that all I remember is the poetic feeling which I experienced while reading, and the evocation of poetic images of bellicose Circassians, sloe-eyed Circassian women, mountains, cliffs, snows, rapid streams, the plane tree . . . The *burka*, dagger and sword also held a far from peripheral place in my mind. These images took shape in my imagination in an extraordinarily poetic way, being embellished upon each recollection. I had already forgotten the poems of Bestuzhev-Marlinsky and Lermontov long before, but each time my mind returned to the images, new poems came into being, each one a thousand times more alluring than the last. I did not even try to convey them in words because I knew it was impossible, but I took secret pleasure in them. Have you ever read verse in a half-mastered language, especially poems you knew were good? Without catching the meaning of every phrase, you continue to read, and from those words which you understand there springs into your head some totally different meaning, not at all clear, to be sure – some foggy meaning that cannot be expressed in words but is all the more beautiful and poetic for that reason. For a long time the Caucasus for me was that poem in an unknown language; and when I delved into its actual significance, I regretted the loss of the invented poem in many respects, while in many other ways I became convinced that reality was better than what I had imagined.[18]

Unconcerned here with either genre or literary mode, Tolstoy allowed "poems" to cover Bestuzhev-Marlinsky's semi-fiction and *A Hero of Our Time*, as well as Lermontov's verse. The term expanded even further to designate the reader's own fantasies stimulated by the literary text. With this latter formulation "poetry" was reduced to daydreams which provide an infantile sort of pleasure at a level where language does not even function ("impossible" to "convey them in words"). In sum, this revealing passage of young Tolstoy's essay sourly employed "poetic" to mean literature which enthralls and fills the reader with ineffable sentiment but makes little sense. Conceptualized as a thick fog of dubious meaning, the inherited textual Caucasus in this assessment became a gigantic "poem" set in opposition to "reality" apprehended by intellect through empirical observation.

PARODY IN *THE COSSACKS*

The Cossacks was Tolstoy's most concerted effort to dissipate "poetry" understood in the comprehensive sense outlined in "Notes on the Caucasus." Although told primarily from the standpoint of the Russian aristocrat Olenin, the novel has an authorial voice often put to documentary uses. Tolstoy plies the reader with linguistic, cultural and historical information in annotations and a lengthy ethnographic sketch of the *stanitsa* (chapter four) interpolated before Olenin arrives. But while the writer thus makes a bid for extra-literary authority, parody in fiction is the main instrument he wields to demystify Russian experience in the territory. Chapter two lines up three literary targets from the past in the revery of Olenin *en route* to the Caucasus from Moscow. The tradition of sublime landscape is signaled by the anticipation of "mountains, precipices, fearful torrents."[19] The hero also forms mental "images of Ammalat-Beks." Finally and in much greater detail comes Olenin's "most precious" fantasy – the acquisition of a savage concubine.

In the war on romanticism *The Cossacks* hits the first target dead center by deflating sentimental travel literature (as Pushkin's *Journey to Arzrum* and Lermontov's *A Hero of Our Time* had already done, of course). Young Tolstoy had covered a leg of his journey to the Caucasus by boat on the Volga, but in fictionalizing the experience he parodically recapitulated the *topoi* of strictly overland transport established in Radozhitsky's seminal *récit de voyage* of the 1820s, "The Road from the Don River to Georgievsk." Like Radozhitsky, Olenin embarks on a literary pilgrimage and impatiently awaits the sight of the snow-capped mountains "about which he had heard so much" (158). As in the travelogue of the 1820s, heavy clouds initially obscure the mountains in *The Cossacks*. Then in conformity to Radozhitsky's old formula, clear weather finally affords Olenin a spectacular view of the Caucasian range.

But after drawing the reader along this familiar path, Tolstoy quashes the clichés of awestruck subjectivity and literary citation still practiced in Russian travelogues of the time. Olenin is not seized by quasi-religious ecstasy at the sight of the snow-capped peaks but rather finds his head swimming, when he begins to comprehend mass in relation to distance. Not a literary echo appears as the mountains penetrate his consciousness to announce an unfamiliar world.[20] Evoked as an elemental but thoroughly secular presence, the range puts all his experience in a different light. Just as the mountains dramatically proclaim a new space, so also do they mark a temporal break between "then" and "now": "All [Olenin's] recollections of Moscow, his bouts of shame and repentance, all the tawdry daydreams of the Caucasus – everything vanished, to return no more" (159).

If the treatment of landscape in *The Cossacks* demonstrates true originality, the romantic theme of erotic conquest in Asia proves trickier. During the journey Olenin daydreams about Circassians rather than Cossack women. He conjures the wish-fulfilling ideal of an abjectly devoted female:

And there she appeared in imagination amidst the mountains – a svelte Circassian slave with a long braid and deep, submissive eyes. He imagined an isolated hut in the mountains with *her* waiting at the door when he came home tired and dusty, straight from the blood and glory of war, to marvel at her kisses, her shoulders, her sweet voice and submissiveness (156).

With an obsessive return to the promise of sexual domination over an utterly "submissive" primitive, Tolstoy attributes to Olenin a fantasy of romantic literature's quintessentially oriental woman – the Circassian love slave who began taking shape in Pushkin's "mountain maid" and found definitive expression in Lermontov's Bela.

Olenin's anticipatory daydream of the Caucasus' exotic sexual opportunities is countered by Tolstoy's anti-romantic plot. Once Olenin reaches the Novomlinskaya *stanitsa*, reality starts piercing his oriental fantasy. No Circassians or other tribeswomen make an appearance in the novel. The erotic yearnings consequently are transferred onto Mariana, the Cossack heroine who is relatively "uncivilized" in the Europeanized Russian's eyes. But if engagingly free of the vices of scientific culture and the *beau monde*, the Cossack women are also completely unmarked by oriental submissiveness. Tolstoy's ethnographic chapter four conveys Rousseauist admiration for them as vigorous, intelligent organizers of domestic and agricultural life – the antithesis of the affected social butterflies the hero left back home.[21] In conformity with such a view, Mariana defies literature's wild slaves of love who fling themselves into self-destructive liaisons with Russians. At best, she shows a bemused interest in Olenin's infatuation, but the cultural gap between them cannot be bridged. A crisis divests the Russian hero of any lingering illusions on that score. When Mariana's local admirer Luka is seriously wounded in a skirmish with Chechens near the novel's end, she rudely rejects Olenin as a superfluous outsider from an alien world.

Distinctive worries about sexual morality creep into Tolstoy's rebellion against the romantic daydream of an uncivilized mistress. Some semblance of the erotically unleashed Caucasus endures in *The Cossacks*. The ethnographic chapter four notes that Cossack women display a "remarkable freedom in their relations with men," and the story bears this out in liaisons between minor female characters and suave Russian aristocrats like Beletsky. The situation is quite ordinary, so that the old Cossack Eroshka proposes to procure Mariana or another local woman for Olenin. As contritely recorded in his diary, Tolstoy himself had bouts of wenching, gambling and drinking while stationed at Starogladkovskaya.[22] But unlike Beletsky, Olenin was not allowed to act out the author's dissipation.

Driven both by parodic purpose and a tormented awareness of his own recurrently losing battles with lust, Tolstoy brought into the literary Caucasus a newly moralistic preoccupation with civilization's role in controlling eros. A prig by comparison to the erotically venturesome Russians in the Caucasus of Pushkin, Bestuzhev-Marlinsky and Lermontov, Olenin places high value on the Christian code of sexual morality. Founded by Old Believers in the seventeenth century, the Grebensk Cossack community belonged formally to Orthodoxy. However, Tolstoy's principal Cossack men embody pagan hedonism and experience none of the moral conflicts which beset Olenin. Repelled by the falsity of the *beau monde* and the aridity of scientific culture, the Europeanized hero is drawn to the instinctual life. And yet he finds the Cossacks' lack of Christian ethics (about killing as well as sex) a shortcoming by comparison to the Russian realm of enlightenment.[23] More pure than Tolstoy knew himself to be, Olenin implicitly censures romantic literature's erotic adventurers in the Caucasus.

But for all its rebellion against the old plot of sexual conquest, *The Cossacks* replicates an important feature of the past by reifying nature in the person of a nubile mountain maid. In an unmailed epistolary manifesto to Russian aristocrats,

Olenin extols Mariana as the natural woman at one with her envigorating, uplifting environment. She personifies the "beauty of the mountains and the sky" (266), the "whole sum of beautiful nature" (269). While never gendering the land, *The Cossacks* thus exhibits the conventional, pastoral impulse to project the Caucasian maiden as the embodiment of the wilderness with which the civilized man ambivalently yearns to merge.

THE INSCRUTABLE SAVAGE

To turn now to the third romantic target which chapter two sets up alongside sublime nature and an oriental mistress, Olenin *en route* to the Caucasus imagines having contact with "Ammalat-Beks," just as he daydreams about a submissive Circassian instead of a Cossack woman. The novel's central cultural clash between Europeanized Russia and the Grebensk *stanitsa* leaves the local Chechens on a secondary plane. However, to the extent that Tolstoy deals with tribesmen, he charts an original course by deflating romanticism's production of surrogate Asian selves.

Romantic fusion with the orient has seduced Olenin. During the journey from Moscow he features the Muslim guerrilla as both the self and the other. First, he imagines "killing and subduing an untold multitude of tribesmen," and then swiftly transfigures himself into a native *dzhigit* at war with tsarist armies (156). Full of parodic force, this passage deftly indicates how romantic literature encouraged readers to identify with dashing Caucasian wild men. Tolstoy cites only Bestuzhev-Marlinsky's surrogate, Ammalat-Bek. However, Olenin's momentary urge to slip into the skin of a Muslim tribesman also contains buried allusions to Lermontov's *alter ego*, Izmail-Bey, and to Pechorin, the Europeanized Russian who so readily activates the "Asia" within. A draft of *The Cossacks* extends Olenin's fantasy of going native: he penetrates the mountains, wins the tribe's acceptance and marries a local beauty who loves him passionately, the "way oriental women love."[24]

By introducing Olenin as a reader in the grips of romantic self-identification with Muslim warriors, Tolstoy lays the ground for another colossal disillusionment. The thrilling machismo of Ammalat-Bek proves to exist in the Caucasus, especially in the person of Luka.[25] However, if able to have a modicum of meaningful exchanges with the Cossacks, the Europeanized hero finds totally impenetrable barriers between himself and the tribesmen. Olenin's knowledge of Chechen life comes almost exclusively through the Cossack braves, reliably cast in the role of cultural mediators. Situated across the Terek from Chechen country, the Grebensk Cossacks shared the tribesmen's ethos of war, could fend in their language, borrowed the term *dzhigit* for themselves and wore similar clothing (the tall sheepskin hat and the *cherkeska*, the "Circassian coat" with cartridge pockets across the chest). Intermarriages between Cossacks and Caucasian tribes also occurred, as stressed by a nineteenth-century Russian traveler who perceived many faces "more than a little Asiatic" in a *stanitsa*.[26] Besides stating such information outright in the expository chapter four, *The Cossacks* artistically succeeds throughout in depicting Novomlinskaya as a culturally mixed zone intersecting both Orthodox Russia and Muslim Chechnia.

The nexus between Cossacks and Chechens is tightened in a politically subversive passage about infanticide. Notably featured in "Izmail-Bey," the killing of tribal children seems to have taken root in Tolstoy's consciousness as an iconic atrocity of war. It figured already in "The Raid" but only as a false alarm (the soldiers' victim turns out to be a squealing goat).[27] Tsarist infanticide returns as an achieved, if unde-picted act in *The Cossacks*. In conversation with Olenin, Eroshka recalls seeing a cradle floating down the Terek during a hunting trek (202). The sight led him to imagine a raid in which "some of your damn soldiers" stormed through houses, terrorized women and smashed a baby's head against a wall. In saying "your" soldiers, Eroshka disclaims tsarist cam-paigns as sadistic assault which unjustly rebounds against the *stanitsy*. Through the relatively "uncivilized" Cossack's words, the Russian military man emerges here as the novel's sole incarnation of horrific bloodlust. Olenin makes no rejoinder about Russia's purportedly humane, Christian values (even though the Cossacks' lack of guilt about killing tribal raiders disturbs him at other points in the novel). By letting Eroshka's characterization of "your damn soldiers" go unchallenged, Tolstoy attributes to the Cossacks and Chechens an honorable code of warfare and a high-spirited bravery not consistent with brutalizing a baby. *The Cossacks* thus takes issue with imperialism's therapeutic fiction of violence as a "savage," alien proclivity to be suppressed by European Russia.

While Tolstoy masterfully constitutes the culturally mixed character of the semi-Asian Cossacks among whom he lived, he displays a notable reticence about the Chechens. Interestingly enough, he had envisioned featuring the tribal milieu extensively. An early draft of the novel was entitled "The Runaway," or "The Fugitive Cossack," and the author continued working on it as late as 1860.[28] In the fugitive's story the hero Luka (or alternatively "Kirka") flees and makes common cause with the Muslim tribesmen after killing a Russian soldier for flirting with his wife. According to an alternate plan, the Cossack fled without murdering the Russian, who was to participate in the search party that penetrates the *aul*, captures the turncoat and brings him back to the *stanitsa*.

For all his interest in the fascinating subject of desertion to Shamil's side, Tolstoy never managed to finish the story, quite probably because literary ghosts of the past kept haunting him. When still attempting to write the Cossack defector's tale, the author noted in his diary in April 1858 that he was continually "blocked at the escape into the mountains."[29] While in the Caucasus, Tolstoy had contact with allied tribesmen in the army, representatives of whom appear in conversation with the narrator in "The Raid." In addition, he visited tribal villages near Starogladkovskaya and had a Chechen *kunak*, Sado Miserbiev. And yet despite these contacts with tribesmen in their native realm, Tolstoy experienced a loss of confidence and artistic inspiration in writing about the subject. Fully aware of the tribal milieux of Pushkin, Bestuzhev-

Marlinsky and Lermontov, Tolstoy failed at this point to find his own way of depicting the Muslim *dzhigit* on home ground.

To put the matter in a more positive light, Tolstoy's writer's block was surely produced, in part, by awareness of an anthropological dilemma barely recognized in the romantic literary Caucasus. Just how was a Russian to penetrate the wild man's culture and mind, in order to write about him reliably? Emboldened by "active imagination," Pushkin had invented Circassians in their *aul*, sight unseen. Bestuzhev-Marlinsky had displayed ethnographic expertise in his Caucasian œuvre but, like Lermontov, had unproblematically inscribed his own psychology in tribesmen. Tolstoy thus found himself confronting the same kind of challenge *vis-à-vis* the Chechens as he faced with respect to spectacular mountain landscape. How could a Russian writer in the 1850s avoid the entrancing modes of his predecessors and fashion a new, fact-oriented representation of the Muslim *dzhigit*?

The Cossacks reflects these anthropological issues by letting Olenin's restricted powers of observation guide treatment of the Chechens. In reaction to the fiery tribal surrogates of Bestuzhev-Marlinsky and Lermontov, Tolstoy sticks to strictly external description. *The Cossacks* announces the deflationary strategy as strongly as possible by first presenting the tribesman as a corpse, a figure with no more inner being to probe. In an episode not including Olenin, Luka shoots the Chechen raider Akhmed-Khan as he tries to cross the Terek (chapter nine). After the killing Tolstoy describes the "svelte, handsome" body, as studied in silence by a group of Cossacks. The narrative voice makes autopsical observations ("The muscular arms lay stiffly next to the ribs. The freshly shaved, bluish round head was thrown back, its wound on the side caked with blood"). Still engaged in his battle with the "poetry" of Caucasian warfare and the *dzhigit*, Tolstoy virtually reduced romanticism's hot-blooded tribesman to a cadaver on a dissecting table.

When Akhmed-Khan's brother comes to claim the body (chapter twenty-one), the author again declines to invent a tribesman's psyche. Olenin exhibits an imperious Russian insensitivity in this episode. First of all, he strides over to take a good look at the corpse. The brother shoots a withering glance at him and speaks abruptly in his native language to a member of his entourage who hastens to cover the dead man's face. Unperturbed, Olenin next decides to strike up a chat with the regal-looking brother. When the Chechen spits contemptuously and ignores him, Olenin attributes his behavior to stupidity or mere incomprehension of Russian. The author clearly distances himself from the blundering ethnocentric hero who judges the tribesman an inscrutable alien. Irony pervades the depiction, and yet the point of view is restricted in part because Tolstoy himself lacked conviction about his personal knowledge of the Chechen's mental life. The tribesman's mind remains *terra incognita* for the author, as well as the dramatis personae of *The Cossacks*. In this respect, the strategy of concerted restriction to the outside conforms to the anatomical depiction of Akhmed-Khan in chapter nine.

Both a rebellion against romanticism and a humble recognition of his limitations as a foreigner, Tolstoy's approach to the tribesmen showed an entirely new concern with difficulties of cross-cultural communication. All previous inventors of the literary Caucasus had glossed over the existence of foreign languages by equipping their speaking tribal protagonists with correct Russian. As recollected by Maksim Maksimych, the first words of Lermontov's Bela are slightly distorted; but her Russian becomes standard thereafter. By contrast to the general tendency, Tolstoy's "The Raid" and *The Cossacks* add an authentic touch by couching the speech of tribesmen in pidgin Russian (just as the novel so successfuly creates individualized voices for the Cossacks themselves). In addition to this linguistic deformation, the very presence of a tribal interpreter in *The Cossacks* further foregrounds language as a barrier between "us" and "them." After Akhmed-Khan's body is ransomed, the ever curious Olenin follows the tribal entourage to the river bank and eagerly asks the interpreter to explain what the dead man's brother has just uttered with a malevolent stare at Luka. As indicated by evasive eyes and vague words, the interpreter obviously misrepresents the statement and laughingly takes his leave.

This exchange between the Russian hero and the interpreter who refuses to say what he knows illustrates Tolstoy's great preoccupation with non-verbal messages and unspoken cultural codes in *The Cossacks*.[30] Olenin completely misreads the Chechen's contempt and lack of interest in him, a tsarist soldier, no less! More generally, however, the Russian is the odd man out. Ignorant of the Chechen language and alien to the local ethos of warfare, he can merely gaze upon the interaction between Cossack and Muslim braves. He is a useless onlooker who lacks all capacity to initiate a cross-cultural dialogue with the tribal other. The exploration of such states of mutual incomprehension and the inquiry into the very possibility of communication between the would-be Russian civilizers and the Muslim tribesmen would make *Hadji Murat* Tolstoy's most original, enduring contribution to the literary Caucasus.

ACCUSED OF ''POETRY''

With mixed success, *The Cossacks* pursued the attack on beguiling literary tradition which Tolstoy first mounted in "The Raid." However, when published in 1863, the novel was widely dismissed as an imitation of past writing, and "poetic" writing, at that. Preoccupied with modernizing the life of the newly emancipated peasantry, the Russian intelligentsia of the time largely frowned on Tolstoy's ambivalent celebration of Cossacks as noble savages untouched by European civilization. In this domestic political context, even somebody with a positive word for *The Cossacks* felt compelled to fault its disharmony with the burning socioeconomic issues of the day. Yakov Polonsky, for example, praised Tolstoy's marvelously "true" presentation of pristine landscape and granted that he was not simply recycling the "romantic Caucasus with romantic heroes."[31] But none the less, Polonsky accused Tolstoy of escaping into delusions of happiness outside civilization, instead of usefully broaching the Russian peasantry's need for enlightenment.

For Tolstoy, surely one of the most exasperating things about responses to *The Cossacks* must have been the recurring references to him as a "poet" or producer of a "poetic" text. The terms appeared as accolades in Pavel Annenkov's review: "Poetry forms the very foundation of his whole picture of Cossack life," wrote the critic, while adding that "dozens of ethnographic articles" could not have captured the *stanitsa* more reliably.[32] However, unlike Annenkov's appreciation of *The Cossacks* as a text both *dulce* and *utile*, radical utilitarians deplored Tolstoy's "poetic" qualities. Now in the hands of Nikolai Chernyshevsky and Nikolai Dobroliubov, the *Contemporary* derided *The Cossacks* as a throwback to the "old school of artists" and a descent into "poetry's abyssmal nadir."[33] Much more extreme than young Tolstoy's own definition of "poetry" as dreamy obfuscation, this vociferous denial of aesthetic values contributed greatly to the aristocratic writer's visceral antipathy for the plebian editors of the journal where he had made his literary debut with *Childhood* in 1852.

The recriminations about "poetic" tendencies seem to have left Tolstoy determined to keep defining his discontinuity with the romantic Caucasus. None of the misreadings of *The Cossacks* elicited any replies from him at the time. However, in the next decade he went back to the source of the 1820s' Caucasian epidemic to deflate Pushkin. Tolstoy now produced his own "The Prisoner of the Caucasus" (1872), a story written in an extremely simple style meant for children but also suitable for freshly literate adults. Although *National Annals* had published excerpts from adolescent Lermontov's identically titled tale in verse in 1859, Tolstoy primarily alluded to Pushkin's seminal poem.[34] In this little narrative Tolstoy confidently declared himself different from the poets but in no way inferior to them: he summoned his predecessors' old plot of love and death in the wilderness and presumed to lay it to rest with his new tale of a resourceful Russian prisoner befriended and freed by a clever little "Tatar" girl of the mountains.[35]

The production of a new Caucasian prisoner's story was an important act of liberation from the anxiety of influence Tolstoy had suffered in his youth. While never settled into a comfortable groove (as his religious crisis of the late 1870s would dramatically affirm), he was now a writer with an international reputation, rather than a novice pursued by shades of Ammalat-Bek, Izmail-Bey, Pechorin and the rest of the romantic Caucasian crew. Tolstoy had laid all three big ghosts to rest – Pushkin, Bestuzhev-Marlinsky and Lermontov. Only in this maturely confident position was he capable of writing *Hadji Murat*, his Caucasian novel which is very frankly "poetic" in its own way.

CHAPTER 14

Post-war appropriation of romanticism

"Well, my dear boy! First I'm going to be your
godfather and then, I promise, I'll be your
matchmaker."
Vasily Nemirovich-Danchenko

The extent of young Tolstoy's failure to displace the inherited literary Caucasus became increasingly apparent in the post-war decades. Far from supplanting his predecessors, Tolstoy was overshadowed by them in this field. Following Shamil's defeat, *The Cossacks*, "The Raid" and "The Wood-felling" died away with virtually no echo. The works inspired no literary imitators and failed to win acceptance as corroborative material in histories of the conquest.[1] In diametrical contrast, hapless versifiers and popular novelists such as Vasily Nemirovich-Danchenko (1844 or 1845–1936) emulated the romantic *élan* of Pushkin, Bestuzhev-Marlinsky and Lermontov after Shamil was vanquished.[2] But even more significantly, "The Prisoner of the Caucasus," "Ammalat-Bek," "Izmail-Bey" and other romantic works were upheld as insightful illuminations of the past and selectively appropriated to constitute the history of the conquest as a civilizing mission.

Epigone belles-lettres and popular history violated romantic discourse by using it to apotheosize the imperialist ideology it had disrupted in its heyday. Young Pushkin, Bestuzhev-Marlinsky and Lermontov had appropriated the Caucasus for their own uses, to be sure. But their writings inscribed passions for revolt and left unresolved a panoply of ideologically unsettling questions about semi-Europeanized Russia's cultural and psychological relations to wild Asia. In the era of

252

conquest history was still open for these writers and their contemporary readerships, uncertain about just how the battle against the tribes would turn out. The epigones who appropriated romanticism after Shamil's surrender had totally different political, cultural and psychological horizons. With the Asian "bandits" beaten at last, Russia was preening its European feathers and formulating economic agendas for the newly acclaimed "paradise" now in its possession.[3] In this self-congratulatory climate, the noble Caucasian savage rebounded but was patronized as never before in his history. The full complexity of this situation was certainly not lost on old Tolstoy: in tackling the Caucasian theme anew at the turn of the century, his *Hadji Murat* blasted Russia's reigning cultural mythology of the civilizing mission, while recuperating violated truths of romantic discourse.

NOSTALGIA FOR THE ROMANTIC CAUCASUS

Russian awareness of the Caucasus in the post-war period was sharply split between a group of experts and the reading public at large. From the 1860s onward, the volume of published documents, history, ethnography and statistics about the dominion grew by quantum leaps. The authors who produced these works occasionally lambasted the literary Caucasus. The historian Nikolai Dubrovin, for example, declared that belles-lettres held Russians in thrall to pure fiction about the territory and its tribes.[4] Somewhat unfairly (as certain twentieth-century specialists would insist), Bestuzhev-Marlinsky was Dubrovin's great *bête noire*, as he was for the ethnographer E. Kozubinsky and the linguist Pyotr Uslar.[5] When Uslar attacked the romantic Caucasus in 1868, he brought into focus the main tension between the intellectual élite and the general population: his major complaint was that "Ammalat-Bek, Seltaneta and all the rest" refused to budge from most Russians' minds.[6] Inattentive to the experts' charge that the romantic Caucasus was mere invention, the average reader simply would not surrender the colorful tribes of Pushkin, Bestuzhev-Marlinsky and Lermontov.

The split between ordinary readers and Caucasian regional specialists became even more pronounced with the rise of literacy in Russia. After the Emancipation of the serfs in 1861 the Russian readership steadily grew to encompass more lower-class townspeople and peasants. Often only semi-educated, these readers predictably displayed a great appetite for simple, exciting chapbook literature.[7] Gradually disseminated to the broadened strata of readers, selected parts of the romantic Caucasus came to enjoy wider sway than ever.

Popular nostalgia for the romance of noble primitivity erupted in Russia immediately after victory over Shamil. One fascinating expression of this mood was adulation of the defeated imam himself. The former leader of the jihad received respectful treatment from Alexander II and Alexander Bariatinsky, the tsarist commander-in-chief who had captured him. Even more interestingly, however, Shamil attracted a great deal of friendly attention from the public at large.[8] People gathered along the route by which he was taken from Dagestan to St. Petersburg, and his hotel in the capital drew a steady stream of curious visitors, including some intent on writing his biography. When Shamil left to take up residence in Kaluga, a festive crowd of Russian men and women gathered in Znamensky Square to bid him farewell. They threw kisses, called out, "We love you!" and invited him to come back to St. Petersburg. To be sure, it was easy for officials to fete the vanquished imam, as though he were an exotic pet. But the unrehearsed public readiness to embrace Shamil was a less patronizing phenomenon. While no doubt attesting to much idle curiosity, the popular acclaim appears to have borne witness to the lingering power of the romantic Caucasus as an Asia happily accommodated in the semi-Europeanized Russian self. Those well-wishers in Znamensky Square were seeking a semblance of the dashing primitives of Pushkin, Bestuzhev-Marlinsky and Lermontov (rather than a sullen brute like Zotov's "last of the Kheaks").

Of course, the romantic nostalgia was not completely unanimous, as notably illustrated by Rostislav Fadeev's popular history *Sixty Years of War in the Caucasus* (1860).[9] A conservative nationalist and industrious journalist, Fadeev constructed a chauvinistic account of Holy Russia's triumph over Muslim "filth." His history and newspaper articles featured the tribes as "rapacious beasts" to be combated for the good of Christian civilization. Without seeing any contradiction, however, Fadeev none the less considered the savages redeemable precisely because they were "Caucasian" in every sense: for all his backwardness, the tribesman "never sank to the level of the Guinea Negro." The Caucasian wild man belonged to "our" superior "Japhetic race" and was basically a "child" who required colonial supervision.

But for all Fadeev's prominence, his pivotal idea of bestial savagery was challenged by other commentators of the era. F. Yukhotnikov's "Letters from the Caucasus," for example, vented Rousseauist doubts about the civilizing mission.[10] Yukhotnikov called the tribesmen "unspoiled" in their natural state, extolled their artistic oral tradition and maintained that Russia had merely brought them vodka, gambling and venereal disease. A contemporaneous, anonymous article titled "The Subjugation of the Caucasus" stated outright that many Russians regretted the end of the war because now the territory's "poetry was dead."[11] The author certainly stood in these ranks, as seen in his praise of the tribesman's lively intelligence, "humane soul" and regal bearing in even the shabbiest garb. Young Pushkin was acclaimed here for recognizing the tribes' verve and "feeling for poetry," even though he had merely "caught a glimpse of the Caucasus." As the allusion to Pushkin underscored, the "poetic" Caucasus for which these post-war Russian readers yearned was quite simply a textual realm of intriguingly shifting boundaries between "us" and "them." Enclosed in print and available for repeated consumption, the romantics' ambivalent Caucasus of conquest was cherished afresh in the much less soul-stirring era of colonial exploitation.

LITERATURE AUTHENTICATED AS HISTORY

In this nostalgic climate, the romantic Caucasus enjoyed a new surge of extra-literary authority in popular imagination. The German writer and translator Friedrich Bodenstedt exhibited the receptivity when he posed the following challenge in an article published in the early 1860s: "Just try to name a single book out of that vast number of thick geographies, histories and other sorts of works about the Caucasus through which a reader can become acquainted with the characteristic nature of those mountains and their inhabitants as vividly and truly as in one of Lermontov's poems."[12] The old urge to take poetry as artful fact thus declared itself alive and well. In the very same period when Tolstoy's *The Cossacks* sought to deflate Lermontov and Bestuzhev-Marlinsky, Bodenstedt recommended poetry as both *dulce* and *utile*, while dismissing the massive corpus of non-fiction as an unmemorable, artless accumulation of words. This yearning for the text which purveys knowledge in a pleasurable form was seconded in the same period by the reviewer of a new Russian history of Chechnia. In words reminiscent of the criticism leveled at Bronevsky in the 1820s, the commentator complained that a "complete absence of literary polish" marred the whole burgeoning field of Caucasian studies.[13] The lack of stylistic felicity in the "thick books" of ethnography, history and geography still provoked dissatisfaction and stirred desires to make literary works serve multiple purposes.

First evinced in the popularity of "The Prisoner of the Caucasus" in the 1820s, the resistance to pedestrian non-fiction and the consequent gravitation toward poetry bespoke a timeless aesthetic predilection. Verse arrests its audience not simply by images or the expression of ideas but by its "unverbalizable pulse," its "non-word language" which cannot be paraphrased or deracinated by reason.[14] As the musical masters of the romantic literary Caucasus, young Pushkin and Lermontov displayed much greater staying-power than the long-winded Bestuzhev-Marlinsky. To be sure the creator of Ammalat-Bek was far from eclipsed in popular imagination in post-war Russia, as Uslar had underlined so unhappily. Despite the intellectual élite's protests, some Russians in the second half of the nineteenth century were even prepared to take Bestuzhev-Marlinsky's sexually uninhibited "mountain goddesses" as authentic Caucasian personages.[15] None the less, at the level of language rather than cultural myth, Bestuzhev-Marlinsky was not nearly so memorable and amenable to citation or recitation as Pushkin and Lermontov were. Not by chance, many educated Russians today never read Bestuzhev-Marlinsky, whereas Pushkin's and Lermontov's Caucasian verse is widely known.

Musically powerful Russian poetry was appropriated for mass dissemination of the ideology of the civilizing mission in the second half of the nineteenth century. No elaborate education is required for the implantation of verse to take place, and indeed an exclusive orientation toward print weakens the memorizing reflex.[16] This general susceptibility to poetry's unverbalizable pulse recommended Pushkin and Lermontov to Russian authors keen on inculcating national pride in the empire. As one striking example, the Circassian heroine's profession of love to the captive in Pushkin's "The Prisoner of the Caucasus" was interpolated into a late edition of Zriakhov's perennial tale *The Russians' Battle with the Kabardinians.*[17] With fond eyes on her future Cossack husband, Zriakhov's "beautiful Mohammedan" delivered Pushkin's unacknowledged verse as an "old Kabardinian song." Young Pushkin's tale about a woman fatally rebuffed by a Byronic Russian was thus plundered to embellish a story of cross-cultural marriage repeatedly issued in the late nineteenth century to endorse the Caucasian conquest as the benevolent march of civilization.

Even more remarkably, Pushkin and Lermontov were requisitioned for little pedagogic manuals. P. Nadezhdin's so-called "study guide" *Nature and People in the Caucasus* (1869) was a pastiche of disparate materials, all treated as equally reliable.[18] Selections from Pushkin's poetry ("The Prisoner of the Caucasus," "The Caucasus") were interwoven with *A Hero of Our Time*, semi-fictional travelogues, natural science and ethnography (including an extract from "Ammalat-Bek"). Imbued with faith in the civilizing mission, *Nature and People in the Caucasus* pieced together a glorious tale about Russian subjugation of wild Asia. E. Voskresensky's schoolbook *The Caucasus through the Works of Pushkin and Lermontov* (1887) followed a similar procedure.[19] Restricted to poetry, this compilation envisioned an audience of pupils (and perhaps semi-educated adults) who even needed a footnote locating the Caucasus. Voskresensky began by explicating the civilizing mission in simple prose and then provided commentary on assembled excerpts from Pushkin and Lermontov. As an illustration of the method, the Circassian in full battle gear was lifted from "The Prisoner of the Caucasus" and juxtaposed to the Russian attack on the tribal village in "Izmail-Bey." Voskresensky's commentary argued that the hostile "savage" accurately captured by Pushkin demanded the ruthless military tactics shown by Lermontov.

In a spirit which violated his sources, Voskresensky quite literally constructed the history of the conquest as one big poem. He might, of course, have profited from the epilogue to "The Prisoner of the Caucasus." Instead, he borrowed the young poet's Circassian brave but deprived him of his ambivalent aura of martial heroism, engagingly simple social relations and native songs. Voskresensky's misappropriation of Lermontov was even more egregious: the excerpt from "Izmail-Bey" naturally omitted the poet's denunciation of Russia as a sinister "new Rome" and his depiction of tsarist soldiers as bloody-handed molesters of tribeswomen.

OLD TOLSTOY AND POPULAR FICTION

During the great age of the novel dominated by Dostoevsky, Tolstoy and Turgenev, the war against Shamil dropped out of sight in Russian literature. The turn of the century, however, brought a new flurry of Caucasian tales and novels by authors now largely, if not completely forgotten.[20] The patriotic spirit of this epigone literature reflected a more pervasive mentality of the time: the centennial of the annexation of Georgia was drawing near, and Russian historians took the occasion to glorify the Caucasian conquest.[21] In tune with the jubilant mood, the era's popular literature rid the romantic Caucasus of restive ambivalence and made it docilely haul the ideology of the civilizing mission.

Two contributions by the immensely popular and prolific historical novelists, Daniel Mordovtsev (1830–1905) and Vasily Nemirovich-Danchenko, merit comment for their interplay with *Hadji Murat*, produced largely in this same period.[22] Although once acclaimed "our Walter Scott," Mordovtsev drew his big following from provincial readers and was generally disdained by sophisticates. His work most pertinent to old Tolstoy was "The Caucasian Hero (A True Story)," a semi-fictional novella about Hadji Murat.[23] As signaled by the parenthetical subtitle, Mordovtsev emulated Bestuzhev-Marlinsky's aspiration to make literature educational as well as fun. To bolster his claim to historical truth, Mordovtsev carefully documented his sources (some of the same Tolstoy used for *Hadji Murat*). But while he had access to a transcription of the autobiography Hadji Murat dictated to a tsarist officer in 1851, Mordovtsev could do no better than invent his "Caucasian hero" as a sorry little vestige of Ammalat-Bek. A handsome, curly-haired fellow given to flowery "oriental" rhetoric, Mordovtsev's Hadji Murat is an inscrutable savage who dies a meaningless death. Why did Hadji Murat defect from Shamil? Why did he try to flee back home, provoking the Russians to pursue and kill him? Mordovtsev could only suggest that a wild man lives by instinct and is inseparable from his native habitat. The *Naturmensch* was, of course, a staple of Bestuzhev-Marlinsky and Lermontov, but Mordovtsev hitched the concept to an absolute faith in the rectitude of the tsarist conquest. A limp incarnation of Asian alterity, this Hadji Murat simply could not fathom Russia's superior civilization and was doomed to die an uncomprehended death.

While Mordovtsev allowed Hadji Murat's Russian killers to vent much hostility toward him ("disgusting savage," "beast," "dog," etc.), Nemirovich-Danchenko's contemporaneous contribution to the Caucasian theme takes the grand prize for patronizing the tribesman as noble savage. Initially famous as a war correspondent during the Russo-Turkish War of 1877–78, Nemirovich-Danchenko increased his celebrity with adventure stories, travelogues, ethnography, memoirs and other genres, to the total of some 250 volumes. His historical novel *The Forgotten Fort* (1897) tells a cross-cultural love story against the background of war against Shamil.[24] At a fort on the Samur river, the local Russian commander's daughter Nina becomes the object of the affections of Amed, a handsome tribesman fighting on the tsarist side. Religious difference naturally poses an obstacle to their union, but Nina's explication of the Gospels sways Amed from Islam. After heroic performance in a decisive battle, Amed is taken to St. Petersburg to have an audience with Nicholas I in the Winter Palace. Friendly as can be, the tsar puts the befuddled tribesman at ease and commends his valor. Nicholas even vows to help the "dear boy" realize his great dream of marrying Nina: once assured that Amed means to convert to Orthodoxy, the tsar promises to be his godfather and matchmaker.

This episode epitomizes the patronizing novel's commitment to a fiction of the empire as a family. Nicholas is ready to gather all the tribesmen into his fatherly embrace, if only they will stop resisting him. He praises them as valiant "knights of the Middle Ages" and wishes they would stop annihilating themselves in the jihad. How much better if they would convert to Orthodoxy and serve the Russian tsar! While Amed exemplifies the "good" tribesman, ready to be assimilated into the empire, Shamil himself is drawn into the scheme. As depicted in the novel's bygone era of warfare, Shamil is a handsome, charismatic leader driven by genuine religious fervor. First glimpsed as a legendary, regal figure on a "golden steed," he dazzles a band of Russian soldiers who crowd their fort's ramparts to see him. The perspective of these admiratory soldiers is Nemirovich-Danchenko's own. An authorial digression near the novel's end proclaims Shamil a towering historical personage, a "giant" and "military genius" with magnificently "savage power." But in the view of *The Forgotten Fort*, even the grandest Asian had to bow to European civilization in the shape of Russia.

Nemirovich-Danchenko's tribute to noble savagery stroked the imperial ego of late nineteenth-century Russians. By patronizing the tribes conquered several decades earlier, the historical novel permitted the "European" victors to fancy themselves a nation of benevolent godfathers and godmothers to culturally inferior Asians. A paean to Nicholas and all "our" other ancestors who effected the purportedly unstoppable march of European enlightenment, *The Forgotten Fort* extolled the conquest as a purely magnanimous force in which Russians should take pride.

As this rapid survey of late nineteenth-century writings has attempted to show, old Tolstoy in *Hadji Murat* tackled a textual enterprise about the civilizing mission which was much vaster than the big romantic "poem" he had spurned in his youth. By the end of the century in Russia, a complete interpenetration of popular history and literature had taken place to form a gigantic imperial epic of European "triumph over obstinate barbarism" in the Caucasus.[25] During the closing decades of the nineteenth century, members of the intellectual élite, such as Adolf Berzhe, kept asserting that the Caucasus was scarcely known to most Russians because they lacked the ability or willingness to perform the "patient labor of specialized researchers."[26] The relevant material was there to be sifted by experts and incorporated into their "thick books." As usual, though, even many of Russia's best educated readers preferred more entertaining, aesthetically enjoyable options. The manuals of Nadezhdin and Voskresensky aimed at the least sophisticated audiences (including school children), but even popular history written strictly for adults footnoted poetry as readily as non-fiction.[27] In the meantime, widely read novelists like Nemirovich-Danchenko and Mordovtsev purported to provide accurate reconstitutions of the past. The biggest of all narratives of conquest had installed itself in old Tolstoy's time: there was no clear-cut division between the historical and literary Caucasus in popular consciousness in the post-war decades of the nineteenth century.

In this context Tolstoy returned to the Caucasian theme in *Hadji Murat* with a more conciliatory attitude toward vintage romanticism than he had held in his youth. Like Berzhe's circle of "specialized researchers," Tolstoy possessed the talent and patience to gather data for his assault on the cultural mythology of the Caucasian war. However, he had lost his notion of "poetry" as the opposite of "fact." No longer plagued by his youthful anxiety of influence, he transposed important features of the romantic Caucasus in his production of Hadji Murat as a noble primitve pitted against the reprehensible Russian élite. Tolstoy thus disappropriated the post-war appropriators of Pushkin, Bestuzhev-Marlinsky and Lermontov. This act restored to romantic discourse its violated capacity to challenge Eurocentric Russian convictions of superiority over the orient.

CHAPTER 15

Tolstoy's confessional indictment

When I got closer, I saw that the little bush was a
"Tatar" like the one whose flower I had picked to no
purpose and thrown away.

Tolstoy

Unlike the politically non-committal Caucasian œuvre of
Tolstoy's earlier days, *Hadji Murat* unequivocally condemned the war against the Muslim tribes. Written between
1896 and 1904, the semi-fictional novel belongs to the era
of the Boer War (1899–1902), an outbreak of hostilities
which inaugurated the twentieth century's long wave of
revolts against colonialism. A glaring demonstration of the
brutality and hypocrisy of "civilizing missions," this current
event surely intensified anti-imperialist sentiment in *Hadji
Murat*.[1] But besides having a new historical perspective on
empire-building, Tolstoy also had evolved his religious and
social thought focused on relations between the peasantry
and lords of Russia. Solidarity with the peasant as the
victim of an unjust sociopolitical system blended in *Hadji
Murat* with sympathy for the Caucasian tribes as a foreign
population senselessly decimated by Russia. The tsarist
state's exercise of abusive power is the story's major concern, condensed in the framing metaphor of the blooming
thistle crushed by a cartwheel.[2] Known as the "Tatar" in
the region of Tolstoy's estate outside Moscow, the colorful
wild plant bears a common Russian misnomer for the
Caucasian tribes and operates as a symbol for the Avar
hero, Hadji Murat.

While Tolstoy's earlier Caucasian œuvre pursued anti-

263

romantic strategies, *Hadji Murat* sought instead to dislodge an officially constituted view of history and force the Russian élite into uncomfortable reassessment of the war. The work approached the tribesman as a culturally muzzled figure who needed a mediator to bring him into authentic dialogue with the Russian readership. Like Tolstoy's very presumption that *he* could grant the Caucasian a voice, his discursive stance in *Hadji Murat* was quite imperious. But of course, the novel's good political intentions are clear as can be. Tolstoy's minimal depiction of Chechens in *The Cossacks* had conveyed wariness of authorial ventriloquism in writing about another's culture. *Hadji Murat* now confidently imagined the "other" side of history, while illuminating how previous Russian writers of literature and history had denied the tribes a voice.

In excoriating the Russian élite, Count Tolstoy did not completely spare himself. He assumed a self-reproachful posture in the novel's frame by despoiling one of the symbolic "Tatar" plants. However, his inclusion in élite culture was more subtly inscribed in the novel's preoccupation with language's embedment in the structure of imperial power. *Hadji Murat* upgraded the orality of the tribes and the Russian peasantry, while devaluing the written word as a tool of dehumanizing state structures. This clash between Europeanized Russia's culture of literacy and the tribal and peasant cultures of speech reached beyond the tale to complicate Tolstoy's own act of writing for readers. More confessional than self-righteous, *Hadji Murat* was a product of book culture turned against itself for therapeutic purposes.

PSEUDO-EPIC REMEMBRANCE

The anti-imperialism of *Hadji Murat* obviously would have had greatest immediacy for Russians at the turn of the century, when Tolstoy laid the work aside. Descendants of actual personages depicted in the novel comprised an especially notable group of potential readers. Roughly a generation younger than the author, these sons and daughters of the dramatis personae had not participated in military or government service during the conquest. Nevertheless, they formed a living link to the past constituted by Tolstoy with so few good words for "our" side. As part of the élite still running the empire at the time of the Boer War and the tsarist expansion into the Far East which led to the Russo-Japanese conflict, how would the Stolypins, Vorontsovs and Bariatinskys have reacted to the depiction of their ancestors' role in the system of power rendered reprehensible in *Hadji Murat*?

This line of speculation points to the novel's envisaged audience of beneficiaries of empire. The élite of old Tolstoy's day never had to fully confront the deeds of its fathers as presented in *Hadji Murat* because an entirely uncensored version of the text did not become available in Russia until the Soviet era.[3] The work simply never reached its historical audience. But *Hadji Murat* anticipates this lost, hypothetical group of addressees as its "ideal readership," a concept which Tolstoy himself had strikingly formulated in his diary in 1852.[4] In the case of *Hadji Murat*, "ideal" primarily entails an acceptance of officially constituted history of the conquest. The novel extrapolates from the immediate period, however, and forces every beneficiary of imperialism into the position of the élite historical audience.

In the frame Tolstoy holds both his confessional and homiletic cards tight to his chest. He assumes an intriguingly ambiguous stance toward the readership by refusing to define the work's genre. After recounting a walk through plowed fields, he lets the crushed thistle stimulate his tale, without yet even mentioning Hadji Murat: "And I was reminded of a story of the Caucasus of long ago, part of which I saw, part of which I heard from eyewitnesses and part of which I imagined. Here is that story as it took shape in my memory and imagination." The cagey avoidance of generic definition is perfectly signaled by an element of the Russian lost in English translation. Tolstoy announces the account as *istoriia*, a word which follows its French model *histoire* to mean both "history" and "story." The English "a story" (*odna istoriia*) should thus be understood to overlap with "an episode of history." This nuance in the Russian leaves doubt about whether the narrative is largely a literary fabrication ("just" a story) or rather the recounting of the actual past. Offered as two things at once, *Hadji Murat* has a typically Tolstoyan double-coded character.[5]

The overlapping codes conform to Bakhtin's definition of the novel and the epic.[6] In accord with novelistic discourse, the frame of *Hadji Murat* links the (hi)story to the present and puts Tolstoy on the same temporal plane as his audience. The author situates himself in the field of representation, depicts an actual event in his life and offers an unexplained symbol which will require interpretation about what the distant era means for "now." The image of the crushed thistle gives a warning that the writer will re-evaluate the past. However, Tolstoy activates a different code by simultaneously striking a pose of epic recollection at the frame's conclusion: he summons the Caucasian conquest as an event of "long ago," a time immediately pinpointed in the tale's first sentence as the "end of 1851." A rather large temporal gap thus opens to suggest that perhaps the distant epoch is finished, has a fixed meaning and is not really going to intrude into the present.

Once the narrative is launched, Tolstoy sustains the epic pose by simulating the flow of memory rather than advertising his extensive research. During his military service in the 1850s he visited Tiflis and became acquainted with Viceroy Vorontsov, Bariatinsky and other people depicted in *Hadji Murat*. The news of Hadji Murat's defection naturally reached Tolstoy at the time. He took little interest in the matter, though, and even judged it an act of treason against Shamil. While Tolstoy undoubtedly had pertinent recollections about the bygone era, *Hadji Murat* was based primarily on the study of published works and archives, correspondence with historians and the collection of personal testimonies about military service in the Caucasus and civilian life in St. Petersburg under Nicholas I. And yet with the exception of the frame's reference to "eyewitnesses," Tolstoy concealed this process of amassing data. Most strikingly, he avoided footnotes (which he had found indispensable in his anti-romantic quest for new truths in his early Caucasian stories and *The Cossacks*). Although *Hadji Murat* sometimes translates foreign words into Russian parenthetically, it has no authorial commentary in its margins. We cannot exclude the possibility that Tolstoy might have added a scholarly apparatus if the novel had gone to press in his lifetime. But this appears highly unlikely in view of the author's concerted substitution of "memory" for scholarly investigation.

By avoiding the footnoter's pedagogic posture, Tolstoy sustains a siren song of epic remembrance sounded to readers in the frame. In an epic mask, the author seems to say, "Let us return to the shared national past together." This implied attitude coaxes the audience to gather round the (hi)story-teller, not to receive instruction but to hear a tale about the "long ago" whose relation to "now" is left so vague as to pose no threat to contemporary Russia's values. After luring readers with an apparently inviting proposition, Tolstoy will spring his trap and inculpate them, as *Hadji Murat* reverses the thrust of epic genre to condemn rather than revere the forefathers.

ENTERING HADJI MURAT'S WORLD

The effort to force the Russian readership into a new relation to the tribes commences in chapter one with a deflation of the elemental mountain man invented in romantic literature and incorporated into official history. In reaction to a reductionist logic of environmental determinism, Tolstoy insists on Hadji Murat's distinctive cultural identity. Devoted to the hero's nocturnal flight to a Chechen village, the first chapter details characteristic architecture and the furnishings of a house, particular types of utensils and foods, the native dress of men and women, and Islam as a respected creed. By avoiding references to landscape, this introduction thwarts a reader prepared to view savage terrain as the mirror of Caucasian *Naturmenschen*. Tolstoy persistently constitutes the cultural rather than "mountain" milieu throughout the novel. Outstanding examples are Hadji Murat's account of his military career (chapters eleven and thirteen), the Chechen Sado's village destroyed in a raid (chapter seventeen), Shamil at Vedeno (chapter nineteen) and Hadji Murat's recollections of his childhood in Dagestan (chapter twenty-three).

Never a mere backdrop of local color, the abundant ethnographic detail is enlivened by the special quality of human relations in the tribal world. From the outset Hadji Murat possesses impressive charismatic authority. In flight from Shamil, he commands loyalty and admiration from his Murid Eldar, Sado and his family, and Bata, the tribesman who agrees to conduct the hero's scouts into Russian territory. Like Sado, proud to risk his life by sheltering Hadji Murat, Bata acts out of devotion and refuses money for his services.

While Hadji Murat will not prove thoroughly immune to dreams of self-aggrandizement through political power, he exists throughout the story as the charismatic fugitive threatened by despotic systems of bureaucratic and proto-bureaucratic authority. In conversation, Tolstoy once called these state structures "two poles of imperious absolutism, the Asian and the European."[7] The despotic governments converge through motifs shared by Nicholas I and Shamil (written edicts, megalomania, political showmanship and religious hypocrisy). In this design Shamil appears in the process of imposing a corrupt, self-serving statecraft onto the social cosmos of direct, authentic human relations in which Hadji Murat is situated in chapter one. On beyond Shamil, Russian tsardom exhibits full-blown bureaucratic authority, most alien to the charismatic hero.

Grounded in the culturally specific, relatively primitive milieu of tribal society, Hadji Murat's personal magnetism is elaborated in encounters with Russians who find him unexpectedly engaging and "childlike." By epitomizing the tribesman's uncorrupted character, "childlike" in Tolstoy's text undercuts Eurocentric notions of Asia's cultural infancy. More decidedly, though, the metaphor of childhood helps repress the hero's erotic force. Hadji Murat is not utterly deprived of virile attractiveness, as demonstrated in the initially unsettling effect he has on Maria Dmitrievna, the mistress of the Russian fort commander at Nukha (chapter eighteen). Nevertheless, Tolstoy's hero is radically distanced from Russian literature's ranks of tribal lady-killers, including Mordovtsev's recent invention of Hadji Murat himself as an oriental swain ("A Caucasian Hero"). Tolstoy casts Hadji Murat in an altogether different mold by accentuating his moral integrity and attachment to his family. Irreproachable in his relations with women, the childlike, charismatic hero is pitted against the polygamist Shamil, sexually promiscuous Nicholas I and other Russian committers of adultery.

THE PEASANT'S WORLD

The envisioned Russian reader is initially plunged into Hadji Murat's cultural realm without being given a point of self-reference. Chapter two then shifts to a group of tsarist soldiers manning a night patrol several kilometers from fort Vozdvizhensk. The Russian peasant enters here as a herald of possible dialogue with the tribesmen. When Hadji Murat's scouts arrive and ask to be conducted to Vorontsov *fils* at the fort, the invented character Avdeev is chosen as one of the escorts. As he starts the mission, he jokingly tells his comrades he will bayonet the tribesmen, if they make a false move. But upon his return he heartily announces that the scouts were "fine fellows" with whom he has had a "nice talk." Avdeev's account makes it clear that the "talk" was comprised of a few words, gestures, tone of voice and a sense of understanding which passes through eye contact. The Russian peasant has managed to surmount the language barrier and learn something about the Chechens' personal lives. A sense of humankind's uniformity strikes him, leading him to conclude, "Really, they're just like Russians." The soldier Nikitin sourly interjects that the tribesmen are treacherous killers, but the remark does not annul Avdeev's experience of cross-cultural communion.

At the same time, however, Avdeev's socially marked idiom implies that Russians are not all alike. The peasant's slightly substandard speech divides him from the anticipated audience – the Russian élite who know how to wield the native tongue correctly in every respect. Tolstoy soon deepens this sociolinguistic dimension of Avdeev's character by specifying that he cannot write and must dictate a letter to his family from his deathbed in the military infirmary (chapter seven).

As *Hadji Murat* proceeds, the gap widens between the peasantry and the envisioned élite audience. The peasant theme resurfaces in chapter eight when Avdeev's family sets to work on a freezing winter morning in their village. Tolstoy's technique conforms to the ethnographic sketch. He lavishes attention on the peasants' clothing, incorporates folkish turns of speech and gives a literally blow-by-blow account of threshing done by a man and two women. Unlike the mowing performed in *Anna Karenina* by the aristocratic hero Levin as a spiritually uplifting *"Arbeitskure,"* the strenuous manual labor in *Hadji Murat* is observed by the narrator exclusively from outside. The account of a typical morning in the life of the mid-nineteenth-century Russian peasantry is pointedly aimed at people of both sexes who may have never looked closely at a threshing-floor and certainly never thought of swinging a flail themselves.[8]

The complex style of *Hadji Murat* is the more pervasive indication of the élite character of the envisioned reader. Sophisticated vocabulary, complicated syntax and untranslated French in conversation between aristocratic characters create a verbal texture which is opaque by comparison to the simple form of writing achieved in Tolstoy's "The Prisoner of the Caucasus" and *Stories for the People*, a series including "How Much Land Does a Man Need?" (1885).

Set in Russian villages and free of bookish language, these tales target an audience of newly literate peasants and lower-class townspeople. By contrast, *Hadji Murat* stylistically resembles *The Death of Ivan Ilych*, as well as *War and Peace* and *Anna Karenina*, the two major novels which Tolstoy's *What Is Art?* categorized as "immoral" because of the class exclusiveness of their language, depicted social milieux and anticipated élite readership. As often noted, writing *Hadji Murat* induced guilt in the author because his admiration for the tribal ethos of war ran contrary to his philosophy of non-resistance to evil and Christian resignation toward death. Likewise, Tolstoy's reversion to his old novelistic idiom apparently struck him as backsliding away from his ideal of moral, universally accessible literature expounded in *What is Art?*

In terms of the envisaged audience *Hadji Murat* did indeed abandon the newly literate whose opportunities as readers Tolstoy had sought to expand through *Stories for the People*. However, as we shall see now in further detail, the aesthetic "sin" of returning to complex artistry in *Hadji Murat* was virtually expiated in its commission since the author had to squarely address upper-class readers in order to implicate them in crimes of the imperial Russian state.

THE READER'S *BEAU MONDE*

Unlike all previous contributions to the literary Caucasus, *Hadji Murat* shows Russia divided into two cultures – the peasants and the élite. Avdeev is the first Russian character to feature prominently, but the anticipated audience could not identify with him. This initial focus on the peasant looks calculated to induce envisioned readers to latch onto home ground once it appears. The Russian élite enters in chapter three in an episode at fort Vozdvizhensk, where Vorontsov *fils* and his wife Maria strive to match their St. Petersburg style of life. At this early point in the novel no opprobrium darkens the little pocket of Russian high society in the Caucasus. Interrupted when the host receives confidential notification of Hadji Murat's defection, the evening of cards is passed in an atmosphere of lighthearted amusement – some trivial gambling among urbane friends, a harmless flirtation between the officer Poltoratsky and Maria Vorontsov, champagne to end the social occasion and banter in French between husband and wife after the guests have gone. The whole strategy invites the sophisticated Russian reader to embrace the milieu culturally rooted in St. Petersburg. After the fugitive Hadji Murat in a Chechen village and the Russian peasant soldiers in the Caucasian wilderness, the home of the Vorontsovs beckons as the envisioned audience's familiar sphere of Europeanized civilization.

But as *Hadji Murat* develops, the audience becomes enmeshed in the mendacity and inhumanity uncovered in upper-class Russia. Instead of being true to the apparently epic proposition of drawing unchastised readers into memory, Tolstoy tips his hand as the judge of the assembled listeners. The (hi)story turns out to be one of the author's characteristic "reader-implicating narratives" which represents the anticipated audience in order to condemn it and push it into self-condemnation.[9] In a narrative design of theme and variations, Tolstoy repeatedly features the soirée as a typical expression of the Russian élite's inauthenticity and moral bankruptcy.[10] A theme of masking and role-playing is particularly pronounced in two instances. Set in Tiflis, chapter ten links the Italian opera with a reception at the palatial home of the Viceroy, Vorontsov *père*. The combined motifs spin a reprehensible air of theatricality around the Russian élite by rendering their values, behavior and attitudes "strange" in the eyes of the Caucasian hero.[11] Bored by the artifice of the actual theater, Hadji Murat is bewildered by the social code of Vorontsov who refuses to discuss "business" at his party and walks away from the hero, "pretending not to hear him" when he raises the subject of negotiating for the rescue of his family held hostage by Shamil. The theme of the theatrical facade which hides a rotten interior reaches its culmination in the presentation of Nicholas I (chapter fifteen). In one episode the tsar actually appears at a masked ball at the Winter Palace in St. Petersburg where he seduces a young woman. But on beyond the lecherous antics of His Highness at the grand soirée, Tolstoy makes the masquerade a comprehensive metaphor for a statecraft which hides murderous tyranny and cruelty behind the exterior of imperial grandeur.

To drive home the point, the long treatment of Nicholas is followed by two short chapters devoted to a raid instigated by the tsar's order to step up warfare in Chechnia. Conducted in a festive spirit of song and camaraderie, the attack razes the village where Hadji Murat found refuge at the (hi)story's beginning. Sado's family suffers the greatest abomination – a small son bayoneted in the back. Still haunted by infanticide as an iconic atrocity of the conquest, old Tolstoy revived this motif from "The Raid" and *The Cossacks*.

After steadily vilifying the Europeanized élite for page after page, *Hadji Murat* slips a noose right around the reader's neck in the second paragraph of chapter twenty-two. Tolstoy now announces that like Viceroy Vorontsov and officials in Petersburg, the "majority of the Russian people" who knew about Hadji Murat's defection considered it a fortunate turn of events in the war or merely found it an interesting *fait divers*, whereas the tribesman himself was experiencing a "dreadful turning-point in his life." This contrastive formulation throws the audience into the killers' camp headed by odious Nicholas. At this stage, readers invited to identify with the *beau monde* have been maneuvered into increasingly damning complicity with the structure of imperial Russian power. Am I not a descendant of these forefathers? Would I not have stood in that "majority," indifferent to Hadji Murat's human problems? Would I not have subscribed to the principle "war is war," as a child-murderer must do (and as the officer Butler will do in the story after seeing the hero's severed head)? These implicit questions would have had an especially urgent ring for the novel's lost historical audience. However, Tolstoy's fierce moral indictment forces all readers to examine their relation to that "majority" of Russians posited as the typically complacent citizenry of an expansionist Eurocentric state.

ORALITY VERSUS PRINT

Hadji Murat tightens the rope around the reader's neck by extending moral opprobrium to the very act of consuming the written word. Tolstoy's *Stories for the People* had allowed peasants and lower-class town dwellers to participate more fully in society's consumption of print. In a transvaluation of this practice *Hadji Murat* makes exclusion from the culture of literacy a point of pride.[12] While having a class component, the negative connotations attached to writing and reading extend beyond the clash of élite and peasant culture within Russia. It is not merely the ability to read French and handle complex syntax which implicates the audience's *beau monde*. Instead, Tolstoy offers the more far-reaching, Rousseauist proposition that the illiterate are morally superior, while writers are dehumanizers and liars prone to a kind of falsification notably manifested in historiography. The written word is devalued as false mediation, while speech is upheld as the conduit of greater truth. This dynamic compromises the envisioned readers of *Hadji Murat* more than ever since they live by the culture of literacy and find themselves with a book in hand.

Hadji Murat puts literacy to shame by commending the peasant and tribal reliance upon speech, as initially signaled by the talk-prone Avdeev's interaction with the Chechen scouts. Writing intrudes into the life of the Russian peasantry as alien power incommensurate to an individual's felt experience. When Avdeev's mother dictates her last letter to her son, writing emerges as the village deacon's professional expertise, pitted against the speaking woman's affectionate, tearful voice. Similarly, Avdeev's own dictated deathbed letter to his family cannot be read by the addressees, who hear it from a local postal clerk. To underline the dehumanizing force of the written word in the peasant's milieu of directly expressed sentiment, the relatives receive an official notification of Avdeev's death in the service of "the tsar, the fatherland and the Orthodox faith." The standard military rhetoric rings especially hollow for the reader, who knows that Avdeev was a random, unnecessary casualty in the conduct of war as theater: eager to seize what looked like an easy opportunity to win distinction for himself and a friend recently demoted to the ranks, the officer Poltoratsky commanded his picket-line into the exchange of fire which left the peasant soldier mortally wounded.

In a related impugnation of the official written word, Avdeev's death is distorted in an army communiqué illustrative of the falsification of history (chapter seven). Not even mentioned by name in the laconic document, the soldier presented as such an amiable fellow by Tolstoy has passed anonymously into statistics ("two of the infantry were wounded, and one killed"). But besides obliterating Avdeev, the communiqué reports a "bayonet attack" not shown in the depiction of the skirmish (chapter five). Was such an attack simply excluded from the narration? Or was it a fabrication, to make the written report more impressive for the military records in Tiflis? Chapter five prepares the audience to take the "bayonet attack" as a lie by propounding a truth in that all-knowing authorial voice which often resounds in Tolstoy's literary works as "absolute language" from outside the novelistic world.[13] The author intervenes to inform readers that hand-to-hand fighting did not occur in the Caucasus in the 1850s and, in any case, never had a valiant character. In a word, Tolstoy dismisses thrilling tales of clashing blades as a widespread, cherished "fiction" of the tsarist military. To expand the censurious notion of "fiction," the rest of the official communiqué reveals a more insidious form of falsification. In a gross exaggeration, the document reckons tribal casualties "about a hundred," although Tolstoy numbered the Chechens around twenty in chapter four. The discrepancy points to the tsarist army's inflation of the body-count of tribesmen killed in action, a prevalent practice which led one Russian veteran to scoff that the sum of dead savages compiled in military statistics would equal the entire tribal population of the Caucasus many times over.[14] The communiqué thus stands as a miniature of the larger, manifold falsification of the Caucasian war which *Hadji Murat* insists has occurred.

To further his depreciation of literacy, Tolstoy depicts both Nicholas I and Shamil as writers instead of talkers. The tsar authors various directives which spell death, while the imam, too, signs a promulgation exhorting the tribesmen to keep resisting the Russians – and, by definition, continue dying for the jihad. Divorced from the dialogic spoken word, each despot has only a few lines of direct discourse. Nicholas even conducts a running inner monologue about his greatness and mutters an aimless string of phonemes. Shamil, too, is largely locked into thoughts about his political image. Furthermore, when he does speak during the audience he grants to Hadji Murat's captive son, four of his seven utterances are *about* writing: "Do you know how to write?" and then the command "write," used repeatedly to outline the menacing letter the boy must send to his father. Beyond Nicholas and Shamil stretch the ranks of secondary characters who produce texts: the imam's adviser Dzhemal-Edin on the Asian side, and in the European sphere, the Minister of War Chernyshev, Vorontsov, General Klugenau and army clerks.

As the provenance of the written word, despotism sets a cultural space which excludes the Caucasian hero as well as the Russian peasantry. Like peasant illiteracy, Hadji Murat's isolation from the official Russian word is accredited as a superior, more authentically human condition. Of course, the division is profoundly deepened since the Caucasian hero has practically no Russian. On this basis Tolstoy elaborates the concern with non-verbal communication first manifested in *Hadji Murat* in Avdeev's "talk" with the Chechen scouts. Hadji Murat is handicapped linguistically but nevertheless grasps the gist of situations through contextual features like tone of voice and gestures. The principle is illustrated in the hero's initial interview with Viceroy Vorontsov, who speaks pious platitudes but radiates mistrust and hostility. Although a speaker's words may sometimes misrepresent what he feels (as in the case of Vorontsov, telling the truth only with his eyes), Tolstoy generally features speech as the most honest medium of communication, unable to lie so readily as a text.

The foremost illiterate in the Russian milieu, Hadji Murat is also the story's chief talker. His orality is asserted at greatest length in a sequence of chapters which juxtapose his dictated autobiography to a letter from the Viceroy to Chernyshev. Chapters eleven and thirteen are comprised almost entirely of direct discourse, as the Caucasian hero gives fluent responses to brief, intermittent questions posed by his interviewer, the interpreter Loris-Melikov. Obviously attaching great importance to this extensive forum for Hadji Murat's voice, Tolstoy reworked the language repeatedly and achieved a vivacity lacking in the pertinent historical document Loris-Melikov prepared in Tiflis.[15] In the novel the simple syntax and colloquial diction convey Hadji Murat's directness and honesty, while well-dramatized incidents from the past and little snatches of quoted speech from other participants in the autobiography make the hero an interesting story-teller. By contrast, Vorontsov's letter (chapter fourteen) confronts the reader with officialdom's chilly formality. With a keen concern for his own prestige, the Viceroy assesses Hadji Murat as a pawn to be used to best advantage for the Russian side. Originally written in French, Vorontsov's actual letter spoke so well for itself that Tolstoy simply incorporated a Russian translation of this document *in toto*.

THE COUNT'S CONFESSION

But if *Hadji Murat* upgrades talk as the more reliable, fully human mode of communication, what then is the author's own condition as a wielder of the pen committing a (hi)story to paper? Notably fond of reading aloud from works-in-progress for family members and friends at his estate, Tolstoy in *Hadji Murat* conveys a certain regret about not actually communicating face-to-face with his audience. This sentiment comes across most strongly in the treatment of the tribes' oral tradition as a form of art which bonds a national community and has vital meaning for the individual.[16] Among the Russians, Hadji Murat gains insight from a tribal folktale about a falcon rejected and killed by his fellows when he tried to return to the fold, wearing jesses he acquired among humans. Tribal songs about heroic death in battle are similarly incorporated as foreshadowings of Hadji Murat's destiny. These samples of authentic Caucasian folklore are complemented by an invented song attributed to Hadji Murat's mother and recollected by the hero as he reviews his past and decides to escape Russian surveillance in order to combat Shamil by himself.[17] In this case, Tolstoy insists upon the naturalness of song-making as part of the tribes' world, while underscoring culturally distinct experiences of childhood.

Although the theme of primitive song was one of the literary Caucasus' oldest traditions, it was newly deployed in *Hadji Murat* against the culture of literacy. As depicted in the novel, orally transmitted poetry belongs to the very fabric of social and personal life. Contemporary Russia's divorce from this ideal is not explicitly deplored by Tolstoy, but the theme of tribal art leaps out of the novel to proclaim what the reading and writing of *Hadji Murat* are *not*. Creatures of a commercialized environment, the novel's envisioned readers buy books by authors who typically remain unseen and unheard. As a rule, this public approaches the literary work as aesthetic experience and entertainment to enjoy in the seclusion of one's home and then lay aside as "just a story." On the other side of the exchange, many modern authors of fiction write largely to make money. After his religious crisis, Tolstoy sought to divorce himself as much as possible from the commercial aspects of authorship. He was fully aware of the financial power of his pen, however, as strikingly illustrated by his determination to finish *Resurrection* and publish it profitably to fund the persecuted Dukhobors' emigration to Canada. In *Hadji Murat* there is no overt self-chastisement about the cash nexus between a contemporary novelist and his public, but Tolstoy's tormented awareness of literature as a business of print-production operates implicitly in the treatment of art's function in the tribes' simpler, more humanly authentic world. The author's professed guilt about writing *literature* once again in *Hadji Murat* thus seems to have been compounded by torment over the historical, cultural necessity of *writing*, period – instead of speaking directly to listeners.

Along with the basic paradox of using literature to proclaim orality's humanly superior character, a larger implication of writing the (hi)story *Hadji Murat* gave Tolstoy pause. Doubts concerning his own reliability as the creator of a text about the past were revealed in a remark about Nicholas. He once wondered in conversation whether he had not "introduced too much subjectivity into the description of the monarch he hated, to the detriment of calm impartiality."[18] Although directed only toward the presentation of the tsar, the question of "impartiality" was equally applicable to the biased treatment of Shamil and Hadji Murat as well. An impossible goal, the concern with "objectivity" expressed Tolstoy's recognition that *Hadji Murat* in its own right was an artful manipulation of language. He knew that his own text was not a "calm" reflection of the past, even as he condemned writers in his narrative for using words to hide the truth.

But if Tolstoy could see his own writing as purposeful misrepresentation, his novel inscribes a moral justification for both him and his readers. The answer to the disingenuous question of "impartiality" lies in the epic ideal of art which assumes a permeating importance in an individual's life. Alienated from the modern norm of literature as entertainment for readers and lucrative business for writers, Tolstoy strives to make *Hadji Murat* mark the consumer indelibly. Didactic purpose removes him from the company of the novel's reprehensibly mendacious writers and turns him into the master misrepresenter who artfully slants his material in the name of moral truth.[19] Of equal importance, however, a confessional dynamic in the attack on the Russian élite affords the author a catharsis.

Tolstoy's dual stance as the judge and the confesser enormously complicates his relation to Hadji Murat. To a large extent, the tribesman is an authorial surrogate endowed with a tenacious attachment to life which old Tolstoy himself felt even "at the edge of the grave," as he put it.[20] But a significant gap between the hero and the author opens through the exercise of an imperious monologism so typical of Tolstoy's art.[21] *Hadji Murat* deprives characters of hegemony by keeping connections between them purely external and orchestrated by the privileged author. Perhaps most noticeably, the Caucasian hero and the Russian peasant Avdeev have no contact or any consciousness of each other. They are aligned strictly in that authoritative field of vision which is Tolstoy's alone. Similarly, the writer likes to lay down the law about characters and events, as illustrated by the passage dismissing hand-to-hand combat as a "fiction." Such purported truths are not reached by the dramatis personae but are imposed from outside by Tolstoy.

Monologic authorial power grows particularly heavy in the narration of Hadji Murat's final days. After dictating his autobiography (chapters eleven and thirteen), the hero has practically nothing else to say and thoroughly retreats into himself in the last three chapters (twenty-three to twenty-five). Sustained to the bitter end, this lapse into silence is rarely broken by a word between Hadji Murat and his Murids during their flight and prolonged battle against Russian forces. The hero's inward turn removes him from dialogue with all the other characters and maximizes Tolstoy's privilege as the omniscient creator who articulates things which he alone knows. This movement culminates in one of the author's most famous attempts to represent death from the inside. After relaying Hadji Murat's final sensation of a big dagger striking his head, Tolstoy describes how the killers stab, trample and decapitate the body. Represented from both inside and outside, this minutely imagined violent death epitomizes the imperious, godlike stance of an author for whom no place is *terra incognita.*

However, Tolstoy's monologic tendencies have a special twist in this historical novel about thwarted cross-cultural communication. Hadji Murat proves unable to make his voice penetrate the tsarist power structure, and his lapse into proud solitude attests to this fact. The terrible futility and loneliness of his position becomes the representative condition of the whole textual world where dialogue fails. Very few direct connections are made within the vast cast of dramatis personae. Foreign languages and cultural codes erect barriers to unmediated communication. Interpreters arc required, and words are wielded regularly in officialdom to distort reality. In this realm of impeded communication the Caucasian hero finds no Russian other able to understand him properly and complement his self. Nobody is there but Tolstoy to orchestrate the story of the elaborately failed cross-cultural dialogue which in its closing episode degenerates into an exchange of bullets.

The hero's death then becomes the ground of a dialogue, as the frame is reasserted in the novel's last sentence ("And that was the death recalled to me by the crushed thistle in the middle of the plowed field"). This shift out of the novel's time compels the audience to contemplate the hitherto unclarified relationship between Tolstoy's experience in the plowed field of the present and Hadji Murat's ordeal of "long ago." The reader is thus asked to assume the job of a survivor who receives Hadji Murat's death as his last act of self-expression, his last word which needs to connect with an interlocutor in order to find its significance.

The reassertion of the frame widens the issues of responsibility and guilt in *Hadji Murat.* Two "Tatars" are destroyed in the (hi)story's opening pages, one by an agricultural laborer and the other by the author. However, both acts of despoilment acquire identical meaning. The hero's primary emblem is the thistle crushed by the unidentified driver of a cart. The plant is described in insistently anthropomorphic terms: it has an "eye gouged out," "it had been eviscerated," its "arm had been cut off." The ostensible stimulator of Tolstoy's flow of "memory" about the Caucasian war, this mangled wild flower is recalled at the narrative's end when Hadji Murat falls like a "thistle, mowed down." As indicated by this closing metaphor of killing as mowing, the whole construct of the tribesman as a plant rests on a jarring notion of agriculture as murder. Before Tolstoy spots the crushed thistle in the frame, he grows oppressed by the vast expanse of the freshly plowed earth and avidly looks for "something living in the dead black field." In this state of mind, he formulates the paradoxical notion of agriculture as the death-dealing pursuit of plowmen who violate the natural state and kill everything in their path. Cast as the wanton plunderer of wild fields, agriculture becomes the analogue of Russia's war against the Caucasian tribes.

But before introducing the thistle ruined by an agricultural laborer, Tolstoy inculpates himself in the symbolic crime against nature. As he recounts gathering the bouquet of wild flowers, he details his own lethal battle with a "Tatar." An entire paragraph is devoted to the effort to pick the resistant plant which is shredded in the act and looks much less "fresh and pretty" when finally plucked. Full of regret about uselessly ravaging a flower so determined to live and "so fine in its proper place," Tolstoy tosses it aside. He thus joins the killers of "Tatars" (even though the agricultural laborers – the cart driver and the mower – are thrust forward in the treatment of Hadji Murat). In fact, by comparison to the evident, if unadmitted, justification of agriculture as a life-sustaining activity which compensates for the destruction of wild plants, the author may well seem the worst despoiler of all because his actions are motivated strictly by the whimsical, aesthetic impulse to add the gaudy thistle to his bouquet of daintier flowers.

Authorial self-projection in relation to the "Tatar" was amplified by Count Tolstoy's eccentric habit of working the fields. Common knowledge in the era when *Hadji Murat* was written, this aspect of his public persona was captured notably in Ilya Repin's "The Plowman." The painting was done during one of the artist's visits to Tolstoy's estate in August 1887 and first exhibited publicly the following year. Dressed in a peasant shirt and cap, the subject guides a horse-drawn plow through a foreground of black and dark brown earth, while another plowman emerges over the crest of a hill in the distant background. The fields seem to stretch endlessly in every direction beyond the frame, and the somber coloration is relieved only by white for the horses and Tolstoy's cap. The composition and the restricted palette produce an impression remarkably similar to the verbal picture of the enormous "dead black field" in the frame of *Hadji Murat*. An image widely disseminated in Russia in periodicals and inexpensive prints, "The Plowman" redoubled Tolstoy's inculpation of himself as an accomplice of the agricultural "murderer" in his Caucasian (hi)story.[22]

As the self-styled killer of one of the symbolic thistles, Tolstoy takes upon himself a burden of guilt about his nation's failure to connect properly and find a *modus vivendi* with the Muslim tribes. The author no doubt remembered how he himself dismissed Hadji Murat back in the 1850s as a scoundrel for betraying Shamil's trust. Old Tolstoy, in other words, must have admitted to himself that he had belonged then to that "majority of the Russian people" who felt idle curiosity about Hadji Murat but had no conception of him as a person deserving sympathy. Tolstoy also no doubt recalled his (grantedly unstable) outlook as a young soldier who thought that war against the tribes might be the only way to safeguard the "civilized lands" of Russia. Such memories do not intrude openly into *Hadji*

Murat. To the contrary, Tolstoy assumes a condemnatory stance toward his anticipated readers. However, as framed by the two thistles destroyed in the domain of the Russian aristocracy, the literary biography of Hadji Murat admonishes the audience to assume upper-class Russian guilt *with* the author as a collective burden. Tolstoy shows himself capriciously annihilating a "Tatar." But of equal importance, he also recognizes the wantonness of his deed and repents on the spot with the words, "I was sorry that I had destroyed to no purpose a flower which had been so fine in its proper place." None of the dramatis personae repents or evolves to achieve self-condemning insight into the killing of Hadji Murat. This leaves Tolstoy as the text's only model of the repentant violator of nature. The confessional import of the work is established precisely by the author's holding his own speech *apart from* and in dialogue with the novelistic world.

The author's despoilment, followed by atonement, is a confessional action which puts him in the position of the reformed sinner who has won the right to preach to others in the hope of prodding them into a similar experience of guilt and moral conversion. The forefathers are denounced in *Hadji Murat* as the perpetrators of atrocities which pass under the name of the march of civilization; but by situating himself in the domain of the wealthy landed gentry in the (hi)story's frame, Count Tolstoy announces that those people are his ancestors, too. The confession about unjustified destruction urges readers to "do as I do" – face your past and present condition as plundering beneficiaries of empire, recognize the conquest of the Caucasian tribes as one of civilization's crimes, and let history not repeat itself.

The self-representation in the frame conveyed Tolstoy's guilt about sharing in the advantages of imperialism which he believed had the same ugly aspect everywhere. As he expressed it in a passage of all-knowing authorial language in a draft of the novel, what occurred in the Caucasus was

what always happens when a state, having large-scale military strength, enters into relations with primitive, small peoples, living their own independent life. Under the pretext of self-defense (even though attacks are always provoked by the powerful neighbor), or the pretext of civilizing the ways of a savage people (even though that savage people is living a life incomparably better and more peaceable than the civilizers'), or else under some other pretext, the servants of large military states commit all sorts of villainy against small peoples, while maintaining that one cannot deal with them otherwise.

That was the situation in the Caucasus. . .when Russian military commanders, seeking to win distinction for themselves and appropriate the spoils of war, invaded peaceful lands, ravaged villages, killed hundreds of people, raped women, rustled thousands of cattle and then blamed the tribesmen for their attacks on Russian possessions [ellipsis mine].[23]

This righteous sense of universality permeates *Hadji Murat*. The moral outlook is totalizing and ultimately ahistorical, so that the novel expands from the specificity of late nineteenth-century Russia to encompass the pursuit of empire in every audience's present.

RECONCILIATION WITH ROMANTICISM

Hadji Murat demonstrated how far Tolstoy had evolved from his former attitude toward romanticism. His symbolization of the Avar hero as a hardy flower was precisely the sort of metaphorical device he had castigated in the 1850s when staging his rebellion against Bestuzhev-Marlinsky and Lermontov. With equal daring, old Tolstoy reactivated his predecessors' major motif of Caucasian tribal song. He put the conception of primitive poetry to a new use, but its very presence in *Hadji Murat* established a significant link with writing of the romantic era. The lengthy, authentic song about dying courageously in the jihad most resembled the superbly versified battle songs of "Ammalat-Bek." Such material was very likely just what Tolstoy had in mind when he told an acquaintance in 1898 that Bestuzhev-Marlinsky was well worth reading, an admission he could not make in his embattled youth.[24] More allusively, *Hadji Murat* acknowledged the "worthiness" of Lermontov, too, by reinforcing the poet's searing insight into war as murder, as seen in "Izmail-Bey," as well as "Valerik."

This selective reconciliation with the romantic heritage evinced old Tolstoy's liberation from his early, rigidly dichotomous thinking about the poetic text as the enemy of fact-oriented truth. In her essay "Pushkin and Pugachev," Marina Tsvetaeva remarked that the poet's novel *The Captain's Daughter* had made a "retort to the archive" by elevating the "high" truth of art over a "low" truth of historical research.[25] The point applies to *Hadji Murat* as well. While still compiling data of possible use for the novel, Tolstoy said that he liked "to be accurate down to the last detail," when dealing with bygone eras.[26] However, *Hadji Murat* fell far short of standards of scholarly investigation. Tolstoy's entire process of researching and ferreting out accurate details was a search for data to corroborate his moral convictions. He disregarded testimony which would have undermined his conceptions of character (on Shamil's religious faith, for instance), while mining his sources for congenial material (the Vorontsovs' little boy hopping onto Hadji Murat's lap, Shamil's antics with his young wife Aminet, Nicholas strutting about at the masquerade). Most tellingly, none of Tolstoy's sources gave him the Hadji Murat he needed. In memoirs published in the 1870s Poltoratsky, for example, claimed that Hadji Murat had died as a "beast in all his ferocity" without ever revealing the "secret" of his temporary *rapprochement* with the Russians.[27] Tolstoy drew extensively on Poltoratsky's memoirs, but he had to annul this version of Hadji Murat as a wild animal whose mind remained *terra incognita*. To paraphrase Tsvetaeva, Tolstoy was sentenced to inventing a more ideal Hadji Murat to serve his anti-imperialist designs, just as *The Captain's Daughter* transformed Pugachev into a subversively attractive outlaw who countered the vicious cutthroat of Pushkin's own well-researched *History of Pugachev*.

In an extremely important respect Tolstoy thus disavowed his youthful resistance to "poetry" and outgrew his related concept of "facts" as objective data which somehow comprise the truth apart from the text in which they appear. He did a massive amount of research to write *Hadji Murat*, but the final product challenged historiography itself as a self-serving manipulation of language within a given structure of political power. Perhaps somewhat paradoxically, the frank subjectivity and metaphorical enhancements of *Hadji Murat* shed more convincing light on the conquest of the Caucasus than any of Tolstoy's youthful exercises in disparaging "poetry" ever did. *Hadji Murat* took artistic license with its material in order to exemplify what the author took for universal truths about language's debasement by political mythologizers, the atrocity of war and the evil of megalomania. Not exactly comparable to any of the fiction and semi-fiction which Pushkin, Bestuzhev-Marlinsky or Lermontov produced about the Caucasus, *Hadji Murat* nevertheless marked an end to Tolstoy's binary thinking about "poetry" as the opposite of "real" knowledge and brought him more into line with Russia's tradition of taking literature as the vehicle of insight superior to what can be found in the non-fictional text.

CHAPTER 16

Concluding observations

My study has stressed the cultural and psychological functions the literary Caucasus assumed as a clarifier of the semi-Europeanized Russian self during the romantic era. The coexistent complexes of inferiority and superiority to the West produced a bifurcation in the works of canonized writers. On the one side, Muslim tribal lands were glorified as citadels of free-spirited, Homeric machismo (naturally complemented by a staple supply of pliant wild maidens in the literary population). On the other side, Georgia was marginalized as a touchy oriental woman. The literary Caucasus was largely the project of Russian men, whose psychological needs it so evidently served. However, both sexes within the romantic era's élite readership could enhance their national esteem by contemplating their internally diversified orient. Effeminate Georgia fed the conceit of Russia's European stature and superiority over Asia. But knowledge of Russia's own Asian roots defied permanent repression, especially when a French consul in Tiflis or a visiting marquis in St. Petersburg was ever ready to castigate the tsars' "rude and barbarous kingdom." Under these conditions, Russians converted the Caucasian tribes into gratifying meanings about their own undeniable cultural and intellectual retardation *vis-à-vis* the West.

This quest for a happy accommodation of Asia was not an aberrant offshoot of the romantic era's exposure to the "wondrous" orient of *la renaissance orientale*. To the contrary, it represented a recurrent dilemma in Russian culture. Ramifications of admirable Caucasian primitivity can be seen, for example, in Scythianism, the pro-Asian conception of Russian

288

identity articulated by various writers in the early twentieth century. Based on the assumption that Russia's national character was split in two, Alexander Blok's definitive verse "Scythians" celebrated precisely the elemental, non-western component, traced back to ancient nomadic hordes of the steppes. With their ineradicable Scythian heritage, Blok's chaotic, slant-eyed Russians pose a potential menace to refined, effete Europe: the native realm is a sphinx with an "Asian snout" turned westward in comingled love and hate. Of course, Blok's outlook on the eve of the 1917 revolution did not merely replicate the romantic era's production of noble Caucasian mountaineers. And yet a similar battle of mixed cultural allegiances was being fought. To paraphrase Bakhtin on discursive rebirths, the poetic word of Scythianism did not forget where it had been.

As nineteenth-century Russian literature's major accreditors of an Asia at one with the national self, noble Caucasian primitives were disrupters, as well as enablers of tsarist imperialism. The romanticized tribes of Pushkin, Bestuzhev-Marlinsky and Lermontov undeniably underwrote certain notions vital to the ideology of the civilizing mission. To recall just one example, Bestuzhev-Marlinsky's "Amma-lat-Bek" set a hegemonic perspective on the tribesman as an intellectual child, asleep until European enlightenment woke him up. The metaphors of Asia's cultural infancy and somnolence recur in nineteenth-century Russian glorifications of the conquest as a victory for Christian civilization, as illustrated in Fadeev's chauvinistic history *Sixty Years of War in the Caucasus*.

However, unlike singleminded extollers of the tribes' subjugation, both Bestuzhev-Marlinsky and Lermontov adumbrated old Tolstoy's declaration that the "glorious triumph over barbarism" was in fact genocidal despoilment, morally and spiritually injurious to its Russian perpetrators. In their engagement with heroic primitivity, the writings of the two military exiles gradually unmasked the self as an institutionalized murderer in tsarist uniform. Intimations of violence as a core of savagery in "us" actually began when Pushkin's "The Prisoner of the Caucasus" juxtaposed Russia's dueling ground to Circassia's "bloody amusements." But with his trope of the "new Parnassus" and his romantic construction of Russian friendship with sublime nature, young Pushkin laid the foundation of the Caucasian Alps – the big discursive wall which secondary poets of the 1820s and sentimental travelers throughout the conquest erected in an effort to shut out imperialism's brutality.

The alpine wall was the site where the soldiers Bestuzhev-Marlinsky and Lermontov inscribed anguished graffiti about transforming Eden into a killing field. "Ammalat-Bek" and Bestuzhev-Marlinsky's *récits de voyage* registered anxiety about the self conscripted by the "angel of death" to usurp paradise. Lermontov's Izmail-Bey has Homeric stature, but the same poem features the tsarist soldier as a "predatory beast" – the routine killer of babies and old people, the sadistic molester of tribeswomen. Military exile then gave Lermontov tragic knowledge of himself as one of the death-dealing Russian "beasts," the very metaphor he employed in depicting battle in "Valerik." These writings all stood in continuity with old Tolstoy's depiction of the Caucasian war as genocidal aggression heavy on the moral conscience of the Russian nation. Not by chance, the three writers who most glaringly exposed the cultural mythology's tension between the alpine sanctuary and the battleground served in the army. One can only wonder whether young Pushkin would have still celebrated war's "black contagion" at the foot of the "new Parnassus" if he had suffered exile in the "southern Siberia's" army.

Of course, no matter how great its resistance to the ideology of the civilizing mission, all the literature stimulated by the Caucasian conquest remained in some sense Russian appropriation. Unrelenting as it is in excoriating "our" side, *Hadji Murat*, too, is a book by a Russian, addressed to Russians. Old Tolstoy produced a culturally distinct voice for the tribesman, but largely in order to administer moral shock-therapy to an envisioned audience of beneficiaries of empire. The basic fact of Russian literary production was enough to make certain representatives of dispossessed Caucasian tribes deny even old Tolstoy their full approval, as we shall see now.

The past holds clues about the various ways the Caucasus' decolonized peoples may respond to nineteenth-century Russian appropriation. To a concerned observer of the late 1860s, the literary Caucasus appeared a strictly monologic cultural enterprise which illiterate tribesmen could not hope to challenge: in lamenting the reading public's refusal to forget "Ammalat-Bek, Seltaneta and all the rest," Pyotr Uslar asserted that writers had been left to "fantasize to their hearts' content" because "tribesmen do not read Russian books and write refutations of them."[1] An investigator of Caucasian tribal languages, Uslar was seeking to open the monologue into dialogue by amassing factual knowledge. Like other experts of the era, he was perhaps too ready to overlook Bestuzhev-Marlinsky's ethnographic competence. None the less, Uslar legitimately called attention to the near non-existence of the authentic tribal word in Russian literature prior to *Hadji Murat*.

Uslar's assertion about tribal silence was overturned already in 1873 when an Ossetian tentatively sought to refute some Russian books. A Russified poet and essayist who was an officer in the tsarist army, Inal Kanukov (1851–99) wrote Russian verse about Caucasian *paysage* which was thoroughly reliant on the old aesthetics of the sublime.[2] Without noticing his own dependence on this literary tradition, however, he raised indignant objections to Russia's cultural mythology of the territory. This occurred in the draft of an article finally published without the following passage:

Former convictions which should be consigned to oblivion leave their traces yet today, thanks to the confidence which the public placed in those fantasy-mongering poets of the 1830s and 1820s, Marlinsky, Lermontov and Pushkin who created bogeys for the Russian readership in the personages of Ammalat-Bek, Kazbich, Mulla-Nur, Izmail-Bey, Hadji Abrek and other monsters. Gullible and accustomed to accepting the authority of these poets who represented life in the Caucasus while knowing scarcely anything about it, the readership took the heroes as actual types.[3]

Quick to spot literature's inadequacies as ethnography, Kanukov took offense at the romantics' volcanic, violent wild men without recognizing how they had been ennobled to accredit Asia for the semi-Europeanized Russian élite.

In the USSR in the 1930s men of Caucasian tribal origins voiced an equally adamant refusal to make any concessions to nineteenth-century Russian writers. The protest raged in the periodical *Revolution and the Mountaineer* during the so-called "proletarian episode" of Soviet literature.[4] In the interest of creating a culture fully appropriate to the workers' society supposedly taking shape in the USSR, the Russian Association of Proletarian Writers (RAPP) launched attacks on literary classics toward the end of the 1920s. What relevance could Pushkin, for instance, possibly have for the new Soviet man? The challenge was readily taken up by the Caucasus' communists with an extra, ethno-cultural interest in purging the classical pantheon. No major contributor to the literary Caucasus escaped the ensuing accusations of misrepresentation. In the words of the Kabardinian author and critic, Dzh. Naloev, even Tolstoy was "not entirely admissible for us."[5] After all, had *Hadji Murat* not failed to divulge the struggle between "feudalism" and "socialism" in the Caucasian war? To correct Tolstoy (while raiding his text), a Soviet Russian playwright transformed Hadji Murat into a radical atheist and proto-Bolshevik in 1934.[6]

The call to formulate "proletarian" tribal discourse about the conquest illustrated how well the Soviet state succeeded in coopting élites of its ethnically diverse republics. But a tribal response to the Russian literary heritage was also articulated in emigration, as typified in the *Caucasian Mountaineer*, a periodical published in Prague in the 1920s. Like their ethnic counterparts who found a *modus vivendi* with the Soviet state, the émigrés were preoccupied with their lack of written national literatures. As just quoted, Naloev maintained that budding authors from the Caucasus should ignore the Russian literary heritage as a matter of principle. But where *could* they find models for writing their own histories and literatures? Grigory Aiollo's article "Somebody Else's Dish Poorly Warmed Over" was a major contribution to this debate in the émigré press. Despite the title's rather belligerent air, Aiollo distinguished Russian "nationalism" from Russian "national spirit" (*narodnost'*) and located literary giants such as Pushkin and Tolstoy in the latter sphere. Most interestingly, Aiollo advised his compatriots to profit from valuable aspects of the nineteenth-century literary Caucasus, even though Russian culture could not provide them any "absolute values": "We are not afraid of these foreign forces, we use them, we are assimilating them."[7] Ready to take sustenance from another's "cuisine," Aiollo foresaw the possibility of a decolonized people's self-actualizing deployment of writings produced in the culture of the imperial overlord (who now called himself "socialist" instead of "tsarist").[8]

Instances of this type of cross-cultural interplay actually occurred in Soviet Russia in later periods. Lermontov's enriching impact on the Kabardinian poet Ali Shogentsukov has been studied, for example.[9] But as one might expect, *Hadji Murat* eventually won the highest possible accolades from the people whose imperialist subjugation it depicted. In memoirs published in 1970 the Lenin-Prize-winning poet of Dagestan, Rasul Hamzatov, remembered how his father had made him read *Hadji Murat* as a boy, translating from Russian into Avar. Filtered through the mother tongue, Tolstoy's castigation of the conquest was fully accepted as the colonized nation's own: according to Hamzatov, the old men of his Dagestan village maintained that only the "Lord Himself" could have authored such a "truthful book."[10]

This quick survey of tribal attitudes toward Russia's literary Caucasus suggests a range of possibilities for the future. Now that the Soviet Union has collapsed, writers and intellectuals of the Caucasus' newly independent states will seek to reappropriate their national histories. The production of counter-history is well underway in Dagestan, for instance, where Shamil is reassuming stature as a national hero after suffering a deep decline into "feudal despotism" in Russian ideology in Stalin's time.[11] Like the Dagestani retrieval of Shamil, other decolonized peoples of the Caucasus will "write back" to tsarist imperialism, through literature as well as non-fiction.[12] Nineteenth-century Russian authors notably deprived Georgia of strong, brave men. But how will Russian culture's heroic Muslim mountaineers fare in the post-colonial era? The past shows options ranging from accepting a Russian writer as the "Lord Himself" to rejecting him *because* of his nationality. Most of the pertinent counter-histories and counter-literatures will take shape between these two extremes and conceivably may deploy selected features of the nineteenth-century Russian literary heritage. First articulated by young Pushkin and variously transposed by Bestuzhev-Marlinsky, Lermontov and old Tolstoy, the resilient Russian expression of affiliation to the Caucasian mountaineers might very well find concordant interlocutors on the "other," decolonized side of history.

Notes

I INTRODUCTION

1. Quoted in G. Semin, *Sevastopol': Istoricheskii ocherk* (Moscow: Voennoe izdatel'stvo, 1955), p. 24.
2. Vano Shaduri, *Dekabristskaia literatura i gruzinskaia obshchestvennost'* (Tbilisi: Zaria Vostoka, 1958), p. 22.
3. S. Vel'tman, *Vostok v khudozhestvennoi literature* (Moscow-Leningrad: Gosudarstvennoe izdatel'stvo, 1928), p. 9; Lidiia Ginzburg, *Tvorcheskii put' Lermontova* (Leningrad: Khudozhestvennaia literatura, 1940), p. 122; and Agil' Gadzhiev, *Kavkaz v russkoi literature pervoi poloviny XIX veka* (Baku: Novaia knizhnaia tipografiia, 1982), pp. 9–10.
4. The standard survey of the nineteenth-century conquest in English remains John F. Baddeley, *The Russian Conquest of the Caucasus* (London: Longmans, Green and Co., 1908). Consult also Paul B. Henze, "Fire and Sword in the Caucasus: The 19th-Century Resistance of the North Caucasian Mountaineers," *Central Asian Survey* 2 (July 1983), 5–44.
5. A. P. Berzhe, "Prisoedinenie Gruzii k Rossii, 1799–1831," *Russkaia starina* 28 (May 1880), 2–3. For pertinent perspectives on empire, see Charles Reynolds, *Modes of Imperialism* (Oxford: Martin Robertson, 1981); Patrick Brantlinger, *Rule of Darkness. British Literature and Imperialism, 1830–1914* (Ithaca: Cornell University, 1988), pp. 7–8; and Edward W. Said, *Culture and Imperialism* (London: Chatto and Windus, 1993), pp. 8–9. As Said's discussion points out, imperialism (unlike colonialism) does not always entail implanting settlements on distant territory.
6. Marc Raeff, *Imperial Russia, 1682–1825. The Coming of Age of Modern Russia* (New York, 1971), pp. 50–60.
7. Marc Raeff, "In the Imperial Manner" in *Catherine the Great. A Profile*, ed. Marc Raeff (New York: Hill and Wang, 1972), pp. 197–200.

295

8. Michael T. Florinsky, *Russia. A History and an Interpretation*, 2 vols. (New York: Macmillan, 1965), vol. i, p. 541.
9. Konstantin F. Shteppa, "The 'Lesser Evil' Formula," *Rewriting Russian History*, ed. C. E. Black (New York: Praeger, 1956), 107–17.
10. On Shamil's varied career in Soviet Russian historiography, see Paul B. Henze, "Un-rewriting History – The Shamil Problem," *Caucasian Review* 6 (1958), 7–29; and Lowell R. Tillett, "Soviet Second Thoughts on Tsarist Colonialism," *Foreign Affairs* 42 (January 1964), 309–19.
11. N. S. Kiniapina, M. M. Bliev and V. V. Degoev, *Kavkaz i Srednaia Aziia vo vneshnei politike Rossii. Vtoraia polovina XVIII–80-e gody XIX v.* (Moscow: MGU, 1984), pp. 9–12.
12. N. Svirin, "Russkaia kolonial'naia literatura," *Literaturnyi kritik* (1934), no. 9, 76–79.
13. Vel'tman,*Vostok v khudozhestvennoi literature*, p. 9. In endorsing Lenin's call to use cinema for propaganda, Vel'tman declared that Asians "think in images" instead of reasoning: pp. 178–80.
14. Split into a Northern Society and Southern Society, the Decembrists were noblemen, army officers and intellectuals who wanted to replace the autocracy. Their proposed strategies and objectives differed, as some favored a constitutional monarchy, while others leaned toward a republic. After the insurrection in St. Petersburg in December 1825, five principal conspirators were hanged and many others exiled to Siberia or transferred to the Caucasus.
15. *Pushkin v vospominaniiakh i rasskazakh sovremennikov*, ed. S. Ia. Gessen (Leningrad: GIKhL, 1936), pp. 611–12, n. 238.
16. L. P. Semenov, *A. S. Pushkin o Kavkaze* (Piatigorsk: Severokavkazskoe kraevoe izdatel'stvo, 1937), pp. 14–24.
17. *Russkie pisateli v nashem krae. Sbornik statei* (Groznyi, 1958); and B. S. Vinogradov, *Russkie pisateli v Checheno-Ingushetii* (Groznyi, 1958). For a more recent contribution to the genre, see L. A. Chereiskii, *Pushkin i Severnyi Kavkaz* (Stavropol': Stavropol'skoe izdatel'stvo, 1986).
18. V. G. Bazanov, *Ocherki dekabristskoi literatury. Publitsistika. Proza. Kritika* (Moscow: GIKhL, 1953); and Shaduri, *Dekabristskaia literatura*.
19. Gadzhiev, *Kavkaz v russkoi literature*, pp. 18–20. See similar dichotomies in R. F. Iusufov, *Dagestan i russkaia literatura kontsa XVIII i pervoi poloviny XIX v.* (Moscow: Nauka, 1964), pp. 83–84; and B. S. Vinogradov, *Kavkaz v russkoi literature 30-kh godov*

XIX veka. (Ocherki) (Groznyi: Checheno-Ingushskoe knizhnoe izdatel'stvo, 1966), p. 98.

20. Edward W. Said, *Orientalism* (New York: Vintage Books, 1979), pp. 14–15, 23–24.

21. Jonathan Arac, "Introduction" in *Macropolitics of Nineteenth-Century Literature: Nationalism, Exoticism, Imperialism*, ed. Jonathan Arac and Harriet Ritvo (Philadelphia: University of Pennsylvania, 1991), p. 1. See also Peter Hulme, *Colonial Encounters. Europe and the Native Caribbean, 1492–1797* (London and New York: Routledge, 1992), pp. 2–12.

22. The quoted phrase comes from the anonymous "Poezdka v Gruziiu," *Moskovskii telegraf* (August 1833), no. 15, 327.

23. Hayden White, "The Noble Savage Theme as Fetish," *Tropics of Discourse. Essays in Cultural Criticism* (Baltimore: Johns Hopkins University, 1978), pp. 183–96.

24. Jonah Ruskin, *The Mythology of Imperialism* (New York: Random House, 1971), pp. 157–58.

25. For a study of this ideological conviction, see Richard Slotkin, *Regeneration through Violence: The Mythology of the American Frontier, 1600–1860* (Middletown, CT: Wesleyan University, 1973).

26. See Gary Saul Morson, "Introduction: Literary History and the Russian Experience" in *Literature and History. Theoretical Problems and Russian Case Studies*, ed. Gary Saul Morson (Stanford: Stanford University, 1986), pp. 1–14; and M. M. Bakhtin, *Estetika slovesnogo tvorchestva* (Moscow: Iskusstvo, 1979), translated as *Speech Genres and Other Late Essays*, trans. Vern W. McGee, ed. Caryl Emerson and Michael Holquist (Austin, TX: University of Texas, 1986): see "Response to a Question from the *Novy Mir* Editorial Staff," pp. 1–9; and "From Notes Made in 1970–71," pp. 139–46.

27. Even in 1844, only 4 percent of the (male) population of a certain Russian province could read: see William Mills Todd III, *Fiction and Society in the Age of Pushkin. Ideology, Institutions and Narrative* (Cambridge, MA and London: Harvard University, 1986), p. 100. On the rise of literacy, consult Jeffrey Brooks, *When Russia Learned to Read. Literacy and Popular Literature, 1861–1917* (Princeton NJ: Princeton University, 1985).

28. For views of ethnography itself as the construction of narratives, see James Clifford and George Marcus (eds.), *Writing Culture* (Berkeley: University of California, 1987).

29. Bakhtin, "Response to a Question from the *Novy Mir* Editorial Staff," pp. 6–7.

30. See treatment of the issue in Elizabeth Freund, *The Return of the*

Reader. Reader-Response Criticism (London and New York: Methuen, 1987), pp. 90–133.

31. Dmitrii Sergeyevich Likhachev, *The National Nature of Russian History* (New York: Harriman Institute, Columbia University, 1990), p. 18.

2 THE POET AND *TERRA INCOGNITA*

Epigraph, V. G. Belinskii, *Polnoe sobranie sochinenii*, 13 vols. (Moscow: Akademiia nauk, 1953–59), vol. VII, p. 372.

1. Belinskii, *Polnoe sobranie sochinenii*, vol. VIII, pp. 376–77. Belinsky tellingly perceived "howling contradictions between a European exterior and an Asian essence" in his own native realm (376).

2. See the discussion of the West in Said, *Culture and Imperialism*, p. 96. Such aspects of Russian writing are stressed in Katya Hokanson, "Literary Imperialism, *Narodnost'* and Pushkin's Invention of the Caucasus," *Russian Review*, forthcoming.

3. For seminal analysis of these impulses and discursive practices, consult Said, *Orientalism*, pp. 31–49. See also Christopher L. Miller, *Blank Darkness. Africanist Discourse in French* (Chicago: University of Chicago, 1985), pp. 6–14; Brantlinger, *Rule of Darkness*, pp. 3–16; and Mary Louise Pratt, *Imperial Eyes. Travel Writing and Transculturation* (London: Routledge, 1992), pp. 6–7.

4. Compare Osip Mandelshtam's view that "instruction is the nerve of prose," in *Modern Russian Poets on Poetry*, ed. Carl R. Proffer, selected and introduced by Joseph Brodsky (Ann Arbor, MI: Ardis, 1984), p. 57.

5. Pushkin, *Sobranie sochinenii v desiati tomakh* (Moscow: GIKhL, 1959–62), vol. IX, p. 39.

6. Pushkin, *Polnoe sobranie sochinenii*, 17 vols. (Leningrad: Akademiia nauk, 1937–59), vol. XII, p. 371.

7. A. Slonimskii, *Masterstvo Pushkina* (Moscow: GIKhL, 1959), p. 217.

8. V. M. Zhirmunskii, *Bairon i Pushkin* (1924; rpt. Leningrad: Nauka, 1978), pp. 28–29, 43–48, 292–331.

9. Paul Debreczeny, "The Reception of Pushkin's Poetic Works in the 1820s: A Study in the Critic's Role," *Slavic Review* 28 (September 1969), 397–98.

10. L. N. Nazarova, "Russkii roman pervogo cherverti XIX veka. Ot sentimental'noi povesti k romanu," *Istoriia russkogo romana*, 2 vols. (Moscow-Leningrad: Akademiia nauk, 1962), vol. I, p. 85.

11. See I. Z. Serman, "Zarozhdenie romana v russkoi literature XVIII veka" in *ibid.*, vol. I, pp. 47–48; and Iu. M. Lotman, *Roman A. S. Pushkina "Evgenii Onegin." Kommentarii. Posobie dlia uchitelia*, 2nd edn. (Leningrad: Prosveshchenie, 1983), p. 215.
12. Todd, *Fiction and Society*, pp. 34–36.
13. B. V. Tomashevskii, *Pushkin*, 2 vols. (Moscow-Leningrad: Akademiia nauk, 1956), vol. I, p. 405; and Iu. N. Tynianov, "Pushkin," *Arkhaisty i novatory* (Leningrad: Priboe, 1929), pp. 253–55.
14. M. M. Bakhtin, "Epic and Novel," *The Dialogic Imagination. Four Essays by Mikhail Bakhtin*, ed. Michael Holquist, trans. Caryl Emerson and Holquist (Austin, TX: University of Texas, 1981), pp. 5–8. See also analysis in Katerina Clark and Michael Holquist, *Mikhail Bakhtin* (Cambridge, MA and London: Harvard University, 1984), pp. 275–77.
15. I. N. Berezin, *Puteshestvie po Dagestanu i Zakavkaz'iu. S kartami, planami i vidami zamechatel'nykh mestakh*, 2nd edn., 2 vols. (Kazan: Universitetskaia tipografiia, 1850–52), vol. II, pp. 51–52.
16. D. S. Mirsky, *Pushkin* (New York: Dutton, 1963), pp. 65–66.
17. M. P. Alekseev, *Etiudy o Marlinskom* (Irkutsk: Universitet Irkutska 1928), p. 144.
18. I. Bessonov, "Zametki dlia budushchikh izdatelei Pushkina," *Otechestvennye zapiski* 45 (April 1846), otd.II, 113.
19. François-René Chateaubriand, *Atala. René* (Paris: Garnier-Flammarion, 1964), p. 58.
20. Paul Austin has argued that Pushkin was "merely providing a poetic variation and paraphrase" of eighteenth-century "empirical accounts" about the Caucasus: see his "The Exotic Prisoner in Russian Romanticism," *Russian Literature* 16-18 (October 1984), 239–41. To all indications, however, those nonfictional writings were hardly read in Russia.
21. Compare Leonard J. Davis, "A Social History of Fact and Fiction: Authorial Disavowal in the Early English Novel" in *Literature and Society*, ed. Edward W. Said (Baltimore and London: Johns Hopkins University, 1980), pp. 125–30.
22. In their introduction to Karamzin's *Pis'ma russkogo puteshestvennika* (Leningrad: Nauka, 1984) Yuri Lotman and Boris Uspensky argue that a fundamentally literary work was pretending to "non-literariness" (*neliteraturnost'*), pp. 534–40, 567–69. See also John Tallmadge, "Voyaging and the Literary Imagination," *Exploration* 7 (1979), 1–16; Percy G. Adams, *Travel Literature and the Evolution of the Novel* (Lexington, KY: University of Kentucky, 1983), pp. 109–47; John Mersereau, Jr., *Russian Romantic Fiction* (Ann Arbor, MI: Ardis, 1983), p. 42; and Germaine Brée,

"Ambiguous Voyage: Mode or Genre," *Genre* 1 (April 1968), 87–96.

23. Adams, *Travel Literature*, p. 45; and Reuel K. Wilson, *The Literary Travelogue. A Comparative Study with Special Relevance to Russian Literature from Fonvizin to Pushkin* (The Hague: Martinus Nijhoff, 1973), p. 12.

24. Lotman and Uspenskii, introduction to *Pis'ma russkogo puteshestvennika*, pp. 561–64; and Wladimir Berelowitch, "Preface" to Nicholaï Karamzine, *Lettres d'un voyageur russe*, ed. Berelowitch (Paris: Quai Voltaire, 1991), pp. 16–17.

25. Lotman and Uspenskii, introduction to *Pis'ma russkogo puteshestvennika*, p. 531. On the kind of information sought by Karamzin's readers, see also Roger B. Anderson, "Karamzin's *Letters of a Russian Traveller*: An Education in Western Sentimentalism" in *Essays on Karamzin, Russian Man of Letters, Political Thinker, Historian, 1766–1826*, ed. J. L. Black (The Hague: Mouton, 1975), pp. 22–23.

26. Wilson, *Literary Travelogue*, pp. 56–62.

27. T. Roboli, "Literatura puteshestvii" in *Russkaia proza. Sbornik statei*, ed. B. M. Eikhenbaum and Iu. N. Tynianov (Leningrad: Academia, 1926), p. 46.

28. Michel Butor, "Traveling and Writing," trans. John Powers and K. Lisker, *Mosaic* 8 (Fall 1974), 1–3.

29. Quoted in *Ocherki po russkoi zhurnalistiki i kritike*, 2 vols. (Leningrad: LGU, 1950), vol. 1, pp. 142–43.

30. Pushkin, *Sobranie sochinenii*, vol. IX, p. 18.

31. Ia. I. Saburov, "Poezdka v Saratov, Astrakhan i na Kavkaz," *Moskovskii nabliudatel'* (May 1835), kn. 2, ch. II, 176–77.

32. Mirsky, *Pushkin*, p. 61; and Mersereau, *Russian Romantic Fiction*, p. 34.

33. Berezin, *Puteshestvie po Dagestanu*, vol. II, p. 2.

34. George Watson, "The Accuracy of Lord Byron," *Critical Quarterly* 7 (Summer 1975), 137–39; and Keith Walker, *Byron's Readers. A Study of Attitudes toward Byron, 1812–1832* (Salzburg: Institut für Anglistik und Amerikanistik, Universität Salzburg, 1979), pp. 4–9.

35. Lord Byron, *The Complete Poetical Works*, ed. Jerome McGann, 6 vols. (Oxford: Oxford University, the Clarendon Press, 1980–91), vol. II, p. 3.

36. Walker, *Byron's Readers*, p. 14.

37. N. P., "Puteshestvie v Berezov i Obdorsk," *Moskovskii telegraf* (1833), no. 13, 76–81.

38. Petr Ivanovich Bartenev, "Pushkin v iuzhnoi Rossii, 1820–23," *Russkii arkhiv* (1866), nos. 8–9, 1102–3, 1111.

39. *Russkaia kriticheskaia literatura o proizvedeniiakh A. S. Pushkina. Khronologicheskii sbornik kritiko-bibliograficheskikh statei*, comp. V. Zelinskii, 7 vols. (Moscow: E. Lissner and Iu. Roman, 1887), vol. 1, p. 102. See also other reviews: pp. 87, 91–92.

40. Frederika von Freygang, "Pis'ma o Kavkaze," *Syn otechestva* (1816), no. 46, ch. 34, 271–77; and I. Eikhfel'd, "Kavkazskaia doroga," *Otechestvennye zapiski* (1821), ch. 6 (253/6), 270–94. "Pis'ma o Kavkaze" was a translated excerpt from Wilhelm and Frederika von Freygang, *Lettres sur le Caucase et la Géorgie, suivies d'une rélation d'un voyage en Perse en 1812*, trans. Struve (Hamburg: Perthes and Besser, 1816).

41. K. Dondua, "Pushkin v gruzinskoi literature" in *Pushkin v mirovoi literature. Sbornik statei* (Leningrad: LGU, 1926), p. 199. The same account of confused Caucasian cartography (dated 1768 rather than 1769) appears in Florinsky, *Russia*, vol. 1, p. 521, n. 1.

42. For an annotated bibliography including works by the eighteenth-century Caucasian explorers, consult M. A. Polievktov, *Evropeiskie puteshestvenniki XVI–XVIII vv. po Kavkazu* (Tiflis: Sakhelgami, 1935).

43. See P. S. Pallas, *Puteshestvie po raznym mestam rossiiskago gosudarstva po poveleniiu Sanktpeterburgskoi imperatorskoi akademii nauk*, trans. Fedor Tomanskii, ch. 3 (St. Petersburg, 1788). Without indicating whether he read Pallas in German, Osip Mandelshtam said the writer seemed to be whistling Mozart as he traveled: see Mandel'shtam, "Zapisnye knizhki. Zametki," *Voprosy literatury* (1968), no. 4, 192.

44. Semen Bronevskii, *Noveishie geograficheskie i istoricheskie izvestiia o Kavkaze*, 2nd. aug. edn., 2 vols. (Moscow: S. Selivanovskii, 1823), vol. 1, pp. ix–x. Iusufov states that a first edition of this book appeared in 1821 but gives no citation: see *Dagestan i russkaia literatura*, p. 44. Only the second edition is cited in M. Miansarov, *Bibliographia Caucasica et Transcaucasica* (St. Petersburg: O. I. Bakst, Gogenfel'den and Co., 1874–76), p. 54.

45. Pushkin, *Sobranie sochinenii*, vol. IX, p. 20.

46. For a thorough survey of the possibilities, consult A. I. Nekrasov, "K voprosu o literaturnykh istochnikakh 'Kavkazskogo plennika' Pushkina" in *Sbornik statei k sorokoletiiu uchenoi deiatel'nosti akademika A. S. Orlova* (Leningrad: Akademiia nauk, 1934), pp. 153–63.

47. Pushkin, *Sobranie sochinenii*, vol. IX, p. 21.

48. On the general issue, see Shari Benstock, "At the Margin of Discourse: Footnotes in the Fictional Text," *PMLA* 98 (January

1983), 204–6, 209; and Lawrence Lipking, "The Marginal Gloss," *Critical Inquiry* 3 (Summer 1977), 609–55.

49. On Karamzin's *History of the Russian State* as a "double text" (literary and scholarly), consult Caryl Emerson, *Boris Godunov. Transpositions of a Russian Theme* (Bloomington, IN: Indiana University, 1986), pp. 31–41.

50. On a similar mode of authentication, see Stephanie Sandler, "The Poetics of Authority in Pushkin's 'André Chenier,'" *Slavic Review* 42 (Summer 1983), 195.

51. Bronevskii, *Noveishie izvestiia o Kavkaze*, vol. I, pp. vii–viii.

52. A. [Bestuzhev-]Marlinskii, *Polnoe sobranie sochinenii*, 3rd edn., 12 vols. (St. Petersburg: III Otdelenie, 1838–39), vol. X, p. 170.

53. *Syn otechestva* (1824), ch. 9, kn. 2, 71.

54. Belinskii, *Polnoe sobranie sochinenii*, vol. VII, p. 373.

55. On General Ermolov's mental library of Latin poetry, see *Aleksei Petrovich Ermolov. Materialy dlia ego biografii*, comp. M. N. Pogodin (Moscow: Katkov and Co., 1863), p. 10. During his military exile Bestuzhev-Marlinsky reported reciting to himself Pushkin, Byron, Dante, Ariosto, Goethe and Walter Scott: see [Bestuzhev-]Marlinskii, *Polnoe sobranie sochinenii*, vol. X, pp. 279–80.

56. P. R. Khanzhonokov, "Rasskaz kavkazskogo veterana o Pushkine," appended in I. K. Enikolopov, *Pushkin na Kavkaze* (Tbilisi: Zaria Vostoka, 1938), pp. 160–66.

57. N. B. Potokskii, "Vstrechi s Aleksandrom Sergeevichem Pushkinym v 1829 godu," appended in Enikolopov, *ibid*, pp. 144–45.

58. P. A. Viazemskii, *Staraia zapisnaia knizhka* (Leningrad: Izdatel'stvo pisatelei, 1929), p. 161.

59. See Brantlinger, *Rule of Darkness*, p. 180; and Andrew Rutherford, "News and the Muse: Press Sources for some of Kipling's Early Verse," *English Literature in Transition, 1880–1920*, 29 (1986, no. 1), 7–16.

60. Quoted by Enikolopov, *Pushkin na Kavkaze*, pp. 79–80.

61. Bulgarin is quoted in Shaduri, *Dekabristskaia literatura*, p. 395.

62. Ivan P. Borozdna, *Poeticheskie ocherki Ukrainy, Odessy i Kryma. Pis'ma v stikhakh k grafu V. P. Z–u* (Moscow: S. Selivanovskii, 1837).

3 IMAGINATIVE GEOGRAPHY

Epigraph, Pushkin, "Kavkazskii plennik," *Sobranie sochinenii*, vol. III, p. 87. (Subsequent citations appear parenthetically in the text.) Pushkin's dedication uses the metrically apt variant "Beshtu," but the poem's first footnote states that the name is "more accurately Beshtau" (which Russians wrote in this non-hyphenated form).

1. A. A. Shishkov, "N. T. A(ksakov)u" in *Poety 1820–1830-kh godov*, ed. L. Ia. Ginzburg, 2nd edn. (Leningrad: Sovetskii pisatel', 1972), vol. i, p. 401. (Cited hereafter as *Poety*.)
2. A similar tendency in British writing about Africa is analyzed in Pratt, *Imperial Eyes*, pp. 51–61.
3. *Ibid.*, p. 100.
4. One of Pushkin's drafts cast the hero as an exile: see Tomashevskii, *Pushkin*, vol. i, pp. 392–93.
5. I. T. Radozhitskii, "Doroga ot reki Dona do Georgievska na prostranstve 500 verst," *Otechestvennye zapiski* (August 1823), no. 40, 343. Cited in several subsequent notes, this monthly journal was published in 1818–19 and 1820–30, primarily under Pavel Svinin's editorship. The better known journal of the same name was founded by Andrei Kraevsky in 1839 and existed until 1884.
6. Alexandre Benningsen, "Muslim Conservative Opposition to the Soviet Regime: The Sufi Brotherhoods in the North Caucasus," in *Soviet Nationality Policies and Practices*, ed. Jeremy R. Azrael (New York: Praeger, 1978), pp. 337–39.
7. Relevant modern studies are Gadzhiev, *Kavkaz v russkoi literature*, pp. 15–19, 118–22; and Iusufov, *Dagestan i russkaia literatura*, pp. 72–75, 144–45.
8. Belinskii, *Polnoe sobranie sochinenii*, vol. ix, p. 298. B. S. Vinogradov argued that Derzhavin reliably depicted snakes engaged in battle or mass copulation: see "Nachalo kavkazskoi temy v russkoi literature," in *Russkaia literatura i Kavkaz*, ed. V. M. Tamakhin (Stavropol', 1974), pp. 20, 25, n. 78.
9. Marjorie Hope Nicolson, *Mountain Gloom and Mountain Glory. The Development of the Aesthetics of the Infinite*, (Ithaca: Cornell University, 1959), pp. 4–38, 59–67.
10. N. Karamzin, *Sochineniia v dvukh tomakh* (Leningrad: Khudozhestvennaia literatura, 1984), vol. i, p. 209.
11. G. R. Derzhavin, *Stikhotvoreniia*, 2nd edn. (Leningrad: Sovetskii pisatel', 1957), pp. 255–59.
12. V. A. Zhukovskii, *Izbrannoe* (Leningrad: Khudozhestvennaia literatura, 1973), p. 70.
13. Pushkin, *Sobranie sochinenii*, vol. ix, p. 55.
14. Victor Brombert, *The Romantic Prison. The French Tradition* (Princeton, NJ: Princeton University, 1978), pp. 3–13. See also Monika Frenkel Greenleaf, "Pushkin's 'Journey to Arzrum':

The Poet at the Border," *Slavic Review* 50 (Winter 1991), 940–41.

15. Pushkin, *Sobranie sochinenii*, vol. IX, p. 30.

16. In my effort to retain Pushkin's meter and rhyme scheme, I have sacrificed "two-headed." This mode of translation requires some paraphrasing, of course, but none the less gives a valid demonstration of rhetoric shared by Zhukovsky and Pushkin.

17. See British cases in Nicolson, *Mountain Gloom and Glory*, pp. 38, 122, 350.

18. For a particularly dense recapitulation of sublime motifs, see L. A. Iakubovich, "Kavkaz" in *Poety*, vol. II, p. 272. See also A. A. Shishkov, "Lonskoi," *Opyty 1828 goda* (Moscow, 1828), pp. 6–8.

19. Dmitrij Čiževskij, *On Romanticism in Slavic Literature* (The Hague: Mouton, 1957), 29–35.

20. See, respectively, S. D. Nechaev, "K G. A. R.–K." in *Poety*, vol. I, p. 101; E. P. Zaitsevskii, "Abaziia" [sic] in *Poety*, vol. I, p. 515; and A. A. Shishkov, "Dagestanskaia uznitsa" in *Dagestan v russkoi literature. Dorevoliutsionnyi period*, ed. Uzdiat Dalgat and Boris Kirdan (Makhachkala: Dagestanskoe knizhnoe izdatel'stvo, 1960), pp. 56, 67.

21. S. D. Nechaev, "Vospominaniia" in *Poety*, vol. I, p. 111, n. 3.

22. K. F. Ryleev, *Polnoe sobranie sochinenii*, 2nd edn. (Leningrad: Sovetskii pisatel', 1971), pp. 91–93.

23. E. P. Rostopchina, "El'brus i ia," *Stikhotvoreniia*, 2nd edn., 4 vols. (St. Petersburg: A. Smirdin, 1857–60), vol. I, pp. 173–75. See other Caucasian poems, pp. 263–65, 269–70.

24. Zaitsevskii, "Abaziia," p. 515.

25. V. I. Grigor'ev, "Beshtau" in *Poety*, vol. I pp. 387; and V. G. Tepliakov, "Kavkaz" in *Poety*, vol. I, pp. 605–7.

26. A. I. Meisner, *Stikhotvoreniia* (Moscow: A. Semen, 1836), pp. 66–68.

27. [Bestuzhev-]Marlinskii, *Polnoe sobranie sochinenii*, vol. X, p. 261.

28. V. I. Grigor'ev, "Vecher na Kavkaze" in *Poety*, vol. I, p. 385.

29. M. Iu. Lermontov, *Sobranie sochinenii v chetyrekh tomakh* (Moscow: Khudozhestvennaia literatura,1983–84), vol. I, pp. 30–31.

30. Reprinted in *Russkie pisateli o Gruzii*, ed. Vano Shaduri, 2 vols. (Tbilisi: Zaria Vostoka, 1948), vol. I, pp. 417–18; vol. I, pp. 419–20, 422–23. On the date of Oznobishin's poem, see Gadzhiev, *Kavkaz v russkoi literature*, pp. 40–41.

31. Lermontov, *Sobranie sochinenii*, vol. I, pp. 76–79.

32. Pushkin, *Sobranie sochinenii*, vol. II, p. 266. In a quatrain which was possibly a self-censored conclusion to "The Caucasus,"

Pushkin correlated the "caged" river and the tribes: "So turbulent freedom is strictured by law, / So government torments a wild people's spirit, / So now does the Caucasus rankle in silence, / So alien power oppresses the land" (*ibid.*, p. 713).

33. A. A. Bestuzhev-Marlinskii, "Ammalat-Bek" in *Povesti i rasskazy* (Moscow: Sovetskaia Rossiia, 1976), pp. 181–82; and V. K. Kiukhel'beker, *Izbrannye proizvedeniia v dvykh tomakh*, 2nd edn. (Moscow-Leningrad: Sovetskii pisatel', 1967), vol. I, pp. 527–28.

34. Lermontov, *Sobranie sochinenii*, vol. I, pp. 43–44. See I. I. Dmitriev, *Polnoe sobranie sochinenii*, 2nd edn. (Leningrad: Sovetskii pisatel', 1967), vol. I, pp. 87–89; and V. I. Grigor'ev's translation of Shtolberg in *Poety*, vol. I, pp. 370–72.

35. Gaston Bachelard, *La poétique de l'espace* (Paris: PUF, 1957), pp. 15–21, 191–207. As an example of topographical distortion, the observer in Pushkin's "The Caucasus" performs the humanly impossible feat of seeing the Aragva and Kura rivers simultaneously: cited in D. S. Blagoi, *Tvorcheskii put' Pushkina (1826–1830)*, (Moscow: Sovetskii pisatel', 1967), pp. 366–67.

36. P. Mukhanov, "Krasnyi most. Vospominanie o Gil'denshtedt [sic] (Pis'mo k R.)," *Moskovskii telegraf* (November 1825), ch. 6, no. 21, otd. II, 61–62.

4 SENTIMENTAL PILGRIMS

Epigraph, Radozhitskii, "Doroga ot reki Dona," 361.

1. *Ibid.*, 343–44.
2. "Rukovodstvo dlia proezhaiushchikh Kavkazskiia gory," *Otechestvennye zapiski* (1822), ch. 12, 212–22.
3. Saburov, "Poezdka v Saratov," 176.
4. Pushkin, *Puteshestvie v Arzrum* in *Sobranie sochinenii*, vol. V, pp. 417–18. On Piatigorsk's gradual transformation, see Laurence Kelly, *Lermontov. Tragedy in the Caucasus* (London: Constable, 1977), p. 69.
5. P. S. [Petr Sumarokov], "Pis'ma s Kavkaza," *Moskovskii telegraf* (May 1830), ch. 33, 183. (The author is identified in Mersereau, *Russian Romantic Fiction*, p. 328, n. 1.)
6. Sumarokov, "Pis'ma s Kavkaza," (June 1830), 320–22.
7. S. D. Nechaev, "Otryvki iz putevykh zapisok o iugo-vostochnoi Rossii," *Moskovskii telegraf* (1826), ch. 7, otd. I, 32.
8. A. Neliubin, "Kratkoe istoricheskoe izvestie o Kavkazskikh mineral'nykh vodakh v Piatigorii [sic]," *Otechestvennye zapiski* (February 1825), ch. 21, 188–89.

9. "Kavkazskiia vody. Pis'mo P. P. Svin'ina k redaktoru, izo Stavropolia," *Otechestvennye zapiski* (July 1825), ch. 23, 250–51.
10. Nechaev, "K G. A. R.–K." in *Poety*, vol. I, p. 101.
11. For two late examples, consult A. Andreev, *Ot Vladikavkaza do Tiflisa* (St. Petersburg: Novosti, 1891), pp. 16, 27, 44–49; and Evgenii Markov, *Ocherki Kavkaza. Kartiny kavkazskoi zhizni, prirody i istorii*, 2nd edn. (St. Petersburg: M. O. Vol'f, 1904), pp. 54, 419–21, 588–89.
12. See Sumarokov, "Pis'ma s Kavkaza," (June 1830), 320.
13. Pushkin, *Puteshestvie v Arzrum*, pp. 422–23. Pushkin may have invented the incident to parody Chateaubriand's allusion to *Atala* in *Itinéraire de Paris à Jérusalem*: see V. L. Komarovich, "K voprosu o zhanre 'Puteshestviia v Arzrum,'" *Vremennik Pushkinskoi kommissii* 3 (1937), 336.
14. Belinskii, *Polnoe sobranie sochinenii*, vol. VII, pp. 713–14.
15. Few Russian women published Caucasian travelogues.
16. Radozhitskii, "Doroga ot reki Dona," 362.
17. *Ibid.*, 371–72. Famous for his oriental subjects, the dancer and choreographer Charles Didelot (1762–1836) worked for extended periods in St. Petersburg.
18. Nechaev, "Otryvki iz putevykh zapisok," 28.
19. *Ibid.*, 29.
20. Karl Gustav Reingardt, "Izvlechenie iz opisaniia puteshestviia v Gruziiu," *Aziatskii vestnik* (May 1825), 339.
21. G. Gerakov, "Puteshestvie k kavkazskim vodam, po Kubanskoi linii i v Taman' (Otryvok iz putevykh zapisok po mnogim Rossiskim guberniiam)," *Severnyi arkhiv* (1823), no. 1, 67.
22. Anon., "Vospominanie o Kavkaze. (Otryvok iz zapisok odnogo puteshestvennika)," *Aziatskii vestnik* (April 1826), 258.
23. For an admonitory reminder that the Caucasus was not bucolic Switzerland, see Eikhfel'd, "Kavkazskaia doroga," 276.
24. "Pis'ma Kh. Sh. k F. Bulgarinu, ili poezdka na Kavkaz," *Severnyi arkhiv* (August 1828), 239.
25. Iu. N. Tynianov, "O 'Puteshestvii v Arzrum,'" *Vremennik Pushkinskoi kommissii* 2 (1936), 57–73; Komarovich, "K voprosu o zhanre 'Puteshestviia v Arzrum,'" 326–38; V. Shklovskii, *Zametki o proze russkikh klassikov*, 2nd edn. (Moscow: Sovetskii pisatel', 1955), pp. 35–40; Gadzhiev, *Kavkaz v russkoi literature pervoi poloviny XIX veka*, pp. 122–27; and Ia. L. Levkovich, "Kavkazskii dnevnik Pushkina," *Pushkin. Issledovaniia i materialy* 11 (1983), 17–22.
26. See Greenleaf, "Pushkin's 'Journey to Arzrum'," 943.
27. Krystyna Pomorska, "Structural Peculiarities in 'Putešestvie v

Arzrum'" in *Alexander Puškin : A Symposium of the 175th Anniversary of His Birth*, ed. Andrej Kodjak and Kiril Taranovsky (New York: New York University, 1976), 119–20.

28. Pushkin, *Puteshestvie v Arzrum*, p. 424. (Subsequent citations appear parenthetically in the text.)

29. P. A. Katenin, "Kavkazskie gory," *Izbrannye proizvedeniia*, 2nd edn. (Moscow-Leningrad: Sovetskii pisatel', 1965), p. 228.

30. I. M. Iazykov, "A. D. Khripkovu" in *Russkie pisateli o Gruzii*, pp. 299–301; V. Zubov, "Iuzhnaia vesna," *Moskovskii nabliudatel'* (July 1835), kn. 2, 245–46; and I. S. Nikitin, "Iug i sever," *Polnoe sobranie sochinenii*, 2nd edn. (Moscow-Leningrad: Sovetskii pisatel', 1965), p. 81.

31. V. Murav'ev, "Stikhi i zhizn' Aleksandra Polezhaeva" in A. I. Polezhaev, *Stikhotvoreniia*. *Poemy* (Moscow: Moskovskii rabochii, 1981), pp. 4, 9–23. The natural son of a rich landowner, Polezhaev was born in 1804 or 1805.

32. Polezhaev, *Stikhotvoreniia*, pp. 136–40. For analysis of this poem's treatment of war, see my chapter 9.

33. Sumarokov, "Pis'ma s Kavkaza," (May 1830), 170.

34. *Ibid.*, (June 1830), 320–22.

35. Grigor'ev, "Pereezd cherez kavkazskiia gory," *Nevskii al'manakh na 1830 god* (St. Petersburg, 1829), 258–61; Baron F. Korf, "Proezd cherez zakavkazskii krai," *Biblioteka dlia chteniia* 29 (1838), ch.1, otd. 1, 19–20; and Prince N. B. Golitsyn, "Pereezd cherez Kavkazskiia Gory," *Biblioteka dlia chteniia* 23 (1837), ch. 7, 19–20.

36. Khersonets [*sic*], "Vzgliad na Gori," *Moskovskii telegraf* (August 1833), 495–96.

37. N. Sk. L. N., "1-e maia 1828 goda. Pereezd iz kreposti Tsalki v gorod Gori, cherez khrebet Erdzhava," *Syn otechestva* 8 (1839), 119–20.

38. [Bestuzhev-]Marlinskii, *Polnoe sobranie sochinenii*, vol. x, pp. 190–92.

39. S. Beliaev, "Dnevnik russkago soldata, byvshago desiat'mesiatsev v plenu u chechentsov," *Biblioteka dlia chteniia* (July 1848), ch. 1, otd. III, 21–48; and Lev Ekel'n, "Iz zapisok russkogo, byvshego v plenu u cherkessov," 19 *Otechestvennye zapiski* (1841), otd. VII, 91–94.

40. E. A. Verderevskii and N. Dunkel'-Velling, *Shamil' v Parizhe i Shamil'poblizhe* (Tiflis: Kantseliariia namestnika Kavkazskago, 1855); and E. Verderevskii , preface to *Plen u Shamilia* (St. Petersburg: Korolev, 1856), pp. 1–2.

41. E. A. Verderevskii, *Ot Zaural'ia do Zakavkaz'ia. Iumoristicheskie,*

sentimental'nye i prakticheskie pis'ma s dorogi (Moscow: V. Gautier, 1857), pp. 116, 122, 136, 191–97, 227–28.

42. *Ibid.*, pp. 116–17.
43. A. A. Bestuzhev-Marlinskii, *Sochineniia v dvukh tomakh* (Moscow: GIKhL, 1958), vol. I, p. 298.
44. Khersonets, "Vzgliad na Gori," 495; and M. Selezhev, *Rukovodstvo k poznaniiu Kavkaza* (St. Petersburg: Morskoi kadetskii korpus, 1847), pp. 16–19.
45. *Vospominaniia graf. A. A. Tolstoi i perepiska L. N. Tolstogo s graf. A. A. Tolstoi, 1857–1903* (St. Petersburg: Tolstovskii muzei, 1911), p. 4.
46. For attributions of oriental indolence to Georgians and Armenians, see Grigor'ev, "Pereezd cherez kavkazskiia gory," 261; and Korf, "Proezd cherez zakavkazskii krai," 45.

5 THE NATIONAL STAKE IN ASIA

Epigraph, Bestuzhev-Marlinskii, *Sochineniia*, vol. II, p. 599.

1. Vinogradov, "Nachalo kavkazskoi temy v russkoi literature," p. 23, n. 33. For analysis of ideological ramifications, see Mark Bassin, "Russia between Europe and Asia: The Ideological Construction of Geographical Space," *Slavic Review* 50 (Spring 1991), 5–13.
2. Reingardt, "Izvlechenie iz opisaniia puteshestviia," 335; and Freygang, *Lettres sur le Caucase*, p. 30.
3. Said, *Orientalism*, pp. 54–55.
4. See Mark Bassin, "Inventing Siberia: Visions of the Russian East in the Early Nineteenth Century," *The American Historical Review* 96 (June 1991), 763–84.
5. V. G. Kiernan, *The Lords of Human Kind. European Attitudes towards the Outside World in the Imperial Age* (1969; rpt. New York: Columbia University, 1986), p. 131; and Raymond Schwab, *La Renaissance orientale* (Paris: Payot, 1950), pp. 13–14, 30.
6. N. M. Lobikova, *Pushkin i Vostok* (Moscow: Nauka, 1974), p. 18.
7. G. S. "Tysiacha i odna noch'," *Aziatskii vestnik* (April 1827), 209.
8. V. Eberman, "Araby i persy v russkoi poezii," *Vostok* (1928), no. 3, 111.
9. Lobikova, *Pushkin i Vostok*, p. 14.
10. Nicholas Riasanovsky, "Asia through Russian Eyes" in *Russia and Asia. Essays on the Influence of Russia on the Asian Peoples*, ed.

Wayne S. Vucinich (Stanford: Hoover Institution of Stanford University, 1972), pp. 8–17; and Seymour Becker, "Russia between East and West: The Intelligentsia, Russian National Identity, and the Asian Borderlands," paper presented at the IV World Congress for Soviet and East European Studies, Harrogate, England, July 1990, pp. 15–24.

11. "O mogushchestve Anglii v vostochnoi Indii," *Vestnik Evropy* 97 (1818), no. 1, 120–23; "O vladychestve Anglii v velikikh Indiakh," *Severnyi arkhiv* (1822), no. 9, 187–98; and "Portial'skii almaznyi rudnik," *Aziatskii vestnik* (February 1826), 118–23.

12. See Svirin, "Russkaia kolonial'naia literatura," 55.

13. "Proekt uchrezhdeniia Rossiiskoi–Zakavkazskoi kompanii," appended in I. Enikolopov, *Griboedov v Gruzii* (Tbilisi: Zaria Vostoka, 1954), pp. 102–9. For official attitudes toward the project, consult S. V. Shastakovich, *Diplomaticheskaia deiatel'nost' A. S. Griboedova* (Moscow, 1960), pp. 193–97.

14. See quotation from the *Tiflis Gazette* in N. Ia. Eidel'man, *Byt' mozhet za khrebtom Kavkaza* (Moscow: Nauka, 1990), p. 150.

15. B. Nikitine, introduction in V. V. Barthold, *La Découverte de l'Asie*, trans. B. Nikitine (Paris: Payot, 1947), p. 12.

16. Compare Emerson, *Boris Godunov*, p. 245, n. 20: "Both culturally and politically Russia had genuine roots in (and boundaries with) Asia, which made the Orient both self and other." See also Charles J. Halperin, *Russia and the Golden Horde. The Mongol Impact on Medieval Russian History* (Bloomington, IN: Indiana University, 1985), pp. 1–20; and Serge Zenkovsky, *Pan-Turkism and Islam in Russia* (Cambridge, MA: Harvard University, 1960), pp. 13–14.

17. Said, *Orientalism*, pp. 113–15.

18. V. V. Bartol'd, "Vostok na russkoi nauke," *Sochineniia* (Moscow: Izdatel'stvo vostochnoi literatury and Nauka, 1963–77), vol. IX, pp. 536–38.

19. Bartol'd, "Istoriia izucheniia Vostoka v Evrope i Rossii," *Sochineniia*, vol. IX, p. 417. This essay points out that Kazan and Astrakhan had provided the tsarist state with Tatar-speaking interpreters for diplomatic missions to Persia since the seventeenth century: see pp. 372–74.

20. *Ibid.*, p. 418.

21. Bartol'd, "Obzor deiatel'nosti fakul'teta vostochnykh iazykov," *Sochineniia*, vol. IX, p. 52. For further details on oriental studies in Kazan, see pp. 43, 80–84.

22. A. Baziiants, N. Kuznetsova and L. Klulagina, *Aziatiskii muzei–*

Institut vostokovedeniia AN SSSR, 1818–1968 (Moscow: Nauka, 1969), pp. 16–20; and Bartol'd, "Obzor," pp. 54–57.

23. On the history, consult Schwab, *La Renaissance orientale*, pp. 16–18; and Said, *Orientalism*, pp. 75–77.

24. S. S. Uvarov, "Mysl' o zavedenii v Rossii Akademii Aziatskoi," *Vestnik Evropy* (1811), no. 1, ch. 55, 32–33.

25. Oriental literature and philology were regularly featured in Russian periodicals of general interest such as the *Herald of Europe*. During 1823–27 the *Herald of Asia* also published a wealth of relevant material, including travelogues.

26. Annual reports of the Société asiatique began appearing in the *Moscow Telegraph* in the 1820s. For examples and a survey of this practice, see "Uspekhi v izsledovanii vostochnoi literatury," *Moskovskii telegraf* 44 (1832), no. 6, 268–89 and no. 7, 419–41. See also *Aziatskii vestnik* 1825 (February), 149–50; (June), 427–28; (September), 205–10 and 377–84; (December), 406–7.

27. Osip Senkovskii, "Ob izuchenii arabskago iazyka," *Sobranie sochinenii* (St. Petersburg: Akademiia nauk, 1858), vol. VII, p. 150. For biographical information, see P. Savelev, "O zhizn' i trudakh Senkovskago" in this edition, vol. 1, pp. xix–xxx.

28. Said, *Orientalism*, pp. 42–43, 80–89; see also Leonid Grossman, "Lermontov i kultury vostoka," *Literaturnoe nasledstvo*, 43/44 (1), (1941), 674, 704–5.

29. A. Richter, "O sostoianii vostochnoi slovesnosti v Rossii," *Aziatskii vestnik* (1825), no. 8, 82–83.

30. On Khudobashev, see Bartol'd, "Obzor," p. 58.

31. "O trudakh Londonskoi kommissii dlia perevodov vostochnykh iazykakh," *Moskovskii telegraf* 48 (1832), no. 24, 510–11.

32. Bartol'd, "Obzor," p. 58.

33. Consult *Rude and Barbarous Kingdom: Russia in the Accounts of Sixteenth-Century English Voyagers*, ed. Lloyd Eason Berry and Robert O. Crummey, (Madison, WI and London: University of Wisconsin, 1968); and *Une infinie brutalité. L'Image de la Russie dans la France des XVI ͤ et XVII ͤ siècles*, ed. Michel Mervaud and Jean-Claude Robert (Paris: Institut d'études slaves, 1991).

34. Jacques-François Gamba, *Voyage dans la Russie méridionale, et particulièrement dans les provinces situés au-delà du Caucase, fait depuis 1820 jusqu'en 1824*, 2 vols. (Paris: C. J. Trouvé, 1826), vol. 1, pp. vii–ix.

35. Marquis de Custine, *La Russie en 1839*, ed. Pierre Nora (Paris: Gallimard, 1975), pp. 120, 176–79, 223. On the political context, see Michel Cadot, *La Russie dans la vie intellectuelle française (1839–1856)*, (Paris: Fayard, 1967).

36. "O literature Arabov," *Vestnik Evropy* (November 1818), ch. 102,

no. 21, 213–15; on oriental poetry, see 178–79, 197–98, 200–3.

37. Lauren Leighton, *Russian Romanticism: Two Essays* (The Hague: Mouton, 1975), p. 61. My subsequent discussion also draws on Leighton's treatment of Pushkin's and Bestuzhev-Marlinsky's responses to Sismondi, pp. 74, 88–94.

38. Leighton, *Russian Romanticism*, pp. 76–77.

39. Hans Rogger, *National Consciousness in Eighteenth-Century Russia* (Cambridge, MA: Harvard University, 1960), pp. 6–67; on Fonvizin, see also pp. 77–84.

40. Isaiah Berlin, *Russian Thinkers* (New York: Penguin, 1979), p. 181.

41. On the great importance of German idealism in Russia at this time, see Berlin, *ibid.*, pp. 136–49; and Neil Cornwell, *The Life, Times and Milieu of V. F. Odoyevsky, 1804–1869* (London: Athlone Press, 1986), pp. 77–80, 91–95.

42. Schwab, *La Renaissance orientale*, p. 198.

43. *Ibid.*, pp. 225–27, 292.

44. Lobikova, *Pushkin i Vostok*, pp. 9–10. Boldyrev was the censor fired for passing Pyotr Chaadaev's "Philosophical Letter."

45. "Moallaka Lebidova," trans. I. Batianov, *Aziatskii vestnik* (1827), no. 1, 32–33.

46. *Teleskop* (1833), ch. 18, no. 23, 395.

47. *Mosvitianin* (October 1855), kn. 1, 154, 162.

48. Orest Somov, *Selected Prose in Russian*, ed. John Mersereau, Jr. and George Harjan (Ann Arbor, MI: University of Michigan, 1974).

49. V. K. Kiukhel'beker, *Sochineniia* (Leningrad: Khudozhestvennaia literatura,1989), pp. 441–42.

50. Quoted in D. I. Belkin, "Pushkinskie stroki o Persii" in *Pushkin v stranakh zarubezhnogo Vostoka. Sbornik statei* (Moscow: Nauka, 1979), p. 177.

51. Bestuzhev-Marlinskii, *Sochineniia*, II, pp. 573–79, 583–97.

52. This paragraph closely follows Malcolm Hamrick Brown, "Native Song and National Consciousness in Nineteenth-Century Russian Music" in *Art and Culture in Nineteenth-Century Russia*, ed. Theofanis George Stavrou (Bloomington, IN: Indiana University, 1983), pp. 67–70. On the song for "Izmail-Bey," see *Lermontovskaia entsiklopediia*, ed. V. A. Manuilov (Moscow: Sovetskaia entsiklopediia, 1981), p. 189.

53. Pushkin, *Sobranie sochinenii*, vol. VI, pp. 264–65.

54. *Ibid.*, vol. IX, p. 148.

55. *Ibid.*, vol. IX, p. 95.

56. Abram Tertz (pseud. Andrei Siniavskii), *Progulki s Pushkinym* (London: Collins and Overseas Publications Interchange, 1975), pp. 130–32.

57. Marina Tsvetaeva, "Pushkin and Pugachev," *A Captive Spirit: Selected Prose*, ed. and trans. J. Marin King (London: Virago, 1983), p. 386.
58. For a similar conclusion about "The Fountain of Bakhchisarai" (but adamantly *not* "The Prisoner of the Caucasus"), see Stephanie Sandler, *Distant Pleasures. Alexander Pushkin and the Writing of Exile* (Stanford: Stanford University, 1989), pp. 179–80.

6 THE PUSHKINIAN MOUNTAINEER

Epigraph, Pushkin, "Kavkazskii plennik," *Sobranie sochinenii*, vol. III, p. 99.

1. Marc Raeff, *Comprendre l'ancien régime russe: Etat et société en Russie impériale* (Paris: Seuil, 1982), pp. 143–46.
2. A. S. Griboedov, "Zagorodnaia poezdka. (Otryvok pis'ma iuzhnogo zhitelia)," *Sochineniia* (Moscow: GIKhL, 1956), p. 413. On the élite's peculiar cultural predicament, see Iu. M. Lotman, "The Poetics of Everyday Behavior in Eighteenth-Century Russian Culture," trans. Andrea Beesing, in *The Semiotics of Russian Culture*, ed. Alexander D. Nakhimovsky and Alice Stone Nakhimovsky (Ithaca, NY and London: Cornell University, 1985), pp. 69–72.
3. Sidney Monas, " 'Self' and 'Other' in Russian Literature," in *The Search for Self-Definition in Russian Literature*, ed. Ewa M. Thompson (Amsterdam: John Benjamins, 1991), pp. 80–83, 91.
4. On Rousseau's reception in Russia with special attention to Pushkin, consult Iu. M. Lotman, "Russo i russkaia kul'tura XVIII–nachala XIX veka" in Rousseau's *Traktaty*, ed. V. S. Alekseev-Popov *et al.* (Moscow: Nauka, 1969), pp. 593–99; and Iu. Lotman and Z. Mints, " 'Chelovek prirody' v russkoi literature XIX veka i 'tsyganskaia tema' u Bloka," *Blokovskii sbornik*, ed. Lotman (Tartu: Tartu University, 1964), 101–7.
5. The passage was designated an "ethnographic essay in verse" in Bazanov, *Ocherki dekabristskoi literatury*, p. 454. See similar arguments in Gadzhiev, *Kavkaz v russkoi literature*, pp. 15–19; and Iusufov, *Dagestan i russkaia literatura*, pp. 72–75, 144–45.
6. Sandler, *Distant Pleasures*, pp. 146–56.
7. Zhirmunskii, *Bairon i Pushkin*, p. 87.
8. Iu. V. Mann, *Poetika russkogo romantizma* (Moscow: Nauka, 1976), p. 53.
9. The song's inauthenticity is underlined in G. A. Gukovskii, *Pushkin i russkie romantiki* (Moscow: Khudozhestvennaia litera-

tura, 1965), p. 286; and S. D. Selivanova, *Nad pushkinskimi rukopisiami* (Moscow: Nauka, 1980), p. 92.

10. On reception of *la théorie des climats* in Russia, see Iusufov, *Dagestan i russkaia literatura*, pp. 47–54.

11. Bronevskii, *Noveishie izvestiia o Kavkaze*, vol. I, pp. 36–37.

12. Zhukovsky's errors were first noted by E. G. Veidenbaum, *Kavkazskie etiudy* in *Kavkazovedenie* (Tiflis: Tsentral'naia knizhnaia torgovlia, 1901), p. 279. One of Zhukovsky's imaginary tribes (the "Bakh") prolonged its textual life in Ryleev, "Pustyn'," *Polnoe sobranie sochinenii*, p. 77.

13. S. G. Bocharov, "'Svoboda' i 'schast'ia' v poezii Pushkina," *Poetika Pushkina. Ocherki* (Moscow: Nauka, 1974), pp. 3–5; and Mann, *Poetika russkogo romantizma*, pp. 46–50.

14. N. V. Gogol', "Neskol'ko slov o Pushkine," *Sobranie sochinenii v semi tomakh* (Moscow: Khudozhestvennaia literatura, 1986), vol. VI, p. 59.

15. On dueling as "a way of winning public esteem" and the possibility that Pushkin had already dueled, see Mirsky, *Pushkin*, p. 29.

16. Tomashevskii, *Pushkin*, vol. I, pp. 408–10; and Gukovskii, *Pushkin i russkie romantiki*, pp. 207–20.

17. Pushkin, *Sobranie sochinenii*, vol. IX, p. 50. In commenting on changes the censor did make, Pushkin wrote that "they served my purpose."

18. Less frequently, women too could identify with the heroic ideal. The celebrated Nadezhda Durova even participated in the Napoleonic wars disguised as a man: consult her book *The Cavalry Maid: Journals of a Russian Officer in the Napoleonic Wars.*, trans. and annotated by Mary F. Zirin (Bloomington, IN: Indiana University, 1989).

19. Lauren G. Leighton, *Alexander Bestuzhev-Marlinsky* (Boston, MA: Twayne, 1975), pp. 19–28. On the Decembrists' prevailing assumption that they would have to resort to violence, see N. A. Guliaev, "O prirode Dekabristskogo romantizma," *Russkii romantizm* (Leningrad: Nauka, 1978), pp. 49–51.

20. Bronevskii, *Noveisheie izvestiia o Kavkaze*, vol. II, p. 130.

21. For the argument that Pushkin produced a subjugated heroine as a "gift" to Raevsky, see Sandler, *Distant Pleasures*, pp. 156–58.

22. Hulme, *Colonial Encounters*, pp. 249–50; and Pratt, *Imperial Eyes*, pp. 96–97.

23. Zelinskii, *Russkaia kriticheskaia literatura o Pushkine*, p. 111.

24. In mystifying the heroine, Viazemsky wrote: "All we know

about her is that she loved, and that is enough for us:" see *ibid.*, p. 104.

25. Compare M. Kagan, "O pushkinskikh poemakh," *V mire Pushkina. Sbornik statei*, ed. S. Mashinskii (Moscow: Sovetskii pisatel', 1974), pp. 102–3; and V. V. Sipovskii, *Pushkin. Zhizn' i tvorchestvo* (St. Petersburg: Trud, 1907), pp. 477–518.

26. Pushkin rehashed the matter in a letter, *Sobranie sochinenii*, vol. IX, pp. 61–62.

27. See Byron quoted in Kiernan, *The Lords of Human Kind*, pp. 137–38; and Ochkin [*sic*], "Plavanie na korable s Lordom Baironom," *Biblioteka dlia chteniia* 3 (1834), kn. 1, otd. II, 19.

28. On the "triumvirate" of "poetry, love and freedom" in young Pushkin's imagination, see Tertz, *Progulki s Pushkinym*, p. 27.

29. A Russified Georgian, Pavel Tsitsianov was Chief Administrator of the Caucasus during 1803–11. General Pyotr Kotliarevsky participated in war against Persia in 1804–13, after which severe wounds forced him to retire. Ermolov was Proconsul of the Caucasus from 1816 to 1827, when Nicholas I recalled him under suspicion of collusion with the Decembrists: see Michael Whittock, "Ermolov, Proconsul of the Caucasus," *Russian Review* 18 (January 1959), 53–60.

30. Tomashevskii, *Pushkin*, vol. I, pp. 406–8. Tomashevsky includes an excerpt from Pestel's *Russkaia pravda* and outlines his dualistic view of Russia.

31. For a relevant discussion of Tocqueville, see Tzvetan Todorov, *Nous et les autres* (Paris: Seuil, 1989), pp. 222–34.

32. A review in *Son of the Fatherland* reprinted all of the epilogue: see Zelinskii, *Russkaia kriticheskaia literatura o Pushkine*, pp. 87–88.

33. Tomashevskii, *Pushkin*, vol. I, p. 425.

34. *Ibid.*, p. 425; and *Le Petit Robert. Dictionnaire universel des noms propres*, ed. Paul Robert (Paris: 1987), p. 523.

35. On the "anthropological tendency" of "The Gypsies," see Iu. Lotman, "Istoki 'Tolstovskogo napravleniia' v russkoi literature 1830-kh godov," *Trudy po russkoi i slavianskoi filologii* 5 (1962), vyp. 119, 15–18.

36. Shishkov, *Opyty*, pp. 4–5.

37. See analysis of this type of discourse in White, "Forms of Wildness," *Tropics of Discourse*, p. 154.

38. "Pis'ma Kh. Sh. k F. Bulgarinu, ili poezdka na Kavkaz," *Severnyi arkhiv* (July 1828), 44–49, 70–74.

39. On Ossian and Homer, see Gukovskii, *Pushkin i russkie romantiki*, pp. 236–41.

40. Bestuzhev-Marlinskii, *Sochineniia*, vol. I, p. 300.
41. Baron Stal′, "Etnograficheskii ocherk cherkesskago naroda," *Kavkazskii sbornik* 21 (1900), otd. II, 100–1.
42. See "Otryvki o Kavkaze" excerpted in "O literaturnoi deiatel′-nosti A. Ia. Iukubovicha," ed. M. K. Azadovskii, *Literaturnoe nasledstvo* 60 (kn. 1), (1956), 272–74.
43. "Cherkes. (Razskaz)," *Nevskii al′manakh na 1829 god*, 260–77.
44. P. A. Viazemskii, *Sochineniia v dvukh tomakh* (Moscow: Khudozhestvennaia literatura, 1982), p. 313.
45. Quoted in M. O. Gershenzon, *Istoriia molodoi Rossii* (Moscow-Petrograd: Gosudarstvennoe izdatel′stvo, 1923), p. 28.
46. N. I. Lorer, *Zapiski dekabrista* (Moscow: Gosudarstvennoe ekonomicheskoe izdatel′stvo, 1931), p. 214.
47. *Ibid.*, pp. 248–49.

7 BESTUZHEV-MARLINSKY'S INTERCHANGE WITH THE
TRIBESMAN

Epigraph, Bestuzhev-Marlinskii, "Ammalat-Bek" in *Povesti i rasskazy*, p. 195. (Subsequent citations appear parenthetically in the text.)

1. Belinskii, *Polnoe sobranie sochinenii*, vol. I, p. 83. For all Belinsky's commentaries, see annotated bibliography in Leighton, *Alexander Bestuzhev-Marlinsky*, p. 151
2. Leighton, *Alexander Bestuzhev-Marlinsky*, p. 106.
3. Mikhail Semevskii, "Aleksandr Aleksandrovich Bestuzhev (Marlinskii), 1798–1837," *Otechestvennye zapiski*, 130 (May 1860), 122 (ellipsis mine).
4. Bestuzhev-Marlinskii, *Sochineniia*, vol. II, pp. 8–59.
5. *Ibid.*, p. 6.
6. While usually remarked by commentators, the writer's ethnographic expertise is treated most extensively in V. Vasil′ev, *Bestuzhev-Marlinskii na Kavkaze* (Krasnodar, 1939), pp. 64–87; Shaduri, *Dekabristskaia literatura*, pp. 315–26; and M. O. Kosven, *Etnografiia i istoriia Kavkaza. Issledovaniia i materialy* (Moscow: Akademiia nauk, 1961), pp. 158–68.
7. [Bestuzhev-]Marlinskii, *Polnoe sobranie sochinenii*, vol. X, p. 20. A subsequent reference appears parenthetically in the text.
8. Leighton, *Alexander Bestuzhev-Marlinsky*, p. 17.
9. The metaphor had appeared in a Crimean poem by Zaitsevsky: see *Poety*, vol. I, pp. 519–21.

10. On distinctions between characters on both the Russian and Dagestani sides, see William Edward Brown, *A History of Russian Literature of the Romantic Period*, 4 vols. (Ann Arbor, MI: Ardis, 1986), vol. II, p. 215.

11. F. V. Bulgarin, "Kartina Turetskoi voiny 1828 godu. (Pis'mo k drugu za granitsu)," *Nevskii al'manakh na 1829 god* (St. Petersburg, 1828), 386–87.

12. [Bestuzhev-]Marlinskii, *Polnoe sobranie sochinenii*, vol. VIII, pp. 231–32.

13. Mann, *Poetika russkogo romantizma*, p. 322.

14. On the type of plot, see Abdul R. JanMohamed, "The Economy of Manichean Allegory: The Function of Racial Difference in Colonialist Literature," *Critical Inquiry* 12 (Autumn 1985), 67; and Brantlinger, *Rule of Darkness*, p. 192.

15. Quoted by Shaduri, *Dekabristskaia literatura*, p. 328.

16. See Steven Marcus, *The Other Victorians* (New York: Basic Books, 1974), pp. 205–6.

17. Such a clash between Christianity and Islam is taken as the tale's basic didactic principle in Mersereau, *Russian Romantic Fiction*, p. 124.

18. See Ermolov's denial of the episode in N. Berg, "Vstrecha moia s A. P. Ermolovym," *Russkii arkhiv* (1872), 1, columns 989–99. Ermolov nevertheless helped circulate "Ammalat-Bek" by anonymously translating it into French in 1835: see the ascription in Antoine-Alexandre Barbier, *Dictionnaire des ouvrages anonymes*, 3rd edn., rev. and aug. by Olivier Barbier, René and Paul Billard (Hildesheim: Georg Olms, 1963), column 138.

19. "Pis'ma Aleksandra Aleksandrovicha Bestuzheva k N. A. i K. A. Polevym, pisannyia v 1831–1837 godakh, s predisloviem," *Russkii vestnik* 32 (1861), no. 3, 307.

20. Dominique O. Mannoni, *Prospero and Caliban: The Psychology of Colonization*, trans. Pamela Powesland (London: Methuen, 1956), p. 21.

21. Lewis Bagby, "Aleksandr Bestužev-Marlinskij's 'Roman i Ol'ga': Generation and Degeneration," *Slavic and East European Journal* 25 (Winter 1981), 9–12.

22. Lauren Leighton, "Bestuzhev-Marlinskii's 'The Frigate *Hope*': A Decembrist Puzzle," *Canadian Slavonic Papers* 22 (June 1980), 174–76, 186.

23. E. P. Rostopchina, "K Serezhe," *Sochineniia*, 2 vols. (St. Petersburg: I. N. Skorokhodov, 1890), vol. I, pp. 1–2. For biographical information, see the introduction by Sergei Suchkov, pp. iii–xiv.

24. V. P. Zhelikhova, *Kavkazskie razskazy* (St. Petersburg: A. F. Devrien, 1895), pp. 28, 58–60, 81.
25. Veidenbaum, *Kavkazskie etiudy*, p. 311.
26. *Ibid.*; and Zhelikhova, *Kavkazskie razskazy*, p. 22.
27. Elizaveta Gan, "Vospominanie o Zheleznovodske," *Polnoe sobranie sochinenii* (St. Petersburg: N. F. Merts, 1905). On the writer's life, see E. S. Nekrasova (comp.), "Elena Andreevna Gan (Zeneida R–va), 1814–1842. Biograficheskii ocherk," *Russkaia starina* 51 (August 1886), 335–56 and (September 1886), 553–76.
28. A. L. Zisserman, *Dvadtsat' piat' let na Kavkaze (1842–1867)*, 2 vols. (St. Petersburg: A. S. Suvorin, 1879), vol. II, p. 3; and vol. I, pp. 1–5, 204–5.
29. I. von der Hoven, "Moe znakomstvo s dekabristami," *Drevnaia i novaia Rossiia* (1877), no. 2, 221.
30. K. P. Belevich, *Stikhi i razskazy* (St. Petersburg: Glazunov, 1895), p. 171; and V. L. Markov, "Vospominaniia ulanskogo korneta," *Nabliudatel'* (1895), no.10, 165–66 and 229. For the same "heroic" expectations without literary allusions, see N. E. Smirnov, *Sovremennye tipy* (St. Petersburg: A. Kaspari, 1870), p. 63.
31. See Bruno Bettelheim on the Nazi Freikorps in the book review "Death Producers," *Times Literary Supplement*, 14–20 April, 1989, 392.
32. Quoted in Alekseev, *Etiudy o Marlinskom*, p. 130, n. 2.
33. *Ibid.*, pp. 132–33, 140.
34. Zisserman, *Dvadtsat' piat' let na Kavkaze*, vol. I, p. 329.
35. For unsupported contentions to this effect, see Iusufov, *Dagestan i russkaia literatura*, pp. 188–89, 222–23.
36. Russian ethnographers of the era considered the Caucasus the cradle of the "white, Caucasian" race: see M. Maksimovich, "O cheloveke," *Teleskop* (September 1831), ch. 5, 8–9.
37. Zisserman, *Dvadtsat' piat' let na Kavkaze*, vol. I, p. 58.
38. A typical nineteenth-century verdict of suicide appears in A. P. Berzhe, "Aleksandr Aleksandrovich Bestuzhev v Piatigorske v 1835 g.," *Russkaia starina* 28 (October 1880), 422. It is possible, however, that the writer was ordered into battle by a general who then promoted a legend of his suicide: see Iu. Levin, "Ob obstoiatel'stvakh smerti A. A. Bestuzheva-Marlinskogo," *Russkaia literatura* (1962), no. 2, 219–22. A scandalous event near the end of Bestuzhev-Marlinsky's life intensified his undeniable despair in exile: after his landlady's daughter was accidentally killed by a pistol kept under his

pillow, the writer was subjected to an official inquiry but absolved of criminal responsibility.

8 EARLY LERMONTOV AND ORIENTAL MACHISMO

Epigraph, Lermontov, "Izmail-Bey," *Sobranie sochinenii*, vol. II, p. 247.

1. Grossman, "Lermontov i kultury vostoka," 681–82.
2. Quoted by Grossman, *ibid.*, 736.
3. Iu. M. Lotman, "Problema Vostoka i Zapada v tvorchestve pozdnego Lermontova" in *Lermontovskii sbornik*, ed. I. S. Chistova *et al.* (Leningrad: Nauka, 1985), pp. 5–11, 22.
4. The censored text appeared in *Otechestvennye zapiski* 27 (1843), otd. I, 1–25. With two small oversights, the deletions are listed in B. V. Tomashevskii's commentary in Lermontov, *Sochineniia v shesti tomakh* (Moscow-Leningrad: Akademiia nauk, 1954–57), vol. III, p. 323.
5. The critic enigmatically counted "Izmail-Bey" among the aesthetically remarkable "facts of the poet's psychic life" (*fakty dukhovnoi lichnosti poeta*): see Belinskii, *Polnoe sobranie sochinenii*, vol. VIII, p. 94.
6. B. M. Eikhenbaum, *Stat'i o Lermontove* (Moscow-Leningrad: Akademiia nauk, 1961), pp. 9–12; and B. T. Udodov, *M. Iu. Lermontov. Khudozhestvennaia individual'nost' i tvorcheskie protsessy* (Voronezh: Voronezh University, 1973), pp. 53–59, 102–5.
7. A. N. Sokolov, *Ocherki po istorii russkoi poemy XVIII i pervoi poloviny XIX veka* (Moscow: MGU, 1955), pp. 593–94. For analysis of Hugo's impact on Lermontov, see E. Duchesne, *Michel Iouriévitch Lermontov. Sa vie et ses œuvres* (Paris: Librairie Plon, 1910), pp. 302–11.
8. S. A. Andreev-Krivich, *Lermontov. Voprosy tvorchestva i biografii* (Moscow: Akademiia nauk, 1954), pp. 73–76, 87–89; and A. P. Semenov, *Lermontov i fol'klor Kavkaza* (Piatigorsk: Ordzhonikidzevskoe kraevedcheskoe izdatel'stvo, 1941); and A. P. Semenov, "Motivy gorskogo fol'klora i byta v poeme Lermontova 'Khadzhi-Abrek'" in *Mikhail Iurievich Lermontov. Sbornik statei i materialov*, ed. A. M. Dokusov *et al.* (Stavropol': Stavropol'skoe khizhnoe izdatel'stvo, 1960), pp. 14–25.
9. U. R. Fokht, *Lermontov. Logika tvorchestva* (Moscow: Nauka, 1975), p. 78.
10. Andreev-Krivich, *Lermontov*, pp. 12–33; A. V. Popov, *Lermontov*

na Kavkaze (Stavropol': Stavropol'skoe knizhnoe izdatel'stvo, 1954), pp. 16–18; and I. L. Andronikov, "Kommentarii" in Lermontov, *Sobranie sochinenii*, vol. II, p. 522.

11. Tomashevskii, commentary in Lermontov, *Sochineniia v shesti tomakh*, vol. III, p. 324. Earlier efforts to relate the song to Caucasian tribal folklore are summarized in V. A. Manuilov, *Roman M. Iu. Lermontova Geroi nashego vremeni. Kommentarii* (Moscow-Leningrad: Prosveshchenie, 1966), pp. 102–3.

12. The parenthetical numerals refer to the part and stanza of "Izmail-Bey."

13. The censor's deletion of the curl in 1843 gave Izmail-Bey a more ruthless air as the seducer of Russian women.

14. On Lermontov and Rousseau, see M. Rozanov, "Baironicheskie motivy v tvorchestve Lermontova" in *Venok Mikhailu Iurievichu Lermontovu. Iubileinyi sbornik* (Moscow-Petrograd: V. V. Dumnov, 1914), pp. 355–75; and Lotman, "Istoki 'Tolstovskogonapravleniia' v russkoi literature 1830-kh godov," pp. 40–45.

15. I. Radozhitskii, "Kyz-Brun. Cherkesskaia povest'," *Otechestvennye zapiski* 32 (1827), 288.

16. The passage's reductive character is noted in Robert Reid, "Ethnotope in Lermontov's Caucasian Poèmy," *Russian Literature* 31 (May 1992), 566.

17. M. Liventsov, "Zapiski damy, byvshei v plenu u gortsev," *Biblioteka dlia chteniia* 149 (May 1858), ch. 1, otd. 1, 38–39.

18. See my chapter 11, p. 202.

19. *Lermontov v vospominaniakh sovremennikov*, ed. V. E. Vatsuro *et al.* (Moscow: Khudozhestvennaia literatura, 1989), pp. 54, 291–92, 364, 400, 416, 432, 442, 444, 446–47, 455, 479.

20. *Akty sobrannye kavkazskoiu arkheograficheskoiu kommissieiu*, ed. A. P. Berzhe *et al.*, 12 vols. (Tiflis: Tipografiia glavnago upravleniia namestnika Kavkaza, 1866–96), vol. IX, p. 346. (Hereafter cited as *Akty KAK*).

21. *Dvizhenie gortsev*, p. 393–94.

22. Zisserman, *Dvadtsat' piat' let na Kavkaze*, vol. I, pp. 48–49.

23. N. A. Dobroliubov, "O znachenii nashikh poslednikh podvigov na Kavkaze," *Sobranie sochinenii v deviati tomakh* (Moscow-Leningrad: GIKhL, 1962–64), vol. V, p. 441.

24. The abduction is dated 1842 in M. Ia. Ol'shevskii, "Kavkaz s 1841 po 1866," *Russkaia starina* 79 (July 1893), 91–92. A later memoir dated the event 1840: see M. N. Chichagova, *Shamil' na Kavkaze i v Rossii. Biograficheskii ocherk* (St. Petersburg: S. Muller and I. Bogel'man, 1889), p. 147.

25. *Dvizhenie gortsev*, pp. 420–21.

26. Lermontov, Letter to A. A. Lopukhin, June 1840, *Sobranie sochinenii*, vol. IV, p. 448.
27. On the distinction between "ideal" and historical readerships, see Peter J. Rabinowitz, "Truth in Fiction: A Reexamination of Audiences," *Critical Inquiry* 4 (Autumn 1977), 134–35. See also Iu. Lotman, "The Text and the Structure of Its Audience," trans. Ann Shukman, *New Literary History* 14 (Autumn 1982), 85.
28. Gan, *Polnoe sobranie sochinenii*, p. 52.
29. Belinskii, *Polnoe sobranie sochinenii*, vol. VII, pp. 648–57, 673.
30. *Ibid.*, pp. 660–61.
31. Berlin, *Russian Thinkers*, pp. 164–81.
32. Belinskii, *Polnoe sobranie sochinenii*, vol. IV, pp. 204, 214–16.
33. See V. Murav'ev's commentary on Belinsky's essay in Polezhaev, *Stikhotvoreniia*, p. 279, n. 8.
34. Belinskii, *Polnoe sobranie sochinenii*, vol. VI, 133–38.
35. In Isaiah Berlin's words, Belinsky "married unsuitably, from sheer misery and loneliness:" see *Russian Thinkers*, p. 155. Belinsky referred to his deprived love life in correspondence: see his *Polnoe sobranie sochinenii*, vol. XI, p. 559; and vol. XII, p. 67.
36. Friedrich Bodenstedt, *Die Völker des Kaukasus und ihre Freiheitskämpfe gegen die Russen* (Frankfurt am Main: Hermann Johann Kessler, 1848), pp. 207–10, 411–35.
37. Friedrich Bodenstedt, *Les Peuples du Caucase et leur guerre d'indépendance contre la Russie*, trans. Prince E. de Salm-Kyrburg, 2nd edn. (Paris: E. Dentu, 1859), p. 78. This edition was not available to me in German.
38. P. A. Efremov, "Biograficheskii ocherk" in Lermontov, *Sochineniia*, 6th edn., 2 vols. (St. Petersburg: Glazunov, 1887), vol. I, pp. xxxiii–xxxiv.
39. Verderevskii, *Plen u Shamilia*, ch. I, p. 1.
40. Chichagova, *Shamil' na Kavkaze i v Rossii*, pp. 127, 146, 157–59.
41. N. A. Volkonskii, "Okonchatel'noe pokorenie vostochnago Kavkaza (1859-i god)," *Kavkazskii sbornik* 4 (1879), 175–76.
42. I. P., "Iz boevykh vospominanii. Raskaz Kurintsa," *Kavkazskii sbornik* 4 (1879), 51–52.

9 LITTLE ORIENTALIZERS

Epigraph, D. Minaev, "Uprek Kavkazy," *Biblioteka dlia chteniia* 42 (1840), ch. I, 72–74.

1. I borrow the French term from Schwab, *La Renaissance orientale*, p. 429.
2. See the quoted phrase in anon., "Tri mesiatsa v plenu u gortsev," *Sovremennik* 10 (July 1848), otd. IV, 5.
3. Belinskii, *Polnoe sobranie sochinenii*, vol. III, p. 357 and editorial commentary, p. 639.
4. Petr Kamenskii, *Povesti i razskazy* (St. Petersburg: III Otdelenie, 1838), ch. pervaia, pp. 1–73.
5. *Dvizhenie gortsev*, p. 396
6. See review of M. Bogdanovich's *Algeriia v noveishee vremia* in *Moskvitianin* (March 1850), no. 7, kn. 1, otd. IV, 103–5; and Cadot, *La Russie dans la vie intellectuelle française*, pp. 12, 345–46.
7. *Dvizhenie gortsev*, p. 58.
8. "Poezdka v Gruziiu," 336–38.
9. Shaduri, *Dekabristskaia literatura*, pp. 328–33.
10. M. Vedeniktov, "Vzgliad na kavkazskikh gortsev," *Syn otechestva* (1837), ch. 188, 57–59.
11. Ia. Saburov, "Kavkaz," *Moskovskii nabliudatel'* (September 1835), kn. 1, ch. IV, 42.
12. George Leighton Ditson, *Circassia, or a Tour to the Caucasus*, rev. edn. (New York: Stringer and Townsend, 1850), p. 275.
13. Iusufov, *Dagestan i russkaia literatura*, pp. 147–53.
14. Vedeniktov, "Vzgliad na kavkazskikh gortsev," 59; Ilia Radozhitskii, "Progulka k kavkazskim mineral'nym vodam," *Otechestvennye zapiski* (February 1824), ch. 17, kn. 46, 209; anon., "Vospominaniia o Kavkaze 1837 goda," *Biblioteka dlia chteniia* 80 (1847), ch.2, otd. III, 61; and Berezin, *Puteshestvie po Dagestanu*, vol. II, p. 97.
15. Lomonosov's Russian "light of Goodness and Beneficence" encompasses symbolic sunshine, stars and fire, while the Turks belong to the "gloom of night," thick smoke, dust and shadow.
16. Polezhaev, *Stikhotvoreniia*, pp. 133–65.
17. A. S. Griboedov, *Sochineniia v stikhakh*, 2nd edn. (Leningrad: Sovetskii pisatel', 1967), pp. 349–52 and commentary, pp. 508–9. The Chegem is a small tributary of the Malka river, slightly south of Piatigorsk.
18. L. Iakubovich, "Cherkes," *Sovremennik*, 9 (1838), otd. VII, 155–56.
19. Prince D. Kropotkin, "Lezginskaia pesnia," *Biblioteka dlia chteniia* 21 (1837), kn. 1, otd. I, 33–34.
20. M. Venediktov [*sic*], "Pesnia zakubanskikh gortsev," *Biblioteka dlia chteniia* 9 (1835), otd. I, 122–23.
21. For Lermontov's translation of Mickiewicz's poem, see Lermon-

tov, *Sobranie sochinenii*, vol. I, pp. 33–34.

22. D. Oznobishin, "Kavkazskoe utro," *Otechestvennye zapiski* 9 (1840), no. 6, otd. III, 151–52.

23. From Sanskrit *dev*, the Persian *div* overlaps with the name for supernatural birds of pagan Slavic mythology which augur ill for the Russians' battle against the Polovtsians in *The Lay of Igor's Campaign*.

24. See a commemorative verse of 1839 in Alekseev, *Etiudy o Marlinskom*, p. 137.

25. Bestuzhev-Marlinskii, *Sochinenii*, vol. II, p. 566.

26. Baron Ekshtein, "O drevnei poezii arabov, do Mugammeda," *Moskovskii telegraf* 41 (1831), no. 19, 352–54.

27. Senkovskii, *Sobranie sochinenii*, vol. VII, pp. 167–70, 194–96.

28. Mentsov [*sic*], "Molodaia aravitianka," *Syn otechestva* 52 (1835), ch. 173, no. 39, 169–70; V. Zubov, "Devy Vostoka," *Moskovskii nabliudatel'* (August 1836), ch. 8, kn. 1, 446–50; M. Vedeniktov, "Vostochnaia krasavitsa," *Syn otechestva* 187 (1837), otd. 1, 368–69; K. Aivulat, "Odaliska," *Otechestvennye zapiski* 61 (May 1841), otd. III, 92; and Bestuzhev-Marlinskii, *Povesti i rasskazy*, pp. 268–76.

29. Aleksandr Shidlovskii, *Grebenskii kazak. Povest'* (St. Petersburg: A. Smirdin, 1831).

30. N. I. Gnedich, *Stikhotvoreniia*, 2nd edn. (Leningrad: Sovetskii pisatel', 1956), pp. 152–53.

31. P. Markov, *Zlomilla i Dobronrava – devy gor, ili vstrecha s kazakom: Kavkazskaia povest' v dvukh chastiakh* (Moscow: Tipografiia Lazarevykh Instituta Vostochnykh Iazykov, 1834).

32. Zriakhov was brought to my attention by Brooks, *When Russia Learned to Read*, p. 222. See my bibliography for editions of the tale I consulted.

33. *Ibid.*, p. 222; and Hulme, *Colonial Encounters*, pp. 257–58.

34. *Moskvitianin*, (July 1850), ch. 4, no. 13, kn. 1, otd. IV, 28–29.

35. See I. Debu, "O nachal'nom ustanovlenii i rasprostranenii kavkazskoi linii," *Otechestvennye zapiski* 49 (May 1824), 281–89. For a study of all Cossackdom's mythic stature, consult Judith Deutsch Kornblatt, *The Cossack Hero in Russian Literature. A Study in Cultural Mythology* (Madison, WI: University of Wisconsin, 1992).

36. V. Zotov, *Poslednii Kheak. Poema* (St. Petersburg: Akademii nauk, 1842).

37. Anon., "Gosudar' Nikolai Pavlovich v avtobiograficheskikh rasskazov byvshego kavkazskogo ofitsera," *Russkii arkhiv* 19 (1881), kn. 2, 235.

38. Ivan Golovin, *The Caucasus* (London: Trübner and Co., 1854), p. 22.
39. Saburov, "Kavkaz," 212–13, 219.
40. For a brief diatribe against Zotov, see Belinskii, *Polnoe sobranie sochinenii*, vol. VI, pp. 394–95.
41. Kamenskii, *Povesti i razskazy*, p. 37. See also Zriakhov's prefatory verse to the "beautiful Mohammedan" tale, *Mosvitianin*, (July 1850), ch. 4, no. 13, kn. 1, otd. IV, 31.
42. Gadzhiev, *Kavkaz v russkoi literature*, p. 30.

10 FEMINIZING THE CAUCASUS

Epigraph, [Bestuzhev-]Marlinskii, *Polnoe sobranie sochinenii*, vol. X, p. 187. (Subsequent citations appear parenthetically in the text.)

1. Hulme, *Colonial Encounters*, pp. xii, 1; Lisa Lowe, "The Orient as a Woman in Flaubert's *Salammbô* and *Voyage en Orient*," *Comparative Literature Studies* 23 (Spring 1986), 44–45; Todorov, *Nous et les autres*, pp. 41–55; and Daphne B. Watson, "The Cross of St George: The Burden of Contemporary Irish Literature" in *Literature and Imperialism*, ed. Robert Giddins (London: Macmillan, 1991), pp. 25–43.
2. For an English translation with analysis, see Louis Pedrotti, "The Scandal of Countess Rostopčina's Polish–Russian Allegory," *Slavic and East European Journal* 30 (Summer 1986), 196–214.
3. George G. Grabowicz, *The Poet as Mythmaker: A Study of Symbolic Meaning in Taras Ševčenko* (Cambridge, MA: Harvard University, 1982), pp. 37–38, 45, 58–59, 64–68.
4. A. Odoevskii, "Brak Gruzii s russkim tsartsvom," *Polnoe sobranie sochinenii* (Leningrad: Sovetskii pisatel', 1958), pp. 178–80.
5. Platon P. Zubov, *Kartina kavkazskago kraia, prinadlezhashchago Rossii, i sopredel'nykh onomu zemel' v istoricheskom, statisticheskom, etnograficheskom, finansovom i torgovom otnosheniiakh*, 2 vols. (St. Petersburg: Konrad Vingeber, 1834), pp. 11–25, 41–47, 54–55, 64–71, 85–86.
6. *Biblioteka dlia chteniia* 26 (1837), ch. 1, otd. V, 2–6.
7. See voluminous annotated bibliographies in N. F. Dubrovin, *Istoriia voiny i vladychestva russkikh na Kavkaze*, 6 vols. (St. Petersburg: Departament udelov, 1871–86), vol. I, kn. 3; and Miansarov, *Bibliographia Caucasica*, otd. 2.
8. "Poezdka v Gruziiu," 353–55; and Prince N. B. Golitsyn,

"Pereezd cherez Kavkazskiia Gory," *Biblioteka dlia chteniia* 23 (1837), ch. 7, 25.

9. N. M., "Vospominaniia o Kavkaze 1837 goda," *Biblioteka dlia chteniia* 81 (March 1847), ch. 3, otd. III, 21–22.

10. Quoted in Enikolopov, *Griboedov v Gruzii*, p. 102.

11. "Poezdka v Gruziiu," 366.

12. "Vospominaniia o Kavkaze (Otryvok iz zapisok odnogo puteshestvennika)," *Aziatskii vestnik* (April 1826), 258.

13. See Bestuzhev-Marlinsky's related discussions of the Caucasus as "terrestrial paradise" (204), a land of "Biblical simplicity" (169) and the "cradle of mankind" (vol. VIII, 245–46).

14. Annette Kolodny, *The Lay of the Land. Metaphor as Experience and History in American Life and Letters* (Chapel Hill, NC: University of North Carolina, 1975), pp. 4–7, 10–70.

15. This argument is pursued in my next chapter as well. For a particularly sly perception of "virgin" nature in Pushkin's "The Prisoner of the Caucasus," see Berezin, *Puteshestvie po Dagestanu*, vol. II, pp. 51–52. Less symbolically loaded references to a virgin Caucasus occur in Saburov, "Kavkaz," 197–98; G. Dzhegitov, "Pir na Kavkaze," *Biblioteka dlia chteniia* 22 (1837), otd. I, 124; Khersonets, "Vzgliad na Gori," 495; Belinskii, *Polnoe sobranie sochinenii*, vol. IV, p. 175; and T. [F. Tornau], "Vospominaniia o Kavkaze i Gruzii," *Russkii vestnik* (1869), no. 2, 103.

16. Agil' Gadzhiev, *Etapy literaturnogo bratstva* (Baku: Iazychy, 1986), pp. 31–57; Gadzhiev, *Kavkaz v russkoi literature*, pp. 72–77; and Bazanov, *Ocherki dekabristskoi literatury*, p. 501. By contrast, Lewis Bagby has called the travelogues "moving accounts of a restless soul in search of stability": see "Bestužev-Marlinskij's 'Mulla Nur': A Muddled Myth to Rekindle Romance," *Russian Literature* 11 (January 1982), 127, n. 1.

17. Dubrovin, *Istoriia voiny i vladychestva*, vol. I, kn. 3, p. 96.

18. N. M., "Vospominaniia o Kavkaze 1837 goda," 21.

19. Count V. Sollogub, "God voennykh deistvii za Kavkazom, 1853–54," *Biblioteka dlia chteniia* 142 (March 1857), ch. 3, otd. II, 4.

20. Meisner, *Stikhotvoreniia*, pp. 77–80.

21. G. I. Uspenskii, *Polnoe sobranie sochinenii*, 10 vols. (Moscow: Akademiia nauk,1940–53), vol. X, part 1, pp. 295–97, 300. The essay was brought to my attention by D. P. Fesenko, "Kritika kapitalizma v kavkazskikh ocherkakh G. Uspenskogo" in *Russkaia literatura i Kavkaz*, pp. 56–63.

22. Shaduri, *Dekabristskaia literatura*, p. 332.

23. The Russian army under Vorontsov's command took the vir-

tually deserted village of Dargo, Shamil's base of operations at the time. During the return march, however, the Russian troops were ambushed by tribesmen and suffered massive casualties in killed and wounded: see Baddeley, *Russian Conquest*, pp. 388–410.

24. *Ermolov*, comp. Pogodin, pp. 279, 282.
25. *Ibid.*, pp. 296–97.
26. See Vorontsov's assessment of the Dargo campaign in *Akty KAK*, vol. x, pp. 288–89. See also reports of General I. F. Paskevich and others in *Dvizhenie gortsev*, pp. 168–72, 192, 283–84. Additional perceptions of Caucasian terrain as Russia's enemy appear in Sollogub, "God voennoi deistvii za Kavkazom," 12; Berezin, *Puteshestvie po Dagestanu*, vol. ii, pp. 92–93; and N. Volkonskii, "Lezginskaia ekspeditsiia (v Didoiskoe obshchestvo) v 1857 godu," *Kavkazskii sbornik* 2 (1897), 219.
27. Nikolai Paul, "Kavkazskie kartiny. Iz zapisok ochevidtsa," *Teleskop* (1833), ch. 16, no. 15, 340–41.
28. *Poety*, vol. ii, p., 272.
29. Shevchenko's long poem "The Caucasus" fiercely protested against the conquest but did not feminize the territory.

11 GEORGIA AS AN ORIENTAL WOMAN

Epigraph, Odocvskii, *Polnoe sobranie sochinenii*, pp. 178–80.

1. See Todorov's discussion of "exotisme et érotisme" in *Nous et les autres*, pp. 41–55. For analysis of woman's duality as the other in narratives of the tropical journey by Lévi-Strauss, Conrad and Baudelaire, see also Cleo McNelly, "Natives, Women, and Claude Lévi-Strauss," *Massachusetts Review*, 16 (Winter 1975), 8–10.
2. See David Marshall Lang, *The Last Years of the Georgian Monarchy, 1658–1832* (New York: Columbia University, 1957), pp. 253–70, 283–84; and Ronald Grigor Suny, *The Making of the Georgian Nation* (London: I. B. Tauris, 1989), pp. 83–84.
3. Georgia was orientalized in a non-romantic but nevertheless noteworthy manner in V. Narezhnyi's *Chernyi god, ili gorskie kniazia* (Moscow, 1829) (*The Black Year, or Mountain Princes*). Narrated in the first person by an Ossetian prince of Persian descent, this novel features Muslims, Zoroastrians, Buddhists, Jews and pagans. It harkens back to traditions of Montesquieu's *Persian Letters* and the Eastern tales of Voltaire to engage in light moral satire of Russian officials: see N. Svirin, "Pervyi russkii roman o Kavkaze," *Znamia* 7 (1935), 224–27, 237–40.

4. Suny, *Making of the Georgian Nation*, pp. 20–21; and, on the impact of Islam, pp. 24–30 , 46–55. See also W. E. D. Allen, *A History of the Georgian People* (London: Kegan Paul, Trench, Trubner and Co., 1932), pp. 73–74, 99, 119, 270–73.

5. Lang, *The Last Years of the Georgian Monarchy*, pp. 52–53, 189. Allen recognized martyrs for the faith among the nobles and also underlined the steady persistence of Christianity among the Georgian peasantry and artisan class, but he claimed that the majority of Georgian princes displayed "cynical indifference" toward religion in this era: "They combined Mussulman polygamy with Christian drunkenness and interested themselves in either religion only to the extent of celebrating with admirable impartiality the feast-days of both," *History of the Georgian People*, p. 272.

6. Quoted in Shaduri, *Dekabristskaia literatura*, p. 347.

7. *Poety*, vol. I, pp. 388–89.

8. Lermontov, *Sobranie sochinenii*, vol. I, pp. 81; vol. II, pp. 51, 83; and Ia. P. Polonskii, *Stikhotvoreniia* (Leningrad: Sovetskii pisatel', 1954), pp. 95, 98. As discussed by Allen, the wearing of the veil in Tiflis reflected the city's long history as a stronghold of Muslim power. By contrast, in country districts, where Christian practices prevailed, the veil was not customary: see *History of the Georgian People*, pp. 98–99, 356.

9. The opposition is stressed in Lobikova, *Pushkin i Vostok*, pp. 49–55.

10. Sandler, *Distant Pleasures*, pp. 173–82.

11. Griboedov, *Sochineniia v stikhakh*, pp. 332–38. For a plot summary published in the Russian press in 1830 by F. Bulgarin (who considered "Georgian Night" a masterpiece), see Shaduri, *Dekabristskaia literatura*, pp. 294–95.

12. Consult poems by Alexander Radishchev in Shaduri, *Russkie pisateli o Gruzii*, vol. I, pp. 14–15. On Medea, see also Bronevskii, *Noveishie izvestiia o Kavkaze*, vol. I, p. viii.

13. A. Khakhanov, "Meskhi," *Etnograficheskoe obozrenie* (1891), kn. 10, no. 3: 36–37. According to pagan belief in mountainous eastern Georgia, the primal demon who revolted from benevolent God was His sister, the creator of the female sex: see G. Charachidze, *Le Système religieux de la Géorgie païenne* (Paris: François Maspero, 1968), pp. 279–81.

14. Charachidze, *Le Système religieux*, p. 654; and on attributes of the Virgin, Khakhanov, "Meskhi," 36.

15. Iraklii Andronikov, *Lermontov. Issledovaniia i nakhodki* (Moscow: Khudozhestvennaia literatura, 1964), pp. 268–70.

16. In a late nineteenth-century version, Tamar finally is exterminated by a valiant Russian soldier who strikes her with a magic button of his uniform: see Khakhanov, "Iz gruzinskikh legend," *Etnograficheskoe obozrenie* (1898), kn. 39, no. 4: 140.
17. Andronikov, *Lermontov*, pp. 252–55.
18. Mann, *Poetika russkogo romantizma*, p. 227, n. 36.
19. On the Demon's rapacious gaze, see Joe Andrew, *Women in Russian Literature, 1780–1863* (London: Macmillan, 1988), pp. 54–60.
20. Griboedov, *Sochineniia v stikhakh*, p. 357; see also Pushkin, *Sobranie sochinenii*, vol. II, pp. 246, 266; Polonskii, *Stikhotvoreniia*, pp. 109–10, 141; and lesser poets anthologized in Shaduri, *Russkie pisateli o Gruzii*, vol. I, pp. 302, 417–18, 422–23. The Darial Pass also figured frequently in literature, as already noted in "Ammalat-Bek."
21. The poetry's fame is underlined in Andronikov, *Lermontov*, p. 241. See also G. Filatov, "Poema M. Iu. Lermontova 'Demon' (k voprosu o znachenii knvkazskoi tematiki)," *Literatura i Kavkaz*, ed. V. Dronov (Stavropol', 1972), pp. 67–69.
22. Lermontov, *Sobranie sochinenii*, vol. II, p. 74.
23. A. A. Shishkov, *Ketevana, ili Gruziia v 1812 godu*, abridged in Shaduri, *Russkie pisateli o Gruzii*.
24. Shishkov, *Ketevana*, p. 426. (Subsequent citations appear parenthetically in the text.)
25. Verderevskii, *Ot Zaural'ia do Zakavkaz'ia*, pp. 170, 206.
26. Although Lermontov's "Rendez-Vous" does not specify the speaker's nationality, he appears Russian by virtue of first-person narration and the depiction of a "Tatar" as an exotic foreigner.
27. L. A. Iakubovich, "Narodnaia gruzinskaia pesnia," in Shaduri, *Russkie pisateli o Gruzii*, p. 420.
28. It is especially notable that the poem induced some Russian women to tell Lermontov flirtatiously that they would like to go flying with his Demon: see *Lermontov v vospominaniiakh sovremennikov*, pp. 205–6.
29. Kamenskii, *Povesti i razskazy*, pp. 102–3.
30. Dzhegitov, "Pir na Kavkaze," 126–27.
31. In reality, when Polonsky wrote this poem, Russia had proved too economically backward itself to realize any major projects for developing Georgia, as stressed in S. and N. Gougouchvili *et al.*, *La Géorgie*, (Paris: PUF, 1983), pp. 116–17. Likewise, as of the mid-1840s, Russia essentially turned a blind eye to slave trade in the Caucasus, much to the exasperation of the British

who were trying to abolish it: see Ehud R. Toledano, *Ottoman Slave Trade and Its Suppression, 1840–90* (Princeton, NJ: Princeton University, 1982), pp. 42, 115–16, 138–42.

32. Ammalat-Bek kills a panther and puts on its skin, and Lermontov's young tribal hero in "Mtsyri" attacks a snow leopard with a club.

33. Enikolopov, *Griboedov v Gruzii*, pp. 15–16; Shaduri, *Dekabristskaia literatura*, pp. 347, 489–97, 516–17; and Stephen F. Jones, "Russian Imperial Administration and the Georgian Nobility: The Georgian Conspiracy of 1832," *Slavonic and East European Review* 65 (January 1987), 61–62.

34. *Lermontov v vospominaniiakh sovremennikov*, p. 48. By contrast to Lermontov, Pushkin in *Journey to Arzrum* acknowledged the valor of Georgians, even as he maligned their intellect: "The Georgians are a nation of warriors. They have proved their bravery under our banners. Their mental capacities still await development" (*Sobranie sochinenii*, vol. v, p. 431). The continuation of the passage attributes a jolly disposition to Georgians, marvels at their great appetite for strong wine and remarks "oriental senselessness" in their poetic songs.

35. The murder naturally made an impression at the time, as seen in Russian documents referring to it as a "bestial" and "barbarous" act, displaying a "vengeance and ferocity unexpected in the female sex": see *Akty KAK*, vol. II, pp. 112, 114–15.

36. Without mentioning any names, the epilogue of Pushkin's "The Prisoner of the Caucasus" refers to the "destruction of Russians" by "vindictive Georgian women," using the plural, interestingly enough, as though such violence were endemic. An old Georgian peasant in Shishkov's *Ketevana* also mentions the murder (p. 453).

12 THE ANGUISHED POET IN UNIFORM

Epigraph, Lermontov, "Valerik," *Sobranie sochinenii*, vol. I, p. 66.

1. *Lermontovskaia entsiklopediia*, pp. 87–90.
2. Lermontov, *Sobranie sochinenii*, vol. IV, p. 427.
3. Grossman, "Lermontov i kultury vostoka," 674.
4. Lermontov, *Sobranie sochinenii*, vol. IV, p. 450.
5. E. Mikhalova, *Proza Lermontova* (Moscow: GIKhL, 1957), pp. 209–10; B. Eikhenbaum, *O proze. Sbornik statei* (Leningrad:

Khudozhestvennaia literatura, 1969), pp. 263–83; and John Garrard, *Lermontov* (Boston, MA: Twayne, 1982), pp. 132–42

6. See Lotman, "Problema Vostoka i Zapada v tvorchestve pozdnego Lermontova," pp. 5–15.

7. Lewis Bagby, "Narrative Double-Voicing in Lermontov's *A Hero of Our Time*," *Slavic and East European Review* 22 (Fall 1979), 273–80; and Todd, *Fiction and Society*, p. 163.

8. Although "Bela" is set in Chechnia, Lermontov retained the traditional romantic obsession with "Circassian" beauties. For pertinent commentary, see S. Durylin, *Geroi nashego vremeni M. Iu. Lermontova* (Moscow: Narkompros, 1940), p. 49–54; and Manuilov, *Roman M. Iu. Lermontova*, pp. 80–81, 88, 91–92.

9. Peter Scotto, "Prisoners of the Caucasus: Ideologies of Imperialism in Lemontov's 'Bela,'" *PMLA* 107 (March 1992), 246–60; and Barbara Heldt, *Terrible Perfection: Women and Russian Literature* (Bloomington, IN: Indiana University, 1987), pp. 29–32.

10. For a recent examination, see Andrew Barratt and A. D. P. Briggs, *A Wicked Irony: The Rhetoric of Lermontov's "A Hero of Our Time"* (Bristol: Bristol Classical Press, 1989).

11. See detailed analysis in Susan Layton, "Lermontov in Combat with *Biblioteka dlia chteniia*," *Cahiers du monde russe et soviétique*, forthcoming. Consult also V. Vatsuro, "Lermontov i Marlinskii" in *Tvorchestvo M. Iu. Lermontova. 150 let so dnia rozhdeniia, 1814–1964*, ed. U. R. Fokht (Moscow: Nauka, 1964), pp. 356–58; and L. S. Dubshan, "O khudozhestvennom reshenii i literaturnom istochnike ognogo iz epizodov povesti 'Bela'" in *Lermontovskii sbornik* (1985), pp. 267–70.

12. Todd, *Fiction and Society*, pp. 147–49.

13. For examples, see anon. book review, *Biblioteka dlia chteniia* 17 (1836), otd. v, 11; and "Podvigi Russkikh za Kuban'iu v 1789 godu," *Otechestvennye zapiski*, 5 (1821), no. 9, 34.

14. Consult Eikhenbaum, *Stat'i o Lermontove*, pp. 243–44; Vladimir Nabokov, "Translator's Introduction," *A Hero of Our Time* (New York: Doubleday, 1958), pp. viii–ix; and Todd, *Fiction and Society*, pp. 149–50.

15. See the developmental assessment of Pechorin in Richard Gregg, "The Cooling of Pechorin: The Skull beneath the Skin," *Slavic Review* 43 (Fall 1984), 387–98.

16. Lermontov, *Geroi nashego vremeni* in *Sobranie sochinenii*, vol. IV, p. 37. (Subsequent citations to the novel appear parenthetically in the text.) I have modified Nabokov's translation.

17. S. Shevyrev, "Geroi nashego vremeni," *Moskvitianin* (1841), ch.1, no. 2, 518, 524 and 533–37.
18. *Russkaia kriticheskaia literatura o proizvedeniiakh M. Iu. Lermontova*, ed. V. Zelinskii, 2 vols. (Moscow: A. G. Kol'chugin, 1897), vol. II, pp. 152.
19. Mikhailova, *Proza Lermontova*, p. 221.
20. Lermontov again used the metaphor of mountains as blushing girls in his fragment of poetic prose, "Blue mountains of the Caucasus, I greet you," *Sobranie sochinenii*, vol. 1, pp. 254–55.
21. Rozanov, "Baironicheskie motivy v tvorchestve Lermontova," 361–62. On parodic echoes of Marlinsky in the passage, see Udodov, *Lermontov*, pp. 595–60.
22. John Mersereau, Jr., *Mikhail Lermontov* (Carbondale, IL: Southern Illinois University, 1962), pp. 122–24; and J. A. Harvie, "The Vulture and the Dove," *Comparative Literature Studies* 18 (March 1981), 27.
23. Cynthia Marsh, "Lermontov and the Romantic Tradition: The Function of Landscape in *A Hero of Our Time*," *Slavonic and East European Review* 66 (January 1988), 45–46.
24. M. Bakhtin, *Problemy poetiki Dostoevskogo*, 4th edn. (Moscow: Sovetskaia Rossiia, 1979), p. 265. For an English translation, see *Problems of Dostoevsky's Poetics*, trans. Caryl Emerson (Minneapolis, MN: University of Minnesota, 1984).
25. See a discussion of British writing in Paul Fussell, *The Great War and Modern Memory* (Oxford: Oxford University, 1975), p. 192.
26. E. M. Pul'khritudova, " 'Valerik' Lermontova i stanovlenie psikhologicheskogo realizma v russkoi literature 30-kh godov XIX veka" in *M. Iu. Lermontov. Sbornik statei i materialov*, ed. L. P. Semenov (Stavropol': Stavropol'skoe knizhnoe izdatel'stvo, 1960), pp. 73–79. See also A. V. Popov, *Lermontov na Kavkaze* (Stavropol': Stavropol'skoe knizhnoe izdatel'stvo,1954), pp. 142–47.
27. See Erich Neumann, *The Great Mother*, trans. Ralph Manheim, 2nd edn. (New York: Bollingen Foundation, 1963), p. 198.
28. *An Age Ago: A Selection of Nineteenth-Century Russian Poetry*, trans. Alan Myers, forward and notes by Joseph Brodsky (London: Penquin, 1989), p. 162.
29. Lermontov, *Sobranie sochinenii*, vol. IV, p. 451.
30. See Belinsky quoted in Lermontov, *Sobranie sochinenii*, vol. I, p. 347.
31. N. Semenov, *Tuzemtsy severo-vostochnago Kavkaza. (Razskazy, ocherki, izsledovaniia, zametki o chechentsakh, kumykakh i nogaitsakh i*

obraztsy poezii etikh narodtsev) (St. Petersburg: A. Khomskii and Co., 1895), pp. 73–75. See also V. A. Geiman, "1845. Vospominaniia," *Kavkazskii sbornik* 3 (1879), 273.
32. Zisserman, *Dvadtsat' piat' let na Kavkaze*, vol. II, pp. 240–41, 326–37. After reading Zisserman, Tolstoy would respond by using the phrase the "poetry of warfare" (*voinstvennaia poeziia*) ironically in *Hadji Murat*.
33. Besides Bestuzhev-Marlinsky's death in combat, Alexander Odoevsky succumbed to typhus while stationed on the Black Sea coast; and Polezhaev died of tuberculosis in a military hospital in Moscow, after deserting his regiment.
34. See Mersereau, *Mikhail Lermontov*, p. 117; and K. N. Grigor'an, *Lermontov i ego roman "Geroi nashego vremeni"* (Leningrad: Nauka, 1975), pp. 219–20. For the verse "Farewell, unwashed Russia," see Lermontov, *Sobranie sochinenii*, vol. I, p. 76.
35. Lermontov, *Sobranie sochinenii.*, vol. IV, p. 436.
36. Belinskii, *Polnoe sobranie sochinenii*, vol. IV, p. 175.
37. Edmund Spencer, *Travels in· Circassia, Krim, Tartary, etc.* (London: H. Colburn, 1837), vol. I, p. 327.
38. Quoted in M. P. Alekseev, "Viktor Giugo i ego russkie znakomstva. Vstrechi. Pis'ma. Vospominaniia," *Literaturnoe nasledstvo* 31–32 (1937), 804.
39. L. N. Tolstoi, *Sobranie sochinenii v dvenadtsati tomakh* (Moscow: Khudozhestvennaia literatura, 1972–76), vol. II, p. 64.

13 TOLSTOY'S REVOLT AGAINST ROMANTICISM

Epigraph, Tolstoi, *Kazaki* in *Sobranie sochinenii*, vol. III, p. 225.
1. Tolstoi, "Zapiski o Kavkaze, Poezdka v Mamakai-Iurt." *Polnoe sobranie sochinenii*, 90 vols. (Moscow: GIKhL, 1928–58), vol. III, pp. 215–17.
2. B. M. Eikhenbaum, *Lev Tolstoi. Kniga pervaia, 50–6oie gody* (Leningrad: Priboi, 1928), p. 180.
3. A classic case of ill-informed ethnography full of Great Russian chauvinism was N. Danilevskii, *Kavkaz i ego gorskie zhiteli v nynyshnem polozhenii* (Moscow: MGU, 1846). For a scornful response to the book, see *Otechestvennye zapiski* 48 (1846), no. 10, otd. VI, 96–97.
4. The newspaper circulated little outside Tiflis: See V. G. Gadzhiev and A. M. Pikman, *Velikie russkie revoliutsionnye demokraty o bor'be gortsev Dagestana i Chechni* (Makhachkala, 1972), p. 51.
5. Zisserman, *Dvadtsat' piat' let na Kavkaze*, vol. I, pp. 328–29.

6. Belinskii, *Polnoe sobranie sochinenii*, vol. I, pp. 135–36.
7. *Ibid.*, vol. IV, p. 174.
8. *Sovremennik*, 26 (1851), otd. v, 68–71.
9. Eikhenbaum, *Lev Tolstoi*, vol. I, pp. 130–38. Eikhenbaum includes an excerpt from Kostenetsky on p. 134.
10. Harold Bloom, *The Anxiety of Influence. A Theory of Poetry* (Oxford: Oxford University, 1973). Tolstoy's embattled stance goes unnoticed in B. Eikhenbaum, "L. Tolstoi na Kavkaze (1851–1853)," *Russkaia literatura* (1962), 52, 56.
11. Tolstoi, *Polnoe sobranie sochinenii*, vol. XLVI, pp. 91, 158–59.
12. *Ibid.*, p. 155.
13. *Ibid.*, vol. LIX, p. 130.
14. Quoted with commentary in N. N. Gusev, *Lev Nikolaevich Tolstoi. Materialy k biografii s 1828 po 1855 god* (Moscow: Akademiia nauk, 1954), p. 328.
15. Tolstoi, *Sobranie sochinenii*, vol. II, p. 14.
16. Tolstoi, *Polnoe sobranie sochinenii*, vol. III, p. 232.
17. Tolstoi, *Sobranie sochinenii*, vol. II, p. 64.
18. Tolstoi, *Polnoe sobranie sochinenii*, vol. III, pp. 215–16. The essay was written in 1852.
19. Tolstoi, *Sobranie sochinenii*, vol. III, p. 156. (Subsequent citations are given parenthetically in the text.)
20. B. M. Eikhenbaum, *Molodoi Tolstoi* (Peterburg: Z. I. Grzhebin, 1922), pp. 111–15.
21. On the Rousseau connection, see Isaiah Berlin, "Tolstoy and Enlightenment" in *Tolstoy: A Collection of Critical Essays*, ed. Ralph E. Matlaw (Englewood Cliffs, NJ: Prentice-Hall, 1967), pp. 30, 37–45.
22. Tolstoi, *Polnoe sobranie sochinenii*, vol. XLVI, pp. 64, 66, 87, 93–94, 162.
23. John Hagen, "Ambivalence in Tolstoy's *The Cossacks*," *Novel* 3 (1969), 44–46; and Robert L. Jackson, "The Archetypal Journey. Aesthetics and Ethical Imperatives in the Art of Tolstoj – *The Cossacks*," *Russian Literature* 11 (May 1982), 389–92.
24. Tolstoi, *Polnoe sobranie sochinenii*, vol. VI, p. 253.
25. Lewis Bagby and Pavel Sigalov, "The Semiotics of Names and Naming in Tolstoj's 'The Cossacks,'" *Slavic and East European Journal* 31 (Winter 1987), 480.
26. M. Ja. Ol'shevskii, "Kavkaz s 1841 po 1866," *Russkaia starina* 78 (June 1893), 592.
27. The soldiers are Don Cossacks, whose officer announces sheepishly to the narrator, "I thought that was a baby they were about to kill."

28. Tolstoi, *Polnoe sobranie sochinenii*, vol. VI, pp. 157–89, 259.
29. *Ibid.*, vol. XLVII, p. 280.
30. See Krystyna Pomorska, "Tolstoy – Contra Semiosis," *International Journal of Slavic Linguistics and Poetics*, nos. 25–26 (1982), 383–90.
31. Quoted in N. N. Gusev, *Lev Nikolaevich Tolstoi. Materialy k biografii s 1855 po 1869* (Moscow: Akademiia nauk, 1957), p. 605.
32. *Ibid.*, p. 606.
33. *Ibid.*
34. V. A. Manuilov, "Kavkazskie rasskazy i povesti L. N. Tolstogo" in Tolstoi, *Kavkazskie rasskazy i povesti* (Voronezh: Tsentral'no-chernozemnoe knizhnoe izdatel'stvo, 1978), p. 27.
35. See N. N. Gusev, *Lev Nikolaevich Tolstoi. Materialy k biografii s 1870 po 1881* (Moscow: Akademiia nauk, 1963), p. 76; and B. M. Eikhenbaum, *Lev Tolstoi. Semidesiatye gody* (Leningrad: Sovetskii pisatel', 1960), pp. 182–83.

14 POST-WAR APPROPRIATION OF ROMANTICISM

Epigraph, V. I. Nemirovich-Danchenko, *Zabytaia krepost'* (L'vov: Stavropigiiskii institut, 1897), p. 462.
1. *The Cossacks* was mentioned in the early twentieth-century travelogue of Markov, *Ocherki Kavkaza*, p. 583.
2. The dreadful epigone poetry of sublime nature and orientalia can be sampled in M. Rosengeim, *Stikhotvoreniia*, 4th edn., 2 vols. (St. Petersburg: M. M. Stasiulevich, 1889), vol. I, pp. 60–61, 222–23; vol. II, pp. 20–23, 171–73; M. I. Lavrov, *Sochineniia* (Moscow: I. N. Kushnerev and Co., 1889), pp. 105; M. I. Lavrov, *Stikhotvoreniia* (Moscow: A. I. Snegirevoi, 1898), ch. 2, pp. 43, 47–48, 246; and V. L. Velichko, *Arabeski. Novyia stikhotvoreniia* (St. Petersburg: P. P. Soikin, 1904), pp. 1, 32–36, 51–58, 72–80.
3. "Pokorenie vostochnogo Kavkaza," *Otechestvennye zapiski* (1860), 101–3; and S. Ryzhov, "Ocherki zapadnogo Zakavkaz'ia," *Otechestvennye zapiski* 128 (January 1860), otd. VI, 12–13; and 129 (March 1860), otd. VI, 8–9. See also the view of the conquest as a civilizing mission in Dobroliubov, "O znachenii nashikh poslednikh podvigov na Kavkaze," pp. 446–47.
4. Dubrovin, *Istoriia voiny i vladychestva*, vol. I, kn.1, p. xiii. Bestuzhev-Marlinsky had posthumous revenge when Dubrovin perceived ethnographic reliability in the author's "Story of a Russian Officer Held Prisoner by Mountain Tribesmen," as

anonymously published in the *Tiflis Gazette* in 1831: see *Istoriia voiny i vladychestva*, vol. I, kn. 3, p. 108.

5. E. I. Kozubinskii (comp.), *Opyt bibliografii dagestanskoi oblasti* (Temir-Khan Shura: V. M. Sorokin, 1895), p. 38. For the countertendency, see Kosven, *Etnografiia i istoriia Kavkaza*, pp. 158–68.

6. P. K. Uslar, *Etnografiia Kavkaza. Iazykoznanie*, vol. II: *Chechenskii iazyk* (Tiflis: Upravlenie Kavkazskago Uchebnago Okruga, 1888), third appendix, pp. 77–78.

7. For a thorough investigation, consult Brooks, *When Russia Learned to Read*.

8. Thomas M. Barrett, "The Remaking of the Lion of Dagestan: Shamil in Captivity," paper delivered at the 20th National Convention of the American Association for the Advancement of Slavic Studies, Honolulu, 1988, pp. 12–17. Barrett calls romantic Russian literature an important "preparation" for Shamil's lionization in defeat.

9. R. A. Fadeev *Shest' desiat let kavkazskoi voiny* (Tiflis: Voenno-pokhodnaia tipografiia Glavnogo Shtaba Kavkazskoi Armii, 1860), pp. 4–18, 24, 37. See also R. Fadeev, *Pis'ma s Kavkaza k redaktory 'Moskovskikh vedomostei'* (St. Petersburg: V. Besobrazov, 1865). Fadeev's popular success was cited in another patriotic history first delivered as public lectures in St. Petersburg: D. I. Romanovskii, *Kavkaz i kavkazskaia voina. Publichnyia lektsii, chitannyia v zale Passazha v 1860 godu* (St. Petersburg: Obshchestvennaia pol'za, 1860), p. 227. But for a private judgment of Fadeev as a writer full of "stupid, shabby adulation and falsehood," see General Nikita Alekseev's letter to Lev Tolstoy, quoted in B. Eikhenbaum, *Lev Tolstoi. Kniga vtoraia, 60-ie gody* (Moscow-Leningrad: GIKhL, 1931), p. 142. Fadeev's politics are treated in Edward C. Thaden, *Conservative Nationalism in Nineteenth-Century Russia* (Seattle: University of Washington, 1964), pp. 146–63.

10. F. V. Iukhotnikov, "Pis'ma s Kavkaza," *Russkoe slovo* (April 1861), otd. III, 9–13.

11. A.V., "Pokorenie Kavkaza," *Russkii vestnik* 27 (June 1860), 348.

12. *Lermontov v vospominaniiakh sovremennikov*, p. 370.

13. *Biblioteka dlia chteniia* 160 (July 1860), ch. 1, "Literaturnaia letopis'," 9–10.

14. Peter Viereck, "Strict Form in Poetry: Would Jacob Wrestle with a Flabby Angel?" *Critical Inquiry* 5 (Winter 1978), 203–11.

15. On the "mountain goddesses," see Belevich, *Stikhi i razskazy*, p. 15, n. 1.

16. Walter Ong, *Orality and Literacy. The Technologizing of the Word* (London: Methuen, 1982), pp. 34–40, 55.
17. *Bitva russkikh c kabardintsami,* 2nd edn., rev. by A. V. Morozov and N. P. Mironov (Moscow: Martynov and Co., 1880), ch. 2, pp. 77–78.
18. P. P. Nadezhdin (comp.), *Priroda i liudi na Kavkaze, po razskazam puteshestvennikov, poeticheskim proizvedeniiam Pushkina, Lermontova, Polonskogo i uchebnym issledovaniiam. Uchebnoe posobie* (St. Petersburg: V. Demakov, 1869), pp. 26–27, 44–46, 58, 76, 144–50. A subsequent edition was transformed but still included literary excerpts: P. P. Nadezhdin (comp.), *Kavkazskii krai. Priroda i liudi,* 2nd edn., rev. and aug. (Tula: E. I. Druzhinina, 1895).
19. E. Voskresenskii (comp.), *Kavkaz po sochineniiam Pushkina i Lermontova* (Moscow: "Nachal'naia shkola" E. N. Tikhomirova, 1887).
20. Zhelikhova, *Kavkazskie razskazy* ; E. I. Novikova-Zarina, *Kavkazskie razskazy (Byl')* (St. Petersburg: D. A. Naumov, 1897); D. Mordovtsev, *Zhelezom i kroviu. Roman iz istorii zavoevaniia Kavkaza pri Ermolove* in *Sobranie sochinenii,* 50 vols. (St. Petersburg: I. F. Merts, 1901–2), vol. XLVIII; and F. F. Tiutchev, *Na gorakh i na dolinakh Dagestana. Roman iz vremen bor'by s Shamilem za vladychestvo na Kavkaze* (St. Petersburg: V. V. Komarov, 1903).
21. *Utverzhdenie russkago vladychestva na Kavkaze, 1801–1901: k stoletiiu prisoedineniia Gruzii k Rossii,* 6 vols., comp. and ed. N. N. Beliavskii and V. A. Potto (Tiflis: Tipografiia shtaba Kavkazskago voennago okruga, 1901–8).
22. Tolstoy's probable familiarity with these works was signaled by L. P. Semenov (ed.), *Kavkaz i Lev Tolstoi. Sbornik* (Vladikavkaz: SERDALO, 1928), p. 20.
23. Mordovtsev, "Kavkazskii geroi. Istoricheskaia byl'," *Sobranie sochinenii,* vol. XLVI, pp. 71–119. See detailed analysis in Susan Layton, "Imagining the Caucasian Hero: Tolstoj vs. Mordovcev," *Slavic and East European Journal* 30 (Spring 1986), 1–17.
24. See further discussion in Susan Layton, "Primitive Despot and Noble Savage: The Two Faces of Shamil in Russian Literature," *Central Asian Survey* 10 (1991), no. 4, 31–45.
25. D. I. Romanovskii, "Gen. Fel'dmarshal kniaz' Aleksandr Ivanovich Bariatinskii i kavkazskaia voina, 1815–1879," *Russkaia starina* 30 (1881), 260–61.
26. Berzhe, "Prisoedinenie Gruzii k Rossii," 1. For other references to public ignorance about the Caucasus, see N. V. Desnitskii, *Rukovodstvo dlia otpravliaiushchikhsia na kavkazskie mineral'nyia vody* (St. Petersburg: Izdanie khizhnago magazina N. N. Tsylova,

1882), first unnumbered page; and Nadezhdin, *Kavkazskii krai*, first unnumbered page of preface.

27. See the treatment of Lermontov's "Izmail-Bey" in Semenov, *Tuzemtsy severo-vostochnago Kavkaza*, p. 73.

15 TOLSTOY'S CONFESSIONAL INDICTMENT

Epigraph, Tolstoi, *Hadji Murat* in *Sobranie sochinenii*, vol. XII, p. 254. (Subsequent citations appear parenthetically in the text.)

1. V. B. Shklovskii, *Lev Tolstoi* (Moscow: Khudozhestvennaia literatura, 1974), p. 626.

2. James B. Woodward, "Tolstoy's 'Hadji Murat': The Evolution of Its Theme and Structure," *Modern Language Review* 68 (July 1973), 871–82.

3. An authoritative version based on Tolstoy's manuscripts was established only in 1950 for the ninety-volume Jubilee edition of the author's works.

4. Tolstoi, *Polnoe sobranie sochinenii*, vol. XLVI, p. 242.

5. See discussion of "Sevastopol Sketches" in Gary Saul Morson, "The Reader as Voyeur: Tolstoi and the Poetics of Didactic Fiction," *Canadian–American Slavic Studies* 12 (Winter 1978), 474–77.

6. Bakhtin, "Epic and Novel," *The Dialogic Imagination*, pp. 13–17, 27.

7. Tolstoi, *Polnoe sobranie sochinenii*, vol. XXXV, p. 622.

8. On the scene's exactitude, see John Bayley, *Tolstoy and the Novel* (New York: Viking, 1966), p. 275.

9. Morson, "The Reader as Voyeur," 479.

10. On the principle of theme and variations, see V. B. Shklovskii, *O teorii prozy* (Moscow-Leningrad: Krug, 1925), pp. 61–64.

11. P. Palievskii, "Realisticheskii metod pozdnego Tolstogo (povest' 'Khadzhi-Murat')," in *Lev Nikolaevich Tolstoi. Sbornik statei o tvorchestve*, ed. N. Gudzii (Moscow: MGU, 1959), vol. II, p. 179.

12. On the traditional values, see Ong, *Orality and Literacy*, pp. 171–75; and Nancy Vogeley, "Defining the 'Colonial Reader': *El Periquillo Sarniento*," *PMLA* 102 (October 1987), 793.

13. Gary Saul Morson, "Tolstoy's Absolute Language" in *Bakhtin. Essays and Dialogues on His Work*, ed. Gary Saul Morson (Chicago and London: University of Chicago, 1986), pp. 128–33.

14. Geiman, "1845 god," 368.

15. Consult Loris-Melikov's text in A. Zisserman (comp.), "Khadji Murat," *Russkaia starina* 30 (March 1881), 668–77.

16. Compare Nancy Dworsky, *"Hadji Murat*: A Summary and a Vision," *Novel* 8 (1975), no. 2, 144–45. Dworsky ventures astray, in my opinion, by reading Tolstoy's own destruction of a "Tatar" thistle as an admission of art's failure in modern society.
17. U. Dalgat, "Gorskie pesni, predanie i skazka v 'Khadzhi-Murate' L. N. Tolstogo i ikh khudozhestvennoe znachenie," *Izvestiia*, 2, vyp. 3: Literatura (Groznyi: Checheno-ingushskii nauchno-issledovatel'skii institut, 1951), 6–23.
18. Quoted in Donald Fanger, "Nazarov's Mother: On the Poetics of Tolstoi's Late Epic," *Canadian–American Slavic Studies* 12 (Winter 1978), 580.
19. The primacy of moral concern is argued in B. Eikhenbaum, "O povesti L. Tolstogo 'Khadzhi-Murat,'" in *Khadzhi-Murat* (Moscow-Leningrad: Detskaia literatura, 1936), p. 170. But for insistence upon the text's historical veracity, see V. A. D'iakov, "Istoricheskie realii 'Khadzhi-Murata,'" *Voprosy istoriiz* (1973), no. 5, 135–48.
20. Fanger, "Nazarov's Mother," 577–79.
21. My ensuing analysis draws on the theoretical discussion of Caryl Emerson, "The Tolstoy Connection in Bakhtin," *PMLA* 100 (January 1985), 72–77.
22. On dissemination of the prints, see *I. E. Repin i L. N. Tolstoi*, comps. S. A. Tolstaia-Esenina and T. V. Rozanova, 4 vols. (Moscow-Leningrad: Iskusstvo, 1948–52), vol. II, part 2, pp. 38, 117–18.
23. Tolstoi, *Polnoe sobranie sochinenii*, vol. XXXV, p. 456.
24. *L. N. Tolstoi v vospominaniiakh sovremennikov*, 2 vols. (Moscow: GIKhL, 1955), vol. I, p. 164.
25. Tsvetaeva, "Pushkin and Pugachev," pp. 394–99.
26. Tolstoi, *Polnoe sobranie sochinenii*, vol. LXIII, p. 353.
27. V. A. Poltoratskii, "Vospominaniia," *Istoricheskii vestnik* 14 (July 1893), 36–38.

16 CONCLUDING OBSERVATIONS

1. Uslar, *Etnografiia Kavkaza*, p. 77. The essay was first published in 1868.
2. Inal Kanukov, *Sochineniia* (Ordzhonikidze: Severo-Ossetinskoe knizhnoe izdatel'stvo, 1963), pp. 235–36, 255–56. I learned of this writer in V. B. Korzun, "M. Iu. Lermontov i literatury gorskikh narodov Severnogo Kavkaza," *Lermontovskii sbornik*, ed. B. S. Vinogradov *et al.* (Groznyi: Checheno-ingushskoe knizhnoe izdatel'stvo, 1964), pp. 104–5.

3. Kanukov, *Sochineniia*, p. 329.
4. See Korzun, "Lermontov i literatury gorskikh narodov," pp. 116–17.
5. Dzh. Naloev, "Ot mertvogo k zhivomu," *Literaturno-khudozhestvennyi sbornik*, vyp. 1: *Kabardino-Balkariia* (Nal'chik: Kabbalknatsizdat, 1933), 81–89.
6. Ia. Apushkin, *Khadzhi-Murat. Geroicheskaia drama v 5 aktakh i 16 kartinakh s interpolatsiiami iz povesti L'va Tolstogo* (Moscow: Tsentral'noe biuro po rasprostraneniiu dramaticheskoi produktsii, 1934).
7. Grigorii Aiollo, "Plokho perevarennoe chuzhoe," *Kavkazskii gorets* (1925), nos. 2–3, 80–81.
8. See the definition of "transculturation" in Pratt, *Imperial Eyes*, pp. 187–88.
9. Korzun, "Lermontov i literatury gorskikh narodov," p. 116.
10. Rasul Gamzatov, *Vernost' talantu* (Moscow: Sovetskaia Rossiia, 1970), p. 7.
11. See various articles in *Central Asia Survey* 10 (1991), no. 1/2.
12. Taken from a statement by Salman Rushdie, the quoted phrase alludes to Bill Ashcroft, Gareth Griffiths and Helen Tiffin, *The Empire Writes Back. Theory and Practice in Post-Colonial Literatures* (London: Routledge, 1989).

Select bibliography

The bibliography has three sections. Because of limitations on space, no section includes all pertinent references contained in my notes. The listing of twentieth-century secondary works highlights methodology, as well as imperialism's impingement on cultural identity.

LITERARY WORKS AND TRAVELOGUES

Berezin, I. N. *Puteshestvie po Dagestanu i Zakavkaz'iu. S kartami, planami i vidami zamechatel'nykh mestakh.* 2 vols. 2nd edn. Kazan, 1850–52.

Bestuzhev-Marlinskii, A. A. *Sochineniia v dvukh tomakh.* Moscow: GIKhL, 1958.

Povesti i rasskazy. Moscow: Sovetskaia Rossiia, 1976.

[Bestuzhev-]Marlinskii. *Polnoe sobranie sochinenii.* 12 vols. 3rd. edn. St. Petersburg: III Otdelenie, 1838–39.

Dagestan v russkoi literature. Dorevoliutsionny period. Comp. Uzdiat Dalgat and Boris Kirdan. Makhachkala, 1960.

Derzhavin, G. R. *Stikhotvoreniia.* 2nd edn. Leningrad: Sovetskii pisatel', 1957.

Gamba, Jacques-François. *Voyage dans la Russie méridionale, et particulièrement dans les provinces situés au-delà du Caucase, fait depuis 1820 jusqu'en 1824.* 2 vols. Paris: C. J. Trouvé, 1826.

Gan, E. A. *Polnoe sobranie sochinenii.* St. Petersburg: N. F. Merts, 1905.

Griboedov, A. S. *Sochineniia.* Moscow: GIKhL, 1956.

Sochineniia v stikhakh. 2nd edn. Leningrad: Sovetskii pisatel', 1967.

Kamenskii, P. *Povesti i razskazy. Chast' pervaia.* St. Petersburg: III Otdelenie, 1838.

Karamzin, N. M. *Izbrannye sochineniia v dvukh tomakh.* Moscow-Leningrad: Khudozhestvennaia literatura, 1964.

Lermontov, M. Iu. *Sobranie sochinenii v chetyrekh tomakh.* Moscow: Khudozhestvennaia literatura, 1983–84.

Markov, P. *Zlomilla i Dobronrava – devy gor, ili vstrecha s kazakom.* Moscow: Tipografiia Lazarevykh Instituta Vostochnykh Iazykov, 1834.

Meisner, A. I. *Stikhotvoreniia.* Moscow: A. Semen, 1836.

Minaev, D. "Uprek Kavkazu," *Biblioteka dlia chteniia* 42 (1840), ch. 1, 72–74.

Mordovtsev, D. L. *Sobranie sochinenii.* 50 vols. St. Petersburg: I. F. Merts, 1901–02.

Nechaev, S. D. "Otryvki iz putevykh zapisok o Iugo-Vostochnoi Rossii," *Moskovskii telegraf* (1826), ch. 7, otd. 1, 26–41.

Nemirovich-Danchenko, V. I. *Zabytaia krepost'.* L'vov: Stavropiliiskii institut, 1897.

Novikova-Zarina, E. I. *Kavkazskie razskazy. (Byl').* St. Petersburg: D. A. Naumov, 1897.

Odoevskii, A. I. *Polnoe sobranie sochinenii.* Leningrad: Sovetskii pisatel', 1958.

Oznobishin, D. "Kavkazskoe utro," *Otechestvennye zapiski* 9 (1840), no. 6, otd. III, 151–52.

Paul, Nikolai. "Kavkazskie kartiny. Iz zapisok ochevidsta," *Teleskop* 1833, ch. 16, no. 15, 321–54.

"Pis'ma Kh. Sh. k F. Bulgarinu ili poezdka na Kavkaz," *Severnyi arkhiv* (July 1828), 40–109; and (August 1828), 194–252.

Poety 1820–1830-kh godov. 2 vols. Ed. L. Ia. Ginzburg. Leningrad: Sovetskii pisatel', 1972.

"Poezdka v Gruziiu," *Moskovskii telegraf* (August 1833), no. 15, 327–67; and no. 16, 410–473.

Polezhaev, A. I. *Stikhotvoreniia. Poemy.* Moscow: Moskovskii rabochii, 1981.

Polonskii, Ia. P. *Stikhotvoreniia.* 2nd edn. Leningrad: Sovetskii pisatel', 1954.

Pushkin, A. S. *Polnoe sobranie sochinenii.* 17 vols. Leningrad: Akademiia nauk, 1937–59.

Sobranie sochinenii v desiati tomakh. Moscow: GIKhL, 1959–62.

Radozhitskii, I. "Doroga ot reki Dona do Georgievska na prostranstve 500 verst," *Otechestvennye zapiski* (August 1823), no. 40, 343–75.

Reingardt, Karl Gustav. "Izvlechenie iz opisaniia puteshestviia v Gruziiu," *Aziatskii vestnik* (May 1825), 333–44.

Rostopchina, E. P. *Stikhotvoreniia.* 2nd edn. 4 vols. St. Petersburg: A. Smirdin, 1857–60.

Sochineniia. 2 vols. St. Petersburg: I. N. Skorokhodov, 1890.

Russkie pisateli o Gruzii. Comp. Vano Shaduri. Tbilisi: Zaria Vostoka, 1948.

Saburov, Ia. "Kavkaz," *Moskovskii nabliudatel'* (July 1835), kn. 2, ch. III, 197–219; and (September 1835), kn. 1, ch. IV, 34–59.

"Poezdka v Saratov, Astrakhan i na Kavkaz," *Moskovskii nabliudatel'* (May 1835), kn. 2, ch. II, 176–229.

Shidlovskii, A. *Grebenskii kazak. Povest'.* St. Petersburg: A. Smirdin, 1831.

Somov, Orest. *Selected Prose in Russian.* Ed. John Mersereau, Jr. and George Harjan. Ann Arbor, MI: University of Michigan, 1974.

P. S. [Petr Sumarokov]. "Pis'ma s Kavkaza," *Moskovskii telegraf* 33 (May 1830), 176–96; and (June 1830), 313–39.

Tolstoi, L. N. *Polnoe sobranie sochinenii.* 90 vols. Moscow: GIKhL, 1928–58.

Sobranie sochinenii v dvenadtsati tomakh. Moscow: Khudozhestvennaia literatura, 1972–76.

Uspenskii, G. I. *Polnoe sobranie sochinenii.* 10 vols. Moscow: Akademiia nauk, 1940–53.

Verderevskii, E. A. *Ot Zaural'ia do Zakavkaz'ia: Iumoristicheskie, sentimental'nye i prakticheskie pis'ma s dorogi.* Moscow: V. Gautier, 1857.

Zhukovskii, V. A. *Izbrannoe.* Leningrad: Khudozhestvennaia literatura, 1973.

Zriakhov, N. *Bitva russkikh s kabardintsami, ili prekrasnaia magometanka umiraiushchaia na grobe svoego muzha Andreia Pobedonostseva.* Moscow: Brat'ia Kupriianovye, 1879.

Bitva russkikh s kabardintsami, ili prekrasnaia magometanka umiraiushchaia na grobe svoego muzha. 2nd edn., rev. by A. V. Morozov and N. P. Mironov. Moscow: Martynov and Co., 1880.

Bitva russkikh s kabardintsami, ili prekrasnaia magometanka umiraiushchaia na grobe svoego muzha. Moscow: I. D. Sytin, 1893.

NINETEENTH-CENTURY SECONDARY WORKS

Belinskii, V. G. *Polnoe sobranie sochinenii.* 13 vols. Moscow: Akademiia nauk, 1953–59.

Berzhe, A. P. "Prisoedinenie Gruzii k Rossii, 1799–1831," *Russkaia starina* 28 (1880).

Bodenstedt, Friedrich. *Die Völker des Kaukasus und ihre Freiheitskämpfe gegen die Russen.* Frankfurt am Main: Hermann Johann Kessler, 1848.

Bronevskii, Semen. *Noveishie geograficheskie i istoricheskie izvestiia o Kavkaze.* 2 vols. 2nd aug. edn. Moscow: S. Selivanovskii, 1823.

Chichagova, M. N. *Shamil' na Kavkaze i v Rossii. Biograficheskii ocherk.* St. Petersburg: S. Muller and I. Bogel'man, 1889.

Dubrovin, N. F. *Istoriia voiny i vladychestva russkikh na Kavkaze.* 6 vols. St. Petersburg: Tipografiia departamenta udelov,1871–86.

Dvizhenie gortsev severo-vostochnogo Kavkaza v 20–50 gg. XIX veka. Sbornik dokumentov. Comp. V. G. Gadzhiev and Kh. Kh. Ramazanov. Makhachkala, 1959.

Aleksei Petrovich Ermolov. Materialy dlia ego biografii. Comp. M. Pogodin. Moscow: Katkov and Co., 1863.

Fadeev, R. A. *Shest'desiat let Kavkazskoi voiny.* Tiflis: Voenno-pokhodnaia tipografiia Glavnogo Shtaba Kavkazskoi Armii, 1860.

Nadezhdin, P. P. (comp.). *Priroda i liudi na Kavkaze, po razskazam puteshestvennikov, poeticheskim proizvedeniiam Pushkina, Lermontova, Polonskogo i uchebnym issledovaniiam. Uchebnoe posobie.* St. Petersburgs: V. Demakov, 1869.

Kavkazskii krai. Priroda i liudi. 2nd edn., rev. and aug. Tula: E. I. Druzhinina, 1895.

Ol'shevskii, M. Ia. "Kavkaz s 1841 po 1866," *Russkaia starina* 78 (June 1893), 573–610; and 79 (July 1893), 89–124.

Romanovskii, D. I. *Kavkaz i kavkazskaia voina. Publichnyia lektsii, chitannyia v zale Passazha v 1860 godu.* St. Petersburg: Tovarishchestvo Obshchestvennogo pol'za, 1860.

Semevskii, M. "Aleksandr Aleksandrovich Bestuzhev (Marlinskii), 1798–1837," *Otechestvennye zapiski* 130 (May 1860), 121–66.

Senkovskii, Osip. *Sobranie sochinenii.* 9 vols. St. Petersburg: Akademiia nauk, 1858–59.

Sismondi, J. C. L. Simonde de. "O literature Arabov," *Vestnik Evropy* (November 1818), ch. 102, no. 21, 175–216.

T. [Tornau, F.]. "Vospominaniia o Kavkaze i Gruzii," *Russkii vestnik* (1869), no. 2.

Uslar, P. K. "Koe-chto o slovesnykh proizvedeniiakh gortsev," in *Etnografiia Kavkaza. Iazykoznanie.* Vol. II: *Chechenskii iazyk.* Tiflis: Upravlenie kavkazskago uchebnago okruga, 1888.

Veidenbaum, E. G. *Kavkazskie etiudy* in *Kavkazovedenie,* vyp. 1. Tiflis: Tsentral'naia knizhnaia torgovlia, 1901.

Verderevskii, E. A. *Plen u Shamilia.* St. Petersburg: Korolev, 1856.

Voskresenskii, E. (comp.). *Kavkaz po sochineniiam Pushkina i Lermontova.* Moscow: "Nachal'naia shkola" E. N. Tikhomirova, 1887.

Zelinskii, V. A. (ed.). *Russkaia kriticheskaia literatura o proizvedeniiakh A. S. Pushkina. Khronologicheskii sbornik kritiko-bibliograficheskikh statei.* 7 vols. Moscow: E. Lissner and Iu. Roman, 1887; rpt. Ann Arbor, MI: University Microfilms, 1967.

Russkaia kriticheskaia literatura o proizvedeniiakh M. Iu. Lermontova. Khronologicheskii sbornik kritiko-bibliograficheskikh statei. 2 vols. Moscow: A. G. Kol'chugin, 1897.

Zisserman, A. L. *Dvadtsat' piat' let na Kavkaze (1842–1867)*. 2 vols. St. Petersburg: A. S. Suvorin, 1879.

Zubov, Platon P. *Kartina kavkazskago kraia, prinadlezhashchago Rossii, i sopredel'nykh onomu zemel' v istoricheskom, statisticheskom, etnograficheskom, finansovom i torgovom otnosheniiakh.* 2 vols. St. Petersburg: Konrad Vingeber, 1834.

TWENTIETH-CENTURY SECONDARY WORKS

Alekseev, M. P. *Etiudy o Marlinskom.* Irkutsk: Universitet Irkutska, 1928.

Andronikov, Iraklii. *Lermontov. Issledovaniia i nakhodki.* Moscow: Khudozhestvennaia literatura, 1964.

Arac, Jonathan and Harriet Ritvo (eds.). *Macropolitics of Nineteenth-Century Literature. Nationalism, Exoticism, Imperialism.* Philadelphia, PA: University of Pennsylvania, 1991.

Ashcroft, Bill, Gareth Griffiths and Helen Tiffin. *The Empire Writes Back. Theory and Practice in Post-Colonial Literatures.* London: Routledge, 1989.

Austin, Paul M. "The Exotic Prisoner in Russian Romanticism," *Russian Literature* 16–18 (October 1984), 217–74.

Baddeley, John. *The Russian Conquest of the Caucasus.* London: Longmans, Green and Co., 1908.

Bagby, Lewis. "Aleksandr Bestužev-Marlinskij's 'Roman i Ol'ga': Generation and Degeneration," *Slavic and East European Journal* 25 (Winter 1981), 1–15.

"Bestužev-Marlinskij's 'Mulla-Nur': a Muddled Myth to Rekindle Romance," *Russian Literature* 11, part 2 (January 1982), 117–28.

Bakhtin, Mikhail. *The Dialogic Imagination. Four Essays by Mikhail Bakhtin.* Ed. Michael Holquist, trans. Caryl Emerson and Holquist. Austin, TX: University of Texas, 1981.

Estetika slovesnogo tvorchestva. Moscow: Iskusstvo, 1979. Translation: *Speech Genres and Other Late Essays.* Trans. Vern W. McGee. Ed. Caryl Emerson and Michael Holquist. Austin, TX: University of Texas, 1986.

Problemy poetiki Dostoevskogo. 4th edn. Moscow: Sovetskaia Rossiia, 1979. Translation: *Problems of Dostoevsky's Poetics.* Ed. and trans. Caryl Emerson. Minneapolis, MN: University of Minnesota, 1984.

Barrett, Thomas M. "The Remaking of the Lion of Dagestan: Shamil in Captivity." Paper delivered at the 20th National Convention of the American Association for the Advancement of Slavic Studies, Honolulu, 1988, 1–25. Published version in *Russian Review*, forthcoming.

Bartol'd, V. V. *Sochineniia*. 9 vols. Moscow: Izdatel'stvo vostochnoi literatury and Nauka, 1964–77.

Bassin, Mark. "Russia Between Europe and Asia: The Ideological Construction of Geographical Space," *Slavic Review* 50 (Spring 1991), 1–17.

"Inventing Siberia: Visions of the Russian East in the Early Nineteenth Century," *American Historical Review* 96 (June 1991), 763–94.

Berlin, Isaiah. *Russian Thinkers.* New York: Penguin, 1978.

Brantlinger, Patrick. *Rule of Darkness. British Literature and Imperialism, 1830–1914.* Ithaca, NY: Cornell University, 1988.

Benningsen, Alexandre. "Muslim Conservative Opposition to the Soviet Regime: The Sufi Brotherhoods in the North Caucasus," in *Soviet Nationality Policies and Practices.* Ed. Jeremy R. Azrael. New York: Praeger, 1978.

Brooks, Jeffrey. *When Russia Learned to Read. Literacy and Popular Literature, 1861–1917.* Princeton, NJ: Princeton University, 1985.

Clark, Katerina and Michael Holquist. *Mikhail Bakhtin.* Cambridge, MA and London: Harvard University, 1984.

Cornwell, Neil. *V. F. Odoyevsky: His Life, Times and Milieu.* London: Athlone Press / Athens, Ohio: Ohio University, 1986.

Dronov, V. (ed.). *Literatura i Kavkaz.* Stavropol', 1972.

Durylin, S. *Geroi nashego vremeni M. Iu. Lermontova.* Moscow: Narkompros, 1940.

Eberman, V. "Araby i persy v russkoi poezii," *Vostok* 3 (1928), 108–25.

Eikhenbaum, B. M. *Molodoi Tolstoi.* Peterburg: Z. I. Grzhebin, 1922.

Stat'i o Lermontove. Moscow-Leningrad: Akademiia nauk, 1961.

Emerson, Caryl. *Boris Godunov. Transpositions of a Russian Theme.* Bloomington, IN: Indiana University, 1986.

"The Tolstoi Connection in Bakhtin," *PLMA* 100 (January 1985), 68–80.

Enikolopov. I. K. *Pushkin na Kavkaze.* Tbilisi: Zaria Vostoka, 1938.

Griboedov v Gruzii. Tbilisi: Zaria Vostok, 1954.

Fokht, U. P. *Lermontov. Logika tvorchestva.* Moscow: Nauka, 1975.

Frenkel, Monika Greenleaf. "Pushkin's 'Journey to Arzrum': The Poet at the Border," *Slavic Review* 50 (Winter 1991), 940–53.

Freund, Elizabeth. *The Return of the Reader. Reader Response Criticism.* London and New York: Methuen, 1987.

Gadzhiev, Agil'. *Kavkaz v russkoi literature pervoi poloviny XIX veka.* Baku: Novaia knizhnaia tipografiia, 1982.

Giddings, Robert (ed.). *Literature and Imperialism*. London: Macmillan, 1991.

Ginzburg, Lidiia. *Tvorcheskii put' Lermontova*. Leningrad: Khudozhestvennaia literatura, 1940.

Grossman, Leonid, "Lermontov i kultury vostoka," *Literaturnoe nasledstvo* 43/44 (I) (1941), 673–744.

Gukovskii, G. A. *Pushkin i russkie romantiki*. Moscow : Khudozhestvennaia literatura, 1965.

Gusev, N. N. *Lev Nikolaevich Tolstoi. Materialy k biografii*. 5 vols. Moscow: Akademiia nauk, 1954–79.

Hokanson, Katya. "Literary Imperialism, *Narodnost'* and Pushkin's Invention of the Caucasus," *Russian Review*, forthcoming.

Hulme, Peter. *Colonial Encounters. Europe and the Native Caribbean, 1492–1797*. London: Routledge, 1992.

Iusufov, R. F. *Dagestan i russkaia literatura kontsa XVIII i pervoi poloviny XIX v*. Moscow: Nauka, 1964.

JanMohamed, Abdul R. "The Economy of Manichean Allegory: The Function of Racial Difference in Colonialist Literature," *Critical Inquiry* 12 (August 1985), 59–87.

Kiernan, V. G. *The Lords of Human Kind. European Attitudes towards the Outside World in the Imperial Age*. 1969; rpt. New York: Columbia University, 1986.

Kornblatt, Judith Deutsch. *The Cossack Hero in Russian Literature. A Study in Cultural Mythology*. Madison, WI: University of Wisconsin, 1992.

Kosven, M. O. *Etnografiia i istoriia Kavkaza. Issledovaniia i materialy*. Moscow, 1961.

Layton, Susan. "Imagining the Caucasian Hero: Tolstoj vs. Mordovcev," *Slavic and East European Journal* 30 (Spring 1986), 1–17.

"Primitive Despot and Noble Savage: The Two Faces of Shamil in Russian Literature," *Central Asian Survey* 10 (1991), no. 4, 31–45.

"Lermontov in Combat with *Biblioteka dlia chteniia*," *Cahiers du monde russe et soviétique*, forthcoming.

Leighton, Lauren G. *Alexander Bestuzhev-Marlinsky*. Boston, MA: Twayne, 1975.

Russian Romanticism. Two Essays. The Hague: Mouton, 1975.

Lobikova, N. M. *Pushkin i Vostok*. Moscow: Nauka, 1974.

Lotman, Iu. M. "Istoki 'Tolstovskogo napravleniia' v russkoi literature 1830-kh godov," *Trudy po russkoi i slavianskoi filologii* 5 (1962), vyp. 119, 3–76.

"Russo i russkaia kul'tura XVIII–nachala XIX veka," in Zh. Zh. Russo (Rousseau), *Traktaty*. Eds. V. S. Alekseev-Popov, Lotman *et al*. Moscow: Nauka, 1969.

"The Text and the Structure of Its Audience," trans. Ann Shukman, *New Literary History* 14 (Autumn 1982), 81–87.

"Problema Vostoka i Zapada v tvorchestve pozdnego Lermontova," in *Lermontovskii sbornik*, ed. I. S. Chistova *et al.* Leningrad: Nauka, 1985.

Lotman, Iu. M. and Z. Mints, " 'Chelovek prirody' v russkoi literature XIX veka i 'tsyganskaia tema' u Bloka," *Blokovskii sbornik*. Ed. Lotman. Tartu: Tartu University, 1964.

Lotman, Iu. M. and B. A. Uspenskii. Introduction to N. M. Karamzin, *Pis'ma russkogo puteshestvennika*. Leningrad: Nauka, 1984.

Lowe, Lisa. "The Orient as Woman in Flaubert's *Salammbô* and *Voyage en Orient*," *Comparative Literature Studies* 23 (Spring 1986), 44–56.

Mann, Iu. V. *Poetika russkogo romantizma*. Moscow: Nauka, 1976.

Mannoni, Dominique. *Prospero and Caliban. The Psychology of Colonization*. Trans. Pamela Powesland. London: Methuen, 1956.

Manuilov, V. A. *Roman M. Iu. Lermontova 'Geroi nashego vremeni'. Kommentarii*. Moscow-Leningrad: Prosveshchenie, 1966.

Miller, Christopher L. *Blank Darkness. Africanist Discourse in French*. Chicago: University of Chicago, 1985.

Monas, Sidney. " 'Self' and 'Other' in Russian Literature," in *The Search for Self-Definition in Russian Literature*. Ed. Ewa M. Thompson. Amsterdam: John Benjamins, 1991.

Morson, Gary Saul. "The Reader as Voyeur: Tolstoi and the Poetics of Didactic Fiction," *Canadian–American Slavic Studies* 12 (Winter 1978), 465–80.

"Introduction: Literary History and the Russian Experience," in *Literature and History. Theoretical Problems and Russian Case Studies*. Ed. Morson. Stanford: Stanford University, 1986.

Nicolson, Marjorie Hope. *Mountain Gloom and Mountain Glory. The Development of the Aesthetics of the Infinite*. Ithaca, NY: Cornell University, 1959.

Ong, Walter. *Orality and Literacy. The Technologizing of the Word*. London: Methuen, 1982.

Pratt, Mary Louise. *Imperial Eyes. Travel Writing and Transculturation*. London: Routledge, 1992.

Raeff, Marc. "In the Imperial Manner" in *Catherine the Great. A Profile*. Ed. Marc Raeff. New York: Hill and Wang, 1972.

Comprendre l'ancien régime russe: Etat et société en Russie impériale. Paris: Seuil, 1982.

Reid, Robert. "Ethnotope in Lermontov's Caucasian *Poèmy*," *Russian Literature* 31 (May 1992), 555–73.

Rhinelander, Jr., Anthony L. H. *Prince Michael Vorontsov: Viceroy to the Tzar*. Buffalo, NY: McGill-Queen's University Press, 1990.

Riasanovsky, Nicholas V. "Asia through Russian Eyes," in *Russia and Asia. Essays on the Influence of Russia on the Asian Peoples*. Ed. Wayne S. Vucinich. Stanford: Hoover Institution of Stanford University, 1972.

Rogger, Hans. *National Consciousness in Eighteenth-Century Russia*. Cambridge, MA: Harvard University, 1960.

Ruskin, Jonah. *The Mythology of Imperialism*. New York: Random House, 1971.

Said, Edward W. *Orientalism*. New York: Vintage Books, 1979.

Culture and Imperialism. London: Chatto and Windus, 1993.

Sandler, Stephanie. *Distant Pleasures. Alexander Pushkin and the Writing of Exile*. Stanford: Stanford University, 1989.

Schwab, Raymond. *La Renaissance orientale*. Paris: Payot, 1950.

Scotto, Peter. "'Prisoners of the Caucasus: Ideologies of Imperialism in Lermontov's 'Bela,'" *PMLA* 107 (March 1992), 246–60.

Semenov, L. P. *Kavkaz i Lev Tolstoi. Sbornik*. Vladikavkaz: SERD-ALO, 1928.

Semenov, L. P. (ed.). *M. Iu. Lermontov. Sbornik statei i materialov*. Stavropol': Stavropol'skoe knizhnoe izdatel'stvo, 1960.

Shaduri, Vano. *Dekabristskaia literatura i gruzinskaia obshchestvennost'*. Tbilisi: Zaria Vostoka, 1958

Shteppa, Konstantin F. "The 'Lesser Evil' Formula," in *Rewriting Russian History*. Ed. C. E. Black. New York: Praeger, 1956.

Slotkin, Richard. *Regeneration through Violence. The Mythology of the American Frontier, 1600–1860*. Middletown, CT: Wesleyan University, 1973.

Svirin, N. "Russkaia kolonial'naia literatura," *Literaturnyi kritik* (1934), no. 9, 51–79.

"Pervyi russkii roman o Kavkaze," *Znamia* (July 1935), 224–42.

Tamakhin, V. M. (ed.). *Russkaia Literatura i Kavkaz*. Stavropol',1974.

Todd III, William Mills. *Fiction and Society in the Age of Pushkin. Ideology, Institutions, and Narrative*. Cambridge, MA and London: Harvard University, 1986.

Todorov, Tzvetan. *Nous et les autres*. Paris: Seuil, 1989.

Tomashevskii, B. V. *Pushkin*. 2 vols. Moscow: Akademiia nauk, 1956, 1961.

Vel'tman, S. *Vostok v khudozhestvennoi literature*. Moscow-Leningrad: Gosudarstvennoe izdatel'stvo, 1928.

Vinogradov, B. S. *Kavkaz v russkoi literature 30-kh godov XIX veka. (Ocherki)*. Grozny: Checheno-Ingushskoe knizhnoe izdatel'stvo, 1966.

Zhirmunskii, V. M. *Bairon i Pushkin*. 1924; rpt. Leningrad: Nauka, 1978.

Index

348

CAMBRIDGE STUDIES IN RUSSIAN LITERATURE

General editor MALCOLM JONES

Editorial board: ANTHONY CROSS, CARYL EMERSON,
HENRY GIFFORD, BARBARA HELDT, G. S. SMITH,
VICTOR TERRAS

Dostoyevsky and the process of literary creation
JACQUES CATTEAU

The poetic imagination of Vyacheslav Ivanov
PAMELA DAVIDSON

Joseph Brodsky
VALENTINA POLUKHINA

Petrushka – the Russian carnival puppet theatre
CATRIONA KELLY

Turgenev
FRANK FRIEDEBERG SEELEY

From the idyll to the novel: Karamzin's sentimentalist prose
GITTA HAMMARBERG

The Brothers Karamazov *and the poetics of memory*
DIANE OENNING THOMPSON

Andrei Platonov
THOMAS SEIFRED

Nabokov's early fiction
JULIAN W. CONNOLLY

Iurii Trifonov
DAVID GILLESPIE

Mikhail Zoshchenko
LINDA HART SCATTON

Andrei Bitov
ELLEN CHANCES

Nikolai Zabolotsky
DARRA GOLDSTEIN

Nietzsche and Soviet Culture
edited by BERNICE GLATZER ROSENTHAL